**University of Washington Publications
on Language and Language Learning**

Volume 1

Research on

Language Teaching

AN ANNOTATED INTERNATIONAL BIBLIOGRAPHY,
1945-64

HOWARD LEE NOSTRAND
DAVID WILLIAM FOSTER
CLAY BENJAMIN CHRISTENSEN

Second edition, revised

Copy 2

1965
UNIVERSITY OF WASHINGTON PRESS
Seattle and London

The research reported herein was performed pursuant to a contract with the
United States Office of Education, Department of Health, Education, and Welfare.

Preface to the Second Edition Revised

ALTHOUGH the original edition of this work is but three years old at this writing, the need for a revised edition in many respects may be traced back to the origins of this project. Aside from the inescapable fact that all bibliographies go out of date rapidly, the *Bibliography of Research on Language Teaching* attempted to fill a vacuum. The fact that no model existed which the editors could follow has meant that at best it is a tentative and exploratory essay at bibliographic control in a field which threatens to defy such control.

Looking at this second edition in the light of the introduction to the first edition written in 1961, Nostrand's statement of intent seems almost inadequate. As he states, the *Bibliography* grew out of the beginnings of the National Defense Education Act Title IV graduate program in language teaching at the University of Washington. It was hoped that the results of the compilation would serve to orient the graduate students of the program in the field of language-teaching research and provide them with guidelines for the research which each was expected to undertake as part of the program. From these modest and immediately utilitarian beginnings the project grew until a published volume became feasible.

Unfortunately, however, the content of the final volume was never able to free itself of these purely local origins. For example, the *Bibliography* was intended to confine itself in scope to "research" items. Neither the faculty guiding the compilation nor the assistants carrying it out were sure of exactly what that key word "research" should mean for this compilation. Should it include the preparation of materials, surveys of enrollment and facilities, opinion by knowledgeable personalities, or only controlled laboratory experimentation? The result was that the end product included a little of everything. Although today none of us holds the final word on what research is, at least we've been able to establish more clear-cut guidelines for this revision.

One of the most serious problems encountered in gathering entries was posed by the modifier "international" in our title. We endeavored to

v

extend our scope beyond the immediate confines of the United States to include, whenever possible, mention of investigation undertaken abroad. We have been criticized for our inability to justify that pretension. The present edition has done a better job of tapping foreign research. One of the difficulties encountered in this regard—indeed, the one which explains the existence of the *Bibliography*—is the lack of bibliographic sources on language-teaching research outside the United States; and even in that country, the existing bibliographic sources are wholly inadequate. The fault lies not so much with the bibliographies as with the discipline. Foreign language-teaching research is by nature interdisciplinary, as can be seen by examining our table of contents, the titles of the journals included and the scope of the headings in the subject index. Add to this the current practice in many of the circles embraced by this research of circulating the results of investigation in mimeographed and dittoed forms and one can easily see how some work is all but impossible to know about except through personal contact.

In retrospect, however, the weakest phase of the undertaking seems to have been that which resulted in Section 8 of the original edition, "Questions in Need of Research." The idea was basically a good one: to solicit from recognized authorities suggestions of avenues for possible investigation and research; in short, to give a compendium of what needed to be done, seen in the light of what we were reporting had been done. We attempted to supplement the questions posed by the researchers contacted by giving a selection of publications which were believed to contain suggestions for actual research. Although this non-bibliographic section has undoubtedly been useful in many quarters, the present edition has foregone suggesting to its users what research they might profitably perform.

On the basis of my own critical evaluation of the preliminary edition of this *Bibliography,* it was easy enough upon entertaining the notion of a revised edition to detail exactly what such a revision would attempt to do.*

The foremost objective was to update the original entries and the volume as a whole. Further objectives were to correct any inaccurate bibliographic information or annotations, and to review the original items and delete those no longer deemed to report "research."

In the preparation of this revision we sent form letters to all authors mentioned in the original volume whose addresses were available in the

---

* Our original project proposal to the U.S. Office of Education was for funds to compile a Supplement which would bring the *Bibliography* up to date, although from the very first a revised edition was in the back of our minds. Time and the cooperation of the University of Washington Press have made the latter possible.

standard directories requesting them to 1) review and criticize the entries under their name, 2) provide us with descriptive annotations for any research which they may have completed in the meantime, and 3) suggest other sources of information: titles, researchers and agencies. We also wrote to many foreign centers of research and to additional domestic sources as they became known to us, many of which were researchers who have appeared since the original publication. We sent follow-up letters to those individuals who were not prompt in replying to our petition. The response to our requests for assistance has been overwhelmingly gratifying apart from several of the more prominent researchers from whom we failed to obtain answers. A diligent attempt has been made to include everything pertinent to the scope of the *Bibliography*. However, owing to the growing amount of research in this field,* and the inability of the traditional bibliographic sources in the field to keep up with it, we can only claim to completeness where the researchers themselves have informed us of their work and provided annotations.

Yet, we could not rely entirely upon the cooperation of the researcher. Although standard sources such as the PMLA *Annual Bibliography, Reader's Guide, Education Index, Psychological Abstracts, Sociological Abstracts,* and *Dissertation Abstracts* proved to be inadequate, either not reporting many items or lagging so far behind our first-hand knowledge of titles as to be only confirmatory, we had recourse to two excellent sources of information, both of which had been of limited assistance in our original undertaking.

Gustave Mathieu's *MLabstracts,* though not yet achieving the bibliographic control needed by the field (a fact which in the end justified this supplement and revision) has proven to be an indispensable aid to us. Coverage is at times sketchy, depending in the main upon contributions, and thoroughly eclectic, including mention not only of solid research and opinion, but also of many articles of inferior quality. Nevertheless, the fact that *MLabstracts* relies on annotations from the authors themselves —one of our own desiderata—has allowed us to borrow items from that source, with Dr. Mathieu's kind permission. If more researchers would contribute to this publication, the field would be far the better for it. In any case, due to *MLabstracts'* limited coverage at present and our more limited criteria for accepting titles, the two publications tend rather to complement each other than to overlap.

---

* If the items of Sections 1 through 7 of the 1962 volume (covering the 17 years from 1945 to 1961) are added to those gathered for the years between 1961 and 1964, one-third would belong to this latter group spanning three years alone— a phenomenal growth in productivity. It is even more impressive when one remembers that we were all the more exclusive in selecting these additional items. By the criteria for the original selection, many more items would have been included.

The other source for many of our entries is a more broadly based undertaking. Western Reserve University's Center for Documentation and Communication Research has grown from a pilot project, when we first had dealings with it, to a permanent installation. The Center has adopted the headings of our subject index for the section of their files dealing with language teaching. This made it relatively easy for the Center to provide us with copies of their collected entries for this area, which included a good number of items which we had not until then known about. Although subsequent correspondence with researchers enabled us to replace some of the Center's entries with entries prepared by the authors involved, many have been retained here with the Center's own annotations, appropriately credited.

Another source must be mentioned, whose influence is not as openly evident. There is little doubt that the National Defense Education Act of 1958 is primarily responsible for the tremendous increase in foreign language-teaching research. Reports of projects which have been completed and descriptions of research in progress form the basis of many items in this work.[1] At the same time, the fact that many N.D.E.A. fellows have been writing dissertations on foreign language teaching has meant an increase in the number of pertinent doctoral dissertations.

I can not say that the problem of discovering foreign research has been adequately solved. Many foreign researchers and research centers were contacted, but only the British and the German (the Deutsches Pädagogisches Zentralinstitut) have complied in any way that may be called satisfying. While both the Library of Congress *East European Acquisition List* and their *Russian Acquisition List* proved fruitless, one publication in particular provided several entries. The van Willigen pamphlet for UNESCO (see Part I, Bibliographies), while eclectic and uneven in its coverage, turned up some research items. If van Willigen's sampling is representative, aside from contrastive studies, European investigation has as yet little to offer in the way of rigorously designed research. But then, Europe has no N.D.E.A. to underwrite potentially important projects. However, the titles mentioned in the UNESCO pamphlet and in the German Zentralinstitut bibliographies indicate an interest and a climate of opinion quite similar to those which preceded and still surround the best research being done in this country.

Lastly, results were obtained by going to the publications themselves, in this case, to the journals. Part II of this *Bibliography* lists the journals publishing pertinent titles.

---

[1] The annotations of these are taken from the official description, unless otherwise indicated. (See Part I, United States Office of Education.)

In reviewing the items to be included in this revised edition, the original as well as the supplemental ones, our guiding criteria for determining what constitutes research have been 1) that the items exemplify the procedures of modern scholarly and scientific investigation; and, 2) that they appear to have significance beyond the limited scope of the instances investigated. In short, our intent was to give as nearly complete a picture as possible of the work which promises to be of significance for foreign language teaching. These criteria demanded the discarding of many of our original items and the rejection of many of the supplemental ones brought to our attention. For example, we felt we could no longer include mention of sets of materials or projects producing instructional materials, except in those rare instances where such projects were designed at the same time to produce theoretical conclusions. Likewise, articles of a partisan nature, formulating opinion rather than presenting research results, were decided to lie outside the scope of this work. Conferences and surveys, on the other hand, are given mention when they constitute research, are preparatory to research, or indicate the trends and results of research. Still, a clear-cut decision often proved extremely difficult. Research dealing directly with foreign language teaching, more related to educational methodology than to the "classic" social and natural sciences, lacks as yet the sophistication of research in psychology, sociology and linguistics. While these fields are exercising an increasing influence upon the research reported by this volume, much of it is a long way from being comparable. Whether or not it should indeed seek to be comparable is a question that will be decided by the directions this research will take in the future, rather than by any of us. I have sought to be as impartial as possible and offer my apologies if I have discarded research that should have been reported.

The user of our *Bibliography* will note that many items by psychologists and linguists have been included, and that the titles of the recurring journals are no longer just those of the language teachers' professional organizations. He will also note a corresponding increase in the number of informally published items, most of them reports of N.D.E.A. projects. Several sections in particular have grown considerably: 2.3, Teaching of Specific Languages; 3.1, General Psychology; 4.1, Applied Linguistics; and 4.3, Theoretical Research. Indeed, the nature of these last three, extending as they do beyond the confines of foreign language teaching, has added the problem of selecting from strictly research items those which are most pertinent to the interests of our users.

We have kept the basic scheme of the 1962 volume, while recognizing that several sections should be added if the number of items were any greater. A future edition may well see separate sections for programmed learning and teaching machines, and a separate section apiece for the teaching of literature and contrastive studies.

Finally, the subject index has been completely redone, with many new headings established and many former ones discarded. Originally, the attempt was made to give as complete a list of main headings as possible, whether or not research existed to include under them. In line with the more strictly bibliographic nature of this edition, the headings under which no entries appeared have been dropped.

This revised edition has been made possible by the kind cooperation of the many scholars and researchers in the field, and especially by the patient assistance of Howard Lee Nostrand, project director, Harriet Frey, editorial assistant, and the University of Washington Library and Department of Romance Languages and Literature, where the work was carried out.

DAVID WILLIAM FOSTER

University of Missouri
Columbia, Missouri

Contents

INTRODUCTION: SOURCES, SCOPE, AND STRUCTURE xv

ANNOTATORS xxv

PART I: BIBLIOGRAPHIES 1

PART II: PERIODICALS AND SERIALS 19

PART III: RESEARCH COMPLETED AND IN PROGRESS 35
   1. Methodology of Research 37
   2. Methods, Materials, and Equipment 41

      2.1 General 41
      2.3 Teaching of Specific Languages 58
         Arabic 58
         Basque 59
         Bengali 59
         Chinese 59
         English 60
         French 71
         German 86
         Hebrew 93
         Italian 93
         Japanese 94
         Latin 94
         Polish 96
         Russian 96
         Spanish 101
         Thai 109
         Urdu 110
      2.5 Auditory and Visual Aids 110
         2.51 Auditory Aids 110
         2.52 Visual Aids 115

Contents

2.53 Audiovisual Aids — 119
2.54 Language Laboratories — 128
2.55 Teaching Machines — 144
2.56 Educational Television — 158
2.7 Evaluation of Achievement in Language Learning — 173
2.9 Specifications for Equipment — 185

3. Psychology of Language and Language Learning — 190

3.1 General — 190
3.3 Aptitude and Prognosis Tests — 216
3.5 Bilingualism — 226
3.7 Sociopsychological Factors of Language Learning — 237

4. Linguistics — 244

4.1 The Use of Linguistic Concepts in Language Teaching — 244
4.3 Theoretical Research with Possible Applications — 258
4.5 The Teaching of Pronunciation — 286

5. Teaching the Cultural and Intercultural Context — 292

6. Languages in the Curriculum — 308

6.1 Elementary School — 308
6.2 First Cycle of Secondary Education — 320
6.3 Second Cycle of Secondary Education — 322
6.4 University — 325
6.5 Language Teaching and General Education — 330
6.6 Specific School Programs — 335

7. Teacher Qualifications and Training — 338

Agencies, Institutions, and Organizations — 345

AUTHOR INDEX — 351

SUBJECT INDEX — 361

Introduction: Sources, Scope, and Structure

THE ANIMATING purposes of this *Bibliography* has been to help researchers find the studies that are sound to build upon, and to help them identify the needs for further research, in areas directly bearing on the improvement of language teaching. Within such areas, we have attempted a world-wide list of all research reports completed since 1945, or in progress when we went to press in October, 1961.

The resulting information on the state of studies will be of use to school and college language teachers and administrators as well as to researchers. The general basis for educational policy and practice is better summarized, however, in the masterly historical syntheses published in the 1960 edition of the *Encyclopedia of Educational Research* (New York: Macmillan Co.), notably the article on modern languages by Emma M. Birkmaier, dated July, 1958, and the article on classical languages by Norman J. DeWitt, dated December, 1957.

Sources

Our attempt at world-wide coverage rests upon several sources of information: the bibliographies we have listed; the indexes of the most pertinent among the listed periodicals; letters to agencies and scholars; and a detailed circular request for official information, sent to each of the embassies and legations in Washington, D.C. This systematic request resulted in careful responses from a few ministries of education, including those of Britain, West Germany, France, Switzerland, and Israel. In other cases it brought only travel folders. Our main chance of completeness, therefore, depended on the bibliographies we used. And these are not likely to be more complete for research on language teaching than are the standard United States bibliographies for the overlapping field of research on educational media. There, a careful analysis,[1] made for

---

[1] Maurice F. Tauber and Oliver L. Lilley, Feasibility Study regarding the Establishment of an Educational Media Research Information Service (New York, Columbia University School of Library Service, 1960, mimeographed). See Section II, Bibliographical Identification of Research Studies in Educational Media, pp. 18-45, particularly p. 43.

the Educational Media Program of the United States Office of Education, has shown that eleven standard sources taken together still omit some 17 per cent of the titles found in a comparatively exhausive list that happened to exist for educational-media research.

The field of language teaching has not been subjected to an exhaustive survey of research. Evelyn Van Eenenaam's annual "Annotated Bibliography of Modern Language Methodology" in the *Modern Language Journal* for 1950 and after, to which we are the most indebted, excludes several of the research fields we have tried to bring together and hence has drawn from fewer sources. *The Bibliography on the Teaching of Modern Languages,* financed by UNESCO in 1955, is chiefly a collection of studies that teachers had found helpful; it makes no claim to cover research. John Carroll's unpublished status study, Research in Second-Language Learning, lists the best twentieth-century American studies up to 1955 in the field of psychology, but in other fields omits contributions essential to a tableau of the best knowledge we have. The articles in the 1960 *Encyclopedia of Educational Research* are accompanied by bibliographies (modern languages, 236 items; classical languages, 51 items). They grow less extensively international, however, toward the end of the period they treat, while this *Bibliography* has more non-English titles for the last few years.

Although the present compilation extends well beyond its predecessors, it is probably still far from complete even for the West; and for the Communist countries, we must expect that it lacks many items of major importance, particularly in linguistics and psychology as they bear upon language teaching. Nevertheless, the researcher in any of the fields we have included should be able to perfect the bibliography of his specialty by starting from the indications he will find of interested persons and centers, and of relevant bibliographies, periodicals, and serials.

One conclusion to be drawn from the present study is that in this field of research, published sources do not suffice for bibliographic control. Some of the best surveys may never be printed, and some of the best research projects are known only through unpublished progress reports until several years after their inception. With the advent of mimeograph and ditto machines the most productive researchers have preferred to keep one another informed by exchanging polycopied reports. This personal correspondence will remain an important mode of communication, even as the number of research centers increases around the globe. The virtue of this device is that it avoids fixing doubtful, tentative conclusions in print, and it protects the few against importune inquiries from would-be researchers.

At the same time, the most impressive result of the present study is to confirm that a great number of areas lack conclusions based upon research. Invaluable human resources are being wasted for lack of answers to open questions about the learner at successive age levels, about each language and its cultural context, and about instructional methods, materials, and equipment. More researchers must be developed. If this can be done, even at some risk of inconveniencing the best researchers, the total energy wasted would be less than at present.

To solve the problem of communication, the professional journals will apparently need to serve bibliographic control more effectively by publishing digests of research in progress, discussions of needed research, and references to published reports. This would not necessarily require added pages. Some types of articles have become repetitious and could be largely discontinued—for example, the testimonial of a local success, reporting practices that have been described before, and the advice on how to teach one's first class, which has been given a score of times with little variation.

As a result of the Tauber-Lilley report, an Educational Media Research Information Service was established on a pilot scale in 1961, at the Western Reserve University Center for Documentation and Communication, with funds provided by the United States Office of Education under Title VII of the National Defense Education Act. This service will meet a part of the need in the language field, and it may pioneer a pattern of information storage and retrieval such as would perfect the present compilation and keep it perpetually up to date, on a world scale, for the use of any researcher or professional journal.

Scope

The beginning date for systematic coverage was set at 1945 because the scant earlier research in this field either is outdated or has been referred to by subsequent investigators. We have, however, included bibliographies and surveys prior to 1945 as well as a few research studies that still seem essential to the present state of knowledge.

The inclusion of uncompleted projects—marked with a star—was necessary since these are a part of the present status of the field. Their inclusion was the more imperative because the questions we ask are rapidly changing and the standards of experimental design are rising. The research now in progress promises to add as much solid knowledge to this field as it has previously acquired in several decades.

Within the period selected for coverage, we have tried to list all experimental research that has been rigorously designed and executed. The severe judgment made by John Carroll in his 1955 status study remains true, however, for the enlarged purview of the present study: "The few studies that have been performed to date are, in the main, either inadequate in experimental design or too limited in scope. On many questions in which second-language teachers have a vital interest, there exists practically no research literature at all" (p. 1).

Professor Carroll's purpose, in this and previous publications and memoranda, was to find any relevant psychological research that met a scientist's standard of experimental design, warning against the unreliability of results reached by less rigorous method. In fulfilling that purpose he has rendered an inestimable service to language teaching.

Our more diffuse purpose, to map the plateau of best knowledge available, has required that we fill in, among the verifiable conclusions, with enlightened opinion.

How broad a plateau to trace out, where to cut it off at each boundary, was a question that had to be settled arbitrarily, for it would take volumes to list all the writings that would enlighten new research and practical judgments in one sector or another of language teaching. We disposed of nonresearch items in several ways.

We endeavored to include any good source lists and surveys of present knowledge in all the areas we selected. We excluded all nonresearch items that discussed essentially experimental problems. Some of these, however, proved to offer suggestive hypotheses, so we decided to list them as documentation in an appendix on problems in need of research.

The hardest questions of proper scope were whether to include experimental research in supporting disciplines, suggestive experiments in the teaching of subjects other than languages, and nonexperimental studies on important problems not amenable to experimental method—the problems, for example, of describing a language or the culture of which it is a part. We made a separate compromise for each area, attempting to give as much help as seemed needed and practicable.

Where the background is voluminous and relatively organized, we have tried to include only studies that seemed unusually pertinent, as in the cases of speech physiology and acoustic phonetics; descriptive linguistics; information theory; the psychology of learning; and the educational properties of media such as still pictures and motion pictures, television, radio, and phonodiscs. Where the background is scant and scattered we have used space generously. Such is the area of programing languages for teaching machines (Section 2.55), and that of descibing the cultural context of a language (Section 5).

Bibliographies are needed of all competent studies that seek to define the institutions, the behavior patterns and personality structures, the history of ideas and tastes, and particularly the unifying themes, of each culture whose language is to be taught. A selective list of such studies, however, calls for the prior steps of systematic collecting and appraising, which could not be extended to these fields in the present project. New projects have been begun in the University of Washington Romance Department to compile this sort of bibliography for the French, Italian, and Hispanic cultures.

We have tried to scan the journals for reviews of research reports, most of which are too specialized to be found in the *Book Review Digest*. Supplements to the present compilation should include such commentaries, which probably will soon be much more numerous since there will be many more reports worth evaluating.

Structure

The categorical scheme of this *Bibliography* arose from its central purpose—to map the plateau of present knowledge and suggest needed research. The scheme was worked out in a seminar for Ph.D. candidates who were developing the interdisciplinary competence requisite for language-teacher training or supervision and whose dissertations were to consist of research on language teaching. The structure of the *Bibliography* has the advantage of being oriented toward its intended use and the disadvantage of not having been built inductively from the data discovered, except of course when these necessitated additional headings. Where a heading proved too large for the materials found, it has been left so in the hope that empty areas will be filled. (Usually, indeed, the corresponding subdivision of the Appendix: Questions in Need of Research, indicates researchable problems that call for the larger rubric.) Such is the case of Section 4.3, Theoretical Research (in linguistics) with Possible Applications, which collected only entries on acoustic phonetics —the one area of that field with a marked experimental orientation.

The categories we have adopted have no permanent validity; in fact they are already obsolescent at some points. For example, we have grouped together "Teaching Machines and Programed Learning," programing having grown up in conjunction with the machines since the first research on the latter, in the 1920's. However, some programed materials now being created, such as Waldo Sweet's Latin lessons, call for only a pencil and paper. Programing thus becomes a field of research quite separate from the development of hardware and distinct from any medium used. It will require a place of its own under teaching methods or under educational psychology.

The classification system hammered out in the seminar, when we compared it with others early in 1960, proved similar to the one adopted for the UNESCO *Bibliography on the Teaching of Modern Languages* (1955). Shortly before his death in July, 1960, we asked Felix H.

Walter, of the UNESCO Department of Education, how the categories could be made compatible with those that would probably be used in a revision of the UNESCO bibliography, then planned tentatively for 1961 or 1962. He suggested only one change, which has been adopted, to make the wording of the subheads under Section 6 understandable and applicable for all countries.

Three other recent schemes for classifying educational research all have advantages over the present classification, as well as over one another. The Index of Subject Headings at the end of the present volume will help the reader find the interconnections brought out by these other schemes.

Maurice Tauber and Oliver Lilley, in their *Feasibility Study,* have produced the most detailed of the three systems. They were concerned, precisely, to facilitate the association of ideas in all possible dimensions. They consequently propose for the educational media a "faceted" classification scheme with four facets—audience, media, program [subject matter], and research [type of investigation]. A point of attack can be chosen on any of the four facets, and all the relevant research items will be "retrieved" from anywhere in the storage system, as though the aspect chosen had been the basis of the classification.

The four facets, as subdivided, will permit ready documentation of topics in several of the areas of the present *Bibliography*—namely, teaching, learning, language, culture, the curriculum, and teacher preparation. For example, teaching methods and the psychology of learning are subdivisions of the audience facet. None of the four facets, on the other hand, gives access to linguistics, theory of cultures, or curriculum building, since the scheme concentrates upon the role of the new media.

The main value of the Tauber-Lilley report for us is that it points out four basic dimensions of education, which tend to be partially hidden by our categories. Audience studies will appear partly in our Section 6, arranged according to age levels; but partly also in Section 3, on the psychology of the learner, and in Section 2, on teaching methods. Media research is well concentrated in Section 2, but subject-matter research is divided into Sections 2, 5 (cultural context), and 6 (curriculum). Methodology of research is treated in Section 1, yet the suggestive illustrations of types of inquiry are scattered through other sections. Since much of the best-designed research is still in progress, and since such items are starred, one can use the stars to find good illustrations of method. If the scope of the present compilation were increased to that envisaged by Messrs. Tauber and Lilley, however, such a device as this would become entirely impracticable.

A second value of the *Feasibility Study* is that the larger of two classi-

fication schedules proposed in it (pp. 82-160) includes not only education but the whole range of the communication arts. The authors call
attention to "the difficulty of isolating many of the aspects of the communication arts from either education or educational media. Many
topics of research interest in entertainment, commercial advertising,
journalism, political campaigning, and other elements of cultural, social,
and economic life are interwoven closely with those of education itself"
(p. 79). The topics in the larger schedule therefore widen our horizon
to show research needs that bear on language teaching but range far
beyond the possibilities one is accustomed to consider.

A different scheme for classifying media research was worked out in
1959, again for the Educational Media Program of the United States
Office of Education, by William H. Allen, Director of Research in the
University of Southern California Department of Cinema and Editor of
Audio Visual Communication Review. This classification, as yet unpublished, was designed for tabulating the numbers of research projects that
have been devoted to each aspect of the educational media; consequently, it serves well to show up the areas needing research.

The tabulation consists of a series of two-dimensional grids. The
media are enumerated on one axis; and on the other, the subdivisions of
another variable, such as "audience conditions," which is broken up into
age levels and group sizes. The boxes of the grid can then show how
many projects have dealt with a given medium as used, let us say, in the
primary grades. For a similar chart, the "objectives of learning" are
enumerated as knowledge, concept development, problem solving, attitudes, motivation, application of learning, and motor skills. Another
chart enumerates practical aspects of each medium's educational use—
comparative effectiveness, classroom use, teacher education, administration, production design, and testing. The practical aspects, in turn, are
compared against the objectives of learning, and so on.

This form of tabulation is recommended to the researcher who wants
to go prospecting systematically for neglected topics. The Tauber-Lilley
report would help him to choose the sets of enumerations he judges most
significant. The present *Bibliography* would tell how many projects
already exist, to be recorded at each intersection on the grid.

The third useful classification scheme was formulated in 1961 by
Alfred Hayes,[2] as groundwork for a projected book-length analysis of
current and needed research on language teaching, commissioned by the

---

[2] Alfred S. Hayes, A Tentative Schematization for Research in the Teaching
of Cross-Cultural Communication (mimeographed); to be published at Purdue
University, Lafayette, Ind., in the proceedings of the Conference on Materials and
Techniques for the Language Laboratory, March 23-25, 1961.

Language Development Program of the United States Office of Education. This scheme aims to bring together all research—from whatever disciplines—that helps to determine how we may best train a person to communicate successfully with persons of a foreign linguistic community.

Dr. Hayes distinguishes two categories as fundamental—*what* and *how* we teach, which are enlightened respectively by "descriptive" and "instrumental" research. This dichotomy, logical as it is, proved impracticable for a bibliography: so many of the items to be listed deal with both methods and materials, that separating the headings results almost in two duplicate listings. The forthcoming book will thus fill needs not met by the present compilation.

The preliminary study, moreover, suggests fields and types of needed research. Mr. Hayes's primary categories—research on *what* and *how* to teach—both subdivide into "theoretical" and "developmental" research, and each further ramifies into two main fields of inquiry with their respective types of research problem. He has related all the fields and types of problem to one another in a chart, which cogently suggests how they can all contribute to a complete and coherent research enterprise on the teaching of cross-cultural communication.

In the light of this integral view, Mr. Hayes also comments on the methods appropriate for the several fields represented on the chart. His remarks and organizing diagram confirm two main observations that one makes, with equal conviction, after examining the first thousand projects submitted under Title VII of the National Defense Education Act—the title devoted to advancing the educational uses of the newer media.

The first observation is that "point-of-application" research, so common in the form of projects to compare the effectiveness of alternative practices—classroom procedures, programed sequences, etc.—should normally be reserved for a final step of evaluating methods, materials, or equipment that the experimenter knows to have been designed on a sound theoretical basis. It is wasteful of human and material resources to "road test" a vehicle built on uncertain engineering principles. We need more fundamental research to establish working principles of language learning, working principles for developing the most teachable "model" of a verb system or a value system, and working principles for evaluating electromechanical aids.

The second observation is that the point-of-application research which tests an isolated resource, such as the single medium of television, soon becomes uselessly repetitious. More research is now needed comparing different combinations of devices, by multivariate or factor analysis. We need to identify the unique contribution of each resource and to determine how each can be used to the best advantage—television in conjunction with group discussion, for example, and with programed self-instruction, or the many other resources, old and new. We need to find out what *system* of resources will accomplish the most in a given environment, and indeed how any manipulable factors among the environmental conditions themselves, such as the attitudes of age mates and the interest of parents, can be brought into the educational system.[3]

The Hayes classification is especially successful in suggesting, through its very structure, the kinds of research needed, while the present study separates methodology (Section 1) from the listing of problems in need of research. (Section 8, the Appendix, omitted from the Second Edition.)

The structure of our Appendix has the same virtues and faults as the *Bibliography* itself. With the exception of 8.1, which is a list of works that survey needed research in the field of language teaching, it recapitulates the headings of the *Bibliography*. The peculiar contribution of this list of research topics lies in the diversity of the perspectives it brings together: it induces the reader to survey the possibilities from contrasting reference points, and warns him against accepting the present most enlightened viewpoint as final. The references cited in the Appendix should enhance this value by suggesting hypotheses in need of conclusive tests. We decided not to attempt formulations of these hypotheses, since the wide range of approaches possible in each case made the added length a questionable improvement. The titles and their classification should suffice to tell the prospective researcher which will be worth perusing for his purpose.

The authors are deeply grateful to the contributors of annotations and to the many librarians, scholars, and officers of governments who have patiently answered requests for information and advice. Rather than trying to list these from the two years of correspondence, we shall endeavor to respond as patiently to the requests of others.

The Romance Department of the University of Washington solicits corrections and additions to the present *Bibliography* and expects to make a supplement available as soon as a substantial number are received.

HOWARD LEE NOSTRAND

Department of Romance Languages and Literature
University of Washington

---

[3] Dr. James J. McPherson of the Educational Media Branch, U.S. Office of Education, has discussed the idea of a system of instructional devices, in a popularized but substantial paper, Let's Look at the Systems Concept of Educational Planning, 1959, 8 pages, ditto, based partly on a French course in the Detroit Public Schools.

ANNOTATORS

BP	Beverly Payne
CBC	Clay Benjamin Christensen
DF	David William Foster
DG	Doris Margaret Glasser
HA	Howard Appel
HLN	Howard Lee Nostrand
JM	Janet Miller
JF	Jeannette Fulmer
JAD	JoAnn Davis (Mrs. JoAnn Creore)
JG	John Alden Green
MJS	Margaret J. Schuddakopf
PK	Paul Kinzel
RK	Robert Kiekel
SJ	Sonia Johanson
SS	Sol Saporta
TD	Thomas Dahl

Other annotators, who have contributed not more than a few notations, are indicated by their full name following their contribution.

SYMBOLS USED

* before a name indicates that the article, book or report was unavailable for annotation.

† before a name indicates that the research reported is still in progress as of August, 1964.

PART I

Bibliographies

Bibliographies

Allen, William H.
"Audio-Visual Communication," *Encyclopedia of Educational Research.* 3rd ed. New York: Macmillan Co., 1960. Pp. 115-37.
    Survey of research in audio-visual communication to January, 1958. Contains a bibliography of 320 items, references to which constitute the bulk of the article. DF

Antier, M.
"Sur l'enseignement des langues vivantes en France. Bibliographie critique," *Revue des langues vivantes,* XXVII (1961), 165-73.

Baker, Hugh Sanford
A Check List of Books and Articles for Teachers of English as a Foreign Language. (NAFSA Studies and Papers, English Language Series, No. 5.) New York: National Association of Foreign Student Advisers, November, 1959.
    Continues certain categories of the Lado bibliography through 1958, 443 items without annotations. Oriented toward use by teachers and foreign-student advisers; lists publications and other bibliographies. DG

Belasco, Simon, Pierre Delattre, and Albert Valdman
"Phonetics," *American Speech,* XXXVI (February, 1961), 69-77.

————.
"Phonetics," *American Speech,* XXXVI (October, 1961), 215-23.

————.
"Phonetics," *American Speech,* XXXVII (February, 1962), 62-70.

————.
"Phonetics," *American Speech,* XXXVII (October, 1962), 222-29.

Bibliographie linguistique des années 1939-1947 [supplemented annually]. Utrecht: Spectrum, 1949-.

3

Birkmaier, Emma M.

"Foreign Languages," *Review of Educational Research,* XXVIII (April, 1958), 127-39.

A bibliographical analysis of publications in the foreign-language field in relation to elementary schools, achievement of articulation, high school and college curriculums, teacher education, interpretation of research, and evaluation of testing. JM

———.

"Modern Languages," *Encyclopedia of Educational Research.* 3rd ed. New York: Macmillan Co., 1960. Pp. 861-88.

Gives a brief history of the teaching of modern languages and explains their role in the United States. Presents three formal investigations of American language curriculum. General postwar aims in language study are viewed, as well as aims in elementary school, high school, and college. Problems of instructions and measures of achievements are treated. There are 236 references supporting the material discussed. JM

See similar article by James B. Tharp in the 1950 edition of the *Encyclopedia.*

Brickman, William W.

"Foreign Language Teaching," *School and Society,* LXXXI (May, 1955), 150-56.

Brown, Paul A.

"Annual Bibliography for 1956," *PMLA,* LXXII (April, 1957), 133-402.

For annotation see below: Brown, "Annual Bibliography for 1958."

———.

"Annual Bibliography for 1957," *PMLA,* LXXIII (April, 1958), 95-364.

———.

"Annual Bibliography for 1958," *PMLA,* LXXIV (May, 1959), 67-336.

These bibliographies have international coverage, including books in English, French, German, Spanish, Italian, Portuguese, Scandinavian, and Dutch. The items come from a master list of about one thousand sources; those considered most useful to scholars are included. BP

Buchanan, M. A., and E. D. MacPhee
An Annotated Bibliography of Modern Language Methodology. Toronto: University of Toronto Press, 1928.

Primary purpose of the book is to indicate research needed and to provide a general plan under which such experimental investigations may be achieved. The work is divided into materials concerning histories, aims and methods, language, the learning process, tests and examinations, sample tests used abroad, and miscellaneous materials. The book is indexed according to authors' names. JM

Buros, Oscar Krisen
Tests in Print, a Comprehensive Bibliography of Tests for Use in Education, Psychology, and Industry. Highland Park, New Jersey: The Gryphon Press, 1961.

Tests in print are listed for 9 languages. Especially valuable for the background to current tests construction are the tests out of print, which list titles in 6 languages, thus giving the field a wide-range of coverage. Included also are Directories and Indexes of publishers and distributors. DF

Carroll, John B.
See 3.1.

Carroll, John B., and S. Earle Richards.
"Instruction in Foreign Languages," *Review of Educational Research,* XXII (April, 1952), 116-35.

This is not a research article in itself. It is connected with the revitalization of language methodology that has been occurring the last six years. In this interest, bibliography and numerous controlled experimental studies are cited. JM

Coleman, Algernon
An Analytical Bibliography of Modern Language Teaching, Vol. III, *1937-1942.* New York: King's Crown Press, 1949.

An 853-item annotated bibliography divided into the following categories: histories and surveys; trends in teaching; psychology of teaching; aims, materials, and methods; curricula; examinations and tests; transfer of training; teacher training; bilingualism; foreign languages for national defense; and publications of the Committee on Modern Languages. JM

Council for Cultural Cooperation
New Research and Techniques for the Benefit of Modern Language Teaching. Strasbourg, 1964 Education in Europe.

Dale, Edgar, and Taher Razik

A Bibliography of Vocabulary Studies. Columbus, Ohio: Publications Office, The Ohio State University, 1964.

A Payne Fund Communications Project, this bibliography includes twenty-six sections of references, on such topics as correlational factors, dictionaries, developmental studies of vocabulary and spelling, frequency of appearance of words, media and methods of acquiring vocabulary, phonetics, reviews and bibliographies, studies of specific vocabularies. There are separate sections on vocabulary content of books, newspapers, periodicals and pamphlets, radio, motion pictures, and comics. There are also many references on tests and testing, grade placement, vocabulary and intelligence, vocabulary and reading, vocabulary research, vocabulary size, vocabulary and spelling as a factor in success or failure, vocabulary in use (studies of words used in writings and conversation), word meanings and definitions. Cross-references and an author index are included. Edgar Dale

De Mandach, André B.

Bibliography of Audio-Visual Aids and Techniques in Language Teaching. Washington, D.C.: National Tape Library, n.d.

Deutsches Pädagogisches Zentralinstitut, Abteilung Dokumentation und Information

Moderner Fremdsprachenunterricht, Literaturzusammenstellung Nr. 11/63. Berlin, March 13, 1963 (ditto).

This bibliography covers the period from 1958-1963 and lists 54 titles from 10 countries. Items which constitute research have been mentioned in the proper sections. DF

―――.

Sprachbildung und Denkschulung im Fremdsprachenunterricht, Literaturzusammenstellung Nr. 48/63. Berlin, October 8, 1963 (ditto).

Covering the period 1958-1963, this bibliography lists 67 titles from 8 countries. Items which constitute research have been mentioned in the proper sections. DF

―――.

Die Vervendung technischer Hilfsmittel im modernen Fremdsprachenunterricht, Literaturzusammenstellung Nr. 13/64. Berlin, April 4, 1964 (ditto).

This bibliography covers the period 1960-1964, and includes mention of 68 articles and books from 11 different countries. Although very little research in the sense of the word which we have given it here is reported, the titles attest to the interest and opinion abroad on this subject. Items which we have adjudged research are included in the proper sections. DF

"Dissertacii po germanskoj i romanskoj filologii i metodike prepodavanija inostrannyh jazykov, zaščiščennye v 1958-1960 g," *Inostrannye jazyki v škole,* No. 3 (1961).

Theses on German and Romance philology and on the method of teaching foreign languages, submitted between 1958 and 1906. From van Willigen, this section.

"Dissertacii po germanskomu i romanskomu jazykoznaniju i metodike prepodavanija inostrannyh jazykov s 1945-1956 gg," *Inostrannye jazki v škole,* No. 1 (1957).

Theses on Germanic and Romance philology and on the method of teaching foreign languages, submitted between 1954 [sic; 1945?]-1956. From van Willigen, this section.

Dissertation Abstracts. Ann Arbor, Mich.: University Microfilms, 1938-.

Doctoral Dissertations Accepted by American Universities. New York: H. W. Wilson, 1934-55.

Dostal, Naida M.
Bibliography and Some Summaries of Research Studies in Foreign Languages Since World War II (mimeographed).
List of twenty-four articles, theses, and books, of which nine are summarized. BP

Education Index. New York: H. W. Wilson, 1932-.

Ferguson, Charles A., and William A. Stewart
Linguistic Reading Lists for Teachers of Modern Languages: French, German, Italian, Russian, Spanish. Washington, D.C.: Center for Applied Linguistics, 1963.
Contains bibliographies of applied linguistics for: French (André Martinet and Stanley Lampach), German (Herbert L. Kufner and William G. Moulton), Italian (Frederick B. Agard and Robert Di Pietro), Russian (Edward Stankiewicz and Dean S. Worth), and Spanish (William A. Stewart). DF

Fleissner, Else M., Juan Marichal, Donald Pitkin, and Ernest J. Simmons
"Four Cultures" (German, Hispanic, Italian, Russian), *PMLA,* LXXIX, No. 4 (September, 1964, part 2), 18-49.

Constitutes revisions of four of the six bibliographies compiled under the direction of Laurence Wylie. See last item in this section.

"Foreign Languages in Elementary Schools: Selected Bibliography," *German Quarterly,* XXVII (May, 1954), 205-7.

Fifteen texts and articles are listed as an aid to the elementary teacher, including such works as those of Andersson, Dunkel, and Ellert. BP

France. Ministère de l'Education Nationale. Direction des Bibliothèques de France
Catalogue des thèses de doctorat soutenues devant les universités françaises, nouvelle sèrie. Paris: Cercle de la Librairie, 1960-.

Frank, Marcella
Annotated Bibliography of Materials for English as a Second Language. Washington, D.C.: National Association of Foreign Student Advisers, April, 1960.

A 335-item annotated bibliography, listing materials for students and teachers—texts (level indicated), workbooks, tests, journals, background readings, bibliographies. Appendix of publisher addresses. DG

"French in the Elementary Classes: Bibliography," *Education,* LXXV (April, 1955), 525-27.

Fry, Edward B., Glenn L. Bryan, and Joseph W. Rigney
"Teaching Machines: An Annotated Bibliography," *Audio-Visual Communication Review,* VIII (1960), Supplement I, 1-80.

Tabulated summary of experiments in teaching-machine field; tabulation of many teaching-machine programs completed or in progress; annotated bibliography of current literature. DG

Gage, William N.
Contrastive Studies in Linguistics: A Bibliographical Checklist. Washington, D.C.: Center for Applied Linguistics of the Modern Language Association, 1962.

Gee, R. D.
Teaching Machines and Programmed Learning, A Guide to the Literature and Other Sources of Information. Roe Green, Hatfield, Hertfordshire, England: Hertfordshire County Council Technical Library and Information Service, Hatfield College of Technology, 1963.

Published in connection with a symposium on Teaching Machines and Further Education held at Hatfield College of Technology on May 3, 1963. The present publication is an extensive bibliography on both teaching machines and programmed learning, as well as references to specific areas of education. References for background readings, further information in indexes and abstracts, and a directory of professional suppliers, both British and American, are included. Research activities in Britain, pertinent organizations and periodicals are listed. DF

Gorokhoff, Boris I.
See Gorokhoff, 2.1.

Gregoire, Sister Mary, O.P.
Foreign Language Periodical Bibliography. River Forest, Ill.: Rosary College, n.d.

Hall, Pauline Cook
"A Bibliography of Spanish Linguistics: Articles in Serial Publications," *Language,* XXXII, No. 4 (October-December, 1956), (part 2), supplement.
    Lists over 1,900 titles from 319 journals for the years 1887-1953. DG

Haugen, Einar I.
See Haugen, 3.5.

Healey, F. G.
Bibliography of Language Laboratories and Mechanized Techniques in Language Teaching. University Education Research Project, Department of Education. University of Manchester, England, March, 1965.
    This bibliography contains a fairly comprehensive selection of recent material (including a few unpublished items as indications of recent trends) concerned with the use of language laboratories, drill techniques and the theory of these, experience of laboratories in use, and a section on critical material, [. . .]. A few items on other mechanized techniques of language teaching are also included. [. . .]. F. G. Healey

————.
Bibliography of Language Teaching. Manchester, England: University of Manchester. University Education Research Project, 1965. (Mimeo)
    Part I, General Theory of Language Teaching, Including Applied Linguistics. Part II, Experimental Work on Language Teaching. Part III, Programmed Learning in Language Teaching. Part IV, Psycholinguistics and Verbal Behaviour, Bilingualism, Proficiency and Aptitude Testing, etc.

Horecky, Paul. The American Council of Learned Societies, New York
    Compilation of "Selected English and West European Language
    Publications on Russia and the Soviet Union: an Annotated Bibliog-
    raphy"; Project No. OE-3-14-001 (National Defense Education Act,
    Title VI), September 1, 1962, to August 31, 1964; $11,250.

        The project provides an up-to-date, selective, annotated bibliog-
raphy of works in English and certain West European languages
dealing with pre-Revolutionary Russia and the U.S.S.R. Dr. Horecky,
the principal investigator and editor, has asked 25 or 30 scholars to
draw up bibliographies for the subject categories of their specializa-
tions. The main headings of the bibliography include (1) general reference aids; (2) the land; (3) the people—demography, ethnology;
(4) history; (5) the State—politics, government, law, diplomatic history, foreign relations; (6) economic and social structure; and (7) intellectual life—language, literature, education, history and ideas, religion, fine arts, theater and cinema, music. The types of publications
included are books, important serials devoted primarily to the area,
and articles when no monographic coverage is available. In large
measure, the coverage consists of English publications (85-90%),
although some French and German works are included (10-15%).
The bibliography is a companion volume to Dr. Horecky's *Basic
Russian Publications: A Selected and Annotated Bibliography on
Russia and the Soviet Union,* prepared under contract SAE-9517
(University of Chicago Press, 1962). DF

Hotyat, Fernand A.
    "Educational Research in French-Speaking Countries of Europe,"
    School Review, LXVI (Autumn, 1958), 313-28.

        This article gives a résumé of recent educational research in
French-speaking countries and is accompanied by a bibliography. BP

Index to American Doctoral Dissertations. Ann Arbor, Mich.: Univer-
    sity Microfilms, 1957-.

Johnston, Marjorie C.
    References on Foreign Languages in the Elementary School. Wash-
    ington, D.C.: U.S. Department of Health, Education, and Welfare,
    Office of Education, 1957.

        This bibliography includes significant material presenting the
philosophy, research, and experiences of those who have observed
language growth in children. The list includes: (1) books, bulletins,
and reports; (2) articles; (3) teachers' guides and resource materials
to French, German, and Spanish. JM (See following entry)

Keesee, Elizabeth
References on Foreign Languages in the Elementary School. Washington, D.C.: U.S. Department of Health, Education, and Welfare, Office of Education, 1963.
This is a revision of and supplement to the above entry.

"Kommentierte Bibliographie ausländischer Zeitschriftenaufsätze zur Methodik des Fremdsprachenunterrichts," *Fremdsprachen Unterricht,* VII (1963), 171-74.

"Kommentierte Bibliographie ausländischer Zeitschriftenaufsätze zur Methodik des Fremdsprachenunterrichts," *Fremdsprachen Unterricht,* VII (1963), 230-37.

Kumata, Hideya
An Inventory of Instructional Television Research. Ann Arbor, Mich.: National Educational Television and Radio Center, 1956.

Lado, Robert
Annotated Bibliography for Teachers of English as a Foreign Language. Washington, D.C.: U.S. Government Printing Office, 1955.
A comprehensive, 720-item bibliography, covering 1945-54 period. Includes background reading, teaching materials, and materials for the student, for thirty-one native languages. Author index. **DG**

Larson, L. C., and Charity E. Runden
Bibliography of Research in Audio-Visual Education and Mass Media, 1930-1950. Bloomington, Ind.: Indiana University Press, 1950.

Leopold, Werner F.
Bibliography of Child Language. Evanston, Ill.: Northwestern University Press, 1952.

McClusky, Frederick D.
The A-V Bibliography. 2nd ed. Dubuque, Iowa: William C. Brown, 1955.

Contains about two thousand items that are not limited in scope or specialized. The organization of references divides the listings into materials regarding elementary and secondary schools and higher education as well as administration and research. There is a preliminary division devoted to the philosophy of teaching and audio-visual teaching materials and uses. **JM**

MLabstracts. Fullerton, Calif.: Department of Foreign Languages and Literatures, California State College at Fullerton, 1961-. [Subscription to four issues: personal, $2.00; institutional, $3.50]

This quarterly publication lists along with the authors' own annotations, titles of publications in the field of modern language teaching. Not confined to strictly research undertakings, it attempts to provide as close a bibliographic control over the field as possible. We have accepted from its issue those items which pertain to the more limited scope of our Bibliography, indicating those borrowings with the note "MLabstract . . ." following the annotation. DF

Modern Language Association of America
Reports of Surveys and Studies in the Teaching of Modern Foreign Languages . . . 1959-1961. New York: Modern Language Association of America, 1962.

A collection of twenty-one studies and reports, many of which are included in this volume. The various reports are also available as separates. DF

Moulton, William G.
"Brief Bibliography on Linguistics, for Foreign Language Teachers," *PMLA,* LXX (April, 1955), 33-35.

Oettinger, Katherine B.
Research Relating to Children. United States Department of Health, Education, and Welfare, Social Security Administration, Children's Bureau, Bulletin No. 9, reported August, 1958-February, 1959.

Includes research in progress or very recently completed. See Carroll, p. 146 and Joly, p. 142. JM

Ohannessian, Sirarpi
Interim Bibliography on the Teaching of English to Speakers of Other Languages. Washington, D.C.: Center for Applied Linguistics of the MLA, November, 1960.

Selective, 140-item annotated bibliography, stressing secondary-school materials but including college- and adult-level materials. Background readings, methodology, and texts listed. More comprehensive bibliography will follow. DG

Ohannessian, Sirarpi, Carol J. Kreidler, and Julia Sableski.
Reference List of Materials for English as a Second Language. Washington, D.C.: Center for Applied Linguistics, 1964.

This work is part one of a two-part project and consists of texts, readers, dictionaries and tests. The second part (to appear late in 1965) consists of background materials in linguistics, the English language, the psychology of language learning, and the methodology of language teaching. Supplements to *Reference List* will be published periodically. The work covers materials produced between the years 1953 and 1963. A number of bibliographies have resulted from the materials accumulated for *Reference List.* Among these bibliographies are *Interim Bibliography on the Teaching of English to Speakers of other Languages, a selected list of 145 items* (published in 1960), *30 Books for Teachers of English as a Foreign Language* (3rd ed., 1963), and *Visual Aids for English as a Second Language* (1964). CBC

Powers, Francis F.
"Selected References on Secondary-School Instruction: Foreign Language," *School Review,* LIII (February, 1945), 116-18.

―――.

"Selected References on Secondary-School Instruction: Foreign Language," *School Review,* LIV (February, 1946), 116-18.

―――.

"Selected References on Secondary-School Instruction: Foreign Language," *School Review,* LV (February, 1947), 116-18.

―――.

"Selected References on Secondary-School Instruction: Foreign Language," *School Review,* LVI (February, 1948), 115-17.

―――.

"Selected References on Secondary-School Instruction: Foreign Language," *School Review,* LVII (February, 1949), 120-21.

―――.

"Selected References on Secondary-School Instruction: Foreign Language," *School Review,* LVIII (February, 1950), 114-16.

―――.

"Selected References on Secondary-School Instruction: Foreign Language," *School Review,* LIX (February, 1951), 117-19.

―――.

"Selected References on Secondary-School Instruction: Foreign Language," *School Review,* LX (February, 1952), 115-19.

―――.

"Selected References on Secondary-School Instruction: Foreign Language," *School Review,* LXI (February, 1953), 116-20.

———.

"Selected References on Secondary-School Instruction: Foreign Language," *School Review,* LXII (February, 1954), 115-19.

———.

"Selected References on Secondary-School Instruction: Foreign Language," *School Review,* LXII (February, 1955), 113-17.

———.

"Selected References on Secondary-School Instruction: Foreign Language," *School Review,* LXIV (February, 1956), 87-89.

Psychological Abstracts. Lancaster, Penn.: American Psychological Association, 1927-.

Registry of Canadian Theses in Education, 1955-1962. Toronto: Research and Information Division, Canadian Education Association, June, 1963.

Research Studies in Education: A Subject Index of Doctoral Dissertations (1941-51) [supplemented]. Bloomington, Ind.: Phi Delta Kappa, 1941-.

Rice, Winthrop H.
"Annotated Bibliography of Modern Language Methodology," *Modern Language Journal,* XXX (May, 1946), 290-308.

———.

"Teaching Foreign Languages," *Review of Educational Research,* XVI (April, 1946), 139-60.
    A discussion of the year's (1945) publishing in the field of foreign-language instruction; bibliography. BP

Romeo, Luigi
A Selected Bibliography on the Application of Linguistics to Modern Language Teaching. Seattle, Wash.: Department of Romance Languages, University of Washington, 1960 (ditto).

Rufsvold, Margaret I., and Carolyn Guss
Guides to Newer Educational Media. Chicago: American Library Association in Cooperation with U.S. Office of Education, 1961.

Sánchez, José
"Twenty Years of Modern Language Laboratory: An Annotated Bibliography," *Modern Language Journal,* XLIII (May, 1959), 188-232.

————.
"Foreign Language Motion Pictures: An Annotated Bibliography,"
Modern Language Journal, XLIV (April, 1960), 177-85.

Schramm, Wilbur
The Research on Programmed Instruction. Washington, D.C.: U.S.
Office of Education, 1964.
Contains abstracts of all research on programmed instruction carried out and prior to Spring, 1963. DF

Sociological Abstracts. Ann Arbor, Mich.: Edwards Bros., 1953-.

Tharp, James B.
*Annotated Bibliographies of Modern Language Methodology for the
Years 1946, 1947, 1948.* Columbus, Ohio: Ohio State University,
1952.

————.
"Foreign Languages, Modern," *Encyclopedia of Educational Research.*
2nd ed. New York: Macmillan Co., 1950. Pp. 464-83.
See Birkmaier item above.

Tharp, James B., *et al.*
"Annotated Bibliography of Modern Language Methodology for
1949," *Modern Language Journal,* XXXV (January, 1951), 53-70.

Toronto Board of Education, Research Department
An Annotated Bibliography of Research Service Publication. Toronto Board of Education, February, 1963 (mimeographed).

Unbegaum, U. N.
A Bibliographical Guide to the Russian Language. London: Oxford
University Press, 1953.

UNESCO
A Bibliography on the Teaching of Modern Languages. (Prepared in
collaboration between the International Federation of Modern Language Teachers, the Modern Language Association of America, and
UNESCO.) (Educational Studies and Documents, No. 13.) Paris:
UNESCO, 1955.
This bibliography, based on items selected and annotated by
teachers themselves, begins listings with the year 1938 and is representative of a wide range of UNESCO states. DF

United States Office of Education. Language Development Program,
National Defense Education Act of 1958.

Completed Research, Studies, and Instructional Materials, List No. 4. Washington, D.C.: U.S. Office of Education, 1964.

Lists 295 completed research studies and instructional materials, and indicates how they may be obtained. This list replaces all previous lists in this series. DF

――――.

National Defense Language Development Program. *Research and Studies Contracted in Fiscal Years 1963 and 1964.* Washington, D.C.: U.S. Government Printing Office, 1964. [Publication no.] OE–12014-64.

U.S. Department of State. External Research Staff
External Research: A List of Current Social Science Research by Private Scholars and Academic Centers. Washington, D.C. 20520, 1952-.

[The 1964 issues state on the introductory page, "Beginning with this edition, there are seven instead of ten lists, the three separate Asian registers having been consolidated, and the Great Britain and Canada list having been incorporated into that of Western Europe." . . .

1.22 USSR and Eastern Europe	4.22 Middle East
2.22 Asia	5.22 Africa
3.22 Western Europe, Great Britain, and Canada	6.22 American Republics
	7.22 International Affairs]

Van Eenenaam, Evelyn
"Annotated Bibliography of Modern Language Methodology for 1950," *Modern Language Journal,* XXXVI (January, 1952), 39-56.

――――.

"Annotated Bibliography of Modern Language Methodology for 1951," *Modern Language Journal,* XXXVII (February, 1953), 85-108.

――――.

"Annotated Bibliography of Modern Language Methodology for 1952," *Modern Language Journal,* XXXVIII (January, 1954), 28-54.

――――.

"Annotated Bibliography of Modern Language Methodology for 1953," *Modern Language Journal,* XXXIX (January, 1955), 27-50.

――――.

"Annotated Bibliography of Modern Language Methodology for 1954," *Modern Language Journal,* XL (February, 1956), 83-104.

————.

"Annotated Bibliography of Modern Language Methodology for 1955," *Modern Language Journal,* XLI (February, 1957), 81-103.

————.

"Annotated Bibliography of Modern Language Methodology for 1956," *Modern Language Journal,* XLII (January, 1958), 27-43.

————.

"Annotated Bibliography of Modern Language Methodology for 1957," *Modern Language Journal,* XLIII (January, 1959), 34-49.

————.

"Annotated Bibliography of Modern Language Methodology for 1958," *Modern Language Journal,* XLIV (January, 1960), 24-42.

————.

"Annotated Bibliography of Modern Language Methodology for 1959," *Modern Language Journal,* XLV (January, 1961), 24-43.

Van Willigen, Daam M.
"Second Language Teaching and Secondary School," *Education Abstracts,* XIII, No. 3 (1961).
    This survey updates the UNESCO entry above present section of this Bibliography. A brief introduction of present trends is followed by a country-by-country survey of foreign language teaching with appropriate annotated bibliography entries. DF

————.

The Teaching of Modern Languages in Primary and Secondary Schools. Paris: UNESCO, 1961.
    This survey, published in French, English, and Spanish, updates the UNESCO entry above, this section. DF

Vinay, J.-P., J. B. Rudnyckyj, W. S. Avis
"Linguistica canadiana: a Linguistic Bibliography for 1961 and Supplement for Previous Years," *Canadian Journal of Linguistics,* VII (Spring, 1962), 113-18.

Williams, Jac L., editor
Bilingualism. A Bibliography with Special Reference to Wales. Aberystwyth, Wales: University College of Wales, 1960.
    Mainly relevant to Welsh-English bilingualism but containing references to many items of more general interest. Introduction, written in Welsh, maintains that most of the attempts made to compare the attainments and achievements of monolingual and bilingual children are of little scientific value because of failure to isolate bilingualism as

the only difference between the groups compared. It concludes that there was at that time no acceptable evidence that bilingualism is detrimental or beneficial to the child's educational development. Jac L. Williams

Wylie, Laurence
"The Culture of France: A Selective and Annotated Bibliography," *Modern Language Journal,* XXXVI (October, 1962), 55-67, same title and text published in *The French Review,* XXXVI, No. 1 (October, 1962), 55-67.
Reprinted from *Six Cultures* . . . , see following item.

Wylie, Laurence, *et al.*
"Six Cultures—(French, German, Hispanic, Italian, Luso-Brazilian, Russian): Selective and Annotated Bibliographies," in Modern Language Association of America, *Reports of Surveys and Studies* . . . See above, this section. For revisions of four of the bibliographies, see Fleissner, Else M. in this section.

PART II

Periodicals and Serials

Periodicals and Serials

ACLS Newsletter. 1949-. New York: American Council of Learned Societies.

Action. 1938-. New York.

Alberta Journal of Educational Research. 1927-. Edmonton: Committee on Educational Research, University of Alberta.

American Academy of Arts and Sciences. *Bulletin.* 1948-. Boston: American Academy of Arts and Sciences.

American Anthropologist. 1899-. Lancaster, Penn.: American Anthropological Association; Anthropological Society of New York; Anthropological Society of Washington; American Ethnological Society of New York.

American Journal of Mental Deficiency. 1896-. Albany, N.Y.: American Association on Mental Deficiency.

American Journal of Psychology. 1887-. Austin, Texas: Department of Psychology, University of Texas.

American Journal of Sociology. 1895-. Chicago: American Sociological Society; University of Chicago.

American Psychologist. 1946-. Washington, D.C.: American Psychological Association.

American School Board Journal. 1891-. Milwaukee, Wis.

American Speech. 1925-. Baltimore.

Américas. Enero, 1940-. New York: Las Américas Pub. Co.

Antioch College Reports. 1960-. Yellow Springs, Ohio: Fels Research Institute for the Study of Human Development.

Audio Engineering Society. 1953-. Utica, N.Y.: Audio Engineering Society.

Audio-Visual Communication Review. 1953-. Washington, D.C.: National Education Association.

Audio-Visual Guide. 1936-. Maplewood, N.J.: N.J. Educational and Recreational Guides.
    Merged with *Educational Screen* to form *Educational Screen and Audio-Visual Guide.*

Audio-Visual Instruction. 1956-. Washington, D.C.: National Education Association of the United States, Department of Audio-Visual Instruction.
    Title varies: Vol. I, Nos. 1-4 (1956) as *Instructional Materials.*

Automated Teaching Bulletin. 1960-. Los Angeles: Rheem Califone Corporation.

AVISO. 1957-. Vienna. Oesterreichische Gesellschaft für audio-visuelle Erziehung.

Babel. 1956-. Melbourne: Modern Language Teachers' Association of Victoria.

Behavioral Science. 1956-. Ann Arbor, Mich.: Mental Health Research Institute, University of Michigan.

Bell Laboratories Record. 1922-. New York.

British Journal of Educational Psychology. 1931-. Birmingham, Eng.: British Psychological Society; Training College Association.

Cahiers de pédagogie expérimentale et de psychologie de l'enfant. Published under the direction of L'Institut des sciences de l'éducation, University of Geneva. Delachaux et Niestlé, 32 rue de Grenelle, 7ᵉ impr. en Suisse.

Cahiers pédagogiques pour l'enseignement du second degré. L'enseignement des langues vivantes. 1945-. Lyons, France.

California Journal of Elementary Education. 1932-. Sacramento, Calif.: State Department of Education.

California Journal of Secondary Education. 1925-. Berkeley, Calif.: California Association of Secondary School Administrators.

California Schools. 1930-. Sacramento, Calif.: State Department of Education.

Canadian Education. 1945-. Toronto: Canadian Education Association.

Canadian Journal of Linguistics. Revue canadienne de linguistique. 1954-. Toronto: Canadian Linguistic Association.

Canadian Journal of Psychology. 1947-. Toronto: Canadian Psychological Association.

Canadian Modern Language Review. 1944-. Toronto: Ontario Modern Language Teachers' Association.

Catholic School Journal. 1901-. Milwaukee, Wis.: Bruce Publishing Co.

Cizi jazyky skole, 1957-. Prague.

Classical Journal. 1905-. Chicago: Classical Association of the Middle West and South; Classical Association of New England.

Clearing House. 1920-. Teaneck, N.J.: Fairleigh Dickinson University.

College and University Business. 1946-. Chicago: Nation's Schools Division.

College Board Review. 1947-. Princeton, N.J.: College Entrance Examination Board.
      Supersedes *College Entrance Examination Board News Bulletin.* 1901-. New York.

College English. 1939-. Chicago: National Council of Teachers of English.

Communications Review. 1945-. Sydney, Australia.

Current Digest of the Soviet Press. 1949-. Washington, D.C.: Joint Committee on Slavic Studies.

Deutsche Zeitschrift für Philosophie, 1953-. Berlin.

The DFL Bulletin. April, 1962-. Boston: Department of Foreign Languages, National Education Association.

Durham Research Review. 1950-. Durham, Eng.: Institute of Education, University of England.

Education. 1880-. Hingham, Mass.: Palmer Co.
      A monthly magazine devoted to the science, art, philosophy, and literature of education.

Education Digest. 1935-. Ann Arbor, Mich.

Éducation nationale. 1946-. Paris: Comité universitaire d'information pédagogique.
Supersedes *France.*

Educational Administration and Supervision. 1915-. Baltimore, Ohio: Warwick and York, Inc.

Educational and Psychological Measurement. 1941-. Chicago: Science Research Associates.

Educational Record. 1920-. Washington, D.C.: American Council on Education.

Educational Records Bulletin. 1928-. New York.

Educational Review. 1948-. Edinburgh; London: Institute of Education, University of Birmingham.

Educational Screen. 1922-. Chicago: Society for Visual Education.

Eight: Newsletter of 8mm Film in Education. 1965. New York: Project in Educational Communication of the Horace Mann-Lincoln Institute of School Experimentation, Teachers College, Columbia University.

Electronics. 1930-. New York: McGraw-Hill Publishing Corp.

Elementary English. 1924-. Champaign, Ill.: National Council of Teachers of English.

Elementary School Journal. 1900-. Chicago: University of Chicago.

Enfance: psychologie, pédagogie, neuropsychiatrie, sociologie. 1948-. Paris: 41 Rue Gay-Lussac.

English Language Teaching Monthly. 1946-. London: British Council.

English Teaching Abstracts. 1961-. London: English Teaching Information Center, British Council.

Erziehung und Unterricht. Vienna: Bundesverlag.

ETC: A Review of General Semantics. 1943-. Chicago: International Society for General Semantics.

The ETL Newsletter. 1959-. Washington, D.C.: Electronic Teaching Laboratories.

Études de linguistique appliquée. 1962-. Paris: Centre de Linguistique Appliquée, Faculté des Lettres, Université de Bescançon.

Exceptional Children. 1934-. Washington, D.C.: International Council for Exceptional Children.
   Published as *Journal of Exceptional Children,* 1935-51.

Explorations: Studies in Culture and Communication. 1953-. Toronto, Ont.

Financing Education. Lexington, Ky.: Bulletin of the Bureau of School Service, College of Education, University of Kentucky.

Foreign Language Bulletin.
   See: *Modern Language Association of America Foreign Language Bulletin.*

Forskning og Dannig.
   Publication information unavailable.

Le français dans le monde. 1961-. Paris.

Le français moderne: Revue de synthèse et de vulgarisation linguistique. 1933-. Paris: 17 Rue de la Rochefoucauld.

French Review. 1927-. Baltimore, Md.: American Association of Teachers of French.

Genetic Psychology Monographs. 1926-. Provincetown, Mass.: Clark University.

Georgetown University Monograph Series on Languages and Linguistics. See: Monograph Series of Language and Linguistics.

German Quarterly. 1928-. Lancaster, Penn.: American Association of Teachers of German.

Harvard Alumni Bulletin. 1898-. Cambridge, Mass.: Wadsworth House.

Harvard Educational Review. 1931-. Cambridge, Mass.: Graduate School of Education, Harvard University; Alumni Association; Harvard Teachers Association.
   Published as *Harvard Teachers Record,* 1931-36.

Harvard Graduate School of Education. *Bulletin.* March, 1958-. Cambridge, Mass.

Higher Education. 1945-. Washington, D.C.: U.S. Office of Education, Division of Higher Education.

High Points—in the Work of the High Schools of New York City. 1919-. Brooklyn, N.Y.: Board of Education.

Hispania. 1918-. Appleton, Wis.: American Association of Teachers of Spanish and Portuguese.

Hollywood Quarterly. 1945-. Berkeley, Calif.: Hollywood Writers Mobilization.
Title varies, appears also as the *Quarterly of Film, Radio, and Television.*

Iazyk i literatura.
Publication information unavailable.

Illinois Education. 1913-. Mount Morris, Ill.: Illinois Education Association.

Indiana University School of Education Bulletin. 1924-. Bloomington.

Inostrannye jazki škole, 1957-. Moscow.

Institute of International Education News Bulletin. 1920-. New York: Institute of International Education.

Institute of Radio Engineers. Transactions. 1955-. Ithaca, N.Y.: Professional Group on Information Theory.

Instructor. 1891-. Dansville, N.Y.: F. A. Owen Publishing Co.

International Journal of American Linguistics. Monographs. 1917-. New York: Columbia University.

International Review of Applied Linguistics in Language Teaching. 1963-. Heidelberg: Julius Groos.

Italica. 1924-. Evanston, Ill.: American Association of Teachers of Italian; Northwestern University.

Items. 1947-. Chicago: Social Science Research Council.

Jewish Education. 1929-. Chicago: National Council for Jewish Education.

Język rosyjski, 1948-. Warsaw.

Jezyki obce w szkole, 1957-. Warsaw.

Journal de psychologie normale et pathologique. 1904-. Paris: Presses universitaires de France.

Journal des professeurs de l'enseignement du second degré. 1947-. Paris.

Journal for Social Research. 1950-. Pretoria: National Council for Social Research.

Journal of Abnormal and Social Psychology. 1906-. Boston; Albany, N.Y.: American Psychopathological Association.

Journal of Applied Psychology. 1917-. Washington, D.C.: American Psychological Association.

Journal of Chemical Education. 1924-49. Easton, Penn.: American Chemical Society, Division of Chemical Education.

Journal of Clinical Psychology. 1945-. Brandon, Vt.

Journal of Communication. 1951-. Tallahassee, Fla.: National Society for the Study of Communication.

Journal of Education. 1875-. Boston: School of Education, Boston University.

Journal of Educational Psychology. 1910-. Washington, D.C.: American Psychological Association.

Journal of Educational Research. 1920-. Madison, Wis.: Educational Research Association.

Journal of Educational Sociology: A Magazine of Theory and Practice. 1927-. Albany, N.Y.: American Viewpoint Society.

Journal of Experimental Education. 1932-. Madison, Wis.: Dembar.

Journal of Experimental Psychology. 1916-. Lancaster, Penn.: American Psychological Association.

Journal of General Psychology: Experimental, Theoretical, Clinical, and and Historical Psychology. 1928-. Worcester, Mass.: Clark University Press.

Journal of Genetic Psychology. 1891-. Provincetown, Mass.: Journal Press.
  Title varies: see *Pedagogical Seminary* and the above title.

Journal of Higher Education. 1930-. Columbus, Ohio: Ohio State University, Bureau of Educational Research.

Journal of Humanistic Psychology. 1961-. Waltham, Mass.: Brandeis University.

Journal of Negro Education. 1932-. Washington, D.C.: Bureau of Educational Research, College of Education, Harvard University.

Journal of Psychology. 1936-. Provincetown, Mass.: Journal Press.

Journal of Social Psychology. 1929-. Provincetown, Mass.: Journal Press.

Journal of Speech and Hearing Disorders. 1936-. Columbus, Ohio: American Speech Correction Association.
Published as *Journal of Speech Disorders,* Nos. 1-12.

Journal of Teacher Education. 1950-. Washington, D.C.: National Education Association of the United States, National Commission on Teacher Education and Professional Standards.

Journal of the Acoustical Society of America. 1929-. Menasha, Wis.

Journal of the AERT. 1951[?]-. Chicago: Association for Education by Radio-Television.

Journal of the Canadian Linguistic Association. 1955-. Beauville, Quebec.

Journal of the Experimental Analysis of Behavior. 1958-. Indianapolis: Society for the Experimental Analysis of Behavior.

Journal of the Society of Motion Picture and Television Engineers. 1916-. Washington, D.C.: Society of Motion Picture and Television Engineers.

Journal of the University Film Producers Association. 1948-. Columbus, Ohio: Department of Photography, Ohio State University.

Journal of Verbal Learning and Verbal Behavior. 1962-. New York: Academic Press.

Journal of the Washington Academy of Science. 1911-. Washington, D.C.

Journalism Quarterly. 1924-. Grand Forks, N.D.; Urbana, Ill.: American Association of Teachers of Journalism; American Association of Schools and Departments of Journalism.

Junior College Journal. 1930-. American Association of Junior Colleges; School of Education, Stanford University.

Kasvatus ja koulu. 1914-. Jyväskylä, etc., Finland.

Kasvatusopillinen aikakauskirja. Helsinki: Suomen Kasvatusopillinen Yhdistys.
Summaries in English.

Kentucky Foreign Language Quarterly. 1954-. Lexington, Ky.: Department of Modern Foreign Languages, University of Kentucky.

Language. 1925-. Baltimore: Linguistic Society of America.

Language and Speech. 1958-. Middlesex, Eng.: Robert Draper.

The Language Laboratory and the Teaching of Literature. 1961-. New York: Modern Language Association Conference.

Language Learning: A Journal of Applied Linguistics. 1948-. Ann Arbor, Mich.: Research Club in Language Learning.

Language Monographs. 1925-. Philadelphia: Linguistic Society of America.
       Supplements to *Language.*

Les langues modernes. 1903-. Paris: Association des professeurs de langues vivantes de l'enseignement public.

Levende Talen, 1914-. Groningen.

Liberal Education. 1915-. Lancaster, Penn.: Association of American Colleges.

Lingua: International Review of General Linguistics. 1947-. Amsterdam: North Holland Publishing Co.

Linguistic Reporter. 1959-. Washington, D.C.: Center for Applied Linguistics.

Le maître phonétique. 1886-. Paris: International Phonetic Association.

Meet the Schools. St. Louis: St. Louis Board of Education.

Menninger Bulletin. 1936-. Topeka, Kan.: Menninger Clinic.

Michigan Education Journal. 1923-. Lansing, Mich.: Michigan Education Association.

Midland Schools. 1885-. Des Moines, Iowa: Iowa State Education Association.

Mitteilungsblatt des allgemeinen deutschen Neuphilologenverbandes. 1886-. Hanover.

MLabstracts. See Part I.

Modern Language Association of America. Foreign Language Bulletin. 1884-. New York: Foreign Language Program.

Modern Language Forum. 1915-. Los Angeles, Calif.: Modern Language Association of Southern California; Department of German, University of Southern California.

Modern Language Journal. 1916-. New York: Federation of Modern Language Teachers' Association; Associations of Modern Language Teachers of the Central West and South.

Modern Languages: A Review of Foreign Letters, Science, and the Arts. 1919-. London: Modern Language Association.

Monograph Series of Language and Linguistics. 1951-. Washington, D.C.: Institute of Languages and Linguistics, Georgetown University. Published materials of the Georgetown Conferences, beginning in 1950.

Montana Education. 1924-. Helena, Mont.: Montana Education Association.

NAEB Journal. 1941-. Urbana, Ill.: National Association of Educational Broadcasters.

National Association of Secondary School Principal's Bulletin. 1917-. Washington, D.C.: National Education Association.

National Education Association Journal. 1923-. Washington, D.C.

National Education Association Research Bulletin. 1923-. Washington, D.C.: Research Division of the National Education Association.

National Elementary Principal. 1921-. Washington, D.C.: National Education Association of the U.S. Department of Elementary School Principals.

Nation's Schools. 1928-. Chicago: Modern Hospital Publishing Co.

Die neueren Sprachen: Zeitschrift für den neusprachlichen Unterricht. 1893-. Marburg in Hessen.

Neuphilologische Zeitschrift. 1949. Berlin.

New York State Education. 1914-. Albany, N.Y.: New York State Teachers' Association.

North Central Association Quarterly. 1926-. Ann Arbor, Mich.: North Central Association of Colleges and Secondary Schools.

Northeast Conference on the Teaching of Foreign Languages. *Reports.* 1954 through 1958, University Microfilms, 313 North First St., Ann Arbor, Mich., 1959-, Materials Center, Modern Language Association of America.

Nova et Vetera. Brussels.

Nueva revista de filología hispánica. 1950-. México, D.F.: Colegio de México.

Ohio Schools. 1923-. Columbus, Ohio: Ohio Education Association.

Ontario Journal of Educational Research. 1958-. Toronto: Department of Educational Research, Ontario College of Education, University of Toronto.

Papers of the Michigan Academy of Science, Arts and Letters. 1921-. New York: Macmillan Co.

Pedagogia. 1953-. Río Piedras: College of Education, University of Puerto Rico.

Pedagogical Seminary and Journal of Genetic Psychology. 1891-. Worcester, Mass.

Pennsylvania School Journal. 1852-. Lancaster, Harrisburg, Penn.: Pennsylvania State Education Association.

Perceptual and Motor Skills. 1949-. Missoula, Mont.: Southern Universities Press.

Personnel and Guidance Journal. 1921-. Easton, Penn.: American Personnel and Guidance Association.
  Title varies.

Phi Delta Kappan. 1918-. Bloomington, Ind.: Phi Delta Kappa.

Phonetica. International Journal of Phonetics. 1957-. Basel.

Pittsburgh Schools. 1926[?]-. Pittsburg, Penn.: Division of Curriculum Development and Research, Board of Public Education.

PMLA. [Publications of the Modern Language Association of America]. 1884/85-. Menasha, Wis.: Modern Language Association of America.

Pour l'ère nouvelle. 1921-. Paris.

Proceedings of the Iowa Academy of Science. 1887/93-. Des Moines, Iowa.

Proceedings of the National Academy of Sciences. 1915-. Washington, D.C.

Programmed Instruction. 1961-. New York: Center for Programed Instruction, Inc.

Psychoanalytic Quarterly. 1932-. Albany, N.Y.: Psychoanalytic Quarterly Press.

Psychological Bulletin. 1904-. Lancaster, Penn.: New York; Princeton, N.J.

Psychological Monographs. 1895-. Washington, D.C.: American Psychological Association.

Psychological Records. 1951-. Granville, Ohio: Denison University.

Publications of the Language Laboratory. 1957-. Ann Arbor, Mich.: University of Michigan.

Quarterly Journal of Speech. 1915-. Chicago: National Association of Teachers of Speech.

Research and Studies. 1950-. Leeds, Eng.: Institute of Education, University of Leeds.

Review of Educational Research. 1931-. Washington, D.C.: American Educational Research Association, a department of the National Education Association.

Revista de educação pública. 1943-. Rio de Janeiro: Secretaria geral de educação e cultura.

Revue belge de psychologie et de pédagogie. Brussels.

Revue des langues vivantes. 1932-. Brussels: Fondation universitaire de Belgique. Flemish title: *Tijdschrift voor levende talen.*

Revue des sciences pédagogiques. Brussels.

Science. New series. 1895-. Cambridge, Mass.

Science News Letter: Weekly Summary of Current Science. 1921-. Washington, D.C.: Science Service.

School and Society. 1915-. New York; Garrison, N.Y.; Lancaster, Penn.: Society for the Advancement of Education.

School Executive. 1881-. New York: American School Publishing Corp.

School Life. 1918-. Washington, D.C.: U.S. Office of Education.

School Management and School Supply and Equipment News. 1932-. New York.

School Review: A Journal of Secondary Education. 1892-. Chicago: Department of Education Publications, University of Chicago.

Der Schüssel: Bild und Ton. 1951-. Vienna: Oesterreichisches Productivitätszentrum.

See and Hear. 1945-. Chicago: O. H. Coelln.

Slavic and East European Journal. 1945[?]-. Detroit: Wayne State University.
Title varies: appears also as *American Association of Teachers of Slavic and East European Languages.*

Social Education. 1937-. Crawfordsville, Ind.: American Historical Association; National Council for the Social Studies.
Social Forces. 1922-. Chapel Hill, N.C.: North Carolina University.

Social Process in Hawaii: 1936-. Honolulu: Romanzo Adams Social Research Laboratory and the Sociology Club of the University of Hawaii.

Social Science Research Council Items. See *Items.*

South African Council for Scientific and Industrial Research. National Institute for Personnel Research. *Journal.* Johannesburg.

Southern Speech Journal. 1935-. Tuscaloosa, Ala.

Sovetskaya Pedagogika. 1937-. Moscow: Akademiya Pedagogicheski- kha Nauk RSFSR.

Speech Monographs: Research Annual. 1934-. Ann Arbor, Mich.: National Association of Teachers of Speech.

Studia Linguistica. 1947-. Lund, Sweden: C.W.K. Gleerup.

System Development Corporation Field Notes. Santa Monica, Calif.: System Development Corporation.

Teacher Education. 1960-. London, Institute of Education, University of London.

Teachers College Journal. 1929-. Terre Haute, Ind.: Indiana State Teachers College, Division of Research.

Teachers College Record. 1900-. New York: Columbia University, Teachers College.

Teaching Tools: The Manual of Classroom Tested Techniques. 1953-. Los Angeles, Calif.: Ver Halen Publishing Co.

Technical Newsletter. St. Charles, Ill.: Du Kane Corporation, Commer- cial Sound Division.

Texas Outlook. 1916-. Fort Worth, Texas: Texas State Teachers' Association.

Times Education Supplement. 1910-. London: Times Education Supplement.

La traduction automatique. Bulletin bimestral de l'Association pour l'Étude et le Développement de la Traduction Automatique et de la Linguistique Appliquée. 1960-. 's-Gravenhage: Mouton.

United States Department of Health, Education and Welfare, Bulletin. 1889-. Washington, D.C.

Universities Quarterly. 1928-. London: Turnstile Press.

University of Kentucky Libraries, Occasional Contributions. 1949-. Lexington, Ky.

University of Manitoba Faculty of Education, Research Bulletin. Winnipeg, Man.

University of Michigan School of Education, Bulletin. October, 1929-. Ann Arbor, Mich.

University of Missouri, Bulletin. 1911-. Columbia, Mo.: Education Series.

Vestnik vysshei shkoly, [1943]-. Moscow: Ministerstvo vysshego i spetsial'nogo obrazovaniia SSSR.

Virginia Journal of Education. 1907-. Richmond, Va.: Virginia Educational Association.

Voprosky Psikhologii. 1955-. Moscow: Akademia Pedagogicheskika Nauk RSFSR.

Vuosikirja/Årsbok, 1960-. Helsinki.

Western Speech. 1937-. Los Angeles: Western Association of Teachers of Speech.

Wisconsin Journal of Education. 1871-. Madison, Wis.: Wisconsin Teachers' Association.

Word. 1945-. New York: Linguistic Circle of New York, Columbia University.

Zakład im Ossolińskich, 1957-. Wroclaw.

Zeitschrift für Phonetik, Sprachwissenschaft und Kommunikationsforschung. 1947-. Berlin: Akademie-Verlag Gmbh.
    Formerly: *Zeitschrift für Phonetik und allgemeine Sprachwissenschaft.*

PART III

Research Completed and in Progress

1. Methodology of Research

See pages xiv-xviii for comments on methods of research. See also Sections 2-7 for discussions and illustrations of methodology as applied to the respective areas of investigation, notably Section 5 for methodology of the study of cultures.

Carpenter, Clarence R.
"A Theoretical Orientation for Instructional Film Research," *Audio-Visual Communication Review,* I (1953), 38-52.

Résumé of some of the research and findings of the Instructional Film Research Program at Pennsylvania State College. Sets up guides for more effective production and use of films. BP

Carroll, John B.
"Research on Teaching Foreign Languages," in N. L. Gage (ed.), *Handbook of Research on Teaching.* Chicago: Rand McNally, 1963. Pp. 1060-1100.

This is a definitive review of research covering many aspects of foreign language teaching and learning. John B. Carroll.

————.

"Research Problems Concerning the Teaching of Foreign Languages to Younger Children," in H. H. Stern (ed.), *Foreign Languages in Primary Education: The Teaching of Foreign or Second Languages to Younger Children.* Hamburg: UNESCO Institute for Education, 1963. Chapter 20.

Delattre, Pierre
See Delattre, 4.3.

Fisher, Ronald A.
The Design of Experiments. London: Oliver and Boyd, 1947.

A discussion of the principles of experimentation with treatment of standardized statistical procedures for reaching unambiguous interpretation. JM

Fry, Edward

"Research Tools: Instrumentation in Educational Research," *Review of Educational Research,* XXV (December, 1960), 513-21.

This article cites a number of different devices that can be used in objective educational research with an emphasis on "teaching machine" type edvices. Extensive bibliography. Edward Fry

Gage, N. L. (ed.).

Handbook of Research on Teaching: A Project of the American Educational Research Association, A Department of the National Education Association. Chicago: Rand McNally, 1963.

"This Handbook is intended as an aid in the training of workers in research on teaching. If it succeeds, it will empower such research workers to begin at a higher level of competence and sophistication, to avoid past mistakes and blind alleys, to capitalize on the best that has been thought and done." From the preface. There are twenty-three chapters, each including a bibliography pertinent to the various subjects treated. Those chapters falling within the scope of this *Bibliography* have been mentioned in their proper place. DF

Glaser, Robert, (ed.).

Training Research and Education. Pittsburgh: University of Pittsburgh Press, 1962.

Good, Carter V.

"Research Methods Bibliography: Selected Bibliography on the Methodology of Educational, Psychological, and Social Research, 1945-1946," *Phi Delta Kappan,* XXVIII (January, 1947), 210-15.

For annotation see final item under Carter V. Good, below.

———.

"Research Methods Bibliography: Selected Bibliography on the Methodology of Educational, Psychological, and Social Research, 1946-1947," *Phi Delta Kappan,* XXIX (November, 1947), 146-52.

———.

"Research Methods Bibliography: Selected Bibliography on the Methodology of Educational, Psychological, and Social Research, 1947-1948," *Phi Delta Kappan,* XXX (September, 1948), 19-26.

———.

"Research Methods Bibliography: Selected Bibliography on the Methodology of Educational, Psychological, and Social Research, 1948-1949," *Phi Delta Kappan,* XXXI (September, 1949), 38-46.

————.

"Research Methods Bibliography: Selected Bibliography on the Methodology of Educational, Psychological, and Social Research, 1949-1950," *Phi Delta Kappan,* XXXII (September, 1950), 11-15, 18-22.

————.

"Research Methods Bibliography: Selected Bibliography on the Methodology of Educational, Psychological, and Social Research, 1950-1951," *Phi Delta Kappan,* XXXIII (September, 1951), 45-52, 61.

Bibliography is divided into four parts: (1) problems, issues, trends, and critiques; (2) library guides, bibliographies, and summaries; (3) collecting, analyzing, interpreting, and reporting data; and (4) organization, supervision, implementation, and support of graduate and research programs. BP

Hayes, Alfred S.

"A Tentative Schematization for Research in the Teaching of Cross-Cultural Communication," *International Journal of American Linguistics,* XXVIII (January, 1963, Part II), 155-67.

In this paper I develop a classification of research activities which, ideally, contribute to teaching materials and methods. The classification is student-oriented, and is addressed to two questions: (1) what do we teach?; (2) How do we teach? Research activities answering the first question are called descriptive research; those answering the second are called instrumental. Within each of these categories the terms "basic" and "applied" research are discarded in favor of theoretical and developmental research respectively. Linguistics and cultural anthropology are prime descriptive categories; psycholinguistics and electromechanics are important instrumental categories. The interrelationships on and within each level of research are treated in detail. A chart is included. Alfred S. Hayes, MLabstract #183.

Lane, Harlan

"Experimentation in the Language Classroom: Guidelines and Suggested Procedures for the Classroom Teachers," *Language Learning,* XII (1962), 115-21.

To stimulate the foreign language teacher to use research methods within the classroom using the techniques and findings of behavioral science. Four classroom experiments are proposed for use as well as suggestions for evaluating the reliability of experiments and the significance of their results. JM

Modern Language Association of America, Committee on Research Activities.
"Aims, Methods, and Materials of Research in the Modern Languages and Literatures," *PMLA,* LXVII (October, 1952), 3-37.

The MLA Committee on Research Activities here outlines and clarifies the objectives of modern language and literature study. BP

Pimsleur, Paul
"Experimental Design in the Language Field," *Modern Language Forum,* XLII (December, 1957), 157-63.

Delineates the essential elements of experimentation for the teacher who wishes objective evidence of the quality of new teaching materials. The article outlines these elements in terms of hypothesis, control, scientific attitude, method, statistical analysis, and consideration of problems of measurement. JM Reprinted in the *MST English Quarterly,* VII, Nos. 3-4 (1958), 8-13.

Stern, J. J.
See Stern, 6.1.

2. Methods, Materials, and Equipment

2.1 General

Agard, Frederick B.
"The University of Chicago Language Investigation: A Report of Progress," *Hispania,* XXX (February, 1947), 45-49.
Preliminary report, by a staff member, of research undertaken to evaluate current experiments in modern foreign-language teaching, with a description of the testing methods, the setting up of norms and control groups, and the methods of checking scores against related data, such as grades in English, grade-point average, etc. Tentative conclusions indicated considerable differences in favor of experimental students in some cases, slight difference in others. More specific findings and conclusions will follow at the end of the final year of research. MJS

Agard, Frederick B., and Harold B. Dunkel
An Investigation of Second Language Teaching. Boston: Ginn and Co., 1948.
Controlled research to secure objective evidence on some questions regarding second-language teaching. Results indicated that superior reading skills are developed in those programs where reading receives the greatest time and emphasis, that oral-aural competence does not automatically create reading ability, and that most students are more highly motivated by oral-aural rather than grammar or reading goals. TD

*Artemov, V. A.
"Kibernetika, teorija kommunikacii i škola [Cybernetics. A Theory of Communications and the School]," *Sovetskaia pedagogika,* XXVI, No. 1 (1962), 26-36.

Beliaev, Boris Vasilevich
"K khavrakteristike zarubezhnoĭ (zapadnoevropeĭskoĭ i amerikanskoĭ)

psikhologii obucheniya inostrannym yazykom [Towards a Characterization of the Foreign (Western-Europe and American) Psychology of Training in Foreign Languages]," *Voprosy psikhologii,* No. 1 (1962), 157-67.

A review of work on the title subject done during the 1st half of the century. The author summarizes current foreign trends mentioning specifically trends toward: (a) practical use of language and not theoretical knowledge; (b) emphasis of thinking directly in the foreign language rather than translating; (c) training in various methods for ascertaining the meaning of a foreign language selection; (d) increased size of units which are taught, e.g., phrases rather than words; (e) training in the spoken language preceding training in the written language; and (f) taking an eclectic approach to language training methods. (92 item bibliography) H. Pick. From *Psychological Abstracts,* 37:3796.

*Benediktov, B. A., and V. E. Jarnatovskaja
"Mezvuzovskie metodiceskie konferencii o metodike prepodavanija inostrannych jazykov [Theoretical-methodological Conference on the Questions of Foreign Language Teaching]," *Vestnik vysshei shkoly,* XVIII, No. 9 (1960), 32-34.

Birkmaier, Emma
An Investigation of the Outcomes in the Eclectic, Reading and Modified Army Method Courses in the Teaching of a Second Language. Unpublished Ph.D. dissertation, University of Minnesota, 1949.

Discusses aural-oral superiority of a control group tested against a group trained by traditional grammar-translation method. BP

Blickenstaff, Channing B.
"Musical Talents and Foreign Language Learning Ability," *Modern Language Journal,* XLVII (December, 1963), 359-63.

In this article I review research answers to this question: Is proficiency in the six *Seashore Measures of Musical Talent* (pitch discrimination, timbre, tonal memory, time, rhythm, and loudness) related to foreign language learning ability? There is good evidence that pitch discrimination is related positively and independently—though modestly—to the auditory comprehension of French and Spanish; timbre discrimination also appears to be related to French auditory comprehension; there is less evidence with respect to tonal memory, but the indications are that it may be unrelated to ability in foreign languages. Finally, the relationships of the remaining Seashore measures have apparently not been investigated, although research on native language abilities indicates that a pattern of small, but consistent relationships may indeed exist for these elements. Channing B. Blickenstaff, MLabstract #647.

Bohlen, Adolf
Methodik des neusprachlichen Unterrichts. Heidelberg: Quelle und Meyer, 1953.

Philosophy, aim, methods, and devices for modern-language instruction (French and English), especially in northwest Germany, up to 1952. Author is director of the Landesinstitut für Neue Sprachen in Münster, Westfalia. Richard Wilkie.

Brooks, Nelson. Yale University, New Haven, Conn.
A Model Plan for the Production of Materials in Foreign Languages; Project No. 8,537 (National Defense Education Act, Title VI), November 27, 1959, to December 31, 1959; $400.

This report covers methods, materials, and patterns for a continuous sequence of study from grades three through twelve in view of the new philosophies of language teaching and the latest developments. BP

————.

Language and Language Learning, 2nd ed. New York: Harcourt, Brace, 1964.

The purpose of the book is to find a more perfect system to teach students language fluency. To accomplish this purpose the author explores what language is, how it works, and how it is learned. BP

Capretz, Pierre J.
Audio-Lingual Techniques for Teaching Foreign Languages; Project No. 9361 (National Defense Education Act, Title VI), February, 1961 to February, 1963, $101,600.

A series of four 60-minute black and white, 16mm sound motion picture films, demonstrating audio-lingual techniques for teaching foreign languages (French, German, Russian and Spanish) at the secondary school level. Distributed by Norwood Films, Washington, D.C., and Audio Visual Center, University of Indiana, Bloomington, Indiana. Pierre J. Capretz

Childers, J. Wesley
Foreign Language Offerings and Enrollments in Public Secondary Schools, Fall 1959. New York: Modern Language Association, 1961.

Gives the public high school enrollments in all foreign languages in the fall of 1959, pointing up the demonstrable effect which the first full year of the National Defense Education Act had upon the offerings and enrollments in foreign languages in the United States. J. Wesley Childers

Curran, Charles A.
"Counseling Skills Adapted to the Learning of Foreign Languages," *Menninger Bulletin,* XXV (March, 1961), 78-93.

In this research project we developed a method of personal communication through a language counselor patterned on counseling skills and relationships to facilitate the learning of four foreign languages simultaneously. As in psychological counseling, the language counselor, a native, offered warmth and security to the person who was able to speak directly and correctly to the group through addressing him first in English and he was then helped to speak the foreign language correctly to the group. We developed five stages in the language counselor-client relationship ranging from client dependence to independence. Subjects were tested before and after each semester with significant language gains in reading and speaking all four languages. We feel that the utilization of this method, based on counseling skills, enabled each subject to speak the foreign language through the native counselor without the tension and threat usually involved in speaking a foreign language. Charles A. Curran.

*DeBlois, Donald
On Foreign Language Teaching—A Structural-Comparative Approach. Unpublished Ph.D. dissertation, Hartford Seminary Foundation (Case Memorial Library of the Hartford Seminary Foundation), n.d.

*Dembowski, Johann
Über einige Fragen des Sprechens und seiner Entwicklung im Lichte kybernetischer Anschauungen [On Some Questions of Speaking and Its Development in the Light of the Observations of Cybernetics]," *Deutsche Zeitschrift für Philosophie,* X (1962), 313-25.

Dunkel, Harold B.
Second Language Learning. Boston: Ginn and Co., 1948.

A critical re-examination of basic knowledge and theory of second-language learning, based on original experimental data and other factual evidence. General theory is stressed rather than classroom practice. Some sections are devoted to elements of aural comprehension and speaking; factors to be considered include student's age, intelligence and background, previous skills, motivation, and his contact with materials and teacher. The appendix refers to Persian materials for the study of language learning—as a method of applying techniques —and the resolutions adopted at the Chicago Language Conference in 1948. Extensive bibliography. JM

Fea, Henry R.
See Russel, 2.1

Gorokhoff, Boris I.
Language Development in the Soviet Union: A Preliminary Survey. Washington, D.C.: U.S. Office of Education, December 11, 1962 (mimeographed).

The above report is designed to be a preliminary review of Soviet language development, for use mainly in determining the need for, and the nature of, further research. It was compiled over five weekends chiefly on the basis of standard Russian reference works and key articles in two leading Soviet journals; thus, it is not a definitive study and findings may be revised after further research. No effort was made to achieve completeness in the bibliographical references. However, it is hoped that this report may serve as an aid in further research in an important and interesting field. From the Postscript to the report.

————.

Review of Language Development in the Soviet Union; Project No. OE-3-14-011 (National Defense Education Act, Title VI), December 1, 1962, to February 15, 1963; $400.

The investigator prepared a brief (50-page), preliminary review of foreign language development in the Soviet Union. This information will aid the planning of foreign language development in the United States by outlining similar activity in the Soviet Union. The report, designed primarily for administrative purposes, will help not only to assess the need for further research in Soviet language development, but also to indicate the main published sources, both in English and Russian, which could be used for such study. The report covers the following subjects: Soviet language policies, development of Soviet minority languages, development of the Russian language, linguistic research, study and teaching, publications, translations, mechanical translation, and languages and foreign policy.

Hamilton, Daniel L.
"Changes in the Teaching of Romance Languages at the University of Texas," *Texas Outlook,* XXXI (June, 1947), 36-37.

A three-year experiment, comparing aural-oral approach with traditional grammar approach through use of textbooks in classes of French and Spanish. No significant differences resulted between the two approaches in the French classes. Some difference noted in Spanish, but the statistics presented are not well verified. JM

Hayes, Alfred S., Takoma Park, Md.
Study and Critical Evaluation of Research and Experimentation Relevant to the Teaching and Learning of Foreign Language; Project No. 9,000 (National Defense Education Act, Title VI), August 8, 1960, to August 7, 1962; $53,865.

Entails a thorough survey and study of the entire range of actual and possible research and experimental activities relevant to the teaching and learning of modern foreign languages, producing a systematic classification of all such research and experimentation, in chart form, and analyses and evaluations of pertinent work, with all projects classified according to the new schematization. From the official description; unpublished, July, 1961. See Hayes, 1.

Johnston, Marjorie C.
"Foreign Language Instruction," *Review of Educational Research,* XXXI (April, 1961), 188-96.

Report reviews research relating to foreign language instruction in the period 1957-1960. Surveys investigating the foreign language curriculum and classroom enrollment in secondary schools; of languages spoken in Hawaii and Africa; and college entrance and degree requirements relating to foreign languages are reported. Research studying methods and materials of instruction including language laboratories and audiovisual aids are indicated. Studies on foreign language instruction in elementary schools are noted. Studies developing aptitude tests for measurement of linguistic ability, and the relationship of ability and motivation to achievement are reported. Report notes the increase in research due to stimulation and sponsorship by the National Defense Education Act of 1958. 63 references. Center for Documentation and Communication Research, Western Reserve University.

Kreusler, Abraham
The Teaching of Modern Foreign Languages in the Soviet Union. Leiden, Holland: E. J. Brill, 1963.

The book is a comprehensive account of the history and methods of teaching modern foreign languages in prerevolutionary Russia and in the Soviet Union. Abraham Kreusler

Lindeman, Louise
"Research in Progress in the Modern Languages and Literatures," *PMLA,* LXXIII (April, 1958), 45-93.

Lumsdaine, A. A.
"Instruments and Media of Instruction," in N. L. Gage (ed.), *Handbook of Research on Teaching.* Chicago: Rand McNally, 1963. Pp. 583-682.
An authoritative survey, with extensive bibliographic references, of research in the area. DF

MacGowan, Kenneth, *et al.*
"Attention, Travaux," *Times Educational Supplement,* March 6, 1964, pp. 565-69.
Although this series of short articles reports no real controlled research, it does describe several programs of foreign language implementation in Great Britain. Particularly important is the Ministry of Education's pilot program, set for late 1964; foreign language teacher training in Dorset, described by its leader, W. B. Seacroft; and Nuffield Foundation's foreign language teaching materials project in the City and the University of Leeds, described by its organizer, A. Spicer. DF

Mackey, William Francis
"Shipboard Language Teaching," *English Language Teaching,* XI (April-June, 1957), 86-97.
This is a series of experiments in mass teaching of languages over short periods to adults travelling between Europe and America and Europe and Australia. The data was gathered in seven Atlantic sailings of 7 to 10 days and two Australian sailings of 27 to 30 days. The latter included a group of some 2,000 learners speaking 15 different national tongues. They were taught to understand about 300 words of oral English in simple question and answer structures and use about 150 of these in simple structures. The five hours a day of instruction were conducted by a single instructor using mass presentation with film-strips and loudspeaker, followed by individual study, demonstration and practice of same material in small groups through techniques of devolution (snoball techniques), and finally review and testing through captionless film-strips. Similar techniques were used in the North Atlantic sailings but instead of attempting to lay the foundations of a new language (French, German, English, Spanish) about ten productive patterns were successfully taught with some useful vocabulary and techniques for fitting new words into the basic structures. William F. Mackey

†———.
A Study of Available Vocabulary. Research in Progress.
Since the frequency and range of concrete nouns have been

shown to lack stability, this important part of any limited vocabulary for language teaching purposes must be determined by other means, the most objective of which seems to be the consensus of a large sample of native speakers in the most usual semantic fields. Therefore, for each of 25 semantic fields concerned with everyday conversation, 2,000 French-speaking subjects were asked (during the years 1962 and 1963) to write 20 names of things. The number of times a word appeared was taken as a measure of its availability. The resulting million words were transferred to punch-cards to be analyzed and classified by an IBM 1410 at the Laval Data Processing Centre. The results are to be compared with those of similar studies being conducted in France, Switzerland, and other parts of Canada. William F. Mackey

†Malcolm, D. J. Educational Testing Service, Princeton, New Jersey
Effects of Teaching Method on CEEB Language Scores. Research in Progress.

The purpose of this research is to obtain evidence concerning the relationship between performance on the CEEB French Test as a whole and on particular item types and the type of language training experienced by candidates, i.e., audiolingual, conventional, or a combination of the two. Progress: By means of a questionnaire, information on instructional methodology was obtained from 338 teachers of French in 95 secondary schools. Each questionnaire has been scored in such a way as to yield an index of the extent to which the teacher uses audiolingual as distinguished from traditional methods of instruction. Using the teacher indices as independent variables, the performance of candidates from the 95 schools in the study on the January 1963 CEEB French Test will be analyzed. The study will be completed in the fall of 1963. (Project supported by the College Entrance Examination Board.) From the ETS *Annual Report,* 1962-63

Michéa, R.
"Limitation et sélection du vocabulaire dans l'enseignement actif des langues vivantes," *Revue des langues vivantes,* XXII (1956), 467-74.

States the general principles underlying vocabulary selection, and explains the meaning of vocabulary limitation, frequently occurring words and common words. The author studies the lexicological and statistical structure of vocabulary lists, and compares the words in such lists with those used in the spoken language. He also deals with automatism and with the teaching of correct and fluent speech. From van Willigen, Part I

Mildenberger, Kenneth W.
See Mildenberger, 7.

Morton, F. Rand
Report on a Pilot Experiment in Second Language Instruction Employing the Concept of "Acoustic Reflex" Conditioning. Cambridge, Mass.: Department of Romance Languages, Harvard University, 1954.
   Summary report of procedures used and results received from a one-semester programed autoinstructional course in spoken American Spanish. The report was subsequently expanded and included in the author's monograph, *The Language Laboratory as a Teaching Machine* (Publications of the Language Laboratory, 1960). See Oinas, Section 2.54.

Moulton, William G.
See Moulton, 4.1.

Mueller, Klaus A.
"Experimentation and Research in the Development of Modern Language Materials and Teaching Methods," *International Journal of American Linguistics,* XXVIII (January 1962, Part II), 92-104.
   In this paper I report the status of experimentation in foreign language teaching techniques and materials at the end of the first semester of a projected four-year program of the Associated Colleges of the Midwest. I describe briefly seven experimental designs which explore the desirability of withholding writing activity during beginning phases of language learning, the efficacy of teaching devices such as language laboratories, the degree of mastery necessary to permit students to advance to new materials, questions of class size, the question of monitored vs. non-monitored lab sessions. I describe in some detail the plan for each of these designs, the problems inherent in them as well as projected solutions. Klaus A. Mueller, MLbstract #210.

Mueller, Klaus A., and William Wiersma, Jr.
"Correlation of Foreign Language Speaking Competency and Grades in Ten Midwestern Liberal Arts Colleges," *Modern Language Journal,* XLVII (December, 1963), 353-55.
   Reports findings which relate audio-lingual competency of students to faculty evaluation of students' overall proficiency in beginning language courses. Five experimental designs are briefly summarized and correlation statistics are presented. The significant finding is that of the four basic language skills, speaking ability receives the

major emphasis in the courses of the ten colleges and speaking competence is reflected in the grades assigned by the instructors. JM

Parker, William Riley
"What's Past Is Prologue," *PMLA,* LXXI (April, 1956), 3-13.

A report on the first six years (1952-56) of the Foreign Language Program of the Modern Language Association of America. During those years, the MLA investigated the extent and character of language teaching in the United States, defined unfilled needs, and established teacher qualifications. It sponsored a summer conference held at the University of Michigan in the summer of 1953 on language and culture in the second-year university course (see MLA Interdisciplinary Seminar, Section 8.5), and generated the project that produced the textbook *Modern Spanish* (New York: Harcourt, Brace and Co., 1960). The program did not directly produce any research in that period on methods, materials, or equipment. HLN

Parker, William Riley, and Robert Graham Sawyer
"Research in Progress in the Modern Languages and Literatures," *PMLA,* LXIII (May, 1948), 138-405.

Pierce, Joe E.
A Method of Teaching Second Languages. Portland, Oregon: Middle East Studies Center, Portland State College, 1963.

The book is a brief manual for the teacher untrained in Linguistics. It explains first phonemics in very simple everyday language and contrasts the English and Turkish phonemic systems. Then there is a discussion of methodology for teaching utilizing the problems common to Turkish speakers for examples in teaching phonology. Then morphology is explained and methods of teaching English to non-native speakers is again illustrated by the errors common to Turks who are learning English. There is a brief discussion of English syntax and a chapter on audio-visual aids, especially with reference to trying to teach in an under developed country. Joe E. Pierce

Poltoratzky, Marianna A.
Methods of Teaching Foreign Languages in the Soviet Union. Washington, D.C.: U.S. Office of Education, 1961.

Research in Library of Congress, Library of U.S. Education Office, and from material sent to me by the Academy of Sciences, USSR (Research Institute of Russian Language). My conclusions are that at the present time the teaching of foreign languages is at a high level in the Soviet Union, special attention being given to the teaching of the English language. The Russian language is taught throughout

Russia, including all national minority groups and the Russian language is taught in all schools of the satellite countries, beginning in elementary school. They used the grammar translation methods until 1959; however, after Khrushchev's visit to the U.S., they introduced the American method of active participation on the audio-lingual. They stress the ability of the spoken language with direct communication with foreign peoples. They also introduced the language lab technique, following the American methods. Marianna A. Poltoratzky

Russell, David H., and Henry R. Fea
"Research on Teaching Reading," Chapter 16 of N. L. Gage (ed.), *Handbook of Research on Teaching.* Chicago: Rand McNally and Co., 1963. Pp. 865-928.
    Section and subsection headings A HISTORICAL BACKGROUND OF READING INSTRUCTION. TEACHING OF IDENTIFICATION AND RECOGNITION: Visual Perception, Auditory Perception, Kinesthetic Perception, Multisensory Perception, Implications for Teaching and Research. TEACHING MEANING: Percepts, Concepts, Verbals. COMPREHENSION ACCORDING TO THE PURPOSES OF THE READER: Critical Reading, Creative Reading. COMPREHENSION ACCORDING TO SUBJECT-MATTER FIELDS: Social Studies, Mathematics, Science, English. THE TEACHER ENCOURAGES INTERPRETATION. CLASSROOM ORGANIZATION: Purposes of Grouping, Types of Grouping, Experiments in Grouping, Individualized Programs. EMERGING PROBLEMS IN RESEARCH ON TEACHING: The Growth of the Mass Media, Television, Other Audio-Visual Devices. Individualization of Instruction, Reading Readiness Reconsidered, The Role of Parents. References, pp. 918-928.

Ryden, Einar R.
Vocabulary as an Index to Learning in a Second Language. Unpublished Ph.D. dissertation, Northwestern University, 1947.
    See annotation on following entry.

———.

"Vocabulary as an Index of Learning in a Second Language," *Journal of Educational Psychology,* XXXIX (November, 1948), 436-40.
    The object of this study is to "provide a rationale and an experimental measuring procedure by which it is possible to evaluate the various methods of teaching in the field of a second language in quantitative terms." Three specific objectives are listed dealing with the relationship of vocabulary as an index to learning. Testing method is described by reference. Three suggestions for further research are listed. JM

Sawyer, Jesse O.
"Foreign Language Instruction," *Review of Educational Research,* XXXIV (April, 1964), 203-10.

This review comments on general trends in language instruction and selects for brief notice some thirty pieces of research spanning the period September 1960 to September 1963. Jesse O. Sawyer

Sawyer, Jesse O., *et al.*
The Utility of Translation and Written Symbols During the First Thirty Hours of Language Study. Berkeley, California: Department of Speech, University of California, July 1962.

In this research project we studied college student acquisition of a second language under oral-aural conditions. The purpose of the experiment was the comparison of three orders of presentation of material and the assessment of the effects of having a text available. None of the variations appeared to have a direct effect on learning or recall of pronunciation, syntax, or meanings. There were indications that students may benefit from training with a text (in normalized phonemics), especially if they are trained in a language laboratory where the motivation and social stimulation may be reduced. Jesse O. Sawyer, MLabstract #316. Final Report

Sawyer, Robert Graham
"Research in Progress in Modern Languages and Literatures," *PMLA,* LXIV (May, 1949), 91-292.

———.

"Research in Progress in Modern Languages and Literatures," *PMLA,* LXV (April, 1950), 123-288.

Scherer, George A. C., and Michael Wertheimer
A Psycholinguistic Experiment in Foreign-Language Teaching. New York: McGraw-Hill, 1964.

An audiolingual and a traditional method of teaching German to 290 beginning college students were compared in a two-year experiment. Student assignment to class sections resulted in groups initially comparable in general ability, language-learning aptitude, sex, age, year in college, motivation for the study of German, and previous experience with German; treatment and testing of the experimental (audiolingual) and control (traditional) students were the same except for the method of teaching employed.

Significant differences in student performance were obtained in many measures. By the end of the first year the experimental students were far better than the controls in speaking and listening, but worse in reading, writing, and translation; by the end of the second year they were still clearly better in speaking but poorer in writing, with the other differences having diminished or disappeared. Composite overall scores for proficiency in the usual language skills did not clearly favor either method at any time in the experiment.

Psycholinguistic measures of ability to "think in German" consistently favored the experimental group; this held on objective scores on a variety of new tests as well as subjective self-ratings by the students. Quality and intensity of motivation were not appreciably different in the two groups, but the experimental displayed more positive attitudes towards Germans and the speaking of German.

While neither method was thus unequivocally superior to the other, the methods did produce sizable differences in various aspects of student performance. M. Wertheimer

Scherer, George A. C., *et al.*
"Reading for Meaning," in William F. Bottiglia (ed.), *Reports of the Working Committees, Northeast Conference on the Teaching of Foreign Languages.* Oxford, Ohio: The American Classical League Service Bureau, Miami University, 1963. Pp. 22-60.

Deals with the problem of teaching reading from first reading of memorized materials, to the reading of contrived materials followed by adapted literary selections and finally to liberation in reading from the usual glosses. George A. C. Scherer

Sebeok, Thomas A., A. S. Hayes, and M. C. Bateson, eds.
Approaches to Semiotics: Cultural Anthropology, Education, Linguistics, Psychiatry, Psychology; Transactions of the Conference on Paralinguistics and Kinesics. The Hague: Mouton, 1964.

See in particular the third section entitled "Paralinguistics and Kinesics: Pedagogical Perspectives," by Alfred S. Hayes, as well as the "Discussion Session on Language Teaching," chairmaned by William R. Parker. DF

Slichenmyer, H. L.
"Arlington Heights, Illinois, Studies Curriculum and Testing, Instruction Assistants, Team Teaching and Modern Technology in Fourteen Projects," *Bulletin of the National Association of Secondary School Principals,* XLV (January, 1961), 41-49.

Report for the Commission on Experimental Study of the Utilization of Staff in the Secondary School. Study of test scores and course grades of high school and college students to determine the effectiveness of experiments involving a language laboratory, audiovisual aids,

remedial mathematics, emphasis on technical aspects in speech instruction, and integrated teaching of English and Latin. Center for Documentation and Communication Research, Western Reserve University.

Starr, Wilmarth H., Mary P. Thompson, and Donald D. Walsh
Modern Foreign Languages and the Academically Talented Student:
Report of a Conference sponsored jointly by the National Education
Association Project on the Academically Talented Student and the
Modern Language Association of America, Foreign Language Pro-
gram. Washington, D.C.: National Education Association Project on
the Academically Talented Student, and New York: Modern Lan-
guage Association of America, Foreign Language Program Research
Center, 1960.

Summary of conclusions reached by members of the Conference
summoned as leaders in the area of modern foreign languages. Discusses the Objectives, the Teacher, the Program, and the Administration as related to the foreign language curriculum. Wilmarth H. Starr

Stone, George Winchester, Jr., and Louise Lindeman
"Research in Progress in the Modern Languages and Literature,"
PMLA, LXXI (April, 1956), 267-345.

Suppes, Patrick and Ruth Weir, The Board of Trustees of Leland Stan-
ford University, Stanford, California
Application of Quantitative Analysis and Computer Data Processing
Technology to Problems of Second-Language Acquisition; Project
No. OE-3-14-020 (National Defense Education Act, Title VI), June
1, 1963, to June 30, 1964; $67,689.

Under U.S. Office Education contract SAE-9514, the contractor
undertook a series of quantitative studies to analyze second-language
learning in terms of stimulus-response theory. The findings have been
published by the Institute for Mathematical Studies in the Social
Sciences, Stanford University. [See Suppes, 3.1, 4.3]

The work performed under this former contract began with a
study of phonological discriminations in syllables and continued
through phoneme and word discriminations in longer contexts. Thereafter the investigators shifted to a study of the acquisition of grammatical concepts, e.g., a gender-case analysis of the learning of three
noun categories in three different cases in Russian, and the roles of
positive and negative transfer.

Under this contract the investigation was extended to other
morphological and syntactical problems, continuing the effort to
develop a quantitative theory of second-language learning. This study

examined five general areas of language learning: (1) component versus pattern learning, (2) order of presentation, (3) reaction time, (4) paired associate learning, and (5) rate of intake.

A secondary result of the research was a body of preliminary data and experience essential to the eventual application of computer technology to the design and presentation of "programmed" (step-increment) self-instructional foreign language courses.

Symposion methodieck en didactiek levende talen. Report of the Verslag Conferentie Wondschoten held at Scheveningen, 1959.

The report of a symposium on the teaching of modern languages organized by the co-operating educational research centres and the Netherlands asociation of modern language teachers. The report gives the text of the speeches and summaries of the discussions. From van Willigen, Part I.

Taylor, Robert E.
"Research in Progress in the Modern Languages and Literatures," *PMLA*, LXVI (April, 1951), 157-311.

———.
"Research in Progress in the Modern Languages and Literatures," *PMLA*, LXVII (April, 1952), 115-336.

Taylor, Robert E., and Trudy K. Railing
"Research in Progress in Modern Languages and Literatures," *PMLA*, LXIX (April, 1954), 203-346.

Templin, Mildred C.
Certain Languages Skills in Children: Their Development and Inter-relationships. Institute of Child Welfare Monograph Series, No. 26. Minneapolis: University of Minnesota Press, 1957.

An experiment that obtained measures of four language skills in children; articulation of speech sounds, sound discrimination, vocabulary, and verbalizations. RK

UNESCO
Modern Languages in the Schools: (Educational Studies and Documents, No. 6.) UNESCO, 1953.

Discusses a seminar conducted in Ceylon on foreign-language instruction. Minimum length of time devoted to foreign-language study in countries outside the United States is four years. Some countries require as much as nine years. United States is at the bottom of the list with an elective of two years. JM

Valverde Z., Luis J.
Pilot Study of Second Language Learning. Los Angeles: School of Education, University of California, 1958 (mimeographed).

Purpose/Scope: 1) to examine the state of Language Learning from a multidisciplinary vantage point; 2) to identify and select some factors which may condition the learning of Spanish (and English) as second languages; and 3) to report the possible correlations and inter-relationships between learning and the target language. Methods: library research; survey, analysis and experimentation. Major Findings: 1) great lag exists in the measurement of English and Spanish as foreign languages, 2) the lag is connected with unscientific views of language teaching-learning, 3) that the science of language must be used in defining what to measure, 4) the native language of the student must be considered in foreign language tests, 5) that more and varied tests are needed adapting the techniques to students of other language backgrounds and measuring more validly the variables involved: 6) that the factor of entrance level is significant for research based on rate of improvement, and 7) that the student's habits, background, experience, interest and motivation, as well as amount of repetition and practice of the target language relate higher with tests scores. Luis J. Valverde Z.

———.

Second Language Teaching and Factors which Condition the Learning of a Modern Foreign Language. Los Angeles: School of Education, University of California, 1958.

Purpose/Scope: to prepare a manual for teachers of English and Spanish (as target languages) which presents an interdisciplinary approach to the teaching and learning problems. Methods: study of socio-psycholinguistic principles as well as sound methodological procedures based on direct experimentation and analysis of various scientific guidelines to language teaching and language learning. Major Findings: that the sciences of linguistics, psychology, psycholinguistics, methodology, and sociology are of paramount importance to a scientific approach to language teaching. That language learning continues to be an overwhelmingly psychological problem and that its subjectivity and complexity becomes more profound when we are referring to foreign language learning. Luis J. Valverde Z.

Varasteh, M.
Some Problems of Teaching Modern Languages in Persian Schools with Suggestions for Their Solution. Ph.D. dissertation, Institute of Education, University of London (printed in Persia, 1956).

Walsh, Donna Rowell
"Research in Progress in Modern Languages and Literatures," *PMLA,*
LXXV (May, 1960), 83-133.

Warfel, Harry R.
Research Projects and Procedures in Modern Languages. Detroit:
Modern Language Audio-Visual Consultation, Wayne State University, December 5, 1958 (unpublished).
    Structural linguistics offers teachers an enriched mode of instruc-
tion. By adapting a child's mode of language learning to the classroom,
the teacher can discard rules, paradigms, and vocabulary extension as
separate topics and emphasize syntax, the system of the language. The
sentence patterns can be practiced, so that case, agreement, tense, and
the various structures (phrase, clause, verbals) can be produced as
automatically in the new as in the native language. Research is needed
in to (1) the sequence of grammatical and sound units and structure
words best suited to the learning process, (2) the subject matter providing the easiest and widest vocabulary, (3) the time necessary for
pattern drill before reading is attempted, (4) the types of drills, and (5)
the types and content of prose readings. The publication of abstracts
of general ideas about language and language teaching is needed.
Harry R. Warfel.

Weir, Ruth
See Suppes, 2.1.

Wykes, Olive, and Catherine M. Berry
"Survey of Language Teaching in Australia," *Babel,* No. 24 (October,
1963), 9-13.
    In this article we describe a survey of the teaching of foreign
languages in Australia undertaken by the Faculty of Education in the
University of Melbourne. The aims of the survey are to discover the
incidence of foreign language teaching in Australian schools and to
examine the evidence based on experiments which supports or refutes
the claims commonly made on the value of foreign languages. Statistics
are being collected from public and private schools showing the proportion of children of one school generation broken into city and
country, boys and girls, Catholic, Protestant and government schools.
The findings are as yet incomplete. Little valid research on the validity
of the claims made for the teaching of foreign languages has been
found. MLabstract #610

2.3: Teaching of Specific Languages

Arabic

Carroll, John B. President and Fellows of Harvard University, Cambridge, Mass.

Research to Determine the Effectiveness of Programed Grafdrils in Teaching the Arabic Writing System; Project No. OE-3-14-006 (National Defense Education Act, Title VI), August 23, 1962, to October 31, 1962; $3,249.

The investigator conducted an experiment designed to test the effectiveness of the "Grafdril" method of teaching the Arabic writing system. The Grafdril method, developed by Dr. John B. Carroll, is a programed drill technique by means of which the student learns to correlate the sound of a word with its written symbol. It was hypothesized that the new method would be particularly helpful to low-aptitude students.

The investigator used two 30-member groups of paid subjects— one experimental and one control—chosen so as to produce a wide range of scores on the Modern Language Aptitude Test in each group and to match each score in one group with a comparable score in the other. The experimental group covered 12 hours of material by the Grafdril method, while the control group received about 13 hours of traditional classroom instruction from a native teacher. At the conclusion of the experiment, both groups were given a proficiency test to determine (a) the effectiveness of the Grafdril method as compared with traditional instruction; (b) its effectiveness for low-aptitude students, as hypothesized; and (c) what further improvements, if any, could be made in the method.

Greis, Naguib Amin Fahmy
See Greis, 4.1.

Khoury, Joseph Farjallah
Arabic Teaching Manual with an Analysis of the Major Problems American High School Students Face in Learning Arabic. Unpublished Ed. D. dissertation, University of Utah, 1961.

This investigation concerned itself with the development of an Arabic teaching manual and an analysis of the major difficulties that American students encounter in trying to learn the Arabic language. [. . .] The Arabic manual was developed for experimental purposes and intended to be a brief guide to the Arabic language. It contained the basic minimum of cultural information, grammar, and vocabulary that was necessary to give the student a general orientation to the language. After putting it into practical use in the classroom it was found necessary to make it more adequate and useful. Consequently [. . .] recommendations were made for revision and improvement. From the abstract.

Basque.

Barrutia, Richard
    See Barrutia, 2.55.

Bengali.

Ray, Punya Sloka. University of Chicago, Chicago, Illinois.
    Project to Study the Dacca Standard and Calcutta Standard Dialects of Bengali and to Produce Preliminary Teaching Materials for the Dacca Dialect (Phase I); Project No. OE–4-14-005 (National Defense Education Act, Title VI), September 1, 1963, to February 28, 1965; $29,020.
        This contract will initiate a project for the study of the Dacca and Calcutta dialects of Bengali and produce teaching materials for the Dacca dialect. The first phase of the project will include a systematic statement of the sound system of the Decca dialect and an analysis of the distinguishing grammatical features of that dialect as compared to the Calcutta dialect. After the analysis is completed, 15 lesson units for teaching the Dacca dialect will be produced. The lesson units will be organized on principles followed in introductory teaching materials for Bengali prepared under a previous contract. Although materials are now available for the study of West Bengali (the Calcutta dialect) none are presently available for the study of the Dacca dialect, spoken in East Pakistan. The study of the Dacca dialect facilitates an understanding of the cultural and linguistic characteristics of East Bengal (Pakistan). Dr. Ray will jointly direct the project with Dr. Edward C. Dimock, Jr., Associate Professor of Linguistics and Oriental Languages and Civilizations.

Chinese

Ai, Joseph W.
    "Report on Psychological Studies of the Chinese Language in the Past Three Decades," *Pedagogical Seminary and Journal of Genetic Psychology,* LXXVI (June, 1950), 207-20.
        Psychological study of simplifying the method for learning the Chinese written language. Since the orthography is not phonetic, what

is the minimum number of characters necessary to an ordinary reading-writing mastery? "Word" vocabulary and factors involved in learning the meanings of the characters are analyzed. There is a comparative study of oral versus silent reading and a measurement of children's ability in silent reading. Test methods are not described; however, resultant statistics are tabulated. Four principles for revising textbooks are given, based on the experimental results. JM

Carroll, John B.
Programmed Self-Instruction in Mandarin Chinese; Observations of Student Progress with an Automated Audio-Visual Instructional Device. Wellesley, Mass.: Language Testing Fund, 1963.

In this report I conclude that most aspects of spoken and written foreign language skills can be effectively taught solely be self-instruction with a specifically constructed audio-visual device, without the aid of an instructor. A programming system adapted for this purpose is described in detail, and results of tryouts of a program covering about nine lessons of Tewksbury's *Speak Chinese* [Malcolm Gardner Tewksbury, *Speak Chinese* (New Haven, Pub. for the Institute of Far Eastern Languages by Yale University Press, 1948)] (plus fifth characters) with twenty-three college-age students are presented. Final achievement of students is, on the average, quite high, but rate of progress is highly related to aptitude as measured by the *Modern Language Aptitude Test*. Student reactions are in general highly favorable to this mode of instruction. While development of FL programmed instructional materials is laborious and expensive, the eventual benefits are thought to be promising and worthwhile. John B. Carroll, MLabstract #554.

Carroll, John B., and Stanley M. Sapon
See Carroll, 3.3.

Morton, F. Rand
See Morton, 2.55.

English

*Al-Haruny, M. M.
Teaching English in the Arabic-Speaking Middle East with Particular Reference to Egypt. Unpublished Master's thesis, Institute of Education, University of London, n.d.

Alhinc, J., M. Clay, and Pierre Roger Léon
See Alhinc, 2.54.

Allwood, Charles S., *et al.*
Experiment i Mullsjö; Anteckningar från ett språkpedagogiskt laboratorium. Stockholm: Hugo Gebers Förlag, 1948.

An action experiment (without control groups) aiming to create an English milieu in a Swedish school, so that the situational cues of, e.g. sports, amateur theatricals, dismantling a bicycle, and discussing art and literature will elicit response in the foreign language; and so that adverse psychological forces—e.g., ethnocentric aversion to a foreign language, and Swedish reserve in the expression of feelings—will be reduced to the minimum. HLN

Asuncion, Nobleza Castro
See Asuncion, 4.1, 4.5.

Baker, Hugh Sanford.
See Baker, Part I.

Bauer, Eric Wolfgang
See Bauer, 2.53.

Bohlen, Adolf
See Bohlen, 2.1.

Bolinger, Dwight L.
See Bolinger, 4.1.

Bratset, Richard E.
See Bratset, 5.

Brault, Gerard J.
See Brault, 7.

Brown, Paul A.
See Brown, Part I.

†Carlos, Lourdes B.
A Comparative Analysis of the Syntax in a Sample of the Speech of Children as a Basis for the Improvement of Teaching English as a Second Language. Unpublished Ed. D. dissertation in progress, University of Indiana.

Carroll, John B.
See Carroll, 2.7.

Chaiyaratana, Chalao
See Chaiyaratana, 3.5.

Chari, Ahalya
"Research in the English Class," *Teacher Education,* VIII (October, 1963), 35-43.

The article outlines the scope of action-researchers in the English class room for Indian Schools and gives practical suggestions regarding possible areas of inquiry. The suggestions are given under two broad categories: (1) those that involve the simple recordings of conditions as they exist (for example, records of the linguistic background of Indian pupils learning English as a Second language); (2) those that involve controlled experimentation, e.g., teaching new vocabulary, teaching the script, relation between speech and reading abilities. It concludes that the value of research that the teacher conducts in class is two-fold: (a) the improvement that it could bring about in the actual practices the teacher is engaged in and (b) the contribution that it could make to the professional growth of the teacher. Ahalya Chari

Condie, Le Roy
An Experiment in Second Language Instruction of Beginning Indian Children in New Mexico Public Schools. Unpublished Ed.D. dissertation, University of New Mexico, 1961.

In this study the experimenter sought to determine whether the achievement of beginning Indian children in learning oral English and in readiness for reading could be improved when teachers were trained in effective techniques of second-language instruction. [. . .] The analysis of results confirmed that significant results had been accomplished in three of the four groups under the conditions introduced by the experimenter. The differences cannot have resulted from errors of sampling, but may tentatively be attributed to superior performance by the experimental groups over the control groups. From the abstract.

Cooper, James G. Territorial College of Guam, Agana, Guam.
Teaching Language Arts to Non-English Speaking Children of Guam; Project No. 477 (U. S. Office of Education, Cooperative Research Branch), October, 1958, to October, 1961.

The major objectives are to determine if and to what extent comprehension of spoken English should precede attempts to teach reading and writing; if general language achievement is greater for those students who first learn conversational English; if unskilled teachers can be taught to teach conversational English to six-year-olds; how growth in language arts can be measured in a bilingual setting. BP

Delattre, Pierre
  See Delattre, 4.3.

de Witte, A. J. J., *et al.*
  See de Witte, 4.1.

El-Bettar, Abdul Kadir Said
  See El-Bettar, 4.1.

Fife, Robert H., and Hershel T. Manuel
  See Fife, 3.5.

†Florander, Jesper
  English in the Elementary School. Research in progress supported by Danmarks Paedagogiske Institut, Emdrupvej 101, Copenhagen NV, Denmark.
  Since 1958 foreign language instruction (especially in English) is compulsory from the sixth schoolyear. The object of the experiments is to find the optimal age level at which to begin this instruction by varying 1) class level, 2) teaching methods, and 3) teaching materials. The start of the instruction varies from the second to the sixth schoolyear. In Experiment E [1959-66, County of Holbaek] 23 classes are involved with 450 pupils, in Experiment F [1959-64, Municipality of Gladsaxe) 96 classes with 2000 pupils, and in Experiment G [1960-64, Town of Rødding] 6 classes with 100 pupils. Jesper Florander

Flores, Francisco Gubaton
  See Flores, 4.1.

Frank, Marcella
  See Frank, Part I.

Fries, Charles C.
  Teaching and Learning English as a Foreign Language. Ann Arbor, Mich.: University of Michigan Press, 1945.
  Presents in nontechnical terms the linguistic approach used in making texts for practical use in teaching. Specific attention is given to problems dealing with English as a foreign language. These problems have been generalized so as to provide fundamental principles of approach applicable to all language learning or teaching. Included is a descriptive analysis of the English sound and structural system and vocabulary; also an outline, in lesson form, of the pronunciation materials included in an intensive course in English for Latin-Americans. JM

Gorosch, Max. Institute of Phonetics, University of Stockholm, Stockholm, Sweden.
English without a Book. Proceedings of the VIIIth International Congress of Linguistics, Oslo, 1958; *Moderna Språk* (Uppsala), No. 4 (1958); stencilled report, December, 1960.

Research in progress on the possibilities of using audio-visual aids—film strips and tape recordings—without a book and without a qualified teacher, to teach children, seven to eleven years old, English as their first foreign language. BP
Initial results presented in the report: research is made in collaboration with Carl-Axel Axelsson and the school of psychologists of the Swedish Board of Education. Walter Johnson

Gorosch, Max, and Carl-Axel Axelsson
English without a Book and without a Teacher, in Primary Schools [Sweden, age 7-11], by Audio-Visual Means: A Bilingual Experiment, Appendix II, n.d. (mimeographed).

Special grants were made by the Royal Board of Education and the Stockholm School Board to produce a sound film strip to teach English to five hundred Swedish primary school students. Results were good. No statistical evaluation. BP

*Greene, Olive
The Problem of the Article in the Teaching and Learning of English as a Foreign Language. Unpublished Master's[?] thesis, Hartford Seminary Foundation (Case Memorial Library of the Hartford Seminary Foundation), n.d.

Guenot, Jean
See Guenot, 2.53.

Guenot, Jean, C. J. Sturge-Moore, and M. Tardy
See Guenot, 2.52.

†Habostad, Knut. Manglerud Skole, Plogveien, Manglerud, Norway. [Preparation of a Programed English Course]. Research in progress.
The basis of this course is J. D. Edmonston's *Here We Are, Books I-III* (Oslo, Norway: Cappelens, 1960-63), and will be used in connection with filmstrips and taperecorders. Like the texts used as the starting point, the course is designed to be used at the elementary school level (grades 5-6-7, ages 11-13). The vocabulary is limited (725 words) and the structures have been carefully selected. The progression of presentation is very slow. Knut Habostad

†Hempleman, David
The Structuring of Possession and Related Problems in the Teaching

of English as a Foreign Language. Ed. D. dissertation in progress, Duke University.

Hill, Leslie A., and R. Derrick S. Fielden
Prepositions and Adverbial Particles in English (An Interim Classification-Structural, Semantic and Graded). London: Oxford University Press, to appear.

This work will cover 62 prepositions and adverbial particles in English. It will divide each up into "learning efforts—new meanings which a foreign student would have to learn as a fresh item in each case. Each "learning effort" is further subdivided according to the structural (semantic) patterns in which it can occur. The authors also suggest a grading of the "learning efforts" within each preposition/ particle, to help teachers, textbook writers, etc. decide on the order in which to introduce each "learning effort" to their students. The work is based on research by the authors. Leslie A. Hill

International Christian University, Audiovisual Center
See International Christian . . . , 2.56.

Jackson, Kenneth L.
See Jackson, 4.1.

Japel, Hans
"Versuche im englishchen Anfangsunterricht, Erfahrungsbericht zu einem Experiment," *Fremdsprachenunterricht,* VIII (April, 1964), 167-73.

Experience from an introductory course of English, on an oral basis, in the 7th forms of 4 urban and 9 rural general schools in the Halle District of the GDR. The lessons were given by experienced teachers and a couple of senior students (future teachers, at the end of their methodological training in the 8th university term). Methodological principles; structure of 12 lessons; results of the "oral approach" (several statistical data) are included. W. Stiehl

Kim, Soon-Han Park
See Kim, 4.1.

Kimizuka, Sumako
See Kimizuka, 4.1.

Kohmoto, Satesaburo
See Kohmoto, 4.1.

*Koumari, A.
Certain Uses of the English Passive Voice and Their Teaching to

Foreign Students. Unpublished Master's thesis, Institute of Education, University of London, n.d.

Koutsoudas, Andreas, and Olympia Koutsoudas
See Koutsoudas, 4.1.

Kruatrachue, Foongfuang
See Kruatrachue, 4.1.

Kuniyuki, Noriko
See Kuniyuki, 2.51.

Lado, Robert
See Lado, Part I; and Lado, 2.7.

Lehn, W. and W. R. Slager
See Lehn and Slager, 4.5.

Lesage, André
See Lesage, 2.53.

*Livesey, Adelis Frances
A Study in Developing a Technique of Method Evaluation in the Teaching of English as a Second Language to Adults in Multilingual Classes. University of British Columbia, Unpublished Masters thesis, 1961.

Lundeen, D. J.
See Lundeen, 4.5.

McArdle, Lois
See McArdle, 2.7.

McIntosh, Lois
See McIntosh, 4.1.

Mackey, William F., and James A. Noonan
"An Experiment in Bilingual Education," *English Language Teaching Monthly,* VI (Summer, 1952), 125-32.

    Purpose was to determine the level of English at which foreigners can chart school subjects, and the quickest, most effective way to start teaching English at this level. Results show that students could study school subjects with a range of fifteen to thirty-five hours of training in English and with a vocabulary as low as 132-370 words. Provisions for these achievements are listed. JM

Manuel, Herschel T.
See Manuel, 2.7.

Marckwardt, Albert H.

"An Experiment in Aural Perception," *English Journal,* XXXIII (April, 1944), 212-14.

Describes testing by English Language Institute in Mexico to discover the reason for the difficulty in teaching a native Spanish speaker to produce the sound *š*. Tests showed a hearing confusion between *č* and *š*. Preliminary exercises in discrimination between these two sounds are essential if the native Spanish speaker is to produce the *š* by imitation. JM

―――.

"Phonemic Bifurcation as an English Teaching Problem," *Papers of the Michigan Academy of Science, Arts, and Letters,* XXXIII (1947), 363-71.

Discusses the methods considered and employed in a series of experiments in aural perception directed toward discovering which of the eight Modern English vowel sounds—i, I, e, ɛ, U, o, ɔ—are heard most accurately by non-English-speaking students with a Spanish-language background, and which are least distinguishable. Results are tabulated and evaluated. Comments are made on the shortcomings of this particular type of experiment. JM

―――.

"Phonemic Structure and Aural Perception," *American Speech,* XXI (April, 1946), 106-11.

This article points out that although the phones *m, n* and *ŋ* are present in both English and Spanish, they occupy different positions in respect to the phonemic structure of the two languages. Tests were devised to determine the accuracy of aural discrimination by native English speakers. The summary lists four aspects of the problem of hearing as an element in language learning. JM

*Mechner, M.

Some Problems of Collocations of Verb and Particle in the Teaching of English as a Foreign Language. Unpublished Master's thesis, Institute of Education, University of London, n.d.

"De methodologie van het Engels als vreemde taal in 1956," *Nova et Vetera,* XXXV, (1957-58), 82-97.

A valuable article on the teaching of English, giving a critical analysis of the principal articles in reviews and other works published in 1956, on methodology, vocabulary, grammar, phonetics, audio-visual aids and textbooks. The question of grammatical structures, comparisons with the mother tongue that should be noted, and the advantages and limitations of the direct method are examined at length. This is followed by a summary of Michéa's views on word frequency and those expressed in an article published in *Taalonderwijs,* in February 1957. From van Willigen, Part I.

Morton, F. Rand
See Morton, 4.1.

Netherlands Didactiekcommissie
See Netherlands . . . , 4.1.

NHK Radio-Television Cultural Research Institute
See NHK Radio-Television . . . , 2.51.

Ohannessian, Sirarpi
See Ohannessian, Part I.

Owen, George
See Owen, 4.5.

Pascasio, Emy Mariano
See Pascasio, 4.1.

Pierce, Joe E.
See Pierce, 2.1.

Poltoratzky, Marianna A.
See Poltoratzky, 2.1.

Sibayan, Bonifacio Padilla
See Sibayan, 4.1.

Sokolov, Alexander N.
See Sokolov, 4.3.

Stensaasen, Svein
"Gjennomføringen av engelskundervisningen i folkeskolen. Fremmedspråksundervisningens stilling i folkeskolen og en undersøking av hvordan denne undervisningen er organisert," *Forskning og Danning,* IV (1958), 125.

A study of the education in English as a foreign language is organized and carried out in Norway. Questions as to the length of the courses, the qualifications of the teachers and the differentiation between the students for the courses are considered. Only elementary-school education is treated. Gunnar Handal

†Sturge-Moore, C. J. Chairman, Centre Audio-Visuel de l'École Normale Supérieure de Saint-Cloud, Saint-Cloud, France

Contrôles d'acquisition de la langue anglaise parlée: une expérience au cours élémentaire 2ème année. Research in progress.

Research on the teaching of English to French 8-year-old children with the help of audio-visual aids. Special attention is being given to the problem of testing achievement. The course consists of tapes, film-strips and pattern drills. The language laboratory is used. This course was specially written for children of this age, as a result of previous research where a course for adults was used. Publication end of 1964 or 1965. C. J. Sturge-Moore

Tan, Jan Cornelis
See Tan, 7.

Tireman, Lloyd S.
1945), 223-27.
"A Study of Fourth-Grade Reading Vocabulary of Native Spanish Speaking Children," *Elementary School Journal,* XLVI (December,

A study to determine the reason for excessive errors in the reading of English by elementary-grade, native Spanish-speaking children. Procedure for testing is described. The responses are statistically recorded. Among the conclusions given us that the native Spanish-speaking child is troubled in recognizing English words in isolation because he cannot pronounce the elements of the words correctly. This conclusion leads to the recommendation of phonetic training for such students. JM

———.

Teaching Spanish-Speaking Children. Albuquerque, N.M.; University of New Mexico Press, 1948.

Indicates that the general methods used to cover specific problems are not adequate in teaching non-English-speaking children in elementary schools. Emphasis here is upon the modifications necessary to cover these special situations. Two chapters are devoted to studies relating to bilingualism and its consideration as a world problem. Approaches to curriculum guidance are divided into prefirst grade, primary, and intermediate grades. There is a generalization on the teaching of Spanish. JM

Uota, Shoji
"Group Learning with Audiovisual Materials," in *Survey of Educational Media Research in the Far East.* Washington, D. C.: U. S. Office of Education, 1963. Pp. 157-58.

Four eighth grade classes in English are given a series of pretests to determine the relative standing of each group. The two lowest classes are treated as the experimental section and the two highest classes as the control section. Each experimental class is further divided into three smaller groups for classroom instruction. One group is taught primarily by visual methods, such as flash cards; another primarily by aural methods, such as tape recordings; and the third by a combination of the two. The control classes are taught by the conventional lecture demonstration method. A comprehensive oral and written examination is administered to all students after the first and second months of instruction. The control groups perform better on the first test, but the experimental groups score substantially better than the control groups on the second test. A further comparison with high, medium and low students, according to pretest results, shows that upper stuednts in the experimental groups do far better than their control group counterparts on both posttests. Center for Documentation and Communication Research, Western Reserve University

Valverde Z., Luis J.

English as a Second Language; Theory and Practice. San Germán, Puerto Rico: Inter American University Press, 1963

This book describes the history, scope, problems, and present state of the study of language—and, in particular, the field of teaching-learning English as a second language—in America. The text is a synthesis of a rapidly developing and expanding area. It is a study on the application of the several disciplines which have contributed to the formulation of new principles and procedures in the realm of English as a secondary language. In it the author has tried to relate the chief concepts, issues, problems and approaches encountered in language study to the essential principles and relationships in the teaching-learning of English. The book is meant to be both theoretical and practical, for successful practice is possible mainly if it is rooted in sound theory. From the publisher's circular

————.

Multi-Disciplinary Bases for the Teaching-Learning of English as a Second Language. Unpublished Ph.D. dissertation, University of California at Los Angeles, 1960.

The purpose of this study was twofold: (1) to present a synthesis and critical analysis of the major contributions that modern descriptive linguistics, psychology, psycholinguistics, and socio-linguistics have made during the last decade to the field of second-language teaching-learning; (2) to formulate an integrated methodology for the teaching of English as a second tongue. From the abstract. This dissertation served as the basis for the immediately preceding entry.

———.
See Valverde Z., 2.1.

Velázquez, Mary D. Rivera de
See Velázquez, 4.1.

Villarreal, Jesse J.
See Villarreal, 2.7.

Xoomsai, M. L. Tooi, and P. Ratamangkala
See Xoomsai, 2.51.

Yorkey, Richard Clements
A Study of the Practical Application of Structural Linguistics to the Teaching of English in Lebanese Elementary Schools. Unpublished Ed.D. dissertation, University of Michigan, 1960.
The purpose of this study is to investigate the ways in which the pedagogical procedures derived from the premises of structural linguistics can be applied to teaching English in Lebanese elementary schools. . . . Areas that require further research are (1) effective methods for teaching reading and writing, (2) structuring the cultural content of teaching materials, (3) determining the pedagogical values of using or not using transcription, (4) differences of methodology for adult as opposed to elementary school students, and (5) the possibility of making an inventory of English grammatical structures on the basis of frequency of occurrence, naturalness, regularity of form, functional load, and with reference to Lebanese Arabic, the degree of learning difficulty. From the abstract

French
Angiolillo, Paul F.
"French for the Feeble-Minded: An Experiment," *Modern Language Journal,* XXVI (April, 1942), 266-71.
The author taught beginning French by the oral method to a group of mentally deficient girls. At the end of a month and a half they had an eighty-word vocabulary; tested a year later they had retained 100 per cent of the work. Author concludes that it is possible to include foreign-language instruction as a recreational activity in institutional care. BP

Baardman, G. G., *et al.*
Voorlopig rapport betreffende onderzoek didactiek Frans. Unpublished report, 1958.
The preliminary report on research in the teaching of French in the Netherlands, carried out under the supervision of D. M. van

Willigen, with a subsidy from the Dutch Organization for Pure Research. From van Willigen, Part I.

Baskin, Samuel
   See Baskin, 2.55.

Beck, Theodore T.
   "Experiment in Teaching French by the Oral-Cultural Approach Method," *Modern Language Journal,* XXXV (December, 1951), 595-601.
      This experiment, using the oral approach, was carried out in two Georgia colleges. Student test scores were compared with secondary-school scores, judging one year of high school work equal to one quarter of university work. College classes (oral method) showed marked superiority over secondary-school pupil scores (traditional method). BP

Bernard, Edward G., and Sarah W. Lorge
   See Bernard, 2.54.

Bohlen, Adolf
   See Bohlen, 2. 1.

Borglum, George P.
   See Borglum, 2.53.

Bovée, Arthur G.
   See Bovée, 3. 1.

Brault, Gerard. Bowdoin College, Brunswick, Maine.
   Revision and Expansion of Bowdoin French Materials; Project No. OE-3-14-009 (National Defense Education Act, Title VI), October 1, 1962, to September 30, 1963; $12,112.
      In 1960, under U.S. Office of Education contract SAE-8889, Bowdoin College produced a series of tape-recording drills to facilitate the learning of "standard" French by persons in the New England States who are native speakers of a variant form of Canadian French. The drills, together with a corresponding *Manual and Workbook for Franco-Americans,* were used successfully in the summers of 1961 and 1962 at NDEA institutes directed by Dr. Brault.
      The present contract provided for the revision and expansion of a version of the Bowdoin French materials written for teaching Franco-American secondary school pupils. The original version of this work, entitled *Cours de langue française destiné aux jeunes Franco-Americains,* had already been used experimentally in a score of New Eng-

land schools since 1961. The new book incorporated all of the special phonetic, structural, and lexical drills devised under SAE-8889 to assist students in perceiving and controlling the differences between Franco-American and standard French. The new contract also provided sufficient copies of the text for extensive trial use in the New England area. From the official description. See Brault, 7.

Brière, Eugène J.
"Improving English Speakers' Pronunciation of French," *Language Learning*, XIII, No. 1 (1963), 33-41.

In this article I report a procedure used to improve articulatory skills by presenting "attainable" pronunciation goals to every student. By contrasting English and French phonemic systems, areas of predicted interference were charted. A "MS" was constructed to record all phonemes on the chart. Students (Ss; N = 24) [were] recorded at the beginning of the quarter. 'Sounds" produced by Ss were phonetically transcribed on individual charts. Regardless of the number missed by each S, no more than three phonemes were taken and presented as pronunciation goals for the quarter. Intensive practice was given in groups. A second recording was made by Ss at the end of the quarter. Ss had intensively practiced only three French phonemes, but showed improved pronunciation of the entire French system. Variations of the procedure are suggested. The question of transfer-learning, stimulus discrimination and generalization is posited. Eugène J. Brière, MLabstract #712

Brown, Paul A.
See Brown, Part I.

Buch, John N.
See Buch, 2.54.

Calvert, F. Irene
"Primary School French," *Modern Languages*, XLIV (September, 1963), 111-13.

In this article I describe an experiment by a lecturer and students in teaching French to thirty-two children aged seven to nine in a primary school once a week, repetition kept up for the rest of the week by the class teacher, not a French specialist. The method, described in some detail, was oral, without visual aids; the language learned was put to use at the end of each lesson in playing a game; certain forms (e.g. the negative) were thus introduced indirectly. Conclusions: optimum length of lesson 20-30 minutes, size of class about 20; children of low general attainment gained confidence through success in

French; University Departments of Education might usefully make more such contributions to Primary School French teaching. F. Irene Calvert, MLabstract, ♯605

Capretz, Pierre J.
See Capretz, 2.1.

Delattre, Pierre
"Une technique audio-linguale d'initiation au français," *Le français dans le monde,* XII (December, 1962), 15-18.
A three week pre-reading program with teacher's book and 12-inch LP record precisely outlined. Graded material *(La belle demoiselle . . .)* is given. Aims at acquiring three types of habits before opening a book: a) Complete articulatory habits; b) Psychological habits of relating sound to meaning without interference of spelling; c) Conversational (grammatical) habits. Pierre Delattre

———.

"A Technique of Aural-Oral Approach," *French Review,* XX (January, 1947), 238-50.
Report on a University of Oklahoma experiment in teaching French. Presentation of methods for teaching psychological, physiological, and grammatical habits. Results showed aural-oral test group subjected to traditional methods. JAD

———.

See Delattre, 4.1, 4.3, 4.5.

de Witte, A. J. J., *et al.*
See de Witte, 4.1.

Dostal, Naida Marich
See Dostal, 2.53.

Dunkel, Harold B., and Roger A. Pillet
See Dunkel and Pillet, 6.1.

†England. Ministry of Education. Department of Education and Science. [The Teaching of French in Primary Schools]. Research in progress.
Plans have been announced by the Department of Education and Science for a pilot scheme in the teaching of French in primary schools. The primary aim of the scheme will be to study in depth the practicability of introducing French into the primary school curriculum in a wide variety of everyday situations. An attempt will be made to throw light on such questions as the feasibility of teaching a modern

language to all primary children from about the age of eight, and on the effects of the early introduction of a modern language on the curriculum as a whole and on the attitudes of both pupils and staff. Information will also be sought on the efficacy of various types of language teaching material and on the effects of the early introduction of language teaching on the training and supply of teachers. A link has been established with the Nuffield Foundation project for the preparation of materials for language teaching, and this material will be used extensively in schools taking part in the Department's scheme. The National Foundation for Educational Research will play an important part in the evaluation of the results of the scheme. P. M. Downie.

Felt, William N.
See Felt, 2.51.

Ferguson, Charles A.
See Ferguson, 4.1.

Ferguson, Charles A., and William A. Stewart
See Ferguson, Part I.

"French in the Elementary Classes: Bibliography."
See "French . . ." Part I.

Garry, Ralph
Summary of Research: Parlons Français I, II, III (videotape edition) and Parlons Français I (film edition). The author, n.d., (mimeographed).

Brief descriptions of seven projects conducted over the period of three years' time to determine the differences in achievement between several classes all using the same materials, but categorized according to type and method of classroom follow-up practice. Major findings for each group are given with reference to students, to teachers and to types of classroom follow-up practice. Complete detailed reports of the research are available upon request from the U. S. Office of Education. DF

Garry, Ralph, and Edna Mauriello
Modern Language Project of the Massachusetts Council for Public Schools, Teachers Training Division: Summary of Research on Parlons Français, Year Two. Washington, D.C.: U. S. Office of Education, 1961.

Three variables are investigated in the televised French instruction of fifth-grade students in Massachusetts schools: the fluency of the teacher conducting the follow-up practice; the type of follow-up practice used (tape-recordings vs. teacher-conducted) and type of teacher training (televised or tape-recorded). Children are pre- and post-tested with a listening comprehension and a fluency test. Analysis of variance is applied to the data. Significant effects and interactions are found in achievement for teacher fluency and type of follow-up practice. Type of teacher training produces no significant differences. Center for Documentation and Communication Research, Western Reserve University.

Gougenheim, Georges, P. Rivenc, R. Michéa, and A. Sauvageot
L'élaboration du français élémentaire. Paris: Didier, 1956.
This study was designed primarily for use in the French colonies to teach a basic French. It is a study of word-usage frequency, research into essential elements according to the environment of the learner, and rational observation. See Mauger and Gougenheim, below. BP

Hall, Robert A., Jr.
See Hall, 4.1.

Halloran, J. H.
"A Four Year Experiment in Esperanto as an Introduction to French," *British Journal of Educational Psychology,* XXII, Part III (November, 1952), 200-4.
Compares a group who studied Esperanto for one year before taking any French, with another group introduced immediately to French. The groups were not kept separate after the first year. Exams in French were administered at end of a four-year period, using eleven different tests. Results: about the same for both groups. JG

Hamilton, Daniel L., and Ernest F. Haden
"Three Years of Experimentation at the University of Texas," *Modern Language Journal,* XXXIV (February, 1950), 85-102.
This was a three-year experiment using different presentations of first-year French and Spanish. In 1946-47, Program A was conducted in the traditional method, Program B emphasized oral-aural work. French Program B proved to be superior to French Program A by 10 per cent. Spanish Program B was superior to Program A by 5 per cent according to test results. Conclusions were that oral-aural sections showed good results but perhaps not as great as assumed generally. In 1947-48, Program D was a systematic presentation of grammar. Program E utilized no formal grammar, relied on pattern practice drills, and reasoned grammar inductively. Conclusions were that Pro-

gram E scores were surprisingly good. French E scored two points higher than French D on test results. A four-week experiment was made in 1948-49 investigating results of different approaches to pronunciation. Conclusions were that (1) physiological description of speech articulation is helpful; (2) it is advantageous to use phonetic symbols in French; and (3) dependence on teacher imitation alone is not advisable. In 1948-49, Program G was set up to stress oral drill and exhaustive study of grammar. Program H featured a quick survey of grammar, followed by a large amount of rapid reading. Test scores showed that students in Program H made higher scores consistently than students in Program G. General conclusions from the three-year experiment were: (1) listening or laboratory sessions obtained good results; (2) emphasis on formal grammar is of doubtful profit; (3) the oral aim is legitimate; (4) pronunciation is improved through use of physiological terms of foreign articulation and use of phonetic symbols in French. BP

Hanzeli, Victor E.
See Hanzeli, 2.53.

Henning, William Andrew
See Henning, 4.5.

Hocking, Elton, Carroll Weisiger, and W. Merle Hill
See Hocking, 3.1.

Johnston, Marjorie C.
See Johnston, Part I.

Kallioinen, Vilho
"Huomioita ranskan kielen ääntämisen opetuksesta suomenkielisille," *Kasvatusopillinen Aikakauskirja,* XCII, No. 5 (1956), 147-53.
    Basing his arguments on phonetic research carried out at the laboratory of the University of Helsinki, the author shows the special difficulties of French pronunication and then discusses ways of overcoming them. From van Willigen, Part I.

Keating, Raymond F.
See Keating, 2.54.

Keeler, Sister Jerome
"Post War Experiment in Teaching First Year French," *French Review,* XXI (February, 1948), 313-16.
    Experimental class, meeting seven hours a week—two of these with native informants, two for lab work with classroom instructor, three for more formal aspects of course—showed greater progress not

only in conversation but also in reading and writing than class meeting
five hours and omitting work with native informants. Experiment
conducted at Mount St. Scholastica College, Atchison, Kansas, with
first-year French class. DG

Keisler, Evan R.
See Keisler, 4.5.

Kern, Edith
See Kern, 2.7.

Kielski, Bolesław
See Kielski, 4.1.

Lambert, Wallace E., *et al.*
See Lambert, 3.7.

Leutenegger, Ralph R., and Theodore H. Mueller
"Auditory Factors and the Acquisition of French Language Mastery,"
Modern Language Journal, XLVIII (March, 1964), 141-46.
    In this research project we attempted to predict ease of difficulty
of mastering French, taught and tested by audio-lingual techniques.
Scores in intelligence and aptitude tests for 31 male and 17 female
beginning college students were used. The variables most highly
correlated with the language laboratory scores were the English Effectiveness Total Score ($r = .55$) and the ACE Linguistic score ($r = .46$).
Of the six Seashore Measures of Musical Talents, *pitch* yielded the
highest correlation ($r = .27$) with the laboratory scores. Multiple
correlation coefficients of .9942 and .7283 were obtained on laboratory
score predictions for females and males respectively. Further data
are being collected on a larger population. Ralph R. Leutenegger and
Theodore H. Mueller, MLabstract #743.

LeVois, Camille J.
See LeVois, 2.53.

Lopato, Esther W.
See Lopato, 6.5.

Lorge, Sarah W.
See Lorge, 2.54.

Mace, Larry
See Mace, 3.1.

Mackey, William F.
See Mackey, 2.1.

MacKinnon, A. R.

"Experimental Study of Learning of French in the Public Schools Undertaken by the Toronto Board of Education," *Ontario Journal of Educational Research,* IV (Autumn, 1961), 43-50.

A pilot study is made in teaching French at the junior high level in Toronto. From 304 pupils three groups are set up, one taught by films, one by an instructor and the third receiving no French instruction. The achievement of the first two groups is compared. Although the teacher group shows a general superiority over the film group, certain anomalies appear in the results: at the end of the seventh week there are no significant differences between the groups, and later differences would appear to be the result of accumulation of errors not corrected in the film presentation. Other aspects of the study are the following: (1) conclusions regarding the effects on the regular school curriculum of introducing another subject; (2) recommendations in the areas of period length, teaching method, selection and motivation of pupils and further research. Center for Documentation and Communication Research, Western Reserve University

Malcolm, D. J.
See Malcolm, 2.1.

Marie Gabrielle, Sister, F.S.E., and Sister Raymond de Jesus, F.S.E.
See Marie Gabrielle, 6.1.

Marty, Fernand
Linguistics Applied to the Beginning French Course. Roanoke, Virginia: Audio-Visual Publications, 1963.

This book contains a phonological, morphological, and structural analysis of contemporary spoken and written French. This analysis leads to a selection of the objectives (terminal behavior) which, the author believes, should be taught in a beginning French course. Fernand Marty

Mauger, Gaston, and Georges Gougenheim
Le français élémentaire: méthode progressive de français parlé. Débutants. 2 vols. Paris: Hachette, 1955, 1956.

These textbooks are based on a new frequency list established by the Commission ministérielle du français élémentaire, after two years' scientific study of everyday spoken French. The words selected for absolute beginners are listed in the first volume, pp. 117-20. (The list lacks two words used in the volume: *lancer and peut-être.)* The remainder of the vocabulary of "le français élémentaire" is listed in the second volume, pp. 115-19. Since the term *élémentaire* tended to be confused with other names and meanings, the name of the list was changed to "le français fondamental." A further advance in the theoretical basis of frequency lists derived from spoken language is expected to be made in the German word count undertaken by J. Alan Pfeffer. See below, Pfeffer, 2.3, German.

*Ministère Français de l'Éducation Nationale
Le français élémentaire. Paris: Centre national de documentation pédagogique, 1955. 67 pages.
 See Mauger and Gougenheim, above, for available version of the frequency list bearing this title.

Morton, F. Rand
 See Morton, 2.55.

Mueller, Theodore
 See Mueller, 2.55, 2.56, 4.5.

Mueller, Theodore, and George P. Borglum
 See Mueller and Borglum, 2.54.

Mueller, Theodore H., and Ralph R. Leutenegger
 See Mueller and Leutenegger, 2.56.

Nostrand, Howard Lee
 See Nostrand, 5, 2.52.

Neale, L. W.
 See Neale, 2.7.

Percival, T. S.
 See Percival, 2.7.

Peters, Mary Olga
 See Peters, 2.54.

Pimsleur, Paul
 See Pimsleur, 2.7, 4.5.

Pimsleur, Paul, Larry Masce, and Evan Keislar
 See Pimsleur, 4.5.

Politzer, Robert L.
 "Auditory Discrimination of French Vowels by English Speakers," *Canadian Journal of Linguistics,* VI, No. 2 (1961), 32-44.
 In this article I presented the results of an auditory discrimination test of French vowels given to first, second and third year students at the University of Michigan. Items testing discrimination between French and English vowels were also included in the test. The results

of the test show that: (1) auditory discrimination between French vowels is controlled by the native system (English), (2) the ability to discriminate between French vowels increases with exposure to French, (3) the ability to identify English sounds as non-French shows no comparable "Automatic" increase and (4) the more advanced students tend to discriminate between French vowels as speech sounds (phonemes) but the beginners discriminate rather on the purely phonetic or non-functional level. Robert L. Politzer, MLabstract #371.

————.

See Politzer, 2.54, 4.1.

Purvis, H.
"A Reading Course in French," *Modern Languages,* XXXIII (September, 1952), 90-95.
    Experiment to investigate the possibility of a reading method for teaching of French. Lacks detailed statistical analysis of test results and comparison of methods. Experimental group superior to control group. TD

————.

"A New Approach to the Teaching of French in Secondary Modern Schools," *Durham Research Review,* IV (September, 1953), 15-22.
    Concerns an experiment comparing two approaches to the teaching of French. One system, called the Modified Direct Method, stressed ability to understand, speak, read, and write French, with stress on oral work and grammar. The second system stressed reading comprehension. It was found that the Reading Method was effective for teaching reading and vocabulary, had a greater educational and cultural value, had a higher surrender value at the end of two years, and aroused more enthusiasm. The Modified Direct Method was significantly better for teaching grammar. JM

Randall, Earle S.
See Randall, 6.1.

Rathee, R. S., and V. V. Mennes
See Rathee, 6.3.

Raybould, A. B.
See Raybould, 3.3.

————.

"Factors Conditioning Achievement in French among a Group of Adolescents; Synopsis of Thesis." *British Journal of Educational Psychology,* XVII (June, 1947), 114-115.

Richardson, G.
See Richardson, 2.52.

Riecks, Donald F., Marie-Georgette, and Howard Lee Nostrand
See Riecks, 5.

Schnurer, Herman, Samuel Baskin, and Robert Boyd
Experiment in French Language Instruction: First Report, 1958-1959. Yellow Springs, Ohio: Antioch College, November, 1959.
First year college French students are grouped and matched for ability, experience, and sex and taught by audiovisual and conventional means. Pre- and posttesting with French achievement, listening and placement tests is accomplished. Students are asked to rate teachers and personal satisfaction with instruction. Analysis is made by chi-square and t test. Results show no significant differences between groups on achievement. The audiovisual group shows significantly higher satisfaction than the conventionally taught group. Center for Documentation and Communication Research, Western Reserve University

————.

Experiment in French Language Instruction; Second Report, 1959-1960. Yellow Springs, Ohio: Antioch College, October, 1960.
A follow-up study of French instruction for college students either by a revised audiovisual instruction method or by conventional teaching procedure. Students are pre- and posttested on achievement, listening, placement tests and a rating scale. Analysis of results by chi-square, t test and F-ratio shows no significant differences in achievement, but significant differences in satisfaction with an economy in instruction time. Center for Documentation and Communication Research, Wester Reserve University

Selvi, Arthur M., *et al.*
See Selvi, *et al.,* 6.1.

Spaulding, Geraldine
See Spaulding, 2.7.

Stevens, Thomas C. Culver-Stockton College, Canton, Missouri.
The Adaptation of the Audio-Lingual Approach to the Teacher of Elementary French in a Small Liberal Arts College (Phase I); Project No. OE-4-14-026 (National Defense Education Act, Title VI), September 3, 1963, to September 2, 1964; $18,045.
The contractor will conduct research and experimentation designed to improve the teaching of modern foreign languages to under-

graduate college students. The project is expected to determine whether the audio-lingual approach to foreign language instruction as developed for larger institutions of higher education may be applied effectively to the small college.

The materials to be used in the project were developed at Indiana University by Dr. Albert Valdman under contract SAE-9498. The students of elementary French comprising the experimental group will spend at least 10 hours per week in contact with the language, including three 30-minute sessions of 4 students or fewer for practice in conversation and a minimum of 8½ hours of individual work in materials prepared by Dr. Valdman. These students will be encouraged to spend additional time studying the materials and to advance through the entire 40 units (normally covering four semesters) at their respective rates of mastering the content. Meanwhile, a control class of 25 students, matched by pretesting, will follow the traditional system of three 50-minute sessions per week, using Dr. Valdman's text. The experimental and control groups will be taught by the same instructor. Phase I provides only for the first year of the experiment.

Strawn, Richard R.
See Strawn, 4.1.

Toronto Board of Education
Experimental Study of Learning French in the Public Schools Undertaken by the Toronto Board of Education: Report No. 1, 1959-60. Toronto, Canada: Board of Education, 1961.

One hundred and two seventh grade pupils learn French through a series of films accompanied by a textbook. A second group of 105 pupils learn French by the conventional method. A group of 97 students, who do not study French, are the controls. Both the film group and the teacher group are matched by achievement, sex, IQ, and foreign language experience and both groups receive four 30-minute periods of instruction for five months. Results of a comprehension test administered after seven weeks of instruction reveal no significant inter-group differences in French achievement. A second comprehension test is administered at the end of the instruction period and repeated following the summer vacation. The teacher group achieves significantly higher scores on both of these tests, but the median score of a group taught French for two semesters during the preceding year is higher than both experimental groups on both tests. An oral test of proficiency in spoken French, administered to both experimental groups at the end of the course, reveals a significantly higher achievement level for the teacher group. A test of verbal reasoning ability is administered at the beginning and end of the experiment to all three groups, but no significant differences are found. 15 references. Center for Documentation and Communication Research, Western Reserve University.

———.

A Follow-up Study of the Effects of Aural-Oral French Instruction in the Elementary School on Pupils' Achievement in a Secondary School Programme. Toronto, Canada: Board of Education, 1962.

This nine month long study is carried out with 354 ninth grade pupils in five schools, half of whom have had previous aural-oral French instruction (the experimental group), and half of whom have had no aural-oral French instruction background (the control group). Students are matched with respect to sex, age, IQ, general achievement and socioeconomic rating. Achievement is measured by an oral proficiency test, administered at the end of the second term, and three end-of-term tests. Although the achievement mean of the experimental group is higher in each case on the oral proficiency test, analysis reveals the difference to be not significant. A further comparison, made between subgroups with and without language laboratory experience, also reveals no significant achievement differences. Analysis by t-test of mean differences on the first and second term tests reveals no significant achievement differences. The subgroup of students without language laboratory experience achieve significantly better on every term test than their matched pairs who receive laboratory experience. It is noted, however, that between the first and second terms the language laboratory subgroup makes a positive mean gain while the non-laboratory group suffers a net loss. 12 references. Center for Documentation and Communication Research, Western Reserve University.

———.

See Toronto Board of Education, 2.56.

Valdman, Albert
See Valdman, 2.55, 6.4.

Weiss, Bernard Joseph
An Investigation of a Synchronous Multilingual Curriculum in a Linguistic Framework. Unpublished Ed. D. dissertation, Wayne State University, 1962.

Purposes: This study was designed to supply information on what happens when children are taught English and French simultaneously and relatedly, especially when these children are not favored by socio-economic factors leading to enhanced academic achievement.

It will also suggest whether or not specially-designed materials will be an adequate substitute for formal teacher-training in foreign-language instruction. The entire program, including block-time and single-period variations, was linguistically-based. [. . .] *Hypotheses:* The investigation was geared primarily to promote the ability to use English through a contrastive-comparative experience with a foreign language. The research hypothesis was: A multilingual program employing linguistic techniques offers a sound basis for growth in the ability to use English. [. . .] *Conclusions:* The block-time program was superior to the single-period program in development of growth in writing expression, but the single-period class surpassed the block-time class in the mastery of English skills. Moreover, slow students surpassed upper-mental-rating students in control of English skills, and boys were superior to girls in the same category. The failure of the data to reject the null-hypothesis on the French test suggests that formal teacher preparation is not a significant factor at this level, and that previous foreign-language training for teachers may have been a distractive element in their multilingual studies; there are also indications that skillful use of audio-visual aids may be useful in assisting pupils and teachers to learn together. From the abstract.

Weldon, Richard C.
See Weldon, 3.7.

Wershow, Irving
Trial Use of the French Program, Foreign Language Institute, University of Florida: Final Report [1963].
   The French Program prepared by Theodore Mueller for ALLP (Audio-Lingual Language Programming) under Professor Rand Morton was used at the Summer Institute of the University of Florida. Compared with previous summer institutes it did not produce any better results. It did, however, prove useful for remedial work in pronunciation and syntax for subminimal participants. It would serve well as an orientation program, especially if it could be administered to the participants in the Spring prior to their coming to the institute. It would prove particularly useful in FLES work for teachers. It permitted the instruction of a larger number of participants (an increase of 50 per cent) without any increase in staff. Theodore Mueller.

Wittenborn, J. Richard, *et al.*
See Wittenborn, 3.1.

Wylie, Laurence
See Wylie, Part I.

German

Altenheim, Margarete R.
"The Relationship of Latin to Achievement in German," *School and Society,* LXXII (November 18, 1950), 326-29.

A study was made at Hunter College to discover if Latin background aided beginning students of German. Achievement was better for all groups with Latin background, and improved progressively with increasing years of previous Latin study. There was a correlation between Latin background and scholastic aptitude scores—the greater the number of years of Latin study, the higher the score. BP

Bauer, Eric Wolfgang
See Bauer, 2.53, 2.54.

Berrett, Donald S., *et al.*
"Report on Special Sections in Elementary German at Indiana University," *German Quarterly,* XIX (January, 1946), 18-28.

A report on the comparison of three methods of approach in teaching German: (1) oral-aural approach by trained linguists with the objective of the transfer of these skills toward a reading objective; (2) a combination of the conversational and the direct approach; (3) an approach through intensive use of text materials. Detailed description of these methods is given. Tables give scores for tests directed toward attainment of vocabulary, speed and comprehension, and grammar. The scores are explained. Seven conclusions are listed. JM

Brewster, Robert R.
Vocabulary Learning Through Reading German Prose (Ebacher Method) With and Without Aural Reinforcement. Richmond, Ind.: Earlham College, June, 1961.

Final Report of a project which set out to compare two groups taught to read German with alternating use of visual method (interlinear glasses), and aural-visual method (simultaneous listening to tape recordings). Procedures alternated every five weeks; individual and group performances analyzed. DF
Final Report available from the author or through Interlibrary Loan of Earlham College.

Brown, G. I., and H. L. Hodgkinson
See Brown, 2.55.

Brown, Paul A.
See Brown, Part I.

Buffington, Albert
"A Reply to Mr. Rovner's 'Appraisal of Teaching Beginning German by Closed-Circuit Television'," *German Quarterly,* XXXIV (March, 1961), 164-73.

Evaluation of television teaching in beginning German at Pennsylvania State College. Achievement compared with that of smaller classes taught by graduate assistants. Student reaction to television teaching. Details of handling instructional situations. Center for Documentation and Communication Research, Western Reserve University. See following item and Rovner, this section.

Buffington, Albert F.
"Teaching Beginning German by Closed Circuit Television," *German Quarterly,* XXXIII (March, 1960), 147-52.

A four-semester experiment at Pennsylvania State University, 1957-59, comparing television instruction of large groups with conventional classroom techniques, showed significantly higher test scores by television groups than by nontelevision, and by full-time television than by part-time television instructed groups. Results attributed to more effective use of visual aids in teaching and error correction, stimulus given by "talk-back" system to improved student preparation and more productive use of class time. Student questionnaire favorable. DG

Capretz, Pierre J.
See Capretz, 2.1.

Conrad, Joseph Lawrence
Study of the Germanic Languages in the Soviet Union (1934-1960). Unpublished Ph.D. dissertation, University of Texas, 1961.

This dissertation investigates the influence of N. Ja. Marr's linguistic theories on students of the Germanic languages in the Soviet Union. In Part I Marr's general theories on the origin and development of language are given, as are his specific notions concerning the Germanic languages. Part II treats the effect of Marr's theories on the dissertations of S. D. Kacnel'son, M. M. Guxman, and A. V. Desnickaja; a discussion of a monograph by V. M. Zirmunskij, who was not influenced by Marr's work, is also included in this section. Part III describes the so-called "stagnation" in linguistics, the increasing disillusionment of Soviet linguists, and the linguistic controversy of 1950. Part IV discusses the conservative position of Soviet linguists after 1950 and the interesting attention given to western methods of linguistic investigation (especially structuralism) after the year 1956. Joseph Lawrence Conrad.

Delattre, Pierre
  See Delattre, 4.1, 4.3, 4.5.

de Witte, A. J. J., *et al.*
  See de Witte, 4.1.

Engler, Leo Francis
  See Engler, 4.1.

Ferguson, Charles A.
  See Ferguson, 4.1.

Ferguson, Charles A., and William A. Stewart
  See Ferguson, Part I.

Ferster, Charles B., and Stanley M. Sapon
  See Ferster and Sapon, 2.55.

Gideon, Sara B.
  See Gideon, 2.51.

Hocking, Elton, Carroll Weisiger, and W. Merle Hill
  See Hocking, 3.1.

Johnston, Marjorie C.
  See Johnston, Part I.

Kufner, Herbert L.
  See Kufner, 4.1.

Lewis, Earl N., Jr.
  See Lewis, 2.54.

Moulton, William G.
  See Moulton, 4.1, 4.5.

Oswald, Victor A., Jr.
  "Progress of Intensive Elementary German at the University of California, Los Angeles," *German Quarterly,* XXIII (May, 1950), 129-34.
    "Intensive" here means the use of aural-oral pattern techniques as a means to an end; the objective is reading. The use of these two phases of training is discussed. Results are given in percentile figures and show that the test scores tend to be higher than with traditional reading methods. JM

Pfeffer, J. Alan. University of Pittsburth, Pittsburgh, Pennsylvania
  Addition of a Semantic Index to the Basic Spoken German Word List; Project No. OE-2-4-036 (National Defense Education Act, Title VI), June 1, 1962 to August 31, 1963; $84,954.

Under contract SAE-8824 with the University of Buffalo, Dr. J. Alan Pfeffer performed field research in the German-speaking area of Europe to produce a *Basic Spoken German Word List* patterned after Gougenheim's *Français fondamental,* and a corresponding book-length *Study* describing in detail the procedures by which the *Word List* was developed. Dr. Pfeffer's investigation has differed from that of Gougenheim in that it is based on two counts of frequency and range: a primary count of all words and a secondary count of the components of the literal compounds in the primary count. The present contract provides for a tertiary count of semantic frequency to reveal the scope of the meanings of each item in the original source materials. It will thus be possible to determine more closely the relative importance to the beginning student of, for example, a word with 19 meanings each of which occurs 10 times as opposed to a word with 5 meanings, each of which occurs 20 times. The *Basic Spoken German Word List,* refined and completed by the semantic index, will provide teachers of German an unequalled basis for unifying the coverage and coordinating the presentation of vocabulary in beginning texts and readers. From the official description.

———.

The Evolution of the Basic Spoken German Word List. Level I.
Preliminary edition and Final Report, to be published in a revised form as part of a volume entitled *The Development of Grunddeutsch,* by Prentice Hall, probably in 1968. The list was derived from a count of spoken words from recorded interviews, a count of concrete terms written by young German-speaking students, supplementary cultural and international items, and adjustments of nouns, verbs, and synonyms. See following four entries. DF

———.

Grunddeutsch. Number 1: Basic Spoken German Word List. Level I.
Englewood, New Jersey: Prentice Hall, 1964.

———.

*Grunddeutsch. Number 2: Basic Spoken German Word List. Level I,
with Semantic Index.* Englewood, New Jersey: Prentice Hall, 1964.
Based on the frequency count in Number 1, q.v., above.

———.

A Spoken German Idiom Count; Project No. OE-4-14-036 (National Defense Education Act, Title VI), September 1, 1963, to August 31, 1964; $39,254.
This contract provides for an investigation and tabulation of

expressions and word patterns most frequently used in contemporary spoken German. The material gathered for the compilation of *A Basic Spoken-German Word List* and Semantic Index, prepared by Dr. Pfeffer under contracts SAE-8824 and OE-2-14-136, will be used for this project. The most common idiomatic expressions will be identified, tabulated according to the frequency of their usage, and correlated and cross-indexed with the *Basic Spoken-German Word List*.

The Spoken-German Idiom Count is expected to contribute considerably to the body of basic resources necessary for developing and revising up-to-date German texts and teaching aids that meet current needs.

———.
(May, 1962), 179-86.
"Grunddeutsch: Werden und Wesen," *German Quarterly,* XXXV Description of projects listed above.

Rathee, R. S., and V. V. Mennes
See Rathee, 6.3.

Reichard, Joseph
"Machines for Language Teaching," *School and Society,* LXXXVIII, (1960), 408.
An experiment is conducted with Oberlin College students to perfect a system under which electro-mechanical machines can be used to supplement the classroom teaching of German language. The aims of the program are to increase the number of students taught by one teacher and to improve the quality of the teaching. A fifty student class is divided into two sections, each of which meets three times a week in the classroom and three times a week in the laboratory. In the laboratory they work with teacher developed taped materials. Results of the final tests indicate that students in the experimental six-hour classes score higher than students taught by standard methods in the regular five-hour German courses. On the basis of this experiment the author plans to develop materials for tapes, films and records. Program will be evaluated by Listening Comprehension Test and tests of speaking ability. Center for Documentation and Communication Research, Western Reserve University.

Rocha e Silva, M. I., and C. B. Ferster
An Experiment in the Teaching of a Second Language. Unpublished multilithed report, n.d.

This report describes a semi-automated method for teaching German derived from "a basic analysis of how verbal behavior develops initially." The program is designed to give a rapid introduction to the basic structures without the aid of the native language. The author's discussion of the program indicates the objectives and devices employed, as well as measurements of the students' progress. They point out the degree to which the program is culture-bound, yet the possibilities which it has for transcription into other languages (i.e., source languages). The successes and limitations of the program are mentioned along with some avenues of possible research for its refinement. DF

Rovner, Philip
"A Appraisal of 'Teaching Beginning German by Closed Circuit Television,'" *German Quarterly,* XXXIV (March, 1961), 154-63.
Evaluation of the methods and success of a TV course in beginning German taught at Pennsylvania State University as presented in an article by Albert F. Buffington *(The German Quarterly,* XXXIII [March, 1960], 147-52 [q.v., this section). Method of comparing linguistic experiments involving establishment of goals, standards of achievement, capability of teaching aids, teacher training and test procedures. Center for Documentation and Communication Research, Western Reserve University.

Ryan, Henry M.
See Ryan, 6.1.

Scherer, George A. C.
"The Forgetting Rate in Learning German," *German Quarterly,* XXX (November, 1957), 275-77.
Deals with the attempt to establish the extent of forgetting during summer vacation. Testing occurs, and the same test is repeated when the students return to begin the second year of study. The test controls are explained and tables are presented. The tentative conclusion is that approximatly one week of class upon return from vacation brings the student back to the level he had attained after a year of learning. JM

————. University of Colorado, Boulder, Colo.
Extended Classroom Experimentation with Varied Sequencing of the Four Skills in German Instruction; Project No. 8,823 (National Defense Education Act, Title VI), June 1, 1960, to September 1, 1962; $75,709.
Two-year experiment to test the hypothesis that reading skill of students trained with stress on spoken language will, after four semes-

ters of college work, equal or surpass that of students trained by conventional grammar-reading method without laboratory work. DG

†————.

Word-Frequency Count in the Modern German Short Story; Project No. OE-4-14-028 (National Defense Education Act, Title VI), December 8, 1963, to June 7, 1965; $18,811.

The contract provides for a word-frequency study based on the modern German short story. Contemporary German writings published since World War II will be examined and a list of about 5,000 words of highest frequency will be compiled. The purpose of the list ultimately is to aid in the compiling of instructional materials for German. In addition it will be useful to linguistic researchers studying changes in language habits, semantic range, and comparative semantics.

Scherer, George A. C., and Michael Wertheimer
"The German Teaching Experiment at the University of Colorado," *German Quarterly,* XXXV (May, 1962), 298-308.

Describes an experiment designed to prove the general superiority of students trained by audio-lingual approach over students trained by traditional approach emphasizing grammar and reading. Procedure of the experiment is described and the methods of testing are interpreted in detail. Results showed superiority in listening and speaking ability for the audio-lingual trained student, whereas they showed insignificant inferiority in reading and writing ability. The students trained traditionally were superior in translation from either language to the other. The audio-lingual students showed greater ability to think in German and a more positive attitudinal orientation toward the language and the German people. JM

————.

See Scherer, 2.1.

Sumner, Francis C.
See Sumner, 2.7.

†Thomas, Joseph V.
Modern Language Department Research Project, Austin Peay State College. Research sponsored by the Tower Club, Clarksville, Tenn., 1963-65(?).

This experiment, underway since September, 1963, aims (1) to devise simple self-drilling devices that can be used in the class, in the lab, or at home for written work; (2) to develop practical self-instructional exercises to be integrated with regular classroom study in elementary German; (3) to compare the relative effectiveness of written and oral laboratory practice in the learning of certain units of study. Joseph V. Thomas

Uttal, William R.
See Uttal, 2.55.

Wittenborn, J. Richard, and Robert P. Larson
"A Factorial Study of Achievement in College German," *Journal of Educational Psychology,* XXXV (January, 1944), 39-48.

A study of achievement in elementary German administered to seventy-nine first-year students at the University of Illinois, involving twenty-two tests. The value of the English Training Test as a measure of aptitude for success in the study of elementary German was established. The rote-memory factor is restricted, and "may be of limited educational significance," at least when rote memory is presented by sound. Tables, analyses, and bibliography. MJS

Zeydel, Edwin H.
"The Teaching of German in the United States from Colonial Times to the Present," in Modern Language Association of America, *Reports of Surveys and Studies . . .* (see Part I.)

Hebrew

Anisfeld, Moshe, and Wallace E. Lambert
See Anisfeld, 3.7.

Kahan, Anne M.
See Kahan, 6.5.

Nardi, Noach
See Nardi, 3.3.

Italian

Di Pietro, Robert J., and Frederick B. Agard
See Di Pietro, 4.1.

Ferguson, Charles A.
See Ferguson, 4.1.

Ferguson, Charles A., and William A. Stewart
See Ferguson, Part I.

Japanese

*Grinder, R. E., A. Otomo, and W. Toyota
Comparisons Between 2nd, 3rd, and 4th Grade Children in the Audio-Lingual Learning of Japanese as a Second Language. Honolulu, Hawaii: Department of Psychology, University of Hawaii, 1961.

Matsumoto, Masatatsu
See Matsumoto, 2.52.

NHK Radio-Television Cultural Research Institute
See NHK Radio-Television . . . , 2.51.

Uemura, Hidekichi
"The Effects of Educational Radio and Related Teaching Methods on Student's Ability in the Japanese Language," in *Survey of Educational Media Research in the Far East*. Washington, D.C.: U.S. Office of Education, 1963. Pp. 109-10.
    Four groups of eighth grade students, totaling 182 in number, participate in this experiment. A selection of 5 programs is made from the radio series "Native Language for Junior High School Students." Group A listens to these programs without teacher participation. Group B also hears the programs and a five-minute postbroadcast summary by the teacher. Group C does not hear the programs but reads the radio scripts and hears them explained by the teacher. Group D simply reads the scripts without any assistance. An examination covering reading, writing and vocabulary is administered to all groups. Group C performs best on the vocabulary and written sections, and there is little difference among the groups on reading. Group A scores the lowest as a whole. This is attributed by the author to the fact that a difficult Japanese character is included in the lessons which requires supplementary illustration. Center for Documentation and Communication Research, Western Reserve University.

Williams, Stanley B., and Harold J. Leavitt
See Williams and Leavitt, 3.3.

Latin

Bailey, Judith A.
See Bailey, 2.55.

Dunkel, Harold B.
See Dunkel, 3.7.

*MacBride, Mary D.
An Experimental Investigation in Winnipeg Schools to Determine the
Extent to Which the Learning of Latin Increases the Comprehension
of English. Unpublished Masters thesis, University of Manitoba
[1961?].

O'Brien, Richard J., S. J., and Neil J. Twombly, S. J.
A Basic Course in Latin. Chicago: Loyola University Press, 1962.

Designed as an elementary Latin text, this work does not explic-
itly purport to be a work of research. As a text it is excellent, embody-
ing many of the features that are today considered effective. Each
lesson contains a brief structural description of the matter to be
learned, followed by pattern practices and additional structural comment, if necessary. "The course is built around a series of twelve nar-
ratives which both provide examples of the structures presented . . .
and at the same time serve as the basis for the pattern practices and
drills for each new structure." (iv) The main theoretical interest of
the book consists in its analyses of Latin structure. The authors have
chosen to use the ecclesiastical pronunciation of Latin, and not the
classical, a decision which has resulted in some interesting differences
in the morphology. Thus the ablative singular can be considered (24)
to have no ending in all declensions. The pronunciation is the only
ecclesiastical element in the book: all else is classical. Morphopho-
nemes replace phonemes at the end of many morphemes: /iulius/ is
composed of iuliO' plus /s/. Discussion of morphemes and morpho-
phonemes is explicit, so that the reader is always aware of the structure of the forms he is learning. Immediate constituent analysis forms
the basis of the syntactic description, much of which differs from the
traditional. Particularly interesting are the discussions of the gernun-
dive (337ff.) and reported discourse (357ff.). The book is a model
application of structural methods of analysis to a highly inflected language. William F. Wyatt, Jr.

———.

An Intermediate Course in Latin—Drills. Chicago: Loyola University
Press, 1964.

This work continues the methods developed in the authors' basic
course, and is intended to provide drills on the reading material in
their *An Intermediate Course in Latin—Readings.* Each section cor-
responds to a section in the reader, and consists of two parts: Latin
questions on the text in the reader (with Latin answers to these questions at the bottom of the same page) designed to enable the student
to grasp fully the meaning of the reading selection without recourse

to translation; structural drills, also based on the reading selections, providing review of grammatical matters. William F. Wyatt, Jr. Although neither this volume nor the preceding constitutes research or reports of research activities, we have included mention of them because we feel that they constitute a significant application of the pattern-drill technique, usually understood to be useful in the teaching of structures orally, to the problems involved in teaching reading comprehension in a foreign language. DF

Rathee, R. S., and V. V. Mennes
  See Rathee, 6.3.

Polish

Vicory, Arthur C.
  See Vicory, 3.1.

Russian

Balogh, István
  See Balogh, 4.1.

Capretz, Pierre J.
  See Capretz, 2.1.

Carton, Aaron S., and John B. Carroll
  The 1959 Summer Russian Language Learning Program. Cambridge, Mass.: Graduate School of Education, Harvard University, 1960 (mimeographed).
  Research results obtained from groups of college students given intensive training in Russian and then sent on a trip to the Soviet Union, all during the summer of 1959. Enormous progress was made in intensive summer training as compared to regular academic training. Tests were developed in Russian. John B. Carroll.

Coleman, Arthur P.
  A Report on the Status of Russian and Other Slavic and East European Languages in the Educational Institutions of the United States, Its Territories, Possessions, and Mandates with Additional Data on Similar Studies in Canada and Latin America. New York: American Association of Teachers of Slavic and East European Languages, and the Columbia University Press, 1948.
  A study to determine if Russian, taught in high school, is acceptable as an entrance credit in colleges, universities, and medical schools.

There is a statistical analysis of survey results. Conclusion shows that high school administrators should not hesitate to introduce the language to the curriculum. JM

Cooper, Franklin S.
See Cooper, 4.5.

Couch, Sanford Gary
The Theoretical and Practical Problems of Teaching the Initial Stage of Russian to Americans. Unpublished Ph.D. dissertation, University of Wisconsin, 1962.

This thesis focuses attention on the pedagogical problems involved in teaching the initial stage of Russian to Americans at high school and college levels, the intial stage being defined as ". . . that part of the learning experience which includes the introduction of the phonetic and orthographic systems of the Russian language." A brief survey of how foreign languages have been taught serves as a point of departure for an investigation of the pedagogical problems of the initial stage as revealed by a comparative analysis of English and Russian phonology and orthography. This is followed by a sequential presentation of Russian phones and graphemes through the use of practice syllables, independent of meaning. The student learns through a series of interrelated learning experiences, each of which is taught without qualification and all of which, when learned in sequence, prepare the student to articulate Russian phones properly and to read Russian words correctly. Chapter 4 discusses how the language laboratory can serve in the teaching of the initial stage with the tape as the informant, the teacher as a tutor. An accompanying tape demonstrates this principle, using the articulations of the sequential presentation. The need for the establishment of a basic minimum vocabulary for the initial stages of Russian language study is discussed and a proposed Lexical Minimum is included. The conclusions indicate that the objective of the initial stage should be to help the student toward the development of an ideolect within the limitations of acceptable Russian pronunciation. From the abstract

Crothers, Edward, Patrick F. Suppes, and Ruth Weir
See Crothers, 2.52.

Crothers, Edward, Ruth Weir, and Patricia Palmer
See Crothers, 2.52.

Doros, Aleksander
See Doros, 4.1.

Ferguson, Charles A.
See Ferguson, 4.1.

Ferguson, Charles A., and William A. Stewart
See Ferguson, Part I.

Gage, William N.
See Gage, 4.1.

Gordon, Oakley J., Keith M. Engar, and Donald R. Shupe
Challenging the Superior Student by Making the Study of Russian Available in the Elementary School Curriculum via Television. Washington, D.C.: U.S. Office of Education, 1963.

Experimental groups containing superior and average fourth and fifth grade pupils are taught Russian via television or by a Russian instructor for three years. Control groups of superior and average fourth and fifth graders are not taught Russian. All the pupils are administered the Pintner-Durost General Ability Test, the Metropolitan Achievement Test, and achievement tests in regular coursework. In addition, teachers complete a behavior check list for each pupil. The experimental pupils are given measures of Russian achievement and measures of interest in the Russian class. Statistical treatment of the data includes correlation coefficients, covariance, and a factor analysis. Conclusions indicate that, regardless of the intellectual ability of the pupils or whether the language is taught via television or with a classroom instructor, the experimental pupils not only gain knowledge of Russian but appear to gain more in regular classroom achievement and behavior than the average and superior control pupils. Center for Documentation and Communication Research, Western Reserve University.

Harding, Francis D., and William S. Jenkins
See Harding, 3.3.

Josselson, Harry H.
The Russian Word Count and Frequency Analysis of Grammatical Categories of Standard Literary Russian. Detroit: Wayne State University Press, 1953.

Presents data dealing with the distribution of vocabulary and structural categories of standard literary Russian, starting with the second quarter of the nineteenth century, including the modern Soviet period. The material is coded according to grammatical construction. Linguistic aspects are also categorized. JM

Kale, Shrikrishna V.
Learning and Retention of English-Russian Vocabulary under Differ-

ent Conditions of Motion-Picture Presentation. University Park, Penn.: Pennsylvania State University, 1953.

A justification of "context learning" with visual representation. Words are more efficiently learned and retained when they are directly associated with the object, actions, or movements that they represent. This is opposed to pairing the foreign-language word with the native-language word. JM

Korwin, Roy
See Korwin, 3.1.

McDonald, Pearl S.
See McDonald, 2.55.

Petrov, Julia A.
"Report on Title VI (NDEA) Activities as They Relate to Improving High School Russian Instruction," *Slavic and East European Journal,* VI (Spring, 1962), 50-57.

Summary of all NDEA Title VI activities relating to the teaching of Russian in the high school, and includes mention of surveys, studies, research and preparation of textbooks. DF

Saltzman, Irving J.
The Construction and Evaluation of a Self-Instructional Program in Russian. Bloomington, Indiana University, n.d.

The purpose of our project was to construct a completely self-instructional, programmed, first semester, college course in Russian. It was hoped that the development of the program would: (1) make available a course which would be suitable for use in high schools and colleges where Russian teachers were not available, (2) provide a useful research tool for studying the learning and teaching of second languages, and (3) yield information about the development of extensive, self-instructional programmed courses. From the abstract. Although this project involved the preparation of materials, it is included in this *Bibliography* because of the theoretical nature of the third objective. See the following item for a discussion of the author's queries along these lines. DF

————.

"Techniques Used in the Construction of a Completely Self-Instructional, One-Semester, Modern College Course in Russian," *International Journal of American Linguistics,* XXIX (April, 1963, Part III), 167-76.

In this article I suggest that there is a fundamental inconsistency in the position of most of the advocates of teaching machines and programmed instruction, viz., they claim that teaching machines can teach virtually everyone, everything, everything faster and better than live teachers, yet they insist the teachers cannot be replaced by machines. I indicated that the goal of our NDEA Title VI project [see preceding entry] is to construct and evaluate a completely self-instructional first semester course in Russian with which to teach high school and college students to read, write, speak and understand spoken Russian. The course consists of programmed texts and tapes and takes about 225 hours to complete. I described the method and rationale of our programming procedures. I pointed out that our course is neither purely traditional nor new-key but that we have attempted to combine these two approaches and derive the benefits of both. I expressed disagreement with Nelson Brooks' opinion with regard to teaching grammar and using translation. I emphasized that there are no data available at the present time to support either his position or mine. I stated that in my opinion our program will greatly facilitate the conduct of research in language learning and teaching. Irving Saltzman, MLabstract #499.

Suppes, Patrick G.
See Suppes, 4.3.

Suppes, Patrick G., Edward Crothers, and Ruth Weir
See Suppes, 3.1.

Szoboszlay, Miklós, *et al.*
As orosz nyelvi kiejtés, irás-, és olvasástanitás módzertana. Budapest: Maison d'édition classique, 1954.
    An indispensable methodological aid to the teaching of Russian, which was made compulsory in Hungarian schools in 1958. This study is of special value in that it is the first Hungarian work on education in which an attempt is made to adopt Pavlov's psychology as the basis for language teaching. From van Willigen, Part I.

Tezza, Joseph S.
The Effects of Listening Training on Audio-Lingual Learning. Unpublished Ed.D. dissertation, University of Pittsburgh, 1962.
    Students in Russian language courses in three Pennsylvania senior high schools are classified according to listening ability as measured by Brown-Carlsen Listening Comprehension Test, Form AM. Students are randomly assigned to three treatment groups: listening, reading exposition, and audio-lingual training. The Brown-Carlsen Listening Comprehension Test, Form BM, and a specially constructed aural-comprehension test of the Russian language are administered after the

training period. Data are analyzed using analysis of variance and multiple correlation analysis. Findings indicate that students who receive listening training do not exhibit greater gains in listening ability nor do they earn significantly greater scores in aural comprehension of the Russian language than do students who receive reading exposition or audio-lingual drills. Initial listening ability influences listening and aural comprehension improvement. Center for Documentation and Communication Research, Western Reserve University.

Twarog, Leon I. Ohio State University, Columbus, Ohio.
Word Count of Spoken Russian: The Soviet Usage; Project No. OE-3-14-028 (National Defense Education Act, Title VI), June 1, 1963, to August 15, 1964; $18,214.

There is at present little uniformity in the vocabulary included in the elementary textbooks used in the United States for teaching the Russian language. This situation leads to serious difficulties in the selection and use of readers and intermediate course materials, produces unfairly disparate results on standardized examinations, and results in dislocation and confusion among students of Russian who transfer from one school or college to another while at the lower levels of study. To help correct the situation, the investigator, Dr. Nicholas P. Vakar, made a word count of contemporary spoken Russian which will guide textbook authors in their selection of basic vocabulary and sentence structures.

Since the usual method of producing such a word count, i.e., taperecording samples of speech, was not possible in the Soviet Union, the investigator sampled the dialog of about one hundred modern (1957-1963) Russian plays. Recent trends have made this approach feasible: the appearance of many plays dealing with contemporary Soviet life and everyday problems, and the reduction of the amount of political jargon in dramatic works. The project lists 500 high-frequency words for first-year Russian courses, a glossary of words having functions and meaning not recorded in standard dictionaries, a table of the frequencies of all vocabulary items, and other useful information.

Unbegaum, U. N.
See Unbegaum, Part I.

Spanish

Andrade, Manuel, John L. Hayman, Jr., and James T. Johnson, Jr.
See Andrade, 2.7.

Barcus, Delbert, John L. Hayman, Jr., and James T. Johnson, Jr.
See Barcus, 2.56.

Bolinger, Dwight L.
See Bolinger, 4.1.

Broady, K. O., C. O. Neidt, and G. B. Childe
See Broady, 2.56.

Brown, Paul A.
See Brown, Part I.

Bundy, Edward Wayne
See Bundy, 2.56.

Capretz, Pierre J.
See Capretz, 2.1.

Cárdenas, Daniel N.
See Cárdenas, 4.1.

Cunning, Carlotta
See Cunning, 2.56.

Delattre, Pierre
See Delattre, 4.1, 4.3, 4.5.

Diebold, A. Richard, Jr.
See Diebold, 3.5.

Donoghue, Mildred R.
See Donoghue, 2.7.

Dufort, Mary R.
See Dufort, 2.7, 6.1.

Feldman, David M.
Final Report [on] Elaboration and Experimental Evaluation of Procedures and Specialized Materials for In-Service Training of Secondary School Teachers of Modern Foreign Language. Boulder: University Extension Division, Correspondence Study, University of Colorado and Washington, D.C.: U.S. Office of Education, 1963.
See following entry.

———.

The Modern Teaching of Spanish. Boulder, Colo.: University Extension Division, Correspondence Study, University of Colorado and Washington, D.C.: U.S. Office of Education, 1963.
An in-service training manual for secondary school teachers of

Spanish, emphasizing the applications of the findings of linguistic science to all phases of instruction in Spanish. Twelve chapters cover such areas as the evaluation, adaptation and creation of audio-lingual materials, the preparation of phonological drills, syntactic drills, culture in the audio-lingual approach, planning the four and six-year sequences in reading and writing in the audio-lingual approach, etc. A separate volume containing a résumé of the experimental use of these materials is also available and has identical bibliographical data [q.v., immediately preceding entry]. An extensive bibliography is included in the manual as well as a special one for the language laboratory in the chapter devoted to labs and their use. David M. Feldman. This publication also includes Barbara Schindler, "The Discussion or Conference as a Learning Method," pp. 157-218.

Ferguson, Charles A.
See Ferguson, 4.1.

Ferguson, Charles A., and William A. Stewart
See Ferguson, Part I.

Foster, Dorothy P., and Clarence M. Williams
"Aural-Oral-Written versus Aural-Oral in Teaching Spanish to Fourth Graders," *Modern Language Journal,* XLIV (April, 1960), 153-57.
    Describes some current studies of modern-language teaching, and presents an experiment to discover whether children, after having learned to understand and pronounce written Spanish words, retain more on oral tests than children who are taught completely orally. The article concludes that the children exposed to written words do not perform as well on experimenters' oral tests. Howard H. Hayden

Gibson, Romain
See Gibson, 2.54.

Giuliano, William
"Aural-oral Proficiency Without Laboratories," *Modern Language Journal,* XLV (April, 1961), 171-73.
    Two classes taught by the writer were compared. In one class aural and oral work preceded formal study of grammar and written work. The other class was taught by the traditional method. Although the first class had had one semester less Spanish, and was a beginner's class, the pupils in this class had better pronunciation than those taught by the traditional method. In identical tests, the first class was superior in dictation and comprehension, while the second class was very slightly superior in grammar. The conclusion reached was

that pupils taught by the oral-aural method could reach a high state of proficiency without the use of laboratories. William Giuliano

Gradisnik, Anthony J.
A Trial Program in Spanish for the Fifth and Six Grades Using Television. Milwaukee: Milwaukee Public School, 1962.

This evaluation attempts to determine the effectiveness of teaching Spanish via television to fifth and sixth graders in all Milwaukee Public Schools. It includes an objective evaluation of public achievement in aural and oral skills and a subjective evaluation of reactions and recommendations of elementary school teachers and principals. These conclusions are based on testing and questionnaire results: 1) Pupils are able to learn basic foreign language patterns and expressions via television; 2) distribution of oral test scores is similar to that generally expected of standardized achievement tests: 3) the quality of telecasts and resource materials seems acceptable to classroom teachers; 4) earlier identification of pupils with foreign language interest and aptitude seems apparent. The Milwaukee Board of School Directors approved the trial program, begun in 1960, as a standard curriculum offering in Spring, 1963. Anthony J. Gradisnik, MLabstract #551. See Milwaukee Public Schools, below, this section.

Gurren, Louise
See Gurren, 4.5.

†Haas, Stanley
A Study of a Method of Teaching Spanish Utilizing Selected Electronic Devices in the Elementary School. Unpublished Ed.D. dissertation in progress, University of California at Berkeley.

Hall, Pauline Cook
See Hall, Part I.

Hamilton, Daniel L., and Ernest F. Haden
See Hamilton and Haden, 2.3, French.

Hayman, John L., Jr.
See Hayman, 2.56.

Hayman, John L., Jr., and James T. Johnson, Jr.
Reading and Writing Results in the Second Year of Research—1961-62. (Denver-Stanford Project on the Context of Instructional Television, Report No. 7) Stanford, Calif.: Institute for Communication Research, Stanford University, May 1963.

Approximately 6,000 sixth graders, all of whom learned Spanish audio-lingually in the fifth grade, are divided into 180 classes. Half of the students begin learning to read and write Spanish in the first semester of the sixth grade and the remainder begin this instruction in the second semester. Both groups are subdivided into two further groups, one learning by lecture-demonstration, the other by programmed text. The text is in two forms, one using small, sequential steps, and the other using larger, less sequential steps. Teachers are rated according to formal training, experience, and workshop attendance on a 20-point scale. Listening comprehension and reading and writing ability are found to be in direct and significant proportion to teacher training and experience. Data are analyzed by covariance and correlation coefficient. It is found that linear, maximum step programs are superior to large step, less sequential programs. Automated instruction proves as effective as the teacher-directed method, especially in the second semester when audio-lingual skills assumed by the program have been solidly implanted. Pupils who begin reading and writing instruction in the first semester of the sixth grade perform better on tests measuring audio-lingual skills at the end of both semesters than pupils who begin study in the second semester. Center for Documentation and Communication Research, Western Reserve University. See Schramm, 2.56, for the original description of this project.

Hohfeld, John M.
An Experiment Employing Two Methods of Teaching Spanish to College Freshmen. Unpublished Ph.D. dissertation, University of Pennsylvania, 1950.

    Discusses controlled experiments to check development of aural-oral skills obtained through the use of audio machines. Results favored the experimental group in aural comprehension and knowledge of Spanish life and culture as well as phonetic accuracy and oral reading ability. JM

†Horn, Thomas D. University of Texas, Austin, Tex.
A Comparison between the Effect of Intensive Oral-Aural Spanish Language Instruction and Intensive Oral-Aural English Language Instruction on the Reading Readiness of Spanish-speaking School Beginners in Grade One. (Project No. 2648, Appendix A: Basic and Applied Research Proposal submitted to the U.S. Commissioner of Education under the Provisions of Public Law 531), June 1964.

    This study tests the hypothesis that there is no difference among the effects of three kinds of oral language instruction on the reading readiness of Spanish-speaking school beginners in grade one: 1) oral-aural English intensive language instruction; 2) oral-aural Spanish intensive language instruction; and 3) no intensive oral-aural language instruction. Comparisons will be made for sex-role and the effects of varying spans of instructional time. (This project has been funded for execution in 1964-65.) CBC

Hunter, Thomas P.
An Analysis of Multivariant Factors in Classroom Structures on Achievement in Spanish in the Third Grade. Bellevue, Wash.: Bellevue Public Schools, to appear late 1964 (multilith).
    A comparison of achievement in classes of varying sizes (approximately 30, 60 and 90 pupils) designated as single, double and triple classes and divided equally into two categories: 1) those taught by one language specialist throughout the year, and 2) those taught by several instructors on a regularly rotated basis. Other comparisons included: 1) morning versus afternoon instruction, and 2) male versus female students. Instruction and materials used were standardized throughout the various groupings. Five tests were administered (excluding a pretest to equate groups), all on IBM mark-sense cards. Thomas P. Hunter

Johnson, Charles E.
See Johnson, 6.1.

Johnson, Charles E., *et al.*
See Johnson, 6.1.

Johnson, Grace Nichols, and Frances Hardy
See Johnson, 2.56.

Johnston, Marjorie C.
See Johnston, Part I.

Larew, Leonor A.
See Larew, 4.5.

Larew, Leonor A., and John J. Lottes
See Larew, 2.51.

"Latin American Studies Program"
See Latin American . . . , 5.

Leavitt, Sturgis E.
"The Teaching of Spanish in the United States," in Modern Language Association of America, *Reports of Surveys and Studies* . . . (see Part I.)

Leino, Walter B., and Louis A. Haak
See Leino, 6.5.

McDonald, Pearl S.
See McDonald, 2.55.

McKinney, James Edward, Jr.
See McKinney, 2.7.

Mate, Hubert E.
See Mate, 2.56.

Maynes, J. Oscar, Jr.
See Maynes, 2.54.

Milwaukee Public Schools
El español en las escuelas primarias, A Report; a trial program in Spanish for the fifth and sixth grades using instructional television. Milwaukee, Wis.: Milwaukee Public Schools, 1962.

This evaluation attempts to determine the effectiveness of teaching Spanish via television to fifth and sixth graders in the Milwaukee Public Schools. It includes an objective evaluation of pupil achievement in aural and oral skills and a subjective evaluation of pupil achievement of reactions and recommendations of elementary school teachers and principals. These conclusions are based on testing and questionnaire results: (1) Pupils are able to learn basic foreign language patterns and expressions via television; (2) distribution of oral test scores is similar to that generally expected of standardized achievement tests; (3) the quality of telecasts and resource materials seems acceptable to classroom teachers; (4) earlier identification of pupils with foreign language interest and aptitude seems apparent. The Milwaukee Board of School Directors approved the trial program, begun in 1960, as a standard curriculum offering in Spring, 1963. Anthony Gradisnik. See Gradisnik, this section.

Morton, F. Rand
See Morton, 2.55.

Mueller, Klaus, and Donald W. Johnson
See Mueller, 6.1.

Mylerberg, Duane W.
See Mylerberg, 4.1.

O'Rourke, Everett
See O'Rourke, 6.5.

Pflieger, Elmer F.
   See Pflieger, 2.56.

Politzer, Robert L., and Charles N. Staubach
   See Politzer, 4.1.

Rathee, R. S., and V. V. Mennes
   See Rathee, 6.3.

Richards, Sumner E., and Joan E. Appel
   "Effects of Written Words in Beginning Spanish," *Modern Language Journal*, XL (March, 1956), 129-33.
      The control group in this study followed a short-term, oral-written course in Spanish. The experimental group received an entirely oral course. On the final tests, the oral group showed superior fluency and pronunciation. Differences in other factors, such as comprehension and vocabulary, were negligible, although they also were in favor of the experimental group. BP

Roberts, Andrew D.
   "Language or Grammar?" *Modern Language Journal,* XXXII (February, 1948), 125-29.
      This study was undertaken to discover if a grammatical framework is necessary to the teaching of a foreign language. Test results from a group of fifty-five indicated that students can learn to express themselves through practice in life-centered situations without first mastering grammatical rules. BP

Sadnavitch, Joseph M., and W. James Popham
   See Sadnavitch, 2.7.

Saporta, Sol
   See Saporta, 4.3.

Schramm, Wilbur, and Kenneth E. Oberholtzer
   See Schramm and Oberholtzer, 2.56.

Stockton, James C.
   See Stockton, 2.52.

Stockwell, Robert P., J. Donald Bowen, and John W. Martin
   See Stockwell, 4.1.

Stowell, Ernest
   See Stowell, 6.5.

Superior Council on Education of Puerto Rico
   Spanish Word Count. London: Waverly House, 1952.
      Concerns word and syntax counts taken from oral sources of

special significance for teachers of Spanish and French. These counts were developed to provide the basis for the preparation of readers for elementary schools in order to rapidly acquire speaking facility of the language. JM

Tracy, Edward
See Tracy, 2.54.

Valverde Z, Luis J.
Guía manual al español. Urbana, Illinois: University of Illinois, 1957.
   Purpose/Scope: to prepare a manual guide for the teaching of spoken Spanish as a second language. Methods: study of linguistics and the principles of foreign language teaching, and experiments with various methods of presentation. Major Findings: an audio-lingual approach is followed: listening and understanding, speaking, reading and writing are the four main language skills presented in a gradual, cumulative and concurrent approach. Luis J. Valverde Z.

————.
See Valverde Z., 2.1.

White, Wayne Hugh
A Comparison of Two Methods of Teaching Beginning Spanish in Junior High School. Unpublished Ed.D. dissertation, University of Arkansas, 1963
   The conclusion of this study is that most of the students who were taught by the Spanish teacher learned more than most of the students taught by tape. However, on the final test students in one of the experimental groups scored as high as the control group and some individual students in each group had high scores. An observation growing out of the study, but not verified by the findings because conditions were not controlled, was that motivation was an important factor in stimulating learning. . . . Another observation was that a multilateral approach would be more effective in teaching a foreign language than the method employed in this study. From the abstract

Thai
Chaiyaratana, Chalao
See Chaiyaratana, 3.5.

Morton, F. Rand
See Morton, 2.55.

Urdu
Barker, M. A. R. McGill University, Quebec, Canada
   A Newspaper Wordcount, Newspaper Reader, and Comprehensive

Course in Urdu (Phase I); Project No. OE-4-14-019 (National Defense Education Act, Title VI), August 15, 1963, to August 14, 1964; $26,650.

The materials for the study of Urdu (one of the three national languages of Pakistan) to be produced under this contract are as follows:

(1) *The Urdu basic course* . . .

(2) *The newspaper wordcount,* which will contain a frequency list in alphabetical order of items occurring in a corpus of approximately 136,000 running words. Appendixes of various kinds (e.g., the frequencies of various types of verbal structures) will be included.

(3) *A reader of newspaper prose* . . .

(4) *The poetry reader* . . .

Items 1, 3, and 4 will be tested during and after production by the Institute of Islamic Studies of McGill University. Phase I involves carrying all the above work through to draft status, followed by trial class use, with subsequent revision of items needing changes.

2.5 Auditory and Visual Aids

2.51 Auditory Aids

Brewster, Robert R.
See Brewster, 2.3 German.

Delattre, Pierre
See Delattre, 2.3 French.

Felt, William N.
"Radio and the Foreign Language Laboratory," *French Review,* XXXIV (May, 1961), 562-66.

Tape recordings of actual French radio programs are used in language laboratories to teach French to an experimental group of college students. The control group is taught the identical material by conventional method. They are tested with an oral and with a vocabulary test at the end of instruction. Laboratory students show marked improvement in aural comprehension when compared with control groups. The use of the laboratory does not seem to have a marked effect on vocabulary test scores. Center for Documentation and Communication Research, Western Reserve University.

Gideon, Sara B.
Aural Comprehension or Auding in Secondary School German. Un-

published Ph.D. dissertation, State College, Pennsylvania State University, 1956.

This is an experimental study at the secondary level of learning through listening. Results showed different teaching methods produced similar results, that German aural comprehension seemed more closely related to length of study than to other factors. Results of auding tests were the same as total German achievement scores in aural-oral sections. BP

Kinney, Jo Ann S.
See Kinney, 3.1.

Kuniyuki, Noriko
"An Analysis of the Learning Effects of the Use of Magnetic Tape Recordings for English Teaching," in *Survey of Educational Media Research in the Far East.* Washington, D.C.: U.S. Office of Education, 1963. Pp. 144-45.

Six eighth grade classes are randomly divided into three experimental groups, totaling 153 students, and three control groups, totaling 143 students. One teacher teaches two experimental and two control groups, and a second teacher teaches one experimental and one control group. Tap recordings, based on the Standardized English textbook, are made by a native speaker of English. The tapes are 14 minutes long and include words, phrases, and sentences. The experimental groups use the tapes three periods per week throughout the semester. During these periods the teacher plays three-minute segments followed by explanation and practice. The control groups use only the text. An objective test is administered at the beginning and end of the semester. No significant differences are discovered between the two methods of presentation. Center for Documentation and Communication Research, Western Reserve University.

Larew, Leonor A., and John J. Lottes
"Tape Recorder Versus the Teacher in the Spanish Class," *Elementary School Journal,* LXII (October 1961-May, 1962), 199-202.

An experimental group of third-grade students is given instruction in Spanish using only a tape-recorder. A control group receives instruction from an experienced language teacher. Both groups are tested midway through and at the end of the instruction period. Data analysis is by means, standard deviations and t-test. Scores on the vocabulary and comprehension tests favor the control group, but no significant differences are found in scores on the articulation tests. Center for Documentation and Communication Research, Western Reserve University.

Leutenegger, Ralph R. University of Florida, Gainesville.
Auditory Factors in Foreign Language Acquisition; Project No. OE–
3-14-024 (National Defense Education Act, Title VI), May 1, 1963,
to September 1, 1963; $3,335.

The investigation was designed to provide more information on
the relationship between a student's auditory skills and his ability to
learn French or Spanish. The general aim of the study was to devise
an instrument for predicting facility or difficulty in learning French
or Spanish.

The subjects for the experiments were students in beginning
French and Spanish courses at the University of Florida. At both the
beginning and the end of a semester's language study, the students
were given the Seashore measures of musical talents, which covers
discrimination of pitch, loudness, rhythm, etc. The investigator then
attempted to relate the Seashore scores to other information on the
students—their previous musical and foreign language experience,
choice of career or college major, sex, sociological backround, etc.
He compared the two sets of Seashore (before and after foreign language study) to determine whether students score higher after a
semester's study of French or Spanish. In addition the study tried to
determine whether any of the Seashore scores, plus intelligence and
aptitude measures, could be used as a predictor of success in learning
a foreign language. (For more precise information, see Leutenegger,
R. R., "Auditory Factors in Foreign Language Aquisition," *Modern
Language Journal,* XLIX (January, 1965), 22-31.

NHK Radio-Television Cultural Research Institute
"The Effects of 'Radio Japanese Classroom'," in *Survey of Educational
Media Research in the Far East.* Washington, D. C.: U. S. Office of
Education, 1963. Pp. 103-4.

Two experimental groups and two control groups are randomly
created using 265 third graders and 300 fifth graders. During the 5
semester course of instruction in Japanese, all groups are taught by
lecture-demonstration, and the experimental groups receive a 30
minute supplementary radio broadcast once a week. The broadcasts
on the third grade level are aimed at the choice and use of nouns and
adjectives and pronunication. At the fifth grade level broadcast
emphasis is on expression, telephone conversation and public loudspeaker announcements. Both broadcasts contain information, demonstration, dialogue, drama, and colloquialisms. Tape recorded tests
of listening ability are administered after the first, second and last
semesters. These constructed tests stress intonation identification,

word identification, and ability to select appropriate oral summaries of stories and dialogues after listening to several alternatives. In half the test periods the experimental groups perform significantly better than the control groups. Performance of all groups is comparatively equal in the remaining test periods. Center for Documentation and Communication Research, Western Reserve University.

————.

"The Listening Effects of 'Radio English Classroom'," in *Survey of Educational Media Research in the Far East*. Washington, D. C.: U. S. Office of Education, 1963. Pp. 102-3.

This experiment is designed to determine the effectiveness of review through educational radio broadcasts over a three semester period. Six experimental and six control groups are randomly created from a total of 534 seventh grade students of English. Both experimental and control groups are taught using a standard textbook. The experimental groups simply review their texts. Tape-recorded multiple-choice achievement tests are administered after each semester. The first-semester test reveals a 5 percent level of significance favoring the experimental group. No significant differences are found on the second semester test. On the third-semester test, a 5 percent level of significance is again found favoring the experimental group. Center for Documentation and Communication Research, Western Reserve University.

Pickrel, Glenn E., *et al.*
"Tape Recordings Are Used to Teach Seventh Grade Students in Westside Junior-Senior High School, Omaha, Nebraska," *National Association of Secondary School Principals Bulletin*, XLII (January, 1958), 81-93.

Describes experiment intended to determine whether Spanish can be taught effectively by tape when the teacher knows no Spanish but learns with the class; and whether instruction is improved when the tape is used by Spanish teachers. The control measures are explained and statistical analysis is thoroughly presented. Results show that in three out of four comparisons, students instructed by a trained Spanish teacher using tapes tested highest. The conclusion points out that regular classroom teachers, untrained in Spanish, can teach effectively when using tapes prepared by Spanish specialists. JM

Popham, W. James
Experimental Appraisal of Tape Recorded Lectures in the College

Classroom; Project No. 474 (National Defense Education Act, Title VII), June 16, 1960, to September 15, 1960; $1,820.

A study to determine the effectiveness of teaching a graduate-level course with a series of tape-recorded lectures. The conclusion shows that lectures by tape are as effective as an instructor who lectures and leads discussion. JM

————.

Experimental Appraisal of Effectiveness of Taped Lectures for College Extension Courses; Project No. 470 (National Defense Education Act, Title VII), August 2, 1960, to August 1, 1961; $2,700.

A study to determine the effect on achievement and attitude of college graduate students instructed by pretaped lectures coupled with discussions led by a graduate assistant. JM

Uemura, Hidekichi
See Uemura, 2.3 Japanese.

Valdman, Albert
See Valdman, 6.4.

White, Wayne Hugh
See White, 2.3 Spanish.

Xoomsai, M. L. Tooi, and P. Ratamangkala
"A Survey of Results of Using School Broadcast as a Teaching Method," in Survey of Educational Media Research in the Far East. Washington, D. C.: U. S. Office of Education, 1963. Pp. 113-14.

An experimental and a control group, each consisting of 1900 students, are formed at the second, third, sixth and seventh grade levels. The experimental group has the benefit of supplementary radio broadcasts, while the control group does not. Second and third graders are taught singing and music appreciation and English is taught to the sixth and seventh graders. Written and oral tests of knowledge, attitude, and appreciation are administered. The radio group at the primary level scores significantly higher, at the .01 percent level, than the non-radio group in music. The radio group of junior high students scores significantly better, at the .01 percent level, in English reading and writing skills. There is no appreciable difference, however, between radio and non-radio groups in aural English skills. Center for Documentation and Communication Research, Western Reserve University.

2.52 Visual Aids

Blayne, Thornton C.
"Building Comprehension in Silent Reading," *Modern Language Journal,* XXIX (April, 1945), 270-76.
First report of controlled experiment at the Menlo Park Public Schools and Junior College at Menlo Park, California. TD

Chatman, Seymour
See Chatman, 2.54.

Cowan, J. Milton
See Cowan, 4.3.

Crothers, Edward, Patrick G. Suppes, and Ruth Weir
Latency Phenomena in the Prolonged Learning of Visual Representations of Russian Sounds. Stanford, Calif.: Institute for Mathematical Studies in the Social Sciences, Stanford University, Technical Report, Psychology Series, to appear.
The authors demonstrate that in learning experiments choice latency data is a valuable adjunct to response probability data. The subject's task was to learn the English equivalents of Russian words in a fifteen-day experiment. Latencies (measured from the onset of the visual display to the response) increased over trials early in the experiment. Then a decline in latency began which continued long after the subject's last error. Latencies were longer on errors than on correct choices. Item analyses relate the features of the Russian words to the choice and latency data. Comparisons are made with the performance of the same subjects on English items. Patrick G. Suppes

Crothers, Edward, Ruth Weir, and Patricia Palmer
The Role of Transcription in the Learning of the Orthographic Representations of Russian Sounds. Stanford, Calif.: Institute for Mathematical Studies in the Social Sciences, Stanford University, Technical Report No. 56, Psychology Series, June, 1963.
Two experiments investigated the learning of the orthographic representations of Russian sounds by American college students with no previous training in Russian. The subjects heard a word and learned to circle the correct multiple choice alternative printed in Cyrillic. Concomitant visual presentation of phonemic transcription did not facilitate learning. Patrick G. Suppes

Guenot, Jean, C. J. Sturge-Moore, and M. Tardy
"Etudes sur la lisibilité des vues fixes," *Études de linguistique appliquée,* I (1961), 104-36.

Preliminary study on the interpretation of film-strips used for teaching English to French adults in conjunction with tapes. Various factors facilitating or hindering the interpretation of these pictures are analysed. Jean Guenot

Hill, Leslie A.
"Colour Slides in Language Teaching," *English Language Teaching,* XV (July-September, 1961), 164-7.

This article reports an experiment made by the Department of Extension Service, Central Institute of Education, Delhi, India, under the guidance of the author, and suggests various ways which were found effective to improve/test the skills of speaking, understanding speech, reading and writing with the help of colour slides. Leslie A. Hill

Hoge, Henry W.
"Visible Pronunciation," *Hispania,* XLII (December, 1959), 559-64.

Concerns the "sound" spectograph—an instrument designed to produce a unique pictorial form for sound. Sound pictures can be "read" as a substitute for hearing. There are six illustrations that picture various vowel and consonant sounds, showing precise analysis of speech sounds. The pictures are analyzed and explained. Advantages and limitations of the machine are mentioned. JM

Kinney, Jo Ann S.
See Kinney, 3.1.

Kopstein, Felix, and Sol Roshal
"Learning Foreign Vocabulary from Pictures vs. Words," *American Psychologist,* IX (1954), 407-8; published also in *Science News Letter,* LXVI (October 16, 1954), 249.

Purpose of the study was to determine whether pictures were a better method for vocabulary learning, if (a) words in response position were foreign and (b) test was given also with English word in stimulus position. Results suggested that foreign vocabulary is acquired more rapidly by using pictures as cues. BP

Lumsdaine, Arthur A.
Ease of Learning with Pictorial and Verbal Symbols. Unpublished Ph. D. dissertation, Stanford University, 1949.
Summarized in Dostal bibliography, Part I.

Matsumoto, Masatatsu
"A Study of the Learning Effects of Audiovisual Methods—Learning Through Slides," in *Survey of Educational Media Research in the Far*

East. Washington, D. C.: U. S. Office of Education, 1963. Pp. 140-41.

Thirty-six fourth grade students are randomly divided into groups. The experiment concerns the teaching of an ancient story in connection with the Japanese language course. Group A, consisting of 18 students, is taught by the following method: introductory explanation of the theme, projection of 19 slides with running commentary, and follow-up consisting of a summary and question-and-answer period. Group B is taught by the teacher through a verbal presentation including the same introductory theme presented to Group A, a story-telling period adapted from the slide commentary, and a follow-up summary similar to the one used with Group A. An objective test, including multiple choice items and arrangement of occurrences according to their proper story sequence, is administered immediately after the presentation and 40 days later. On the immediate recall test Group A scores an average of 2.2 points higher out of 100 than Group B, a non-significant difference. On the delayed recall test, however, Group A scores an average 11.8 higher, significant at the .05 level. Center for Documentation and Communication Research, Western Reserve University.

Miller, James Dale
The Visual Adjunct in Foreign-Language Teaching. Unpublished Ph. D. dissertation, University of Utah, 1964.

Conclusions summarized in *Chilton-Didier Foreign Language Newsletter.* Philadelphia, XX, No. 4 (Winter 1964-65) as follows: The analyses indicated that: 1) The filmstrip visual methodology was found to result in higher mean proficiency scores in five of the six categories, i.e., each method by listening, reading, and speaking skills. In only one group having to do with the speaking skill did the non-visual method indicate a slightly higher score. 2) Differences significant at the .001 level were found in favor of the filmstrip visual methodology for listening over the method wherein no visuals were used. 3) Differences significant at the .05 level were found in favor of the visual approach for the reading skill. 4) Speaking yielded only a .10 level of significance, which cannot be considered as conclusive. 5) No significant differences were found in favor of low-aptitude students. 6) According to the student survey instrument, students in the visual methodology groups: (a) appeared to have higher class morale; (b) indicated greater interest in continuing French study; (c) seemed to have fewer problems understanding the language; and (d) expressed greater satisfaction in cultural learnings.

Morehouse, Ward. University of the State of New York, Albany, New York.

Survey and Cataloguing of Slide Materials in South Asian Language and Area Studies (Phase 1); Project No. OE-4-14-027 (National Defense Education Act, Title VI), December 4, 1963, to November 30, 1964; $11,450.

The principal investigators will begin a project to develop a set of color slides on South Asian cultures for use in South Asian language and area studies. There is a widely-recognized need for visual aids that illustrate South Asian cultures. Phase I of the project calls for examining and assembling relevant slide materials in the United States (re-photographing when necessary), preparing a basic set of slides, and devising an index for the collection. The draft catalog and preliminary set of slides will be available to major university centers of South Asian Studies, including seven NDEA Language and Area Centers. Comments and evaluation by center faculties will provide guidelines for the second phase of the project, the production of a comprehensive catalog and a complete set of 750 color slides based on existing and newly photographed materials. Professor Morehouse will direct the project, and Professor Spink will conduct the collection, photographing, and classification of the slides.

Richardson, G.

"An Experiment in the Use of Filmstrip in the Teaching of French," *Durham Research Review,* II (September, 1957), 142-50.

Describes an experiment carried out in a provincial grammar school, using as subjects two groups of children of "nearly the same age, ability, and level of achievement." The control group was taught by a "normal active, oral method." The experimental group was taught by a method that stressed a visual approach, whenever possible, and that used filmstrips for teaching free composition and concrete vocabulary. The research concerned (a) the effectiveness of filmstrip presentation of visual material, as compared with presentation via the printed picture, in the teaching of free composition; (b) the relative effectiveness of visual presentation as a method of teaching vocabulary; (c) whether any improvement in learning, observed in connection with (a) or (b), was offset by poorer learning in some other aspect of the language. Results showed that the filmstrip method was superior in teaching free composition and a concrete vocabulary (if the words taught had been made the main subject of a frame and if the words were tested by direct association). The group taught by this method was superior in the achievement of French-English translation to the group taught by the orthodox method. There was evidence to suggest that the less intelligent pupils benefited most from the filmstrip method. The results also showed that under certain conditions the use of filmstrip in language teaching is profitable in conjunction with an "active, oral method." No significant difference existed between the two methods with respect to abstract vocabulary, concrete vocabulary that was not made the main subject of a frame, purely auditory comprehension of spoken or written French, dictation, or grammar. The weakness of the experiment was the smallness of the groups tested, and the numerous variables introduced. Statistical results are presented. JM

Stockton, James C.
"Flashcard Experiment for Teaching Spanish in the Fifth Grade," *Hispania,* XLII (December, 1959), 590-94.
This experiment studies the question: "Does the presentation of the printed Spanish word to children of the fifth grade, along with the spoken word, have an advantage over the spoken method alone?" Control methods are carefully established. Four tables show testing results, which establish an affirmative answer to the question. JM

2.53 Audiovisual Aids

Allen, William H.
"Research on Film Use: Class Preparation," *Audio-Visual Communication Review,* III (Summer, 1955), 183-96.
Results of studies show that learning from instructional films is increased if teacher employs various motivating techniques on her students before showing film. BP

————.
"Audio-Visual Materials," *Review of Educational Research,* XXVI (April, 1956), 125-56.
Discussion of research of previous ten years in audio-visual techniques for teaching; bibliography attached. BP

————.
"Research on Film Use: Student Participation," *Audio-Visual Communication Review,* V (Spring, 1957), 423-50.
Presentation of numerous studies concerning the variables in the use of films. This research stresses "participation" in the aspects of recitation, mental practice, rehearsal, knowledge of results, verbalization, discussion, and note taking. Clear-cut definitions of these techniques, however, await further experimentation. Conclusion of

the study shows verbalization of response and furnishing knowledge of results to be the most effective of the participation techniques. Twenty-seven references are listed. JM
See Allen, Part I.

Allen, William H., and Morton S. Malter
"Research Related to Audio-Visual Administration," *The School Administrator and His Audio-Visual Program, 1954 Yearbook.* Washintgon, D.C.: Department of Audio-Visual Instruction, National Education Association, 1954. Pp. 266-84.

Refers to three past studies covering the period from 1923 to 1946. Materials, equipment, and building facilities are discussed. Problems of personnel, curriculum, and distribution of materials are presented. A 52-item bibliography is included. JM

Bauer, Eric Wolfgang
"Audiovisual Aids and Language Teaching in the USSR," *Audiovisual Communication Review,* November-December, 1960, pp. 295-99.

This article is a review of recent Soviet research in the field of audiovisual media and language-teaching methods. BP

———.

"Das Fernsehen und seine Möglichkeiten für Schule and Volksbildung," *AVISO,* No. 2 (1958).

An investigation of the effect of audiovisual media in teaching English in the Vienna schools. Conducted in 1954-55; tested 3,190 high school students. Later extended to a third year. Eric W. Bauer

———.

"New Avenues of International Cooperation in Audiovisual Language Teaching," *Audio-Visual Communication Review,* XI (September-October, 1963), 200-206.

Report on recent research and presentations given at the First International Colloquy on Audiovisual Aids and the Teaching of Languages, held in Antwerp, Belgium, April 3-7, 1963. Special Reference to Audio-Aids, The Electronic Ear, Sensory Stimulation, Visualisation and Language Laboratory Techniques. Eric W. Bauer

Bern, Henry A.
"New Directions in Audio-Visual Communications: Toward Educational Engineering," *Indiana University School of Education Bulletin,* XXXVI (November, 1960), 4-19.

The implications of educational engineering for improved audiovisual communication are discussed. Findings include the engineering origin of recent theories of audio-visual communication and the influence of human engineering research upon audio-visual research. Summaries of research in progress on the following aspects are presented: the effect of problem-setting questions on rate and amount of learning in programming teaching machines; the effect of screen size and image size and contrast on perception; the effect of various types of stimuli upon foreign language learning; the usefulness of videotape recorders in teaching education. 30 references. Center for Documentation and Communication Research, Western Reserve University.

Borglum, George P.
"AV-Active French," *National Education Association Journal,* XLVII (November, 1958), 566-68.
    This is a description of a program at Wayne University using color slides synchronized with tapes to teach French. Studies show that audiovisual sections were 50 per cent better in speaking ability at end of one year than standard classes. BP

————.

Modern Language and Audio-Visual Research Project. Detroit: Wayne State University, March, 1964.
    This Final Report on the project describes the research activities involved in the development of an integrated program in French at Wayne State University. Included are chapters on the history of the project and cooperative research with project materials. An extensive chapter is given over to "Motivational Factors in the Study of French" and contains the results of a study conducted for the project by an outside agency. A teacher evaluation of the *Aspects de France* film series for intermediate classes is also included. DF

————.

"Modern Language Audio-Visual Project," *Modern Language Journal,* XLII (November, 1958), 325-28.
    Audiovisual use of combination slide and motion-picture technique in teaching beginning language. BP

*Candelaria, Martin
Significant Developments in Teaching Foreign Languages and the Important Contributions of Audio-Visual Aids. Unpublished Ph. D. dissertation, University of Denver, 1950.

Carroll, John B.
See Carroll, 2.3, Chinese; 3.1.

Cline, Marion, Jr.
Improving Language Arts of Bilinguals through Audiovisual Aids.
El Paso: Texas Western College, 1962[?].
The achievement of the 1959 experimentals at the end of 1960 far exceeded normal expectancy. This could be attributable to the Westinghouse or Hawthorne effect. They achieved better than the repetitives in comprehension, total reading, and total arithmetic. The repetitives gained more in vocabulary, mechanics of English, spelling, and total language with one month less instruction. *Recommendations.* Further study is needed with more closely matched groups for a longer period of time and with the teaching of all experimentals by one teacher. A comparative study should be made between Spanish-American and Indian pupils using Anglo-American as controls. The effects of audiovisuals in earlier grades should also be tested. From the abstract.

Cooper, Franklin S.
See Cooper, 4.3.

Deutsches Pädagogisches Zentralinstitut, Abteilung Dokumentation und Information.
See Deutsches Pädagogisches Zentralinstitut . . . , Part I.

Dostal, Naida Marich
Audio-Visual Second-Language Learning: A Historical Review and Comparative Evaluation of the Use of Audio-Visual Instructional Materials and Teaching Techniques in First Year High School French. Unpublished Ed. D. dissertation, Wayne State University, 1960.
The experimental population consists of 282 pupils in high school French classes. They are tested at the end of the first and second semesters using experimental audiovisual tests and the Cooperative French Test. The experimental group using audiovisual instructional materials and teaching techniques surpasses the control group in speaking ability by the end of the second semester. However, the control group is superior in reading, vocabulary and grammar at a very high level of significance. Center for Documentation and Communication Research, Western Reserve University.

————.

Research Report: An Evaluation of the Use of Audio-Visual Teaching Techniques and the French Pilot Instructional Materials in First Year High School French. Wayne State University, 1958.
Gives definition and purpose of the study. Methodology is described in reference to control groups, teacher background, instruc-

tional materials, and testing instruments. The findings are discussed. Conclusions cannot be fully drawn until analysis is complete. However, the statistical evidence—which was shown by slides and is not presented in the report—showed that students taught by audiovisual materials and techniques held their own in reading, writing, and comprehension. They show superiority in speaking ability. JM

Forsdale, Louis, and Gerald Dykstra
"An Experimental Method of Teaching Foreign Languages by Means of 8mm Sound Films in Cartridge-Loading Projectors," *Language Learning*, XIII (1963), 5-10.
   The authors describe a trial procedure at Teachers College, Columbia University using student-operated equipment in both laboratory and classroom situations. The equipment consists of sound films which allow the student to engage in conversations with characters appearing in the film. The films and the program in which they are used are described. DF

Guenot, Jean
Pédagogie audio-visuelle des débuts de l'anglais: une expérience d'enseignement à des adultes. Unpublished Ph.D. dissertation, Sorbonne, 1963.
   See following entry.

———.
Pédagogie audio-visuelle des débuts de l'anglais: une expérience d'enseignement à des adultes. Paris: Sabri, 1964.
   Report on the teaching of English as a foreign language to French adults at the language laboratory at Saint-Cloud. Study bearing on: conditioning, visual semantics, audio-lingual imitation problems, testing and evaluation according to the various aspects of the language being tested (first level: phonology and semantic accuracy; second level: morphosyntactic correctness; third level: spontaneous elocution). Film strips and tapes were used as experimental material. Jean Guenot

Haas, Stanley
See Haas, 2.3 Spanish.

Hanzeli, Victor E., and A. E. Creore
A Comparative Evaluation of Two Modern Methods for Teaching a Spoken Language; Final Report Submitted to the United States Office of Education. Grant No. 745016.09. Seattle, Wash.: Department of Romance Languages and Literature, University of Washington, 1960.

Final conclusions show that the experimental group was superior to the control group in achievements of pronunciation and aural comprehension—the motivation was greater. The knowledge of English was not as important in the transfer to French as in the control group. The achievements in reading and writing were inferior to those of the control group and also to national standards. Balanced progress in the four language skills is not equivalent to that of methods used with the control group. Comment on the test battery itself shows that it was not completely satisfactory. JM

Hayes, Alfred S. 715 Gilbert Street, Takoma Park, Md.
A Survey of Needed Research for the Development of the Use of Electromechanical Aids in the Teaching of Foreign Languages; Project No. 8,578 (National Defense Education Act, Title VI), February 8, 1960, to August 31, 1960; $12,600.

Investigation to determine needed research in problems involving electromechanical aids, and to identify persons qualified to do such research. Based on survey of language labs purchased with NDEA Title III funds and other recent installations. DG

*Hoban, Charles F., Jr., and Edward B. Vanormer
Instructional Film Research, 1918-1950. Port Washington, Long Island, N. Y.: Technical Report No. SDC 269-7-19; Instructional Film Research Program, Special Devices Center, Pennsylvania State University, December, 1950.

This report was prepared for the Special Devices Center in the Human Engineering Division of the Office of Naval Research, under contract with Pennsylvania State College (later, University). Subsequent research reports, numbered up to SCD269-7-35, were detailed, and all 35 reports were summarized in January, 1953, in a binder titled *Instructional Film Research Reports; Rapid Mass Learning* (Technical Report No. SCD 269-7-36; [Port Washington, Long Island, N. Y.: Special Devices Center]). HLN

Jakobovits, Leon A.
See Jakobovits, 3.1.

Johnson, Charles E.
See Johnson, 6.1.

Kale, Shrikrishna V., and J. H. Grosslight
Exploratory Studies in the Use of Pictures and Sound for Teaching Foreign Language Vocabulary. Port Washington, Long Island, N. Y.: Technical Report SDC 269-7-53; Special Devices Center, Pennsylvania State University, August, 1955.

A study of learning Russian vocabulary under several conditions: pictures plus titles versus titles only; motion versus still pictures, sound versus silent pictures. It was found that (a) pictures of an object or act were an aid to vocabulary learning; (b) still pictures are as effective as moving pictures; (c) pronunciation of words by a narrator seemed to inhibit learning to write words. See William H. Allen, Part I. BP

Larson, L. C., and Charity E. Runden
See Larson, Part I.

†Lesage, André, Centre Audio-Visual de l'École Normale Supérieure de Saint-Cloud, Saint-Cloud, France.

Le passage de la langue orale à la langue écrite dans un enseignement audio-visuel de l'anglais à des enfants de 8 ans. Research in progress.

Research on the teaching of English to 8-year-old French children with audio-visual aids. Special attention is given to the teaching of written English after 130 hours spent in purely audio-lingual and audio-visual teaching conditions. New material has to be prepared, implemented, produced and tested; a new method has to be defined experimentally. Jean Guenot

LeVois, Camille J.
"The Use of Aural-Oral Materials and Methods in High School French," *French Review,* XXIII (February, 1950), 308-13.

Report on experiment at the University High School, State University of Iowa, comparing achievements of two groups taught French by different methods: experimental group, in which aural-oral skills were presented by mim-mem method as prerequisite to reading; and control group, taught reading for two years by conventional method, then introduced to aural-oral activities in third and fourth years. Aural comprehension and reading ability of both groups surpassed college norms on standardized tests. The difference in I.Q. between the two groups, the different lengths of time spent in studying the language, and the small number of subjects make results of questionable value. DG

Long, Arthur L.
"Recent Experimental Investigations Dealing with Effectiveness of Audio-Visual Modes of Presentation," *Educational Administration and Supervision,* XXXI (February, 1945), 65-78.

A summary of studies reported in the field of educational motion pictures from 1939-44. Forty-five reports form the basis of the study. They are classified under seven general headings that refer to effectiveness in teaching, developing attitudes, valuating films, etc. A 77-item bibliography is included. JM

MacKinnon, A. R.
See MacKinnon, 2.3 French.

Motzko, Gertraud
"Die Bedeutung audiovisueller Hilfen für das Gedächtnis," *Erziehung und Unterricht,* 1956, 138-42.

An attempt to show, through psychological tests, what different results are obtained from the teaching of nursery rhymes (e.g. Mary had a little lamb) according to whether no audio-visual aids are used, or whether recording or films are employed. An assessment is made of the number of spelling mistakes that are due to faulty sight or hearing or to lack of grammatical knowledge. The conclusion is that recordings and films substantially reduce the number of mistakes of all kinds. From van Willigen, Part I.

Newmark, Gerald
A New Design for Teaching Foreign Languages Using Dramatic Motion Pictures and Programmed Learning Materials. Santa Monica, California: System Development Corporation, 9 November, 1962.

I describe a plan for integrating combinations of media, materials, and techniques in a total instructional design. Research is proposed to compare the effects on student motivation, achievement, and retention of the following three variables: 1. Type of instruction (fluent teacher, non-fluent, student self-instruction), 2. Sequence of instruction (extended period of listening comprehension preceding speaking, comprehension and speaking together), 3. Type of materials (programmed materials alone, programmed materials and motion pictures.). Gerald Newmark

Nostrand, Howard Lee, and Donald F. Riecks, University of Washington, Seattle, Washington
An Experiment in Filmed Recitations for Use in Teaching French: Providing an Opportunity for the French Student to Experience Vivid Examples of Good Literature; Project No. OE-4-14-010 (National Defense Education Act, Title VI), July 15, 1963, to July 14, 1964; $10,336.

Chief outcomes: (1) a color film of the actor Pierre Viala reciting 17 French selections (all poems except a monolgue and a brief short story) totaling 41 minutes; (2) a *Cultural Commentary* containing suggestions for teaching the poems and indications of the aspects of

French culture they exemplify; and (3) a critique based on experimental use of the materials in early 1965 in elementary, secondary, and undergraduate education.

Pervy, Adolphe
L'audio-vision et l'enseignement des langues vivantes. Unpublished Ph. D. dissertation, Laval University, 1949.

Analysis of the ten learning factors of most impact experimentally known; qualitative description of these factors, experimental and bibliographical data, and discussion of their integration in: (1) natural language learning situations such as a child 2 to 4 years of age learning his native language: (2) audio-visual language learning situations determined by special language teaching films: (3) traditional modern language classroom situations. Among the many avenues of investigations opened by the above working hypothesis the following problems were quantitatively studied, using the experimental method: experimental measurement of number of words learned from one single projection of a language film teaching 100 words, by high school students of 21 different U. S. high schools; experimental measure of number of words learned in function of number of times a language teaching film is projected. Results: the two first projections yield the most learning. After the fifth projection learning slows down considerably. Other measurements: (A) amounts of forgetting, 36 days after learning 100 words from a French language teaching film; (B) number of times a specific film teaching 100 words has to be projected in order that an average learning of 100 per cent be reached by the various high school semestrial levels; (C) quantitative measure of attitude deterioration, in function of number of repetitions of projection of same language teaching film. Experiments conducted with first semester and fourth semester high school groups. Adolphe Pervy

Reams, Mary H.
"An Experimental Study Comparing the Visual Accompaniments of Word Identification and the Auditory Experience of Word Intelligibility," *Southern Speech Journal*, XVII (1952), 174-77.

Experimental study of two hypotheses: one is concerned with the relative intelligibility values and the visual identification value of words, both being said by the same speaker; the other is concerned with the relationship between the relative intelligibility of words heard in noise and the identification values of pronunciation of those same words when articulatory movements are viewed by normal-hearing adults. Control methods are outlined in general. Results of the study are indicated. JM

Rosselot, LaVelle. Otterbein College, Westerville, Ohio.
Evaluation of the Otterbein College Film-Text Method of Teaching
French, at Five Ohio Institutions; Project No. 8,617 (National Defense
Education Act, Title VI), March 1, 1960, to June 30, 1961; $38,560.
Two-year project, using control groups, to evaluate the method
at both high school and college levels by testing achievement in several
areas. Results will be tabulated in a final statistical report. As of
August, 1964 no final report is known to exist. DG

Rufsvold, Margaret I., and Carolyn Guss
See Rufsvold and Guss, Part I.

*Rusowicz, Mieczyslaw
"Sprodki techniczne w nauczaniu jezyko obcych na podstawie
doswiadczen w Zwiazku Radziockim [Technical Devices for Foreign
Language Teaching in the Principles of Accumulated Experimentation
in the Soviet Union]," *Jezyki obce w szkole,* V (1961), 170-76.

Sturge-Moore, C. J.
See Sturge-Moore, 2.3 English.

Toronto Board of Education
See Toronto Board of Education, 2.3 French.

Uota, Shoji
See Uota, 2.3 English.

2.54 Language Laboratories

Alhinc, J. M. Clay, and Pierre Roger Léon
"Le laboratoire de langues et la classe audio-visuelle dans une expérience d'enseignement accéléré de l'anglais parlé au Centre de Linguistique Appliquée de l'Université de Besançon," *Études de linguistique appliquée,* I (January, 1962), 156-67.
Description of an accelerated English course for beginning adults
conducted in cooperation with the ENS of Saint Cloud. The program
employs a strictly direct method, utilizing films and phonetic transcription, pattern drills for grammatical acquisition and the language lab.
The discussion is divided into two parts: phonetic conditioning and
systematic acquisition of linguistic structures. A program of regular
testing of the students' progress is included. While the present article
describes no actual research but rather a tentative program, the authors
indicate that further such programs will enable them to compile a body
of statistically valid observations, presumably toward the end of creat-
ing a more solid program built upon the principles of applied linguistics. DF

Allen, Edward David
"The Effects of the Language Laboratory on the Development of Skill in a Foreign Language," *Modern Language Journal,* XLIV (December, 1960), 355-58.

In this experiment fifty-four French and Spanish pupils were divided into two groups of equal ability. Experimental group spent 20 per cent of class time during year in lab. End-of-year tests showed experimental group achieved higher scores in reading, vocabulary, and grammar. BP

Banathy, Bela H.
A Test of Significance of the Class-Laboratory. Paper delivered at the 1963 Annual Meeting of the Modern Language Association (General Phonetics Group).

The assumption entertained in the experiment was that the introduction of audio-lingual electronic potential (CLAB) into the foreign language class, and a program dveloped to make use of this potential would make a significant difference in language proficiency. The performance of the experimental groups of the two language programs involved was found to be significantly better (.05 level of confidence) than that of the control groups. Bela H. Banathy

Bauer, Eric Wolfgang
An Experimental Study of the Achievement in Learning a Foreign Language through Comparison of Classes Taught with and without Audio-Aids of the Language Laboratory. Unpublished Master's thesis, DePauw University, 1959.

Outlines procedure and results of experiment comparing achievement of two German classes—one taught with audio-visual aids to supplement classroom work, one without. Classes equated on basis of mental ability and placement scores. Results of three written tests show no statistically significant differences, but indicate the aural-oral drill practice of tape-recorded grammar exercises raises considerably the achievment of the very good student, and gives increased achievement and incentive to the poor and average students. Experimental class showed over-all gain in long-range retention. Results of the oral test show significant difference in pronunciation. Opinion questionnaire on motivation showed some interference due to "complicated mechanism of the tape recorder"; need for good ventilation and soundproofing; necessity of close correlation of lab exercises and classroom teaching units, and for varied material for lab use. Conclusions: Audio aids bring a 20 to 30 per cent increase in mechanics of expression, vocabulary, and grammar, and as much as 50 per cent in oral work. Unless they are carefully prepared and integrated, audio aids can produce negative results in grammar. Visual aids increased short-range retention, but not long-range retention; however, they did increase student motivation. Suggests additional research experiments with larger groups over a longer period of time; comparative study of use of language lab under different conditions. Extensive bibliography, statistical tables. DG

————.

"A Study of the Effectiveness of Two Language Laboratory Conditions in the Teaching of Second Year German," *International Review of Applied Linguistics in Language Teaching,* to appear.

The purpose of this study was to determine which of two laboratory conditions, group-controlled, would yield higher performances. The results of Test I indicated that the performance of the controlled group showed a highly significant superiority in the lab-oral and lab-dictation areas. A slight trend favoring the controlled group in the written area was also apparent. Test II results indicate a slight trend in the lab-oral favoring the controlled group. In the written and lab-dictation areas of Test II there was a slight trend favoring the uncontrolled group. The results have indicated that a one semester program of 16-18 weeks for second year Foreign Language Instruction should begin with four- to six-week periods of controlled group laboratory-practice integrated into the total curriculum. This initial period should primarily consist of audio-lingual practice (which has proved superior under the controlled group condition in both tests). Dictation practice should also be stressed as a secondary objective in order to develop a high degree of writing skill and comprehension ability. At the conclusion of this four-six week controlled group laboratory condition the class schedule should provide for *equal* concurrent use of the two conditions (controlled *and* uncontrolled) during the remainder of the semester. A facultative increase of the controlled group condition in the proportion of controlled vs. uncontrolled instills the formation of highly efficient work habits and motivation during the initial controlled group condition and the latter utilizes carry-over of the habits formed in the uncontrolled group condition. Eric W. Bauer

————.

See Bauer, 2.53, 4.1.

Bernard, Edward G., and Sarah W. Lorge
The Relative Effectiveness of Four Types of Language Laboratory Experience. Research supported in part by the New York State Education Department, 1962-63.

A study of comparative gains made by groups of pupils using two types of language laboratory equipment in each of two time patterns. Types of equipment studied were: audio-active (non-recording) and recording-playback (tape recorder at each student station; student records and plays back his own speech). Time patterns were: one laboratory session a week, and twenty-minutes-daily laboratory sessions. Laboratory sessions were part of the regularly scheduled class periods. The four laboratory groups (recording-playback daily, recording-playback once a week, non-recording daily, non-recording once a week) were compared with each other and also with a group of classes using no electronic equipment. Seventeen classes in second-year French, in ten New York City high schools, were the experimental population. Areas investigated were: speech characteristics, comprehension of rapidly- and slowly-spoken French, and conventional skills measured by a paper-and-pencil test. Taped speech tests, administered at beginning and end of the year, were rated under conditions of anonymity by native French experts. In overall quality of speech, all laboratory groups made greater gains than the group using no electronic equipment. The group using recording-playback equipment twenty minutes daily outranked all other groups at the highly significant level of .01, and made the greatest gains also in pronunciation and intonation in which areas the no-electronic-equipment group made the least gains. In comprehension of rapidly-spoken French the greatest gains were again made by the recording-playback-twenty-minutes-daily group. This same group also made greatest gains in total performance on the standardized test of conventional skills (the Cooperative French Test), outranking the no-electronic-equipment group and the other laboratory groups. Recording experience appears to have beneficial effect on comprehension as well as speech. Type of equipment and amount of use both have important influence on what is accomplished in language laboratory work. Sarah W. Lorge.

———.

The Use of the Language Laboratory in the Teaching of French in Secondary Schools. Research supported by the New York State Education Department, 1959-62.

Groups of students who used language laboratories for 60 minutes a week taken from their regularly-assigned class contact periods were compared with groups who did not use the laboratory at all, in their study of first-, second-, and third-year French. Areas of investigation were: comprehension of French spoken at two rates of speed; speaking skills; and conventional skills of silent-reading comprehension; vocabulary; and grammatical concepts. Areas were identified where differences occurred, attributable to the lab work, at various levels of advancement. First-year lab students developed superiority in fluency of speech. Second-year lab groups developed superiority in fluency and intonation. Third-year groups developed superiority in comprehension of rapidly- and slowly-spoken French. At all levels, laboratory and non-laboratory groups performed equally well in standardized tests of conventional skills (Cooperative French Tests) despite the fact that sixty minutes per week of class time were replaced by that amount of laboratory work. Motivational factors appear to be involved: in three separate groups which were studied, lab students elected the optional fourth-year course in approximately twice as great proportion as non-laboratory students. The research was conducted in two high schools in New York City. Sarah W. Lorge.

Brushwood, John S., and Paul C. Polmantier
"The Effectiveness of the Audio-Laboratory in Elementary Modern Language Courses," *University of Missouri Bulletin,* LIV (May 22, 1953), 14.

Compares results of testing two groups of freshmen college students: group one following traditional courses—survey of grammar, some reading, *no* planned oral-aural program; group two following a new course, which included "a planned approach to the attainment of an aural-oral objective." Results published in this bulletin: "The experimental had greater tested aural achievement than did the control groups while doing as well as, or slightly better than, the control groups on the tested traditional objectives of reading, vocabulary, and grammar." JG

Buch, John N.
Using Variation of Language Laboratory Equipment with High School Students in Beginning French. Harrisburg, Pa.: Department of Public Instruction, 1963.

In this research project we found that a group using the audioactive equipment 80 per cent of the time and the record facilities 20 per cent of the time achieved superior results in comprehension of the spoken word, structural accuracy, and speaking fluency. No significant differences resulted among the four groups on mastery of traditional skills. Practically, the findings of this study would support an installation of 24 or 30 pupil stations equipped with the record playback feature. John N. Buch, MLabstract #555.

Buchelt, Walter
"Über die Entwicklung von Kabinetten für den Fremdsprachenunterricht," *Fremdsprachenunterricht,* VIII (March, 1964), 133-46.
Methods of using the language laboratory in the general school. Measures taken in the GDR to set up modern language laboratories. Description of a language laboratory and the technical equipment. The methodology of teaching in the language laboratory. Interrelations between the various types of teaching aids in language teaching. Conclusions concerning the equipment of standard language laboratories at general schools in the German Democratic Republic. W. Stiehl

Chatman, Seymour
"Report on Possible Applications of Sound Spectrography in the Language Laboratory," *System Development Corporation Field Note,* FN-6817 (August 20, 1962), 1-10.
In this report I suggest the possibility of experiments to automize the language laboratory. The present state of the art of mechanical speech recognition is such that automatization is a distinct possibility, both in respect to phenomena like intonation and stress and to individual segmental phonemes. By way of example, I compare two spectrograms of the same utterance, one by a native speaker of English and another by a Korean student who is just beginning to study English. It seems obvious that relevant information from the spectrographic output could be converted into a pedagogically useful display, and three exploratory experiments are suggested to test the efficacy of possible displays. Seymour Chatman, MLabstract #362.

Conwell, Marilyn
"An Evaluation of the Keating Report," *Bulletin of the National Association of Secondary School Principals,* XLVIII (March, 1964), 104-15.
A factual analysis of Mr. Keating's study [q.v., this section]; its scope, methods, statistics, and conclusions. Findings: Mr. Keating's controls are not consistently applied, the student group under examination is too heterogeneous to permit valid conclusions, the testing procedures are inefficient and inappropriate, the findings are misreported to the extent of omitting over 1,600 from important statistical tables, the conclusions are biased by overgeneralization. Furthermore, Mr. Keating ignores the fundamental use of the laboratory, and the necessity of teacher training to the success of any new program. Marilyn Conwell

Crossman, David M.
"Reports of the Keating Report," *American School and University,* XXXVI (December, 1963), 35, 38.

In this report I evaluated a research study by Raymond F. Keating [q.v., this section] entitled *A Study of the Effectiveness of Language Laboratories,* published by the Institute of Administrative Research, Teachers College, Columbia University, in 1963. I criticized Mr. Keating for not being concerned with the way in which the sample labs were being used, for supplying no data about the use of commercial versus locally prepared material, for assuming that higher paid teachers use language laboratories better than lower paid teachers, for making insufficient attempt to insure comparability between lab and no-lab schools, and for failing to pretest to establish a reference base. This study perhaps accurately assessed an existing situation, but has little inferential value. David M. Crossman, MLabstract #664.

Delattre, Pierre C.
"Testing Students' Progress in the Language Laboratory," *Automated Teaching Bulletin,* I (Summer, 1960), 21-31.

This is a description of the exercises and testing and an evaluation of amount learned from language laboratory by students at the French Institute at the University of Colorado, in the summer of 1959. BP

Deutsches Pädagogisches Zentralinstitut, Abteilung Dokumentation und Information.
See Deutsches Pädagogisches Zentralinstitut . . . , Part I.

Edling, Jack V., *et al.*
"Reports on the Keating Report," *American School and University,* XXXVI (December, 1963), 33-38.

In this article six experts in the fields of audio-visual and language instruction take issue with a nationally-publicized study. It is contended that data in the Keating report do not, in themselves, constitute a major condemnation of language laboratories. The design of the Keating study [q.v., this section] is simple and open to criticism. With the exception of the manner in which the speech production data were reported, the measurement devices and sampling procedures employed in the study may be justified. Jack V. Edling, MLabstract #685.

Felt, William N.
See Felt, 2.51.

Freeman, M. Z., and M. Buka
See Freeman, 2.9.

Gaarder, A. Bruce, and Joseph C. Hutchinson
Brief Analysis of the Keating Report. Washington, D.C.: U.S. Office
of Education, 1963.
   In this paper we present ten comments on Keating's study [q.v.,
this section]. 1. The effectiveness of the LL depends on how it is used,
not on its mere presence. Effective use involves five factors: (a)
Teachers interested and skilled in using equipment and materials; (b)
Materials which develop listening-speaking skills and closely integrate
class and LL learning; (c) Testing and grading with due weight on
achievement in listening-speaking; (d) Student practice sessions adequate in frequency and length; (e) Equipment of good quality. Unfortunately, Keating made no attempt to evaluate these five variables.
2. To the extent it was used, the LL taught almost as well as the teachers did. 3. Keating's data was for '61-'62. Adequate FL materials, designed for use in class and LL in high schools appeared in '61 for
Level I, '62 and '63 for Levels II and III, and Level IV is not yet
available. 4. Adequate standardized tests of listening-speaking in the
schools will be available in '64 MLA-ETS. 5. In the twenty-one
schools covered, modal use of LLs was only one period per week. Yet
in 866 schools elsewhere, LL practice sessions were 3-5 times per
week in 37 per cent, 2 per week in 36 per cent, and 1 per week in only
27 per cent. A 1963 NYC study in ten high schools documents dramatic gains achieved by *regular, frequent* LL practice. 6. LL and
non-LL designations did not indicate whether or not recorded materials were used in classwork. 7. LLs are primarily for developing
listening-speaking skills, only secondarily for reading. 8. The pronunciation test used was of questionable validity and not adequate to test
speaking. 9. LLs were widely accepted before NDEA by those com-
mitted to developing oral skills. 10. Schools have spent for LLs about
$15 million of Federal funds under Title III NDEA. The "nine digits"
figure is obviously exaggerated. MLabstract, #602.

Gibson, Romain (Mrs. Rodney E.)
   "Tape Recordings Experiment Is Expanded in Westside Junior and
Senior High Schools, Omaha, Nebraska," *National Association of
Secondary School Principals Bulletin,* XLIII (January, 1959), 49-72.
   A study to verify the effectiveness of tape teaching in conversa-
tional Spanish in classrooms where the teachers know no Spanish.
Seven hypotheses are listed. Control group organization is clarified,
using seventh- and eighth-grade students. Complete statistical infor-
mation is presented. Testing was done at the end of each semester. At
the end of the year, the written and oral test showed no significant

difference in the scores achieved by groups studying by tapes whose teachers knew no Spanish, and the control group, which was taught by a Spanish teacher, in the seventh grade. Second-year conversational Spanish in the eighth grade was not put on a statistical basis. The purpose of the study was to determine what would happen due to teacher and pupil turnover. Test groups are again described. Conclusion was that a second year is not feasible if the class is of medium or low ability and the teacher knows no Spanish or has not been in the program previously. Some of the students were well enough qualified to have been doing regular first-year high school Spanish, being ready to go on with second-year high school Spanish upon entering high school. Language-laboratory experiments were not completed for Spanish. Conclusions are affirmative for the use of laboratories in comprehension and writing of French. Results and benefits as well as limitations are discussed. The article also itemizes cost of materials for laboratory facilities. Savings in use of trained personnel, larger groupings, and materials are discussed. Eight points are listed considering advantages of tape teaching. Problems are pointed out; future plans are described. JM   See Pickrel, 2.51.

Giuliano, William
See Giuliano, 2.3 Spanish.

Grittner, Frank
"Shortcomings of Language Laboratory Findings in the IAR-Research Bulletin," *Modern Language Journal,* XLVIII (April, 1964), 207-10.
    In this article I point out the more glaring flaws in the *IAR-Research Bulletin* and raise objections to the practice of bulk mailing a three-page brochure of "preliminary findings" nearly a year in advance of publishing the 60-page *Keating Report* [q.v., this section]. One of the flaws would seem sufficient to discredit the entire report since, by its own admission, it measures *failure* to use laboratory rather than *use* of laboratory. ("The modal practice was one period per week.") Incredibly, this shortcoming is passed off with the remark that "it is hard to see how more frequent periods in the laboratory would change the outcome!" Among the many other flaws discussed are: (1) The manner of evaluation is not consistent with the usual objectives of laboratory work. (2) Important variables are not mentioned, are uncontrolled, or are lightly set aside by means of questionable assumptions. (3) Other studies which contradict this one were not taken into account. Frank Grittner, MLabstract #726.

Guenot, Jean
See Guenot, 2.53.

Hayes, Alfred S.
"Notes on Current Research." Chapter 3, pp. 60-77, of Elton Hocking. *Language Laboratory and Language Learning*. Washington, D.C.: Department of Audiovisual Instruction, National Education Association of the United States, 1964. $4.50.

A well-informed, selective account of research on language laboratories, completed or in progress in 1963. HLN

Hocking, Elton. Purdue University, Lafayette, Ind.
Comparative Effectiveness of Language Laboratory Equipment, February, 1960, to June, 1961.

Compares the achievement of students using the language laboratory for responding to exercises with activated earphones and recording their response to playback. Results to be released through Educational Facilities Laboratories. HLN

———.

"The Power of Babel," *Modern Language Journal,* XXXVI (May, 1952), 239-41.

Description of Purdue language-laboratory research at Purdue University on the use of the speedreaders, opaque projector, and oral-aural machines in the language laboratory. JG

Hutchinson, Joseph C.
"The Language Laboratory, How Effective Is It?" *School Life,* XLVI (January-February, 1964), 14-17, 39-41.

See Gaarder, this section.

Keating, Raymond F.
A Study of the Effectiveness of Language Laboratories. New York: Institute of Administrative Research, Teachers College, Columbia University, 1963.

More than five thousand students of French in twenty-one school districts of the Metropolitan School Study Council were tested in three language skills: reading comprehension, listening comprehension, and speech production. The total number of students was distributed among two groups, a language laboratory group and a no-laboratory group at each of four levels of experience, that is, years of French instruction. In only one instance, that of speech production scores at Level 1, was there found significant difference that favored the language laboratory group. Significant differences that favored the no-laboratory group predominated and appeared in connection with each language skill tested. When comparisons were made using students within the same I.Q. band, or class, significant differences favoring the no-laboratory group of students were found almost exclusively with students at the upper end of the I.Q. distribution. Thus, at least in this study, high I.Q. students were found to be the most severely disadvantaged by the inclusion of the laboratory in the instructional program. Students of average I.Q. were found, within the limits of the measures and comparisons made in this study, to be relatively unaffected by the inclusion of the laboratory in the instructional program. While this study does not purport to demonstrate that the language laboratory cannot be used effectively, it does show that in schools of the Metropolitan School Study Council, a group of schools characterized by competent and well-prepared teachers, better results in certain important skill areas are being achieved in instructional situations which do not use the language laboratory. Raymond F. Keating, MLabstract #549.

*Léon, Pierre Roger
Méthodologie de l'orthophonie au laboratoire de langues. Unpublished Doctorat de l'Université dissertation, University of Besançon, 1960.

Leutenegger, Ralph R., and Theodore H. Mueller
See Leutenegger and Mueller, 2.3 French.

Lewis, Earl N., Jr.
Experimentation to Develop More Effective Methods of Teaching Foreign Languages with Electromechanical Aids. Baton Rouge, La.: Louisiana State University, August, 1961. Also in Modern Language Association of America *Reports and Surveys* . . . (see Part I).
    Comparison of two elementary German classes—one using integrated class and laboratory procedures to free teacher from routine drill sessions and allow him to spend time in less routine work with students, the other using conventional homework as class supplement. Complements Reichard experiment at Oberlin (q.v., 2.3 German). DG

Lorge, Sarah W.
"Report of Study on Foreign-Language Laboratories in Secondary Schools," *Audio-Visual Communication Review,* XI (May-June, 1963), 70.
    A population of 713 secondary school students are divided into experimental and control groups to learn French over a three-year period. A language laboratory of 32 stations with 14 tape recorder stations is used. Students are administered the following tests at the beginning, middle, and end of the year: a Listening-Directions Picture

Test to measure listening comprehension; a question-answer test to measure the student's ability to make prompt, correct responses to questions; and the Cooperative French Test to measure student's reading, vocabulary, and grammar. Results indicate that students using language laboratory learn French without detriment to the traditional skills of reading and writing; and that listening comprehension is not improved by the language laboratory. However, language laboratory results in definite gains in student's speaking competency and student's interest in French. Center for Documentation and Communication Research, Western Reserve University. See Bernard, this section.

Mathieu, Gustave

"[Editorial Comment on Keating's *A Study of the Effectiveness of the Language Laboratories*]," *MLabstracts,* No. 11 (November, 1963), 2.

[The following is appended to MLabstract #549. See Keating, this section.] The above abstract represents verbatim the "Summary" of Mr. Keating's study. The "Summary" is section II of Chapter V, "Concluding Observations and Summary." The following excerpts from section I, "Concluding Observations" are necessary for a fuller appreciation of the "Summary" since they underline Mr. Keating's statistical findings that the laboratory is worthless unless used properly: "No attempt was made in the present study to indicate what results would be obtained under some ideal and highly creative program of language instruction into which the laboratory had been integrated according to organizational principles not yet widely accepted." (p. 37) "Most districts reported that students spent only one classroom period per week in the laboratory. Only one district stated that the time a student spent in the laboratory contributed to an actual increase in the total regularly scheduled class time spent with the target language. (p. 38) ". . . Even the limited amount of information about these programs obtained by surveying the local districts must be considered merely suggestive of the use to which the laboratory was put during the period of study. Not only the validity but also the reliability of this information might be questioned." (p. 38) ". . . It would seem fairly clear that in few cases, if any, was the introduction of the laboratory accompanied by the emergence of any new principles of organization for instruction. Only one district, for example adopted a plan for using the laboratory in such a way that time regularly spent in the laboratory would not merely replace regularly scheduled time spent with the target language." (pp. 38-39) It should also be noted that the "speech production" test is actually a pronunciation test. Why condemn the jet plane if it crashes because the airline did not properly train its propeller plane pilots to fly the new machine and understand the principles on which it works? Gustave Mathieu

Maynes, J. Oscar, Jr.
An Experiment to Gauge the Effectiveness of the Audio-Lingual Method and the Language Lab. Glendale High School, Glendale, Arizona. Unpublished report.

An eighteen week experiment intending to prove the effectiveness of the language laboratory in teaching the four fundamental abilities using Spanish. The experimental group memorized unwritten dialogues; grammar was taught in relation to the dialogues and reinforced by pattern drills; the laboratory facilities aided in overlearning; the emphasis was on speaking and understanding. The control group received the traditional training in which reading and writing was the primary stress. In contrast to the passivity shown by the control group, the experimental group demonstrated enthusiasm and active participation. The tabulated results of examinations show this group to have achieved the highest score. JM

Moore, Patricia [Sister John Marguerite, S.N.D. de N.]
"A Language Laboratory Experiment in Junior High School," *Modern Language Journal,* XLVI (October, 1962), 269-71.

The aim of this experiment was to investigate the value of the language laboratory as a supplement to an already established FL program on the junior high school level. A class of sixteen homogeneously grouped seventh graders served as subjects. Aural and written pretests, based completely on class material, served as instruments in matched pairing. The control group continued regular classwork, while the experimental group received two supplementary thirty minute periods of laboratory practice and review drill every week for six weeks. Retesting with the same instrument and teacher observation showed that the experimental group gained over the control group in audio-lingual and writing skills in both testing and classroom situations. Patricia Moore

Mueller, Klaus A.
See 2.1.

Mueller, Theodore, and George P. Borglum
"Language Laboratory and Target Language," *French Review,* XXIX (February, 1956), 322-31.

Controlled experiment at Wayne University resulting in correlation of grades of first-year French students with minimal and maximal language-lab experience. Strong trend toward positive correlation observed. Effects of increased lab work include improved grades, higher reading comprehension and total score on ACE Cooperative French Test, increased confidence, and increased motivation for home study. Psychological learning principles of lab drill are analyzed. DG

Oinas, Felix J. (ed).

"Language Teaching Today," *International Journal of American Linguistics,* Part II, Vol. XXVI, No. 4 (October, 1960).

Report of the Language Laboratory Conference held at Indiana University, January 22-23, 1960. The volume is a compilation of twenty-three papers presented at the conference. In general, the material discusses the theoretical problems in audiovisual methods and techniques in teaching a foreign language as centered in the language laboratory. In particular, on pp. 77-94, Pierre Delattre discusses details of testing students' progress in the laboratory. Patterns used in testing are presented, as well as a mimicry test, which can be used for objective measurement of progress in pronunciation. Rand Morton describes (pp. 113-17) experiments based on linguistic theories that make use of tape recordings. These experiments are directed toward teaching Spanish. JM

Peters, Mary Olga

"Report of an Experiment in the Teaching of Beginners' French," *Teachers College Journal,* XXII (November, 1950), 26 ff.

Compares two small groups, A and B, both using same beginning French texts. Group A also attended language laboratory. Unexpected result: Group B surpassed Group A. Peters suggests that the lab was inadequately handled. JG

Pimsleur, Paul

See Pimsleur, 4.5.

Politzer, Robert L.

"Assiduity and Achievement," *Modern Language Journal,* XLIV (January, 1960), 14-16.

This study is concerned with two problems: (1) the relationship of student effort to achievement, and (2) use of the language lab and achievement. The author compares a beginning French group at Harvard without a lab to a group at Michigan with a lab. He found in both groups that the A student was a high-aptitude student rather than a hard worker. In the Harvard group the C student put in the most hours of work. In the Michigan group, hours spent in the lab related directly to success in the course. He concludes that, owing to different student aptitudes, the language lab is a necessity. BP

Porter, John J., and Sally F. Porter
"A Critique of the Keating Report," *Modern Language Journal,*
XLVIII (April, 1964), 195-97.

The authors critically analyzed the Keating Report on the effectiveness of language laboratory instruction in foreign languages. Specifically, the intelligence test levels used as a control variable by Dr.
Keating cannot be equivalent with the several I.Q. tests used; his
statistical procedures were incorrect for the experimental design used;
differences in attainment between his groups are too small to be significant in light of his sample size; finally, the tabular presentation of
his results reveals several sections where his entries of common groups
in different tables sum to different totals. The authors concluded that
Dr. Keating's results are not useful in evaluating the instructional
adequacy of the language laboratory. John J. Porter, MLabstract
810.

Reichard, Joseph
See Reichard, 2.3 German.

Siliakus, H. J.
"The Effectiveness of the Language Laboratory—Two Reports,"
Babel, No. 26 (July, 1964), 19-26.

Author reviews two studies of the effectiveness of the language
laboratory: the Keating Report and the New York City Reports. As
copies of these are not easily available in Australia, the author briefly
sketches the circumstances under which the studies were conducted,
their findings and conclusions. He comments on each of these reports,
drawing attention to their weaknesses and to some of the more puz-
zling results. In the case of the Keating Report, the author argues
that the study loses its value because of a lack of precise information
about materials, equipment, and teacher preparation, and because of
some doubtful testing procedures. The New York City investigation
was well designed and documented. Stress is made of the obvious
increase in motivation and enthusiasm of the students, of the credit-
able performance of the control group. The author concludes from
this the need for superior equipment and frequent practice. The article ends by stressing the need for more well-designed experiments.
H. J. Siliakus, MLabstract # 817.

Stack, Edward M.
"Laboratories—The Effectiveness Controversy," *Modern Language
Journal,* XLVIII (April, 1964), 189-94.

In this article I contrast two reports on the effectiveness of the language laboratory. The 'Keating Report,' [see Keating,] this section while tacitly admitting that the lab successfully performs its function, is flawed by technical failures of research (failure to define, to take account of teaching techniques and programs, to use applicable and valid tests) and is written in negativistic terms which mislead the casual reader into the false conclusion that labs in general are ineffective. The adverse effect of this report, directed to administrators, might be combatted by the careful, well-documented objective studies made by New York City (Mrs. Sarah Lorge) [see Bernard, this section] Bureau of A-V Instruction. This NYC report conclusively shows the advantage of audiolingual lab work in that it increases speech skills without diminishing 'traditional' grammatical skills. Edward M. Stack, MLabstract #702.

————.

"The Keating Report: The Case of the Missing Subtitle," *The ETL Newsletter,* IV (November, 1963), 1-7.

    This is a review of Raymond F. Keating's *A Study of the Effectiveness of Language Laboratories,* [q.v., this section]. Mr. Stack takes the report to task for its failure to indicate the limited scope of the study and the investigational techniques employed, and suggests the addition of the subtitle "In Certain Schools of the Metropolitan School Study Council Using Unevaluated Programs." The reviewer goes on to justify his subtitle on the basis of the reports. In essence, his basic criticism is that the report would have one believe as significant and applicable to all laboratory programs, including well-run ones, its conclusion that schools using ineffective (by Mr. Stack's evaluation) laboratory programs contribute little to the foreign-language learning situation. DF

Sturge-Moore, C. J.
See Sturge-Moore, 2.3 English.

Thomas, Joseph V.
See Thomas, 2.3 German.

Throop, Joseph F., *et al.*
See Throop, 2.56.

Tracy, Edward. Easton Area Joint High School System, Easton, Conn. An Experimental Project to Measure Certain Facets of Language Growth for High School Students in Beginning Spanish When Variations of Language Laboratory Equipment are Utilized in the Instructional Process; Project No. 759 (National Defense Education Act,

Title VII), May, 1961, to September, 1962; total cost $32,360; federal funds, $14,855.

Evidence as to the merit of record playback in each language-laboratory booth is unknown. This experiment will measure student growth in relationship to use of record playback, in the areas of pronunciation accuracy, comprehension of spoken word, speaking fluency, and structural accuracy. BP

Walsh, Donald D.

"The Language Laboratory: A Report on Two Conferences, November 27-28, 1960 and December 18-19, 1960," in Modern Language Association of America, *Reports of Surveys and Studies . . .* (see Part I.)

Young, Clarence W., and Charles A. Choquette

An Experimental Study of the Relative Effectiveness of Four Systems of Language Laboratory Equipment in Teaching French Pronunciation. Hamilton, New York: Colgate University, 1963.

Three experiments were performed, one with college, one with senior high school, and one with junior high school subjects. In each experiment there were four treatments: (1) Activated headphones (2) Inactivated headphones (3) Inactivated headphones with long-delay playbacks (4) Inactivated headphones with short-delay playbacks. Improvement was measured in each training session and after six training sessions. Activated headphones were superior for performance, but no superiority for any treatment was found for learning. College subjects were equivalent to high school subjects in improvement during training sessions, but did not retain improvement as well. Clarence W. Young

2.55 Teaching Machines

Asher, James J. San Jose State College, San Jose, Calif.

Factors within the Program of a Teaching Machine Which Influence Foreign Learning; Project No. 578 (National Defense Education Act, Title VII), June 10, 1960, to September 9, 1961; $8,947.

A study of the effects of sequence of visual and audio elements upon the amount and transfer of learning. Half of the subjects will learn vocabulary items through visual presentation, relearn them through aural presentation, and will interpret a passage presented aurally. The other half will learn the items through aural presentation, relearn through visual presentation, and interpret a passage presented visually. JM

————.

Sensory Interrelationships in Vocabulary and Syntactic Learning. Paper given at the First Conference of Language Programmers, University of Michigan, Ann Arbor, Mich., April, 1961.

————. San Jose State College, San Jose, Calif.

Continued Development of a Theoretical Model for Programmed Learning of Languages; Project No. 873 (National Defense Education Act, Title VII), November 1, 1961, to September 1, 1963; $23,651.54.

Objectives of the project: (a) to trace the causal relationship between concept guessing behavior and language learning; (b) to replicate the sensory research of the author (see above entry) in order to increase the generality of findings by showing that the results apply to languages in different language families; and (c) to continue the development of a theoretical model of language learning entitled, "A neofield theory of learning the $1+n$ language." From this research more powerful strategies will be developed for programing the automated teaching of foreign languages and other verbal materials. JM

Bailey, Judith A. Hollins College, Roanoke, Va.

Experimental Investigation of the Use of Automated Instructional Devices in Teaching Elementary Latin; Project No. 534 (National Defense Education Act, Title VII), June 16, 1960, to June 15, 1961; $2,800.

A study of the effectiveness of mechanical teaching devices in teaching Latin classes by comparison with student achievement in groups taught by an instructor. JM

Barcus, Delbert, John L. Hayman, and James T. Johnson

See Barcus, 2.56.

Barlow, John A. Earlham College, Richmond, Ind.

New Instruction Media: Self-Instruction, Guided Instruction and the Role of the Teacher; Project No. 143 (National Defense Education Act, Title VII), July 1, 1959, to June 30, 1962; $140,542.

Exploration of the use and adaptation of mechanical and electronic instructional devices for individual student self-instruction. Courses to be programed include elementary Russian. A contrastable situation will be established in which one group will be taught by the devices for two years, and the second group, having previously received conventional instruction, will continue on the devices. Control groups are to be matched by tests and/or previous grade records. Treatment of data will consist of such techniques as trend analysis, tests of significance of differences, and comparison to establish norms. DF

Barrutia, Richard
"A Suggested Branch Program for Foreign Languages," *Hispania,*
XLVII (May, 1964), 342-50.
　　The author describes an automated branching program and
device that permits teaching material selected on the basis of the type
of student response. This type of program is significant because it
has a built in selective unit which has four separate alternatives, one if
the response is correct, and separate sequences for each of the possible
three incorrect responses. The language used in this experimental unit
of the program conducted at the University of Arizona is Basque.
Hubert Molina

Baskin, Samuel. Office of Educational Research, Antioch College, Yellow Springs, Ohio.
"Experiment in French Language Instruction," *Antioch College Reports,* October, 1960.
　　A two-year study to learn if new methods using mechanical instruction along with trained student assistants produce as much learning achievement as the conventional method taught by a course instructor. The findings favor the achievements of students taught by the
audiovisual mechanical methods. JM

Bauer, Eric Wolfgang
See Bauer, 4.1.

Bern, Henry A.
See Bern, 2.53.

Bryan, Quentin R. Inglewood Unified School District, Inglewood, California.
Experimental Use of Audio-Lingual Self-Instructional Course in
Spoken American Spanish; Project No. OE-4-14-029 (National
Defense Education Act, Title VI), October 15, 1963, to August 31,
1964; $7,259.
　　This contract provides for the testing of a self-instructional programmed course in spoken Spanish, developed under contract OE-3-
14-012 at the University of Michigan by Dr. F. Rand Morton. The
project is being undertaken in anticipation of the need for additional
foreign language teachers at the beginning of the 1965-66 school year
when, by State law, foreign language instruction is made mandatory in
the sixth grade in California schools.
　　Thirteen elementary school teachers will participate in the course.
They will be provided with complete sets of materials and tape recordings and, working in their own spare time, will proceed each at his

own rate. Periodic meetings with a trained supervising Spanish instructor will be held to evaluate progress and discuss specific problems. Upon satisfactory completion of the course, the participants will receive two units of college credit from the California State College at Palos Verdes.

The project will help to determine the extent to which persons without previous knowledge of Spanish can acquire a command of the foreign language, or persons with an insufficient knowledge can improve their skill, by using self-instructional, programmed materials.

Buiten, Roger, and Harlan Lane
A Language Teaching System with Real-Time Error Discrimination and Feedback. [Unpublished paper (dittoed), 1964.]

[Research on the perception of relative pitch, loudness (stress), and tempo (rhythm) of the segmental units in spoken languages has led to experimentation with a computer-controlled teaching machine called SAID, Speech Auto-Instructional Device.—HLN

"SAID is an electro-mechanical device which performs three significant functions in conditioning prosodic accuracy in a second language. First, pattern sentences which are considered standards in prosodic performance are presented to the student by tape recording. These sentences are programmed in the best known sequence for teaching prosody in the target language to a speaker of a given native language. After the student hears the pattern sentence, he is instructed to imitate it. Second, the device processes the student's imitation, and instantaneously evaluates its acceptability on the basis of its three distinct prosodic features: pitch, loudness, and tempo. Third, SAID immediately feeds back to the student, by means of a visual display, the degree to which his imitation is unacceptable. The display indicates to the student how he must modify his next imitation in each or all of the prosodic features in order to make the imitation more acceptable. This process of presentation-evaluation-display repeats itself until the prosody of the student's imitation is acceptable."—p. 6.] See Lane, this section, and Lane, 4.3.

Carpenter, Clarence R., and Leslie P. Greenhill
Comparative Research on Methods and Media for Presenting Programmed Courses in Mathematics and English. A Cooperative Project by The University Division of Instructional Services and The Departments of Mathematics and English at The Pennsylvania State University . . . University Park, Penn.: The Pennsylvania State University, March, 1963.

The present publication discusses the "New" Media and Programmed Learning, giving a description of six experiments involving Mathematics and English: 1) Comparison of External-pacing and Self-pacing of Programmed Instruction in Mathematics Using Different Methods of Presentation; 2) An Experimental Comparison of Differential Rates of Pacing Programmed Mathematics; 3) Adaptation and Evaluation of a Programmed Mathematics Course for Televised Presentation; 4) Paired vs. Individual Study of Programmed Instruction in Contemporary Algebra; 5) Comparisons of Televised with Teaching Machine and Televised with Instructor Presentations of English Grammar; 6) Effects of Personality-Pairing on the Performance of Students in a Programmed Course in English Grammar. The report is concluded by a section, which might offer possibilities of application to language learning, entitled Observations, Judgments, and Suggestions for Further Research. DF   See Carpenter, 1; Greenhill, this section, and 2.55.

Carpenter, F.
"The Teaching Machine," *Recent Research and Developments and Their Implications for Teacher Education.* Thirteenth Yearbook; Chicago: American Association of Colleges for Teacher Education, February, 1960.

    Defines self-instruction devices. Points out relative lack of controlled experiments on their use, shortcomings of reported studies, need for large-scale studies. Suggests the following research problems in theory of teaching-machine learning: effect of errors, need for overt response, rearrangements, fundamental principles of programming. Discusses educational and methodological implications of self-instruction devices—presentation time, identification of learning difficulties, grading procedures, school space allotment, teacher preparation. Outlines assumptions underlying Skinnerian point of view; contrasts lecture method with potential of machine teaching. DG

Carroll, John B.
See Carroll, 2.3 Arabic, 2.3 Chinese.

Ferster, Charles B., and Stanley M. Sapon
"An Application of Recent Developments in Psychology to the Teaching of German," *Harvard Educational Review,* XXVIII (1958), 58-69; also in A. A. Lumsdaine and R. Galser (eds.), *Teaching Machines and Programmed Learning: A Source Book.* Washington, D.C.: Department of Audio-Visual Instruction, National Education Association, 1960. Pp. 173-85.

    Description of experiment applying psychological theory to the teaching of German through the use of semiautomatic, mechanical teaching devices. Masked answers are revealed for immediate self-scoring. Six of the twenty-eight original subjects completed a course equivalent to the conventional semester course in beginning German. Nonstandardized achievement tests on specific material are given; scores are reported without statistical interpretation; the time difference required for mastery by two methods was insignificant. DG

Fry, Edward B.
"Teaching Machines: An Investigation of Constructed Versus Multiple-Choice Methods of Response," *Automated Teaching Bulletin,* I (December, 1959), 11-12.

A dissertation abstract discussing the comparison of mechanical devices, one of which requires the student to construct his own answer, the other device requiring only recognition responses. Pilot study showed better test results from students who were required to construct responses. However, longer training time was necessary. JM

————.

See Fry, 1.

Galanter, Eugene H. (ed)
Automatic Teaching: The State of the Art. New York: John Wiley and Sons, 1959.

Papers and abstracts prepared for a symposium at the University of Pennsylvania, sponsored by the Air Force Office of Scientific Research, concerning the machine instruction of servicemen. First published book in teaching-machine field. Reference is made to some experimental studies; main concern is psychological learning theory as it applies to teaching machines. Reviews: J. A. Barlow, *Harvard Educational Review,* 1960 (factual summary); E. Z. Rothkopf, *Contemporary Psychology,* V (1960), 104-5; L. S. Reid, *Science,* CXXXI (1960), 29-30 (suggests potential of teaching machine as a research tool). DG

Gavurin, Edward L., and Virginia M. Donahue
"Logical Sequence and Random Sequence," *Automated Teaching Bulletin,* Vol. I (Spring, 1961).

This research validates the basic assumption that subject matter is most effectively presented in logical sequence for acquisition, but no definite conclusion could be drawn concerning retention. BP

Gee, R. D.
See Gee, Part I.

Greenhill, Leslie P. Pennsylvania State University, University Park, Pennsylvania.
Research on the Presentation of Programed Instruction to Large Groups over Closed Circuit Television; Project No. 736,116 (National Defense Education Act, Title VII), August, 1960 to March, 1963, no information on funds.

This research project may have implications for language learning. Leslie P. Greenhill See Carpenter, 1, and this section; Greenhill, 2.56.

Habostad, Knut
See Habostad, 2.3 English.

Hanzeli, Victor E.
Report on the First Conference of Language Programmers. Seattle: University of Washington, May 12, 1961 (ditto).

Contains abstracts of eight papers presented at a programmers' conference held at the University of Michigan in April, 1961: (1) George L. Geis, Reinforcements in Programming; (2) Ted Mueller, Programming in the Morphemic Structures in French; (3) John Gilpin, A Versatile Apparatus for Audio Self-Instruction, Called the "Polyaudio"; (4) Stanley M. Sapon, Some Reflections on Models of Linguistic Structure and Language Programming; (5) F. Marty, Self-Instruction Programs Should Have Variable Sequences; (6) M. I. Moraud, Programming Basic French; (7) Paul Pimsleur, Programming Acoustic Discriminatory Skills; (8) Donald C. Reiff, Molecular Analysis of Spanish Phonology. Other papers are also mentioned. Impressions of the author at the conclusion of the conference were: practically all the existing materials—programs and hardware—are still experimental; the minimal-step approach to learning is in question. JM See Morton, "Programming . . ." this section.

Hayman, John L., Jr., and James T. Johnson, Jr.
See Hayman, 2.3 Spanish.

Heinberg, Paul. University of Iowa, Iowa City, Iowa
Phonetics Program. Research supported by the Mast Development Co., Inc., February 1, 1963 to February 1, 1964; funds as needed.

Development and evaluation of a 2400 frame phonetic transcription program for use with principal investigator's audio-visual, automated instructional device, the Auvitor. Program designed to serve as prerequisite for automated, foreign language instruction. Paul Heinberg

———.

Voice Training Program. Research in progress supported by North-western Bell Telephone Co., February 1, 1963 to June 1, 1964; $18,500.

Development and evaluation of a 677 frame voice quality and a 367 frame pitch-intonation audio-visual, automated program for use with principal investigator's audio-visual devices: the Auvitor and Reinforcement Panel. Paul Heinberg

Lane, Harlan

"Programmed Learning of a Second Language," *International Review of Applied Linguistics*, II (November, 1964), 249-301.

The processes of programmed learning of a foreign language are examined according to the principles of operant conditioning (i.e., the shaping of the learner's behavior) which is basic to the techniques of programming. The methods used in diverse programs to condition formal repertories (imitation, transcription, reading, and the taking of dictation) and to condition thematic repertories (intraverbal responses, tacts [verbal response to a nonverbal stimulus], and mands [demands, commands, and other verbal operants involving a charac-teristic consequence]) are interpreted in the light of the experimental evidence for the behavioral processes involved: discrimination of stimuli and differentiation of responses. From the abstract.

———.

"Teaching Machines and Programmed Learning," *Harvard Educa-tional Review*, XXXI (1961), 469-476.

———.

See Lane, 2.9.

Lumsdaine, Arthur A., and Robert Glaser (eds.)

Teaching Machines and Programmed Learning: A Source Book. Washington, D.C.: Department of Audio-Visual Instruction, National Education Association, 1960.

A symposium of 47 articles on teaching by machine, followed by a 110-page annotated compilation of papers on the subject, a 28-page bibliography, and index. Introduction to each section sketches history of teaching machines, the application of psychological learning theory to programed learning, contributions from military and other sources, recent experiments, and studies. Only a few of the articles deal spe-cifically with foreign-language teaching; however, the basic principles of machine teaching discussed are applicable to any field. Topics dis-cussed include presentation time, identification of learning difficulties, grading procedures, effect of different teaching rules on programing methods, maintenance of electronic equipment, use of error response, theory of learning efficiency. Of special interest to language teachers are the Skinner article on verbal behavior and the Smith article on programing. DG

Marty, Fernand

Programing a Basic Foreign Language Course—Prospects for Self-Instruction. Hollins College, Va.: Hollins College, 1962.

The author defines programing as the process of organizing material in such a way that the student acquires the desired linguistic skills or terminal behavior in a minimum of time and with a maximum of efficiency. Dr. Marty presents twelve points which are essential to good programing. He discusses Total Self-Instruction, listing drawbacks due to the lack of a student-teacher relationship; and then presents techniques of self-evaluation through contrastive presentation designed to overcome this lack. With a partial self-instruction course, the student would spend 10% of his time with a teacher. There is a description of the course which includes discussions of techniques and devices. JM

McDonald, Pearl S. Arlington County Public Schools, Arlington, Virginia.

Experimental Use of Self-Instructional Courses in Russian and Spanish by Secondary School Students; Project No. OE-3-14-033 (National Defense Education Act, Title VI), June 13, 1963, to September 30, 1963; $7294.

The Arlington County Public Schools tested the effectiveness of a set of student workbooks and tape-recordings for Spanish and Russian produced in 1962 by the University of Michigan under contract with the U.S. Office of Education. All previous testing programs used adult subjects.

Twelve students from Yorktown High School served as the subjects for the experiment, 6 taking the Spanish course and 6 enrolling for Russian. Each student, selected for high scholastic ability but not necessarily for language aptitude, had no previous training in the language he was studying. The students worked at least 5 hours a day, Monday through Friday, for a 10-week period. They were tested on their listening and speaking ability at the end of the experiment, and the results of these tests, along with other information about the students (such as scores on achievement, aptitude, and intelligence tests and a record of daily attendance on the project) was included in a final report submitted to the Office of Education.

Morton, F. Rand. Regents of the University of Michigan, Ann Arbor, Michigan.

Development and Testing of Self-Instructional Programs ["A-LLP"] in Chinese, French, Spanish, and Thai; Project No. OE-3-14-012 (National Defense Education Act, Title VI), October 15, 1962 to January 15, 1964; $155,116.

Under U.S. Office of Education contract SAE-8938, the University of Michigan prepared self-instructional language courses for Russian, Spanish, and Thai. The courses, consisting of tape recordings, transcriptions of the recordings, and student workbooks, included the following sections (tasks):

Russian and Spanish
Task   I—Auditory perception and discrimination
Task   II—Active control of the sound system
Task III—Perception and control of structural signifiers
Task IV—Control of syntactical patterns, together with lexical
            meaning

Thai
Tasks I and II as above

Initial experimental use indicated modifications would be extremely useful. This contract, produced a complete revision of the Spanish and Thai, and the addition of parallel courses in Mandarin Chinese and French, having the following modifications and additions:

1. More intensive analysis of verbal behavior.
2. The use of "reinforcement" and "shaping" procedures developed too late under the previous contract for incorporation in first courses.
3. Closer analysis of the phonological and structural characteristics of the languages.
4. Instead of the discrete, four-task linear progression of the first courses, the revisions will utilize "spiral" programing which will reduce considerably the introduction of semantic meaning of each successive segment of the course.
5. Addition of a Task V, extended discourse, to the Spanish and French, and, if feasible, to the Chinese courses.
6. Research on the teaching of intonation.
7. Construction and utilization of a prototype electro-mechanical teaching device.

The senior programers are Dr. Kou P'ing Chou, University of Wisconsin, for Chinese, and Dr. Theodore Mueller, University of Akron, for French.

———.

"Programming of Audio-Lingual Language Skills for Self-Instructional Presentation," *Publications of the Language Laboratory,* VI (1961), 35-40.
    Available from the author. This publication contains reports described by Victor E. Hanzeli, this section.

———.

"The Teaching Machine and the Teaching of Languages: A Report on Tomorrow," *PMLA,* LXXVI, Part 2 (September, 1960), 1-6.
    Report on research thus far undertaken in applying the concept of the automated self-instruction device to the teaching of spoken languages. F. Rand Morton

Mueller, Theodore. University of Akron, Akron, Ohio.
    French by Programed Learning; Project No. OE-4-14-013 (National Defense Education Act, Title VI), August 15, 1963, to August 14, 1964; $10,636.
    The project was designed to test the effectiveness of a self-instructional course in beginning French during the 1963-64 academic year, among regular students at the University and working adults enrolled in its Community College. The tape-recorded materials were developed under contract OE-3-14-012 by the University of Michigan. The 30 college students participating in the project were scheduled for at least 10 hours each week in the language laboratory where they used the self-instructional materials. In addition, they had regularly scheduled sessions with instructors on pronunciation and other aspects of the customary course in a modern foreign language. Achievement tests were administered periodically to measure the group's achievement.
    The 20 Community College participants worked with the materials at home, using their own tape recorders. After finishing each study unit, they reported to the language laboratory where they demonstrated their progress. There were no formal classes. However, the students were able to meet with their instructor by appointment. These adults were also given the same tests administered to the regular college students.

———.

"Programming Morphemic Structures: The Concept of Minute Steps," *Publications of the Language Laboratory,* VI (1961), 41-52.
    The article demonstrates first attempts at programming the syntax in the series of tapes *La Structure de la langue française.* [q.v., Borg-

lum, Section 2.3, French, of this *Bibliography*.] The exercises in these tapes progress by small steps, using a basic one hundred sentences as the vocabulary. Repeated use of the same elementary vocabulary eliminates meaning as a difficulty in learning the structure of the language. Theodore Mueller

———.

See Mueller, 2.56.

New Teaching Aids for the American Classroom: A Symposium on the State of Research in Instructional TV and Tutorial Machines Held November 13 and 14, 1959. Institute for Communication Research, Stanford University, 1960.

In general, the material is concerned with the strategy and tactics of research in the field of mechanical instruction. The papers included discuss the classroom of tomorrow, research background—summing up the present state of learning theory—and research foreground, which suggests advance research and development of materials and techniques. JM

Newmark, Gerald. Systems Development Corp., Santa Monica, Calif. Research in Programmed Instruction in Spanish With Seventh-Grade Students; Project No. OE7-140000-181 (National Defense Education Act, Title VII), June 29, 1964.

While the author implies in his conclusions that the materials and techniques could have been more sophisticated, the experiment indicates that on the seventh grade level relatively few students have the capacity or motivation for independent study. Hubert Molina

———.

See Newmark, 2.53, 6.1.

Porter, Donald
"A Report on Instructional Devices in Foreign Language Teaching," *Teaching Machines and Programmed Learning,* ed. A. A. Lumsdaine and Robert Glaser. Washington, D.C.: National Education Association, 1960. Pp. 186-205.

Critical analysis of teaching-machine use and the development of self-instructional language packages. Principles for selection and programing. Emphasis on functions of various audiovisual devices for use in second-language learning as well as application of reinforcement and programing concepts to the requirements of language-teaching devices. Includes a bibliography of 467 items. Center for Documentation and Communication Research, Western Reserve University.

Rocha e Silva, M. I., and C. B. Ferster
See Rocha, 2.3 German.

Saltzman, Irving J.
"Programmed Self-Instruction and Second Language Learning," *International Review of Applied Linguistics,* I, No. 2 (1963), 104-14.

In this article I described our research in connection with our NDEA Title VII project to develop a completely self-instructional, programmed, first semester college course in Russian. Four experiments using a short section of the program were described. Our future research plans using the entire program were described in detail. I emphasized the important use of self-instructional programs as an aid to the conduct of research in the area of second language teaching and learning. Irving J. Saltzman, MLabstract #716.

————.
See Saltzman, 2.3 Russian.

Schramm, Wilbur L.
See Schramm, Part I, 2.56.

Silberman, Harry F., and John Coulson
"A Draft Summary of Findings in an Exploratory Teaching Machine Study," *Automated Teaching Bulletin,* I (December, 1959), 35-38.

Discusses testing of (1) modes of response; (2) size of steps between successive items to be taught; (3) item sequence. Method of testing is outlined and results analyzed. Groups tested by recall responses required more time than those tested by recognition responses. More learning was acquired by groups who learned material in more items but smaller steps. More study is required on the problem of item sequence. JM

Stolurow, Lawrence M.
See Stolurow, 3.1.

Swets, John A.
See Swets, 4.3.

TEMAC.
Programmed Learning Materials Report No. 2. Wilmette, Ill.: Encyclopaedia Britannica, April, 1961.

Concerns the process of programing materials in mathematics and foreign languages or the breaking down of the structure of these subjects into small, related parts. This is considered a "new approach." The design of the experiment relating to the structure analysis is explained and evaluated. The student learning rate and per cent of failures is discussed. Retention of material is reported as 90 per cent. JM

Thomas, Joseph V.
See Thomas, 2.3 German.

Turner, Raymond
"Deus Ex Machina," *Modern Language Journal,* XLII (February, 1958), 396-98.

This was a limited experiment contrasting results of traditional teaching methods with machine-teaching results. Of the experimental group, under machine-teaching conditions with 27-28 language-contact hours, ¼ qualified for advanced standing at the university. Of the entering freshmen scores after 360 contact hours under traditional methods, the lower quartile ranked below the lower quartile of the experimental group. Considering differences of time and preparation, the experimental-group media are not significantly lower. BP

Uttal, William R.
My Teacher Has Three Arms. Research Paper RC-788. Yorktown Heights, New York: I. B. M. Corp., September 15, 1962.

IBM 650, a computerized adaptive teaching machine, is described with its mechanical components and programming for teaching stenotypy, German, and psychological statistics to small groups of college students. Though the results of the pilot studies are preliminary, findings indicate great acceleration of learning time associated with what is apparently an equivalent increase in the students' acquisition of new information. The problems of experimental control and computer requirements are both discussed. 12 references. Center for Documentation and Communication Research, Western Reserve University.

Valdman, Albert
"Breaking the Lockstep," *International Journal of American Linguistics,* XXIX (April, 1963, Part III), 147-59.

In this article I describe the type of pedagogical material used in conjunction with a partially self-instructional French basic course presently being tried out at Indiana University. This material—which has been revised and modified extensively—can be characterized as preprogrammed materials in that the structures taught have been reduced to very small steps and, wherever possible, correct responses are confirmed immediately. I also present tentative comparisons in pronunciation accuracy between the experimental group and a group of French majors; these show that, although phonology drill as relegated to the autodidactic component, the experimental group as a whole performed as well as the advanced students. Albert Valdman, MLabstract #493. This is a preliminary description of the research project under Mr. Valdman's name, 6.4.

———.

"Toward Self-Instruction in Foreign Language Learning," *International Review of Applied Linguistics in Language Teaching,* to appear.
This is a description of research being done on the project described under Dr. Valdman's name, 6.4.

2.56 Educational Television
Andrade, Manuel, *et al.*
See Andrade, 2.7.

Barcus, Delbert, John L. Hayman, Jr., and James T. Johnson, Jr.
Development of Programed Learning Materials for use with Televised Spanish Instruction. Denver-Stanford Project on the Context of Instructional Television: Report No. 4. Stanford, Calif.: Institute for Communication Research, Stanford University, November, 1961.
This reports preliminary results of a project involving the teaching of Spanish to some 12,000 fifth and sixth graders in Denver via televised programed materials and supplementary conventional classroom methods. It describes only the development of the first 672 frames—about one-third of the total anticipated program. Comparisons of achievement are made and results are analyzed by rank correlations. It is concluded that pupils definitely learn from the automated instruction program, but the real value of the program cannot be assessed until it is compared to more conventional teacher-directed instruction. The results also indicate that factors other than ability and outside of the program itself affect learning, and that further research in this is obviously needed. 5 references. Center for Documentation and Communication Research, Western Reserve University.

See Delbert Barcus, "The Spanish Program," in *Four Case Studies of Programed Instruction.* New York City: Fund for the Advancement of Education, 1964. Pp. 34-37.

Belson, William A.
See Belson, 3.7.

Bern, Henry A.
See Bern, 2.53.

Borglum, George P. (ed.).
Second Annual Consultation Modern Language Audio-Visual Project.

Wayne, Ind.: Audio-Visual Materials Consultation Bureau, Wayne State University, 1957.

Discusses experimentation in the use of television and film in teaching foreign languages. Preliminary work indicates that lab experience increases students' memory span in vocabulary and sentence patterns. JM

Broady, K. O., C. O. Neidt, and G. B. Childs
The Nebraska Experimental Program in the Use of Television and Correspondence Study, 1957-1958. Lincoln, Nebraska: University of Nebraska, 1958.

An exploratory experiment with high school students with comparable ability in various size schools in Nebraska. Some are taught algebra, geometry, physics, English, general math, Spanish and art by television and correspondence while others are taught by regular classroom methods. Analysis of pre- and posttesting data by covariance analysis indicates that achievement is related to subject taught and sometimes to school size and type of instruction. Center for Documentation and Communication Research, Western Reserve University.

Brown, G. I., and H. L. Hodgkinson
"A Note Concerning 'An Application of Recent Developments in Psychology to the Teaching of German' by C. B. Ferster and S. M. Sapon," in A. A. Lumsdaine and Robert Glaser (eds.), *Teaching Machines and Programmed Learning*. Washington, D.C.: National Education Association, 1960. Pp. 592-94. Also in *Harvard Educational Review*, XXVIII (Spring, 1958), 156-7.

A criticism is made of an article by C. B. Ferster and S. M. Sapon concerning an experimental study of teaching German with a teaching machine. Criticism of the authors' evaluation of the project is in terms of their methodology: i.e. failing to describe or account for a considerable dropout of students, failing to provide sufficient means of comparison, such as standardized tests or a control group, and failing to explain lesson difficulty or to accurately calculate teaching time. Center for Documentation and Communication Research, Western Reserve University. See Ferster and Sapon, 2.55.

Buffington, Albert
See Buffington, 2.3 German.

Bundy, Edward Wayne
An Experimental Study of the Relative Effectiveness of Television Presentational Techniques and Conventional Classroom Procedures in Promoting Initial Comprehension of Basic Verb Form Concepts in

Elementary Spanish. Unpublished Ph.D. dissertation, University of Michigan, 1960.

The purpose of the study was to determine the relative effectiveness of specialized television presentational techniques and conventional classroom procedures in promoting initial comprehension of critical basic Spanish verb form concepts. [. . .] The basic relative effectiveness comparison was in terms of initial comprehension of concept, as measured by a teacher-designed test, employing real subjects in a realistic situation, seeking to compare presentational techniques rather than mode-of-presentation alone. This comparison involved: (1) TV—*television presentational techniques,* [. . .] and (2) CR—*conventional classroom procedures.* [. . . From the] findings, it is apparent that complex language word form concepts can be communicated by specialized television presentational techniques fully as effectively as—and very probably more effectively than—by conventional classroom procedures. Moreover, in view of the overwhelming consistency of trend favoring TV—and the implications of various other factors—the findings seem reasonably indicative beyond this minimal conclusion. The implications relevant to language-teaching by television are: (1) that more effective communication of such foreign language concepts may be expected through these TV techniques than through CR procedures, and (2) that the alternative of teaching languages by TV when increased enrollments make present procedures impracticable should produce achievement full equivalent—and probably superior—to that produced by CR procedures, and hence that the use of TV techniques in teaching languages is desirable, not merely acceptable in time of future need. [. . .] From the abstract.

———.

"Television and the Learning of Spanish Verbs," *The Impact of Educational Television,* Urbana, Ill.: University of Illinois Press, 1960. Pp. 125-42.

The study compares the effectiveness of television presentation with classroom procedures, in the teaching of basic concepts of Spanish verb forms. The results somewhat favored the effectiveness of the television techniques. The author suggests possibilities as to why the findings were not more statistically significant. He also lists implications of the findings. Further research is recommended. JM

Carpenter, Clarence R., and Leslie P. Greenhill
See Carpenter, 2.55.

Cassirer, Henry R.
Television Teaching Today. Paris: UNESCO, 1960.

A survey is made of the development of TV teaching in United States, including a description of the role of FCC, NAEB, and NETRC, and national distribution of stations. Details of experiences in Hagerstown, Maryland, Philadelphia, "Delmarva," and elsewhere are included. Role of television in school, college, and community; closed circuit and broadcast television. Techniques and costs of production and reception. Examples and evaluation of application in sciences, humanities, and modern languages. Applications in teacher, professional, and technical training and adult education. Problems of coordination between producer, television teacher, classroom teacher and student. Enrichment vs. direct teaching. Center for Documentation and Communication Research, Western Reserve University.

Cunning, Carlotta
Educational Television in the Kansas City, Missouri, Public Schools. Kansas City, Mo.: Kansas City Public Schools, June, 1961.

A report is made on the third year of use of open circuit television for teaching beginning Spanish to third grade pupils, science in fifth grade, general science in seventh and eighth grades, and citizenship in ninth grade classes. Comparisons are made with conventionally taught classes. Tests include the Peltier-Durost, a science test and the California Test of Social and Related Sciences. Results are analyzed by variance, with t-tests of significance. A summary of responses of principals, teachers and pupils to questionnaires, and recommendations for the use of television are presented. Results indicate televised instruction has been at least as effective as, and in some cases more effective than, the instruction in regular classes. Center for Documentation and Communication Research, Western Reserve University.

Garry, Ralph
See Garry, 2.3 French.

Garry, Ralph, and Edna Mauriello
See Garry, 2.3 French.

Gordon, Oakley J., Keith M. Engar, and Donald R. Shupe
See Gordon, 2.3 Russian.

Gradnisnik, Anthony J.
See Gradnisnik, 2.3 Spanish.

Greenhill, Leslie P., *et al.*
"Further Studies of the Use of Television for University Teaching," *Audio-Visual Communication Review,* IV (Summer, 1956), 200-15.

Results of study at Pennsylvania State College on closed-circuit

television in university teaching. General findings were that students did as well as those in traditional classes. BP
(See Greenhill, 2.55.)

Hayman, John L., Jr.
"Viewer Location and Learning in Instructional Television," *Audio-Visual Communication Review*, XI (May-June, 1963), 27-31.

An experiment is conducted with 577 fourth graders to determine the effects of viewer location relative to the television on learning. With one exception, the television set is either at the front center or side center of the room. The exception has the television set in a corner. The subjects are divided into three groups: those in a center position, those in a side position, and those in a back position. Three lessons in Spanish are video taped for the study. All students are tested for comprehension and speaking ability. Data analysis by covariance indicates that pupils in the center position perform best on the listening comprehension test, though differences are quite small. On the speaking test, however, both pupils in the center and at the back perform significantly better than those at the side. It is concluded that viewer location relative to television screen is definitely a factor in learning from instructional television. Center for Documentation and Communication Research, Western Reserve University.

Hayman, John L., Jr., and James T. Johnson, Jr.
Audio-Lingual Results in the Second Year of Research—1961-62. (Denver-Stanford Project on the Context of Instructional Television, Report No. 8) Stanford, Calif.: Institute for Communication Research, Stanford University, June 1963.

The project concerns the development of understanding and speaking skills in elementary school Spanish instruction. Both fifth and sixth grade pupils in the project see a 15-minute television lesson concerned with these skills, and, based on the first year's results, all pupils receive 15 minutes of teacher-directed, eclectic classroom practice following the television lesson. Among other things the results showed the relative effectiveness of each instructional method, including use of electronic aids, depended on the classroom teacher's prior training and experience. CBC

————.

"Exact vs. Varied Repetition in Educational Television," *Audio-Visual Communication Review,* XI, No. 4 (July-Aug. 1963), 8.

A second viewing of Spanish TV lessons (that is, exact repetition of these lessons) was evaluated under three conditions: compared to a single viewing and no other practice; compared to a single viewing and teacher-directed classroom practice (varied repetition); and, as an addition to a single viewing and classroom practice, compared to these conditions used alone. The second viewing significantly increased learning when there was no other practice. It was not as effective as teacher-directed classroom practice, however, and its ability to increase learning when added to classroom practice varied inversely with the experience and preparation of the classroom teacher.

These results fit a very neat pattern if one assumes a positive relationship between the effectiveness of the classroom teacher and his experience and preparation. Teachers repeated the content first given in the original showing of the TV lesson, but their manner of presentation was different from that on TV, and their instruction was adjusted to the needs of individual pupils in the class. The more experience and preparation the teachers had, therefore (if the assumption is granted), the more effective was the varied and individually adjusted repetition they handled. Exact repetition in teaching Spanish by television is shown by these results to be a potent variable, but it is not as potent as a *skillfully presented* varied repetition by the classroom teacher. John L. Hayman, Jr.

Data on the above project:
Funding Agency: US Office of Education—Title VII, NDEA
Code Number: 7-14-1380-083
Dates: January 1960 through June 1964
Funds: Denver Public Schools: $198,722; Stanford University: $110,000 (approx.)

———.

A Further Search for Elements of Tomorrow's Classroom. (Denver-Stanford Project on the Context of Instructional Television, Report No. 12) Stanford, Calif.: Institute for Communication Research, Stanford University, July 1964.

During the last year of the active research for this project, 1962-63, seven teachers were removed from the experimental design and given free rein in *how* they were to present the televised Spanish lessons. This report presents the detailed records which they kept of their activities, and draws several noteworthy conclusions, referred to as "imaginative ideas": "1) automated instruction should be an integrated part of a larger program rather than a separate entity, and, in line with this use of it, pupils should complete a specific number of frames each lesson period and should not proceed at their own rates; 2) the written and spoken language should be taught together so far as possible with artificial separation of the two skills eliminated; 3) communication between pupils in the second language should be encouraged through devices which allow the pupils to teach each other, so to speak; 4) foreign language can be made more interesting and meaningful by using it in other subject areas such as geography, reading, and arithmetic." (From the Summary). The report reaffirms the necessity to individualize all programs of this nature, acknowledging that while mass instruction devices can make an enormous contribution they alone are not enough. The various experiments of this project have demonstrated the value of the teacher, and in the opinion of the researchers, underlined the great influence which the teacher exerts on the pupil. DF

———.

Research in Retrospect: Administrative Memoranda of the Denver-Stanford Research Project. Report No. 11. Stanford, California: Institute for Communication Research, Stanford University, June, 1964.

See Hayman, "The Context of Instructional Television . . . ," this section. The present report deals with the how of the project in the hopes that the information reported will be of practical assistance to the school administrator. DF

———.

"Research on the Context of Instructional Television," *School Life,* XLV, No. 6 (Apr., 1963), 4.

This article summarizes, as of April 1963, the scope of the Denver-Stanford Project, the results to date, and future plans. The project involved teaching Spanish to fifth and sixth grade pupils in the Denver Public Schools. Television was the basic instructional device, and the research objective was increased learning through various classroom and home activities. Conclusions reported include these: eclectic practice, including structure, dialogue, and narrative drills, is best for the classroom follow-up to TV; parents working at home can effectively help their children learn a second language; reading and writing should be introduced no later than the beginning of the second year of instruction; automated instruction can be a significant help in the reading and writing phase, though it cannot do the complete job; overall, the TV plus related activities approach is quite effective. John L. Hayman, Jr.

Data on the above project:
Funding Agency: US Office of Education—Title VII, NDEA.
Code Number: 7-14-1380-083.

Dates: January 1960 through June 1964
Funds: Denver Public Schools: $198,722; Stanford University: $110,000 (approx.)

_____

Results of the First Year's Research in the Denver-Stanford Project. (Denver-Stanford Project on The Context of Instructional Television: Report No. 5) Stanford, California: Institute for Communication Research, Stanford University, January, 1962.

Fifth grade pupils in Denver, Colorado public schools are taught Spanish in groups by TV and combinations of different types of home activity. Analysis of test results by covariance analysis indicates that achievement is significantly influenced by evening viewing and parent help. Center for Documentation and Communication Research, Western Reserve University. See Schramm, this section.

_____.

Third Year Results in the Denver-Stanford Project. (Denver-Stanford Project on the Context of Instructional Television, Report No. 10) Stanford, Calif.: Institute for Communication Research, Stanford University, March 1964.

During 1962-63, the last year of active research in the Denver-Stanford Project, work was continued at both the fifth and sixth grades. The fifth grade instruction was concerned entirely with the development of listening and speaking skills. At sixth grade, the research was directed mainly toward evaluating methods of teaching reading and writing. Results at fifth grade suggested that electronic aids, especially those with feedback (that is, where the child records and listens to his own voice), are a desirable addition to the classroom Spanish program. The sixth grade results confirmed that a combination of automated and teacher-directed reading and writing instruction would be superior to either method alone.

Hayman, John L., Jr., James T. Johnson, Jr., and Alan E. Mayers
Causative Factors and Learning Related to Parent Participation. Report No. 13, Denver-Stanford Project on the Context of Instructional Television. Denver, Denver Public Schools and Stanford, Institute for Communication Research, Stanford University, September, 1964 (mimeo).

Interviews were conducted with parents who participated with their children in the Denver-Stanford project in an attempt to show why children of these parents performed observably and significantly better. Results showed that children did better whose parents viewed the TV lessons with them and who practiced Spanish with them. The use of neither the guidebook nor the phonograph records specifically designed for parental participation had any direct effect on performance. Education of parents and especially their formal training in Spanish proved to be significant factors. Investigation also showed that although background factors alone might have accounted for high child performance, parental participation alone would and did improve the child's performance. DF

Himmler, Merwin L.
An Analysis and Evaluation of a Television Demonstration of the Teaching of Fifth Grade Reading, Arithmetic, and French. Unpublished Ph. D. dissertation, University of Pittsburgh, 1957.
This study is an analysis and evaluation of a demonstration program teaching fifth-grade reading, arithmetic, and French. Some of the findings were as follows: there is little observable difference in the effectiveness of television and regular instruction; pupil interest is high; reading was more suitable to the medium than arithmetic and French. Lessons provide in-service training for teachers. BP

International Christian University, Audiovisual Center
"The effects of 'Television English Classroom for the Seventh Grade," in *Survey of Educational Media Research in the Far East*. Washington, D. C.: U. S. Office of Education, 1963. Pp. 116-17.
One hundred eighty seventh graders from two schools are randomly divided into two control and two experimental groups at each school. The experimental groups view the television program "Television English Classroom for the Seventh Grade" once a week for twenty minutes over a period of two semesters. A ten-minute follow-up including a question and answer period, follows each broadcast. The broadcasts are made by a native speaker of English. The control group does not receive the television series. One teacher at each school conducts classes for both the experimental and control groups. An examination including a tape-recorded oral test, a written test, and a measurement of motivation and attitude is administered as a pretest and after the first and second semesters. There is no significant difference between experimental and control groups in each of the three sections of the test at any of the three test periods. Center for Documentation and Communication Research, Western Reserve University.

Johnson, Charles E.
See Johnson, 6.1.

Johnson, Grace Nichols, and Frances Hardy
The Big Picture: The Norfolk City Experiment in Instructional Television. Norfolk, Virginia: Norfolk City Public Schools, June, 1960.

Results are given for a study extending over a three year period during which in-school telecasts are used for direct teaching. Lessons are presented over commercial station in science, history, geometry, mathematics, a survey humanities program and in Spanish. Details are given of pre- and post-test methods, of selection and training of teachers, of administration of the classes, and of results in achievement, presented according to race and sex. Pupils are selected for evaluation from fifth and sixth grades, junior and senior high schools in the city of Norfolk, Virginia. Statistical results are analyzed by covariance. Pupil, teacher, parent and principal attitudes are measured by questionnaires. Details of responses are presented, general conclusions drawn and recommendations made. Center for Documentation and Communication Research, Western Reserve University.

Johnson, James T., Jr.
See Hayman, 2.56.

Keller, Robert J.
See Keller, 7.

Kumata, Hideya
See Kumata, Part I.

Mate, Hubert E.
"Spanish on Television at the University of Alabama," *Hispania,* XLI (September, 1958), 415-18.

Report of an experiment in teaching elementary Spanish on television to college and high school students. Assignments and tests disclose that at the end of one year, college students did at least as well in the written work as their counterparts on the campus with the same assignments and tests. Satisfactory progress in oral Spanish was reported for those students interviewed. MJS

Mauriello, Edna A.
An Appraisal of Three Variables in the Teaching of Conversational French by Television to Fourth Grade Children. Unpublished Ph.D. dissertation, Boston University, 1961.

Appraises effectiveness of teacher-training programs by investigating certain of its effects on the skill developed by fourth-grade children in an elementary course of conversational French. Forty classes of children in the metropolitan Boston area participate; half the teachers are trained by a weekly television program, the remaining teachers have no television training. Study shows that televised teacher training, plus teacher-directed practice, plus a reasonably fluent teacher will produce significant increases in achievement. Center for Documentation and Communication Research, Western Reserve University.

Mayers, Alan E.
See Hayman, 2.56.

Mendeloff, Henry
"Aural Placement by Television," *Modern Language Journal,* XLVII (March, 1963), 110-13.
  The article describes an experiment in aural placement by television at the University of Maryland. The test was devised by the author for adaptation to French, German, and Spanish. Norms were derived by pre-testing university students on Levels II, III, and IV. The success of the experiment demonstrated the feasibility of aural placement by television. The scores achieved by entering students indicated the invalidity of the traditional placement ratio of "one high school year equals one college semester." Henry Mendeloff

Milwaukee Public Schools
See Milwaukee Public Schools, 2.3 Spanish.

Mueller, Klaus, and Donald W. Johnson
See Mueller, 6.1.

Mueller, Theodore
"French by TV—The Teacher and the Machine," *French Review* XXXV (December, 1961), 185-90.
  In this article I present the reasons for the content and the development of a three semester course in beginning French. I discuss the advantages and shortcomings of TV in teaching a skill, the role and limitations of visuals, student participation, the nature of language, the principles in learning a skill and their application to TV, the contributions made by the science of communication which separates "code" from "message," the contributions from psychology, particularly programed learning as used in the teaching machine, TV as a step towards self instruction, student acceptance of TV as a teaching medium and the results obtained. Some research in student attitude and its relevancy in learning was initiated. Theodore Mueller, MLabstract #168. See also, Mueller, below.

†————.

TV and Mass-Instruction Experiments. Research in progress supported by the Ford Foundation and the State of Florida.

Language was taught with emphasis on the code, but the student had knowledge of the sentences that were used. There was content to the sentences; the message, however, was so simple that the student paid little or no attention to it. TV and Mass Instruction Experiment: Fifty-one video tapes were produced for First Semester French; forty-five video tapes were produced for Second Semester French; forty-five video tapes were produced for Third Semester French. These materials were used in classes from 1959 through 1963. Results: The Overall results were about the same as with smaller classes and an instructor. The pronunciation for many students, however, did suffer in the TV instruction due to the lack of control on the part of an instructor. Theodore Mueller.

Mueller, Theodore H., and Ralph R. Leutenegger
"Some Inferences about an Intensified Oral Approach to the Teaching of French Based on a Study of Course Drop-Outs," *Modern Language Journal,* XLVIII (February, 1964), 91-94.

In this article we investigate why students drop out of the elementary French course, taught by TV. Through a questionnaire the students were asked how they evaluate TV as a teaching medium. The students who had dropped out were interviewed. Acoustic proficiency data consisting of the Seashore Measure of Musical Talents were available, which demonstrated interesting differences in hearing discrimination particularly in Tonal Memory and Time sub-tests. Emphasis on audio-lingual learning seems to be a frustrating experience for students with little training in oral perception or memory work. Discrepancies in four of the Seashore Measures indicate that these students had too much trouble with learning through the ear exclusively. Theodore H. Mueller and Ralph R. Leutenegger, MLabstract #709.

National Educational Television and Radio Center.
The Impact of Educational Television, ed. Wilbur Schramm. Urbana, Ill.: University of Illinois Press, 1960.

The chapters of this book are based on research that investigates the attitudes, motivations, viewing habits, and the degree of learning of the viewers; the audience composition; and the presentational patterns of educational television programing. Pages 229-47 are devoted to a theory concerning the interdependence of the relative potency of the program messsage and its relative comprehensibility. JM

Pflieger, Elmer, F.

The Television Teaching Project: Report for the Year 1957-1958. Detroit, Michigan: Detroit Public Schools, 1959.

Report on the second year of experimentation with ETV, sponsored by the Fund for the Advancement of Education. Public school children at the elementary and secondary level are taught American literature, health, science, Spanish or world history by ETV. They are matched with a control group for IQ, pre-test ability and other factors. Scores on achievement tests and listening tests are compared using the t-test. The two year experience of the Television Teaching Project gives definite support to the proposition that pupils can learn subject-matter by television in larger-than-normal classes as well as by conventional teaching methods. Center for Documentation and Communication Research, Western Reserve University.

Randall, Earle S.

See Randall, 6.1.

Reid, J. Richard

"An Exploratory Survey of Foreign Language Teaching by Television in the United States," in *Reports of Surveys and Studies in the Teaching of Modern Foreign Languages ... 1959-1961*. New York: The Modern Language Association of America, 1961. Pp. 197-211.

A survey of foreign language teaching by instructional television in the United States is reported. Information is obtained through questionnaires, personal visits to language program projects, and interviews with television teachers, classroom teachers, school administrators, television personnel, and students. The use of television in conjunction with other audio-visual media, such as moving pictures, recordings, and language laboratories is reported. The role of television in the FLES program, college experimentation, and rural high schools is noted. Aims, methods, technical procedures, and presentations, are reported. Foreign language telecourses are listed. The program is evaluated, recommendations are made, and research in progress is noted. Center for Documentation and Communication Research, Western Reserve University.

A Report of the Seminar on the Uses of Television in Education. Conducted by the Subcommittee on Television of the Commission on Research and Service, North Central Association of Colleges and Secondary Schools, Chicago, Ill., December 3-6, 1959, under contract with the United States Office of Education. Washington, D. C.: U.S. Office of Education, 1959.

"The Contractor conducted a seminar in Chicago, Illinois, on December 3-6, 1959, to identify significant principles and practices in the uses of television for educational purposes. The seminar was composed of representatives from colleges and secondary schools, administrators, faculty, staff, technicians, audiovisual specialists, board of control members, students, representative citizens, and related professional organizations, i.e., National Association of Educational Broadcasters, National Educational Television and Radio Center, Department of Audio-Visual Instruction (NEA), etc. The report of this conference seminar was critically reviewed by a follow-up conference, November 12-14, 1960, in Columbus, Ohio. . . . The seminar report on principles and practices, as revised at the follow-up conference, is available from the Contractor."—From official description, March, 1961.

Rovner, Philip
See Rovner, 2.3 German.

Schramm, Wilbur, Kenneth E. Oberholtzer, *et al.*
The Context of Instructional Television. Summary Report of Research Findings, The Denver-Stanford Project. Denver, Colorado and Stanford, California, Denver Public Schools and Stanford University, June, 1964.

This Final Report concerns the end results of experimentation and investigation from 1960 to 1964. The Conclusions report the pattern which has been established for Denver's future teaching of elementary school Spanish and go into the implications which the findings have for other educators and researchers. The principal investigators feel that their project has "demonstrated that an effective context can be built for instructional television" and that "even a teacher inexperienced in Spanish could learn to manage efficiently the combination of activities built around television." Furthermore, "this experience has proved that the parent can participate effectively in a course built around television." "This study adds to the growing evidence that programmed instruction, of certain kinds and under suitable conditions, can be used effectively in schools. An extensive Appendix of results is included." DF See Hayman, this section, for other publications pertinent to this project.

Silagyi, Dezo Vincent
A Critical Analysis of Attitudes of Selected Elementary Students Toward Television Teaching in the Detroit Television Teaching Project. Unpublished Ed.D. dissertation, Wayne State University, 1961.

The experimental population consists of 2840 pupils enrolled in larger-than-normal classes. Subject areas covered are conversational French and Spanish, science and health. A pupil opinionnaire is formulated and results are subjected to a chi-square analysis. Pupil attitudes towards television teaching are investigated in the following areas: television teaching in general, physical setting, personal relationships, achievement and technical and productive aspects. In general, student attitude is favorable and they feel that they achieve as much in a television class as in a regular one. Center for Documention and Communication Research, Western Reserve University.

Stake, Robert E.
The Effect of Television Instruction on Individual Learning Curves. Washington, D. C.: U.S. Department of Health, Education, and Welfare, Office of Education, November, 1959. Cooperative Research Project No. 573.
　　Twenty-three students in five high schools taught Spanish for one year by closed-circuit television. Control groups included thirty-one students in three small high schools, ninety-six students in one large high school in a Spanish-speaking community, and fourteen college students. Weekly vocabulary quizzes and Cooperative Spanish Test administered. Achievement of television students found to be inferior. Includes bibliography of thirteen references. Center for Documentation and Communication Research, Western Reserve University.

Throop, Joseph F., Lewis T. Assini, and George W. Buguslavsky
The Effectiveness of Laboratory Instruction in Strength of Materials by Closed-Circuit Television. Troy, N. Y.: Rensselaer Polytechnic Institute, November 8, 1958 (mimeographed).
　　A 41-page report of an experiment designed to test the practicability of substituting televised laboratory demonstrations for actual student-group laboratory experimentation. The objective was to impart an understanding of the mechanical behavior of engineering materials rather than to train students in the techniques of materials testing. DF

Toronto Board of Education
An Experimental Study of Television as a Medium of French Instruction. Toronto: Toronto Board of Education, 1962.
　　French Through Pictures was shown to one group through closed-circuit television. The other group used the book *French Through Pictures* and heard tape-recordings over the school P.A.

system. The instructional content of both techniques was the same. Both groups received additional instruction from an itinerant teacher. Other variables studied were Grade 7 versus Grade 8 performance, four fifteen-minute periods versus two thirty-minute periods per week, and the expressed attitudes of the students towards language learning and its importance. A variety of tests were used and samples of these tests are included. The results indicated significantly higher scores for (a) the book-tape method, (b) Grade 8 students, (c) two thirty-minute periods, (d) students learning French as a third language, (e) students considering language their favourite and/or an important subject, (f) students who were certain about their future plans. From An Annotated Bibliography of Research Service Publications, see above, Part I, Toronto Board of Education.

Ulrich, John H.
"An Experimental Study of the Acquisition of Information from Three Types of Recorded Television Presentations," *Speech Monographs,* XXIV (March, 1957), 39-45.

Based upon Ph.D. dissertation, State University of Iowa, 1955. "Specifically, this investigation was designed to determine whether eighth grade pupils retained more information from observing a kinescope recording of a lecture without visual aids, one with aids handled by the lecturer, or the same lecture with aids that were merely flashed on the screen." Conclusion: "Eighth grade pupils immediately recall more information from a kinescope recording of a lecture . . . supported by poster-type visual aids. . . ." JG

2.7 Evaluation of Achievement in Language Learning

Andrade, Manuel, John L. Hayman, Jr., and James T. Johnson, Jr.
"Measurement of Listening Comprehension in Elementary-School Spanish Instruction," *Elementary School Journal,* LXIV (Nov. 1963), 10.

Data on the above project:
Funding Agency: US Office of Education—Title VII, NDEA
Code Number: 7-14-1380-083
Dates: January 1960 through June 1964
Funds. Denver Public Schools: $198,722; Stanford University: $110,00 (approx.)

One activity of the Denver-Stanford project was the development of fifth and sixth grade Spanish listening comprehension tests. Several problems related to the peculiarities of testing in the early, entirely audio-lingual stages of a FLES program, are discussed, and methods of overcoming them are described. Technical criteria—validity, reliability, discrimination, comprehensiveness, and difficulty range—were found to depend on careful and detailed analysis of course content, exact specification of course objectives, and extensive pretesting. It was further found that all aspects of language learning, including vocabulary, acquisition, verb usage, article agreement, adjective agreement, word order, and structure, could best be measured through picture items which require the pupil to match a picture on an answer sheet to a spoken statement. John L. Hayman, Jr.

————.

Measurement of Speaking Skills in Elementary Level Spanish Instruction. (Denver-Stanford Project on the Context of Instructional Television, Report Number 9) Stanford, Calif.: Institute for Communication Research Stanford University, July, 1963.

This report describes the development of three tests to be used to measure the ability of 5th and 6th graders in Spanish. Discussed also are the ways in which certain problems of scoring and measurement revealed during the construction of tests were dealt with. Development of the tests was completed during the 1960-61 school year. Used since, the tests have been found satisfactory. This report is one of a number of progress reports on the Denver-Stanford Project on the Context of Instructional Television, headed by Kenneth E. Oberholtzer for the Denver Public Schools and Wilbur Schramm for Stanford University. DF

*Beezhold, F. W.
"Factor analyses of Language Achievement Tests," *Journal of the National Institute of Personnel Research,* VI (1956), 63-73.

Breckwoldt, John P.
An Attempt to Measure Academic Achievement Efficiency. (Denver-Stanford Project on the Context of Instructional Television, Report No. 6) Stanford, Calif.: Institute for Communication Research, Stanford University, March 1962.

This study explored the possibility of constructing a personality inventory which would predict academic achievement efficiency among fifth graders in the Denver-Stanford project. No significant correlations or differences in personality traits were obtained through the measurements used in this study. CBC

Brooks, Nelson. Yale University, New Haven, Conn.
Foreign Language Tests for School and College; Project No. 8,827

(National Defense Education Act, Title VI), June 15, 1960, to June 4, 1963; $588,255 [FY60 $225,201; FY61, $201,638; FY62 $161,386].

The language tests being developed will be at two levels—high school and college—and test listening, speaking, reading, and writing abilities of German, Italian, French, Russian, and Spanish. BP

Buros, Oscar Krisen
See Buros, Part I.

Carroll, Brendan J.
See Carroll, 2.3 English.

————.

"An English Language Survey in West Africa," *English Language Teaching,* XVI (July, 1962), 205-10.

In this article I describe a survey made in Ghana to compare the rates at which African and English children acquire a mastery of English, and to isolate certain problems of cross-cultural testing. 150 young African children were examined in five tests—Word Recognition, Sentence Structure, Vocabulary, Dictation and Writing Fluency. These results were related to the test norms and to the performances of a control group of English children. Interesting group and test differences are found and illustrated numerically and graphically. The African children performed best in Writing Fluency (average quotient 71), and worst in Vocabulary (average quotient 34), with an overall average quotient of 56 (English norm 100). Brendan J. Carroll, MLabstract #338.

Carroll, John B. President and Fellows of Harvard University, Cambridge, Mass.

Foreign Language Proficiency of Language Majors Near Graduation from College (Phase I); Project No. OE-4-14-048 (National Defense Education Act, Title VI), March 15, 1964 to October 31, 1964; $30,983.

A pilot survey of foreign language proficiency of some 1,000 foreign language majors graduating in the spring of 1964 from Harvard University, Radcliffe College, and colleges and universities in New York State will be conducted. The pilot survey is Phase I of a project to measure the proficiency of some 8,000 language majors graduating from colleges and universities throughout the country in the spring of 1965. The project will involve administration of the *Modern Language Association Foreign Language Proficiency Tests for Teachers and Advanced Students* in five commonly taught languages and correlation of the scores with scales of language proficiency developed by the State Department's Foreign Service Institute. The MLA tests measure foreign language reading, writing, listening, and speaking abilities, as well as knowledge of the world area where the language is spoken. Preparation of the tests received Federal support under another Office of Education contract. The Foreign Service Institute tests provide a means of translating numerical scores into descriptive evaluations of language proficiency ranging from "ability to use limited social expressions and language for travel requirements" to "fluency in the foreign language." Additional survey data will be obtained through use of a short modern language aptitude test and information supplied by questionnaires on students' foreign language background and goals.

————.

"Fundamental Considerations in Testing for English Language Proficiency of Foreign Student," in *Testing the English Proficiency of Foreign Students* [Report of a conference, May, 1961, sponsored by the Center for Applied Linguistics]. Washington, D. C.: Center for Applied Linguistics, 1961. Pp. 30-40.

Discussion of purpose of testing, kinds of competencies to be tested, controls for extraneous influences, problems of sampling and of source interpretation. Methodology is stressed. John B. Carroll

Carroll, John B., Aaron S. Carton and Claudia P. Wilds.

An Investigation of "Cloze" Items in the Measurement of Achievement in Foreign Languages. A Report of Research Conducted under a Grant from the College Entrance Examination Board. Cambridge, Mass.: Laboratory for Research in Instruction, Graduate School of Education, April, 1959 (mimeo).

An attempt to develop a ready method for constructing achievement tests in any language by use of the "cloze procedure," i.e. requiring subjects to guess words or other units deleted systematically from texts. Study involved French and German tests. Found special ability to guess deletions was too much of an interfering factor; hence concluded this method not appropriate for general use. John B. Carroll.

Cloos, Robert I.

A Comprehensive Study of Fourteen Predictors of Success in the Audio-Lingual Approach to First-Year German at the High School Level. Unpublished Ed.D. dissertation, Rutgers, The State University of New Jersey, 1964.

Fourteen measures of 122 public high school students used as predictors of success: (1) Otis IQ, (2) Grade Point Average, (3) five sub-scores and total raw score on the *Brown-Carlsen Listening Comprehension Test*, and (4) five sub-scores and total raw score on the Carroll-Sapon *Modern Language Aptitude Test*. The criterion measure, obtained after seven months of instruction, was the total raw score on the *Modern Language Association Cooperative Foreign Language Test: German—Form LA*. Computer analysis provided inter-correlations and regression analyses which were used to test the extent of relationship between the predictors and the criterion. The predictors were all found to be significantly related, at the one per cent level, to the criterion. The *MLAT* indicated the highest correlation. The female subjects achieved a higher mean total raw score than the males on the *MLAT*, as well as on three sections of the criterion. However, the degree of difference in achievement by males and females was found to be not significant. Prior out-of-school experience in German was found to have played a significant part in the achievement of the subjects of this study. Robert I. Cloos, MLabstract # 840

Dickens, Milton, and Frederick Williams
An Experimental Application of "CLOZE" Procedure and Attitude Measures to Listening Comprehension," *Speech Monographs*, XXXI (June, 1964), 103-08.

An application of the "cloze" procedure (having respondents replace deleted words) to sound tapes of oral messages for the purpose of comprehension measurement. This procedure demonstrated high reliability and correlation with separate measures of language ability. A secondary focus upon attitude toward message topic as a variable revealed its relative independence from measures of comprehension. Milton Dickens, MLabstract # 826

Dodson, C. J.
Oral Examinations. Aberystwyth, Wales: Faculty of Education, University College of Wales, 1963.

A report of an investigation into problems of standardization of oral examinations in modern languages. Encouraging results were obtained by counting words and errors in examinations recorded by the teacher on a tape recorder. Jac L. Williams

*Donoghue, Mildred R.
Measuring Achievement in Listening Skills of First Year Spanish. Unpublished Ed. D. dissertation in progress, University of California at Los Angeles.

Dufort, Mary R.

"An Audio-Comprehension Ability Test for FL Programs in the Elementary School," *California Journal of Elementary Education,* XXX (November, 1961), 121-28.

In this article I describe the "Audio Comprehension Ability Test —Spanish" (ACAT) which I constructed to measure the audio achievement of fourth, fifth and sixth grade subjects in a FLES research study. A variety of ways of testing audio comprehension is presented. Reasons are discussed for selection of the types of items used in the three parts of the ACAT. Trial administration, item analysis, reliability and validity of the instrument are discussed. Results of the research study are not included in this article. Mary R. Dufort, MLabstract #290.

Dyer, Henry S.

"Validity of CEEB Placement Test in French," *College Board Review,* I (Spring, 1947), 1, 12-15.

Validity of tests was shown to be high when achievement of test group on exam correlated closely to final achievement in French course. BP

———.

"The Effect of Recency of Training on the College Board French Scores," *School and Society,* LXX (August 13, 1949), 105-6.

Small study made at Harvard to test the decrease in French scores on the CEEB in relation to years of time elapsed since study. Decrease was sufficiently great to show that scaling the results is meaningless unless one regards the recency of the students' training. It is interesting to note that the greater the number of years of Latin study, the higher the student scored on Scholastic Aptitude Test. BP

Fife, Robert H., and Herschel T. Manuel

See Fife, 3.5

Kern, Edith

"FLES Testing," *French Review,* XXXIII (October, 1959), 45-52.

Results of tests given to eight hundred students in twenty-eight classes of fourth-grade level after thirty hours of televised French lessons. There was a strong correlation between achievement and intelligence. There was little correlation between the achievement of the students and teacher training in foreign language. None of the classroom teachers participating was qualified to teach French. Hypothesis: There may be a connection between the *interest* of the classroom teachers and pupil achievement. Testing by television is possible and should be investigated further. MJS

Lado, Robert
Language Testing: The Construction and Use of Foreign Language Tests, A Teacher's Book. London: Longmans, Green, and Co., 1961.
"A comprehensive introduction to the construction and use of foreign language tests. It incorporates modern linguistic knowledge into language testing as one of its chief contributions. . . . The material is primarily intended for teachers of foreign languages and of English as a foreign language."—From the Preface. DF

————.
Measurement in English as a Foreign Language with Special Reference to Spanish-Speaking Adults. Unpublished Ph.D. dissertation, University of Michigan, 1950.
Summarized in Dostal, p. 7

Lorge, Irving, and L. K. Diamond
"The English Proficiency of Foreign Students," *Journal of Higher Education,* XXV (January, 1954), 19-26.
Description and analyses of tests devised at the Institute of Psychological Research, Teachers College, Columbia University, to determine (a) if there are particular aspects of English usage more or less difficult for all foreign students, or for certain groups, and (b) whether foreign students are favored on English vocabulary tests containing words related to their own vernacular. Two parallel forms, each comprising four subtests, are used for placement purposes. The study examines the performance of 459 students with respect to usage according to their native language grouping, compares performances, and gives tables of results. The Romance-language grouping did better on words of Latin over Germanic origin, but the German-language group did not do better on words of Germanic origin, rather, did better on words of Greek origin. MJS

McArdle, Lois
"TOEFL: Program for the Testing of English as a Foreign Language," *Linguistic Reporter,* VI (June, 1964), 2-3.
Description of the establishment and objectives of the test. There are five subtests: Listening Comprehension, Structure, Vocabulary, Reading Comprehension, Writing Ability. The article goes on to describe the steps taken to determine test validity and reliability. Further trial uses of the test are planned. The program is sponsored by the Center for Applied Linguistics. DF

McKinney, James Edward, Jr.
The Development of an Auditory Comprehension Test for Use at the Completion of the Second Semester of College Spanish. Unpublished Ed. D. dissertation, Purdue University, 1961.

The purpose of this investigation was to develop an instrument to measure students' achievement in auditory comprehension of Spanish at the end of two semesters of instruction and to study the relationship that the scores obtained on this test had with scores on tests designed to measure other variables in language behavior. The variables selected in Spanish were achievement in reading, vocabulary, and grammar. The scores on these variables were obtained from the *Cooperative Achievement Test*. In addition to the study of the relationship of these elements in foreign language learning, a study of the relationship between scores on the auditory comprehension test and *The Purdue Orientation Test in English* was made. [. . .] The assumption that there is a need for tests of auditory comprehension seems to be justified. Although the correlation coefficients of the reading skills, as measured by the *Cooperative Achievement Test* and auditory comprehension show that there exists a significant relationship between the two, they are not sufficiently high to warrant the assumption that achievement in the various skills are equal. From the abstract.

Malcolm, D. J.
See Malcolm, 2.1.

Manuel, Herschel T.
The Preparation and Evaluation of Inter-Language Testing Materials. University of Texas, Austin, Texas, 1963[?].

Reports construction of a new series of Inter-American Tests of General Ability and Tests of Reading in parallel English and Spanish editions. Includes interpretive and evaluative data. Herschel T. Manuel

————.
"Use of Parallel Tests in the Study of Foreign Language Teaching," *Educational and Psychological Monthly*, XIII, No. 3 (1953), 431-36.

Discussion of possibilities of interlanguage comparisons, i.e., English and Spanish through the use of parallel tests. Percentage tables are given, scoring as to vocabulary and comprehension, supporting the hypothesis that a student tends to learn a foreign language in proportion to the mastery of his own language. JM

"The MLAS Cooperative Classroom Testing Program," *Modern Language Journal*, XLVII (May, 1963), 212.

The Modern Language Association and the Educational Testing Service in Princeton, N.J. (Mirian M. Vryan, ETS Program Director) are currently collaborating in the design and preparation of a new series of tests of competence in five languages—French, German, Italian, Russian, and Spanish—for use in grades 7 through 14. The tests will measure four separate skills—listening, speaking, reading, and writing—at two levels, lower and higher. The lower-level tests will be suitable for use with students who have completed one or two years of language study at the secondary school level, or the equivalent in semesters of study at the college level. The higher-level tests are intended for use with secondary school students with three or four years of language study, and with third and fourth semester language students. There will be two forms of each test in each language, making a total of 80 tests. The tests will reflect recent developments in the approach to modern foreign language teaching. MLabstract #491.

Mueller, Klaus A., and William Wiersma, Jr.
See Mueller, 2.1.

Neale, L. W.
"The Development of Reading Ability in French and Its Measurement in the Grammar School Course," *Durham Research Review,* IV (September, 1953), 9-14.

Concerns the development of an achievement test for silent reading in French. Charts are presented as proof of reliability of the tests developed. Reference material is listed. JM

Sadnavitch, Joseph M., and W. James Popham
"Measurement of Spanish Achievement in the Elementary School," *Modern Language Journal,* XLVI (November, 1961), 297-99.

The purpose of this article was to describe the development of a measuring device designed specifically to evaluate achievement in conversational Spanish programs at the elementary school level. According to accepted standards of test construction, the *Spanish Comprehension Test* appears to satisfy the minimum recommendations and suggests potentiality for the measurement of achievement at the elementary school level. Even though this instrument evidenced limitations of large scale standardization and more adequate validity procedures, it appeared to indicate value for school systems wishing to study elementary programs in conversational Spanish. This instrument also indicated the feasibility of a method for measuring achievement of this type in other foreign language areas. Joseph M. Sadnavitch and W. James Popham, MLabstract #151.

Schenck, Ethel A.

The Cheydleur Studies of Testing and Teaching in Modern Foreign Languages. Madison, Wis.: Dembar Publications, 1952.

This material is based on research work done by Frederick D. Cheydleur from 1919 to 1949. The statistical evidence presented is therefore supported by large-scale numbers within each experiment. This booklet discusses the procedures for experimental testing for placement, attainment, and evaluation of teaching. Also presented are standardized test results in basic language courses from 1943 to 1949. The appendix contains sample tests. JM

———.

Studies of Testing and Teaching in Modern Foreign Languages. Madison, Wis.: Dembar Publications, 1952.

Finds that guidance-placement examinations increase effectiveness of university language programs by reducing the percentage of failures and dropouts. This was a twenty-year experiment. JM

Spencer, Richard E.

"The Relative Effectiveness of Earphones and Loudspeakers as a Means of Presenting a Listening Test in a Foreign Language," *Modern Language Journal,* XLVIII (October, 1964).

Commercial language laboratories rely upon the use of earphones through which stimulus material is presented. Actual foreign language speakers are not heard through earphones, however, nor are the usual listening comprehension language tests which are normally presented over loudspeaker systems. There is a difference, then, between the learning situation, the testing of the learning, and actual communication with foreign materials. In this study two groups were tested with a listening comprehension test in German (College Board Tests), with either earphones, or loudspeakers. The results show that the performance on the listening test for the earphone group was superior (significant to the .07 level of confidence). The media through which students are tested affects test results significantly. Richard E. Spencer, MLabstract # 790

Starr, Wilmarth H.

"MLA Foreign Language Proficiency Tests for Teachers and Advanced Students," *PMLA,* LXXVII (September, 1962, Part 2), 31-42.

A final report to the profession of the history, purposes, statistical findings, and uses of the tests through the period of test development and their final forms. Wilmarth H. Starr

————.

MLA Proficiency Tests for Teachers and Advanced Students. Princeton, N.J.: Educational Testing Service.

Available to qualified users only. These tests measure the proficiency of modern foreign-language teachers in the seven areas of listening comprehension, speaking, reading, writing, analysis of the language, culture, and professional preparation. Tests are available for French, Spanish, Italian, German, and Russian. Wilmarth Starr

Stodola, Quentin, Donald F. Schwartz, Ralph H. Kolstoe
Administering a Listening Comprehension Test Through Use of Teacher-Readers, Sound Film and Tape Recordings. Fargo: North Dakota State University, 1962.

"A major purpose of the experiment was to find out whether or not in a typical school situation there is enough variation in reading abilities among teachers giving a listening test so as to have a significant effect on test results. It was also hoped to find out if variability among scores for comparable class units could be reduced by using other methods of test administration. Listening tests were administered to the Fargo Public School pupils at three different levels of difficulty: high school, junior high school, and elementary school. At each grade, the test was given by four different methods [regular, trained, movie, audio] to groups of five class units to which pupils and teachers had been assigned on a random basis." From the Summary. Findings are that only on the high school level (where tests administered to the movie group had significantly higher scores) was there any variation attributable to the various methods of test administration. There is a section of suggestions for Further Research. DF

Strain, Jeris E.
"Difficulties in Measuring Pronunciation Improvement," *Language Learning,* XIII, Nos. 3-4 (1963), 217-24.

An experiment intended to measure pronunciation improvement (recognition level) among Japanese college students of English. The discussion treats (1) experiment design, (2) data collection preparation, and presentation (two graphs are included), and (3) analysis. Its purpose is (1) to suggest criteria and procedures for experiments, (2) to survey variables that should be considered in experiments, and (3) to raise several questions that others interested in experimentation might also undertake to investigate. Jeris E. Strain, MLabstract # 767

Sturge-Moore, C. J.
See Sturge-Moore, 2.3 English.

Sumner, Francis C.

"Relation of Grades in German Reading Vocabulary to the Method of Testing," *Modern Language Journal,* XXXIII (March, 1949), 238-40.

Tests were devised to measure German vocabulary after two months of instruction designed to equip students to sight-read in psychology. Conclusions from test results were that (1) grades vary from A to failure depending greatly on the method of testing; (2) test methods that involve mainly recognition yield higher grades than those involving reproduction; (3) tests that require English equivalents for German words yield lowest scores; and (4) teachers of sight translation must equip students to produce English words for German equivalents. BP

Valette, Rebecca M.

"The Use of the Dictée in the French Language Classroom," *Modern Language Journal,* XLVIII (November, 1964), 431-34.

In this article I examine the reliability of the dictée both as a testing technique and a teaching technique for beginning French courses taught by an audio-lingual method. In the experiment, 120 college students were divided into two groups which differed only in that the first group was given a daily dictation. The analysis of performance on a common final examination indicates that (a) the dictée constitutes a valid test of overall language skills only for students with little practice in dictation, and that (b) emphasis on dictation develops proficiency in that skill alone without leading to proportional proficiency in other aspects of language learning. Rebecca M. Valette, MLabstract # 851

Van Riper, Charles

An Investigation of Differential Binaural Stimulation in the Teaching of a Foreign Language. Washington, D.C.: U.S. Department of Health, Education, and Welfare, Office of Education, October, 1960. Cooperative Research Project No. 739.

Study of the reliability and validity of college instructors' evaluations of student adequacy in pronouncing Spanish and the effectiveness of dichotic as opposed to binaural stimulation in a language laboratory over a two-semester period. No significant difference between dichotic and binaural stimulation in teaching Spanish pronunciation. Objective measures of pronunciation adequacy suggested. Includes bibliography of eleven references. Center for Documentation and Communication Research, Western Reserve University.

Vicory, Arthur C.

See Vicory, 3.1.

2.9 Specifications for Equipment

Buch, John N.
See Buch, 2.54.

Buka, M., M. Z. Freeman, W. N. Locke
"Language Learning and Frequency Response," *International Journal of American Linguisics,* XXVIII (January, 1962, Part II), 62-79.

An attempt is made to determine the effect of high frequency response characteristics of language laboratory equipment on ability to discriminate between pairs of consonants and vowels in French and German. 90 pairs were used with paid groups of high-school subjects who had studied no French or German. Results showed that as high frequency response is cut back from 7300 cycles per second (the maximum for the system) to 5000 cycles, then 3000 cycles, the subjects were prevented from perceiving an increasing number of phonemic contrasts in French and German. The effect was more noticeable for German. William N. Locke

Delattre, Pierre
"Quality in Tape Recording and Voicing," *International Journal of American Linguistics,* XXIX (April, 1963, Part III), 55-59.

Language teachers must learn to discriminate between good and bad tapes. The listening and recording quality of their language laboratory must be good; the pattern drills of their learning sequences may be well composed; if the tape is not well recorded acoustically and phonetically, teaching conditions are still poor. This paper is in two parts. In the first part it indicates what sound frequencies must be present in the tape for certain fricative consonants to be well identified. It describes simple acoustic experiments which should aid an amateur in recognizing the quality of *sh, s, th,* and *f* frictions. In the second part it presents seven precepts to be observed by a voicer when he records language material; the last two are: the voicer must either be a phonetician or be trained by one; otherwise he cannot be consistent in treating the unstable *e,* the liaisons, the phrasing, etc., as in realistic speech. In addition, like a professional actor, the voicer must be trained to mentally hear the rhythm and the intonation far enough ahead of himself to read words as he would *speak* them in a real situation. Pierre Delattre, MLabstract #494.

Freeman, M. Z., and M. Buka
"Language Learning and Frequency Response II," to appear.

An attempt is made to determine the effect of low frequency response characteristics of language laboratory equipment on ability to discriminate between pairs of consonants and vowels in French and German. 90 pairs were used with paid groups of high-school subjects who had studied no French or German. Results showed that as low frequency response is cut back from 50 cycles per second (the minimum for the system) to 500 cycles, then 1000 cycles, the subjects were prevented from perceiving an increasing number of phonemic contrasts in French and German. The effect was more noticeable for German. William N. Locke. See Buka, 4.5, and this section.

Gonzalez, Simon
Planning Foreign Language Laboratory Facilities for Secondary Schools. Unpublished Ed. D. dissertation, Stanford University, 1962.

This study encompasses the investigation of a method of instruction and the facilities which will make employment of that methodology most effective and efficient. It endeavors specifically to develop educational specifications which may be used as a guide for school administrators, school board members, teachers, and architects in the planning and designing of foreign language laboratories for secondary schools. From the abstract.

Hayes, Alfred S.
Language Laboratory Facilities: Technical Guide for the Selection, Purchase, Use and Maintenance. Washington, D.C.: Office of Education, U.S. Department of Health, Education, and Welfare, 1963.

Prepared for the Electronic Industries Association, this is a comprehensive guide covering all aspects of implementing and maintaining a language laboratory. Various systems are discussed and extensive consideration is given to general and specific technical specifications. Testing and servicing the language laboratory is discussed. An appendix gives a sample procurement specification. Although several briefer treatments have appeared dealing with language laboratory design and, to a certain extent, with technical specifications, Mr. Hayes' pamphlet is the most extended and undoubtedly a very reliable treatment of this subject, making a very needed contribution to the subject. DF

Kopp, James
A New Determination of the Pure Tone Equal-Loudness Contours for Earphone Listening, in Experimental Analysis of the Control of Speech Production and Perception, Progress Report No. 3: February 1, 1962, to April 1, 1963.

Pure tones which were of constant intensity and continuously variable frequency were presented to subjects by means of an earphone. The subject compensated for loudness changes by adjusting a potentiometer. Sound pressure at the eardrum was maintained at a nominally constant level by means of a compressor feedback system in which the voltage applied to the subject's earphone was inverse to the output of a matched earphone mounted on a standard artificial ear. Preliminary contours from two subjects obtained by this method were variable across subjects but quite reliable for individual subjects. James Kopp See Harlan L. Lane, this section.

[Lane, Harlan L.]

Initial Specifications for a Speech Auto-Instructional Device, in Experimental Analysis of the Control of Speech Production and Perception. Progress Report No. 3: February 1, 1962, to April 1, 1963. Ann Arbor, Michigan: Behavior Analysis Laboratory, Department of Psychology, University of Michigan, April 1, 1963[?] (multilithed).

A speech auto-instructional device (hereinafter called SAID) will be constructed and assembled from existing components for the purpose of teaching the prosodic features of speech to human speakers. Basically, SAID will be an electronic and electro-mechanical device that will serve the following overall functions: (a) *recording and playback* of a sequence of model patterns for presentation to the subject. (b) electronic *analysis* of certain parameters of simple and complex acoustic signals from two sources (the recorded mode and the subject). (c) electronic *comparison* of these parameter sets in time. (d) *display* of parameter mismatch for instructional and research purposes. Harlan L. Lane

————.

. . . Preliminary Manual for the Speech Auto-Instructional Device, a system for conditioning fluency in the prosodic features of speech. Progress Report No. 5: November 1, 1963, to February 1, 1964. Ann Arbor, Mich.: Behavior Analysis Laboratory, Department of Psychology, University of Michigan, February, 1964 (multilithed).

See Harlan L. Lane, above, Initial Specifications . . . "The Speech Auto-Instructional Device is a computer-based speech training system. It is designed to provide maximum versatility in the conduct of research on conditioning fluency in the prosodic features of speech, in order to provide (1) specifications for an effective and economical device to teach those skills, and (2) basic information on the control of speech production and perception." This manual goes on to describe the subsystems of the device, and the system and program operation. Figures of the subsystems are appended. DF

Leidy, Thomas Ross

Achievement in Modern Languages as a Function of Variations in

Language Laboratory Facilities. Unpublished Ph.D. dissertation, Purdue University, 1963.

Two basic experimental situations were investigated. In the first, the achievement of students assigned to a large (60 place) language laboratory was compared with that of students assigned to a standard size (30 place) laboratory. In the second, the achievement of students assigned to audio-active and non-record laboratory booths was compared with that of students assigned to the standard record-playback booths. . . . Results of the analyses revealed no systematic differences in either experimental situations. In certain instances significant differences between treatments were observed but they were consistently overshadowed by differences of even greater magnitude within treatment groups. Further research is now in progress. From the abstract.

Lewis, Earl N., Jr.
See Lewis, 2.54.

Morton, F. Rand
"Initial Mechanico-Electronic Specifications for a Prototype Audio-Visual Teaching Machine Designed for Self-Instructional Use in the Audio-Lingual Learning of Foreign Languages," *Publications of the Language Laboratory,* Vol. III (1959).

Analysis of the mechanicoelectronic requirements of a machine capable of implementing the concept of step-increment learning of habitual verbal behaviors in students of second or foreign languages and intended as a supplement to the specifications previously established by Carroll and Silvern. F. Rand Morton

————.

"Recent Advances in Language Laboratory Equipment for Teaching and Research: The College Language Laboratory," *Publications of the Language Laboratory,* V (1961), 1-24.

Suggests categorizing the different mechanicoelectronic components useful in language teaching and research, and surveys existing equipment with regard to its pedagogical effectiveness. F. Rand Morton

Taylor, E. H.
"Performance Criteria and Design Considerations for Language Laboratory Systems," *Technical Newsletter* (DuKane Corporation), No. 110 (March, 1960).

Relationship of language laboratory and design of telephone systems, showing differences and standards. Conclusions on specifications: magnetic microphones should not be used in language-teaching facilities; top quality dynamic or "sealed" crystal-type headsets are preferable. Total system-performance criteria: frequency response: 200-8, 500 cycles plus 4 db; noise (unweighted): 45 db below program level of 75 db; distortion: no more than 3 per cent THD (total harmonic distortion) in the band 200-3, 500 cycles. JAD

————.

Architectural Design Consideration for Language Laboratories. St. Charles, Ill.: DuKane Corporation, August, 1960.

The article covers the subject of design for listening booths, and the architectural consideration of window and floor areas, as well as the transmission and absorption of sound. JM

Young, Clarence W.
See Young, 2.54.

3. Psychology of Language and Language Learning

3.1 General

Al-Karbouli, Hamad D.
Interference as a Function of Certain Factors in Learning Two Foreign Languages Contiguously. Unpublished Ph. D. dissertation, Indiana University, 1961.

Experiment with ninety high school students to find out if there is a significant difference in amount of recall between the groups to which the initial (Arabic) and the interpolated (Persian) learning are taught by the same teacher and those to which the initial learning is taught by one teacher and the interpolated learning by another. Effects distributing the teaching-method variables among different groups are determined. The groups in which the materials were taught by different teachers and those in which the material was varied for initial and interpolated learning were found to achieve significantly better recall. Center for Documentation and Communication Research, Western Reserve University.

Anisfeld, Moshe
See Anisfeld, 4.3.

Asher, James J.
"Evidence for 'Genuine' One-Trial Learning," *International Review of Applied Linguistics in Language Teaching*, I (1963), 98-103.

Evidence was presented to support a one-trial learning hypothesis. The data suggested that the closer an item was to being learned on the first presentation, the higher the probability that the item would be retained. Conversely, the more repetitions necessary *before* an item was learned, the less likely it was that the item would be retained. The phenomenon held for language samples taken from Spanish, Japanese, and Russian. Implications were discussed for the traditional repetition learning theory and the newer theory of all-or-none learning. James J. Asher

————.

The High Velocity Process of Logic in Verbal Training. Paper read at the California Research Association, Palo Alto, California, March 1961. The contents are reported in Bradley C. Fallentine, Experimental Validation of Constructs with the Theory, "A Neo-field Theory of Learning the 1 + n Language." Unpublished Master's Thesis, San Jose State College, 1961.

This study was a test of the hypothesis that a high-velocity process of logic underlies the interference effects in verbal learning. Classic studies of interference tend to conclude that "noise," or interference, is maximum when one tries to learn new responses to old stimuli. This generalization was modified by predicting that noise will decrease as the logical relationship between the old and new responses is increased. With nonsense syllables as the S-R learning task and college undergraduates ($N = 17$) as subjects, the experiment confirmed the hypothesis. J. J. Asher

————.

Sensory Interrelationships in the Automated Teaching of Foreign Languages. Paper read at the First Conference of Language Programmers, University of Michigan, Ann Arbor, Mich., April, 1961.

Three experiments were designed to determine (a) the effects of learning symbolic material—vocabulary items in Spanish—through one sense modality, then relearning the same material through a different sense modality; and (b) the transfer effects from elements—vocabulary items—to patterning of the elements—syntactic material consisting of sentences and stories composed from the vocabulary items. Two samples of undergraduate college students ($N = 80$) with no training in Spanish, learned and relearned 92 vocabulary items, under conditions including (a) paired-associate versus recognition learning, (b) pictures versus English words as stimuli, and (c) simultaneous versus sequential presentation of visual materials. Active acquisition of the languages was required in that all responses were in the foreign language and were either written or spoken. Novel methodological techniques allowing random access to the visual and aural materials are described in detail. Under all conditions, subjects who learned visually and relearned aurally achieved a superior performance in comparison to subjects who learned aurally and relearned visually. "Superior" means (a) significantly less persistent error in initial learning, (b) significantly less unique error in relearning, and (c) significantly greater transfer to syntactic comprehension. Other factors found to have an important relationship to language learning were

sensory dominance and guessing behavior. A series of theoretical constructs were suggested as possible explanations for the intersensory differences. J. J. Asher
  See Asher, 2.55.

————.

"Towards a Neo-field Theory of Behavior," *Journal of Humanistic Psychology,* to appear.

This article explores the problem of theory-construction within the field of psychology. The basic idea is that it may be autistic thinking to expect theoretical models in psychology to contain built-in algorithms as is characteristic of theories in mathematics and the physical sciences. Then, a new approach to theory building is illustrated with an application to the problem of achieving listening fluency in a foreign language such as Japanese with a procedure which approximates one-trial learning. James J. Asher.

————.

"Vision and Audition in Language Learning," *Perceptual and Motor Skills.* XIX (1964), 255-300.

The primary purpose was to present data for the transfer of learning from one sensory modality to another, specifically the relationship between vision and audition. The parameter was a range of natural languages including Spanish, Japanese, Russian, Turkish, and Persian. The secondary purpose was to suggest some theoretical constructs which may account for the data, and the third purpose was to explore certain side issues such as pronunciation shock and the validity of predictors for paired-associate learning. There was positive transfer of large magnitude from *vision to audition* for Spanish, Japanese, Turkish, or Persian, but a small, negative transfer for Russian. There was positive transfer from *audition to vision* for Spanish, Japanese, and Russian, but transfer was neutral for Turkish and negative for Persian. The magnitude of the positive transfer was usually higher from vision to audition than audition to vision. Much of the transfer data seemed to be accounted for with a *phonetic fit hypothesis* and a *central mediation hypothesis of sensory process.* The first concept, that of phonetic fit, postulates that positive transfer will be a function of the congruent match between the spoken and written language. The greater the congruency, the higher the probability of positive transfer between sensory channels. The second concept, the central mediation hypothesis, suggests that the direction and amount of transfer is a function of data processing *not* as the sensory receptor level, but at some centralized location in the brain. From the Summary at the head of the article.

Banathy, Bela H.
Measurement of Aptitude in Foreign Language Learning: An "S" Factor Model. Paper presented at the 1963 annual meeting of the Western Psychological Association.

In contrast with existing "G" (general) factor model of language aptitude tests an "S" factor model was presented which conceptualizes success in foreign language learning as a function of factors specific to particular languages or language families. The "S" factor model suggests a test-structure of five dimensions which are closely tied to the linguistic characteristics of specific languages. Bela H. Banathy

Barik, Henri C., and Wallace E. Lambert
"Conditioning of Complex Verbal Sequences," *Canadian Journal of Psychology*, XIV (June, 1960), 87-95.

Describes experiments that investigate the conditioning of a complex verbal response by means of selective reinforcement. Eight references are included. JM

Bauer, Eric Wolfgang. Indiana University, Bloomington, Ind.
An Exploratory Investigation of "Sensory Image Types" in Foreign Language Learning; Project No. 690 (National Defense Education Act, Title VII), January 1, 1961, to December 31, 1961; $3,252.

Problem: Experimental evidence points to presumable existence of at least three groups of learners—the visual, the auditory, and the "combined" types. Objectives: (1) an analysis of three "sensory-image types" in foreign-language learning; (2) an analysis of effectiveness of individualized programs in relation to three sensory-image groups of learners. BP

Beliaev, Boris Vasilevich
Ocherki po psikhologii obucheniia inostrannym iasykam [Essays on the Psychology of Teaching Foreign Languages]. Moscow, U.S.S.R.: RSFSR Ministry of Education, 1959. Also *The Psychology of Teaching Foreign Languages,* Oxford, N.Y.: Pergamon, 1963.

This book on the psychology of teaching and learning foreign languages is intended for use by foreign language teachers and students of languages in pedagogical institutes. I. D. London. From *Psychological Abstracts*, 37:1867.
See the companion volume: *On Teaching Russian,* by C. V. James. New York: Macmillan Co., 1963.

Belson, William A.
"Learning and Attitude Changes Resulting from Viewing a Television Series *Bon Voyage*," *British Journal of Educational Psychology*, Part I, Vol. XXVI (February, 1956).

Purpose of study was to determine to what extent aims of program were achieved. Results showed viewers had learned words and phrases, but had greater fear of language difficulties and of visiting France generally. BP

Benesh, Marijana, Ernest Kramer, and Harlan L. Lane
See Benesh, 5.

Bousfield, Weston A., and Burton H. Cohen
"The Occurrence of Clustering in the Recall of Randomly Arranged Words of Different Frequencies of Usage," *Journal of General Psychology*, LII (January, 1955), 83-95.

Controlled experiment with undergraduate students, using two simultaneous lists of randomly arranged words. JAD

Bovée, Arthur G.
"A Study of the Relationship between Visual Thought Comprehension in English and in French," *French Review*, XXI (December, 1947), 120-23.

Testing 232 twelve- to eighteen-year-olds at the University of Chicago Lab School for comparative reading ability in English and French, using Thorndike-McCall reading test and a similarly constructed French adaptation, showed decreasing differences in ability to read the two for study purposes throughout the four-year program. Statistical tables show results. Suggests more readily available alternate test material. DG

————.

"The Relationship between Audio and Visual Thought Comprehension in French," *French Review*, XXI (February, 1948), 300-305.

Audio comprehension tests appropriate to four years of courses were correlated with visual thought comprehension. Correlation for 205 seventh- to tenth-grade pupils at University of Chicago Lab School was .792, indicating reading in larger thought groups may be a carry-over from the aural approach. Suggests more extensive research at a less specialized institution. DG

Bovée, Arthur G., and G. J. Froelich
"Some Observations on the Relationship between Mental Ability and Achievement in French," *School Review*, LIII (November, 1945), 534-37; *Modern Language Journal*, XXX (October, 1946), 333-36.

Data from intelligence tests and scores on Cooperative French tests were compared to see if there was any correlation. It was found that extremely weak achievement in first- and second-year courses was related to low intelligence; that strong achievement in first-year course had only negligible relationship to mental ability. In advanced courses requiring individual initiative, achievement again correlated with intelligence. Investigators suggest that attention be given mental ratings when counseling continuation of work in French. BP

Brosnahan, L. F.
"Some Aspects of the Child's Mastery of the Sounds in a Foster-Language," *Studia Linguistica,* XIV (1960), 85-94.

General similarity of the vocal tract in human beings is but one of the factors which account for the ease by which a child acquires the phonemic and phonetic habits of a foster-language community. Overlap of *champs de dispersion* of phonemes, universal facts of phonemic-phonetic structure, and especially the process of acculturation of the child to the foster community are significant contributing factors. From Simon Belasco, *et al.,* February, 1962, Part I.

Brown, Charles T.
"Studies in Listening Comprehension," *Speech Monographs,* XXVI (November, 1959), 288-94.

In this research project I studied the role of anticipatory set in listening, the importance of theoretical interest in listening, and the importance of word association in listening. The Educational Testing Service Test of Listening Comprehension was used to measure listening ability. The data indicate that listener anticipation of the purposed of a message is an important factor in comprehension. The data show that high theoretical interest, as measured by the Allport, Vernon, Lindzy *Study of Values* [Gordon Willard Allport, and Philip E. Vernon, *Study of Values* (Boston: Houghton Mifflin, 1931)] tends to assure good listening comprehension. The reverse is not true. The data do not indicate a relation between the quantity of word association and listening comprehension. Charles T. Brown, MLabstract #295.

Brown, Roger W.
"Linguistic Determinism and the Part of Speech," *Journal of Abnormal and Social Psychology,* LV (July, 1957), 1-5.

Investigation of thesis that grammatical features of a language can affect cognition, here concerning allocation of words to a part of speech. Comparison of semantic distinction between noun and verb in adult and child speech. Experiment to test distinction by children. JAD

Brown, Roger W., and Eric H. Lenneberg
"A Study in Language and Cognition," *Journal of Abnormal and Social Psychology*, XLIX (July, 1954), 454-62.

Discussion of Whorf thesis that "the world is differently experienced and conceived in different linguistic communities." Experiment in recognition of color and codability of color in English and suggested relationship of experiment to similar ones in different languages. JAD

Brown, Roger, and Ursula Bellugi
"Three Processes in the Child's Acquisition of Syntax," *Harvard Educational Review*. XXXIV, No. 2 (1964), 133-151.

The study describes three processes involved in the child's acquisition of syntax. It is shown that of these processes, the induction of latent structure is by far the most complex. It is possible that this process will prove to be a deterent on any learning theory thus far conceived by psychology. CBC

Carroll, John B.
An Application of Psycholinguistics in Language Teaching: An Audio-Visual Instructional Device. A paper prepared for the Twelfth Annual Round Table Meeting on Linguistics and Language Studies, Institute of Language and Linguistics, Georgetown University, Washington, D.C., April 21-22, 1961 (mimeographed).

Carroll describes the machine he designed for audiovisual instruction of foreign languages, and how material is programed for the machine. BP

————.

"Communication Theory, Linguistics and Psycholinguistics," *Review of Educational Research*, XXVIII (April, 1958), 79-88.

A bibliographical analysis referring to the three subjects cited in the title of the article. JM

————.

Language and Thought. Englewood Cliffs, New Jersey: Prentice-Hall, Inc., 1964.

This work combines the disciplines of linguistics and psychology as an introductory view to the psychology of language. A basic notion of phonology, morphology, and syntax of language is presented as a description of speech utterances. Speech is analyzed as a consequence of some kind of thought or cognition, even though language structure may channel or influence thought. The major breakdown of contents are: (1) the learning of language, (2) aspects of language behavior, (3) individual differences in language behavior, (4) cognition and thinking, and (5) language and cognition. CBC

———.

"Language Development," in C. W. Harris (ed.), *Encyclopedia of Educational Research,* third edition. New York, Macmillan, 1960. Pp. 744-52.

In this article I review research and theory relating to the development of language in the child, considering the following topics: the nature of language, the language learning process, methodology of research, aspects of language development, stages of development, conditions affecting language development, the functions of language in the life of child, and implications for language-arts teaching. John B. Carroll, MLabstract #357.

———.

"Some Psychological Effects of Language Structure," in Paul H. Hoch (ed.), *Psychopathology of Communication.* New York: Grune and Stratton, 1958. Pp. 28-36.

Rejects as improbable both the null hypothesis "that there is no relation (other than a trivial one) between language structure and cognitive process," and the mold theory of Sapir and Whorf, that "our perceptions are possible only within the 'molds' provided by [the] language structure" that we have learned. Proposes for investigation a "lattice theory": that language structure is like a lattice or screen through which we see the world of our experience; it predisposes one to make certain discriminations, but does not prevent one from making any others. HLN

———.

Southwest Project in Comparative Psycholinguistics. (Sponsored by the Committee on Linguistics and Psychology.)

Purpose: To make experimental tests of the general hypothesis that the structure of language affects thought and behavior in different ways for speaking of different languages. DG

———.

The Study of Language. Cambridge, Mass.: Harvard University Press, 1953.

See especially chapter 3 on psycholinguistics. Discusses the nature of language behavior. Shows relationship between behavior and structural units. Implication of the Shannon-Weaver communication theory. Also reports on research on the strength of linguistic response, the child's learning of morphology and syntax, and individual differences in linguistic response. Daniel F. Delakas

Carroll, John B., and Joseph B. Casagrande
"The Effect of Linguistic Classifications on Sorting Behavior," in Eleanor E. Raccoby *et al.* (eds.), *Readings in Social Psychology.* New York: Henry Holt and Co., 1958. Pp. 18-32.

Discusses two experiments designed to explore the linguistic relativity hypothesis, i.e., a person's behavior is a function of the language he speaks. One experiment deals with the manner in which drawings are associated with actions by Hopi-language speakers as compared with English speakers. Methodology and limitations are explained, and tables are presented. In general, the hypothesis seems to be supported. Recommendations for improvement of methodology are listed. The second experiment attempts to show that behavior can be influenced by grammatical phenomena as well as lexical and semantic phenomena. The tests were applied to Navaho-speaking children. A specific hypothesis was formulated. Testing required a revision of the hypothesis, but in general the influence of grammatical phenomena was supported. JM

Carton, Aaron S. New York University, New York, New York.
The "Method of Inference" in Foreign Language Comprehension, Learning, and Retention (Phase I); Project No. OE-4-14-021 (National Defense Education Act, Title VI), September 9, 1963, to September 8, 1964; $40,768.

The contractor is conducting research and experimentation to develop procedures for encouraging and systematizing the use of inference and analogy in the learning of foreign languages. For the purpose of this study, inference and analogy involve the processes whereby one learns the meaning and use of new words and linguistic structures through perception of partial similarities to previously learned expressions.

The project's initial phase involves recruitment of personnel and enlisting the cooperation of selected secondary schools, followed by development of teaching techniques and test materials. The project staff and teacher-experimenters will plan the second phase of the project, application of the methods in selected high schools, at a workshop during the spring and summer of 1964.

Curran, Charles A.
See Curran, 2.1.

Doob, Leonard W.
"The Effect of Language on Verbal Expression and Recall," *American Anthropologist,* LIX (February, 1957), 88-100.

Controlled experiment with African and Afrikaaner secondary-school students of English, testing effect of English on verbal expression and recall. Statistical analysis of results and evaluation. JAD

Fox, Bernard, and Joseph Rabbin
"The Retention of Material Presented during Sleep," *Journal of Experimental Psychology,* XLIII (1952), 75-79.

Report of an experiment performed with pretested groups in a controlled situation to determine if hearing material during sleep facilitated learning. A list of Chinese words was used with the problem to remember English equivalents. The facilitation group learned the list correctly in a smaller number of trials than did the control group, or the group where wrong answers were presented during sleep instead of correct answers, as to the facilitation group, or music, as to the interference group. The authors concluded that learning can occur during sleep. Bibliography. MJS

Gibson, Eleanor J., *et al.*
See Gibson, 4.3.

Hall, Edward T.
See Hall, 5.

Hocking, Elton, Carroll Weisiger, and W. Merle Hill
Disordered Communication Processes Associated with Foreign Language Learning. Lafayette, Ind.: Purdue University, December, 1962 (mimeographed).

Final Report of the project described on pp. 125-26, 1962 volume of this Bibliography. Three separate studies are described: An Experimental Study of the Relation Between Auditory Discrimination Abilities and the Learning of French Pronunciation, The Prediction of Academic Achievement in First-Semester College German, Studies in the Psychology of Learning. DF

Howes, Davis
"On the Relation between the Probability of a Word as an Association and in General Linguistic Usage," *Journal of Abnormal and Social Psychology,* LIV (January 1957), 75-85.

Question: Does the specialized nature of the instructional set and other conditions attendant upon the experimental situation invalidate the word-association experiment as a method for quantitative analysis of linguistic behavior? In order to test this, an experiment was carried out on one property of language. The distribution of word frequencies was selected. Statistical analysis indicates a person's selection of words is not affected by the artificial laboratory situation required for the association experiment. Log tables shown. MJS

Hoyt, William George
The Effect on Learning of Auditory Material Presented During Sleep. Unpublished Masters thesis, George Washington University, 1953.

An attempt is made to determine whether learning Chinese-English word pairs is affected by material presented during sleep if sleeping subjects are observed during the period of presentation and if the sequence of presented word pairs is systematically varied. The subjects are twenty undergraduate and graduate students at George Washington University. Three experimental groups are formed, the facilitation group (who learn ten paired English-Chinese words during sleep), the interference group (presented ten unpaired words during sleep), and the control group (no material presented during sleep). A comparison of the posttest learning scores shows that the difference in mean number of trials between the facilitation and interference groups is not only insignificant but indicates a greater degree of learning for the latter group. Center for Documentation and Communication Research, Western Reserve University.

Jakobovits, Leon A.
Effects of Repeated Stimulation on Cognitive Aspects of Behavior: Some Experiments on the Phenomenon of Semantic Satiation. Unpublished Ph.D. dissertation, McGill University, 1962.

Gives a theoretical analysis within the behavioral psychology tradition of cognitive activity. Reports of experiments on the effects of repeated presentation of linguistic symbols upon learning and problem solving. The main thesis relates to the detrimental effects of too much repetition. Leon A. Jakobovits.

————.

The Effects of Repetition in Stuttering: A Theoretical Analysis. Paper presented at the Fifth Regional Conference of The Speech and Hearing Society of the Province of Quebec, Montreal, Canada, May, 1963.

A theoretical analysis of stuttering in terms of the concept of semantic satiation. Includes research proposals. Is relevant to the problem of language teaching of abnormal individuals. Leon A. Jakobivits. Copy obtainable from the author at the Department of Psychology, McGill University, Montreal, Quebec, Canada.

———.

"Stimulus Characteristics as Determinants of Semantic Changes with Repeated Presentation," *American Journal of Psychology,* to appear.

Experimental findings on the changes in meaning which occur with repeated presentation of words and objects and pictures. Is relevant to language teaching methods (especially the audio-visual techniques). Leon A. Jakobovits

Jakobovits, Leon A., and Wallace E. Lambert
Semantic Satiation in an Addition Task. Montreal: McGill University, September, 1960 (ditto).

An investigation to extend the concept of semantic satiation. As a more objective testing method, mathematical symbols were used instead of language symbols. The results support the idea that oral repetition of the symbol by the subject causes the loss of the meaning of that symbol. Nine references are included. JM

†Jakobovits, Leon, and William F. Mackey, Laval University, Quebec, Canada
A Psycholinguistic Study of Measurable Factors in Second-Language Learning. Research in progress.

This study aims to base its results on techniques for the measurement of individual variations in the mastery of foreign phonetic features, morphological and lexical rates of intake and the comparative learnability of items and structures presented ostensibly, pictorially, differentially and in various types of verbal contexts. William F. Mackey

Kilpatrick, Joel Fred
A Differential Analysis of Language and Nonlanguage Abilities of Seventh-Grade Boys and Girls. Unpublished Ed. D. dissertation, University of Texas, 1961.

The purpose of this investigation was to determine if certain cognitive and noncognitive measures of seventh-grade boys and girls are related significantly to language and nonlanguage abilities. The Ss were 126 boys and 126 girls selected on the basis of differential combinations of low, average, and high CTMM Language and Nonlanguage IQ. Sixteen cognitive and 13 noncognitive measures were analyzed in a 2x3x3 analysis of variance design. [...] The findings of this investigation suggest strongly that cognitive measures of seventh-grade boys and girls are associated significantly but differentially to the levels of L and N represented in this experimental population. From the abstract.

Kinney, Jo Ann S.
"Discrimination in Auditory and Visual Patterns," *American Journal of Psychology,* LXXIV (December, 1961), 529-41.

The effect of two variables on temporal discrimination in auditory patterns and on spatial discrimination in visual patterns was measured. The two variables were the type of pattern, or the manner in which the elements were combined, and the degree of separation between elements. The patterns were transformed between the two senses by making frequency in audition comparable to the vertical dimension of visual space, and time in audition comparable to the horizontal dimension of visual space. Temporal discrimination in auditory patterns was better when the elements in the pattern were of relatively near frequencies than when they were widely separated. This outcome was in accord with the visual result of better spatial discrimination when the elements were close together in the vertical dimension than when they were far apart. Jo Ann S. Kinney.

Korchin, S. J., and S. Levine
"Anxiety and Verbal Learning," *Journal of Abnormal and Social Psychology,* LIV (1957), 234-40.

Does anxiety facilitate and organize behavior, particularly with respect to learning, or does it tend to disruptive effects? The verbal-learning tests consisted of two parts—word associates and false equations—and two groups received the tests under different conditions; those with lower anxiety performed better than those with higher anxiety, especially on the word association tests. Tables, scores, discussion, and bibliography. MJS

Korwin, Roy
The Learning and Retention of Material Presented by Means of Multiple-Choice Items. Unpublished Ph.D. dissertation, Indiana University, 1962.

Subjects in nine treatment groups are taught Russian words using programed workbooks containing multiple-choice items. The number of incorrect alternatives is varied (2, 3, and 2) and three levels of difficulty of items are employed. A recall and a recognition test are administered after instruction. A significant increase in time taken to complete the learning phase is found as the number and difficulty of the alternatives increases, but no significant differences in recall or retention are found. Center for Documentation and Communication Research, Western Reserve University.

Lambert, Philip

"Should Parents Study Languages Too?" *Elementary School Journal,* LX (December, 1959), 124-27.

The study inquires into the effect of parental reinforcement on the learning of French. One experiment intends to determine if a child who is taking French does better if one of his parents is studying the language at the same time. The conclusion was that there was no influence. A second experiment intends to find out if children whose parents already know some French learn better than children whose parents know little or no French. Analysis here shows no difference. The article concludes with a discussion of possibilities for the results in terms of the parental problems. Recommendations for further experiments are suggested. JM

Lambert, Wallace E.

"Psychological Approaches to the Study of Language. Part I: On Learning, Thinking and Human Abilities," *Modern Language Journal,* XLVII (February, 1963), 51-62.

This paper introduces contemporary psychological theories and associated research efforts dealing with language. Two contrasting theories of learning are reviewed, that of B. F. skinner on verbal behavior, and that of C. E. Osgood on the learning of meanings. Finally, the theories and research of J. Carroll and C. A. Ferguson on human aptitudes and abilities were discussed and related to language learning abilities. Implications of each of these movements in psychology for teachers of foreign languages were alluded to. Wallace E. Lambert, MLabstract #523.

————.

"Psychological Approaches to the Study of Language. Part II: On Second-Language Learning and Bilingualism," *Modern Language Journal,* XLVII (March, 1963), 114-21.

In this part, a review is presented of psychological studies of second-language learning and bilingualism, in particular those carried out at McGill University. As in the first part, an attempt was made to relate psychological approaches to the study of language to the problems faced by language teachers and to encourage them to become better acquainted with these movements. Wallace E. Lambert, MLabstract #524.

Lambert, Wallace E., and Sandra F. Witelson

Concurrent and Consecutive Orders of Learning Two Languages. Montreal: McGill University [1960?] (ditto).

A study to measure the comparative difficulty of acquiring a foreign vocabulary concurrently with the native language or consecutively. The method of the experiment was to simulate certain features of actual language learning by using colors and nonsense words as symbols and referents. Results show that concurrent learning is more time-consuming but is much more accurate in recall testing. Evaluation of testing methods and of the results is discussed. There are sixteen references listed. JM

†Lambert, Wallace E., and Grace Yeni-Komshian. McGill University, Montreal, Canada.
Concurrent and Consecutive Modes of Learning Two Languages. Research in progress, McGill University.

Lane, Harlan L.
"Temporal and Intensive Properties of Human Vocal Responding under a Schedule of Reinforcement," *Journal of the Experimental Analysis of Behavior,* III (1960), 183-192.

————.

"Acquisition and Transfer in Auditory Discrimination," *American Journal of Psychology,* LXXVII (1964), 240-48.

When auditory discrimination training is undertaken with human adults the effect of their prior history of reinforcement is certain to play a major role in the course of learning. This history may manifest itself in the extensive control of discriminative behavior observed at the outset of training, or it may appear as a discontinuity in the development of differential responding—an abrupt increase to nearly complete stimulus control. There seem to be few, if any, auditory continua that do not sample, at least in part, the subject's prior discriminative repertory. Harlan L. Lane

————.

"Differential Reinforcement of Vocal Duration," *Journal of the Experimental Analysis of Behavior,* VII (1964), 107-15.

The effects of differential reinforcement of vocal duration were examined in a series of experiments in which a total of 28 subjects emitted a single vowel each time a light was flashed. After establishing a baseline duration under continuous reinforcement (in which pennies were dispensed to *S*), the experimenter selectively reinforced those responses with durations greater than criterion. When ten successive responses were reinforced, a new criterion was determined and the experiment continued. The criterion for reinforcement was varied in the six experiments; it ranged from 80 to 120 per cent of the mean duration of precurrent responding, according to one of six schedules.

Differential reinforcement effected a large and systematic change in the duration of vocal responding as low as the responses selected for reinforcement had a sufficiently high probability of occurrence. Harlan L. Lane. The research reported herein is related to the project under Mr. Lane's name, 4.3.

Lane, Harlan L., and James L. Kopp
"The Effects of Response-Dependent and Independent Reinforcement in Extending Stimulus Control," *Psychological Records*, XIV, No. 1 (1964), 81-87.

Auditory generalization gradients of response probability and latency were obtained from human Ss under three conditions: (a) discrimination training was given to 500 cps tones at 56 and 74 db, and followed by generalization testing over eleven different intensity levels at 3 db intervals from 50 to 80 db (SPL); (b) an additional phase was interpolated between discrimination training and generalization testing, in which stimuli adjacent to the training stimuli were presented (62, 65, 68, and 71 db). All stimuli were followed by reinforcement and *there was no overt responding* during the interpolated phase; (c) the treatment was identical with that of (b), except that S gave an overt response during the interpolated phase. Differences in discrimination training failed to differentiate in generalization testing the group which received only the initial training phase and was then tested (control group) from the group which was presented with the additional stimuli of the interpolated phase and reinforced after each stimulus, independent of responding. Harlan L. Lane
The research reported herein is related to the project under Mr. Lane's name, 9.3.

Lane, Harlan L., and Bruce Schneider
"Methods for Self-Shaping Echoic Behavior," *Modern Language Journal*, XLVII (April, 1963), 154-60.

Six methods are described for the self-shaping of a minimal echoic operant in a foreign language and their effects on two parameters of stimulus-response correspondence are noted. During self-shaping, in which subjects imitated repeated presentations of a Thai toneme, the duration and pitch slope of echoic vocal responses stabilized at some value. This "steady state" did not necessarily have the same parameter values as those of the discriminative stimulus. The most effective method for self-shaping of response duration involved the use of a digital display. Echoic accuracy was highest and variability least when the display was present, and directly following its removal. Accuracy was poorest and variability greatest during the pre-test, prior to the introduction of the display, and in a post-test in which both the auditory stimulus and the display were removed. The efficacy of the technique is attributed to the simplification of the discriminative task required in self-shaping. Harlan L. Lane

———.

See Lane, 4.3.

Lane, Harlan L., and P. G. Shinkman
"Methods and Findings in an Analysis of a Vocal Operant," *Journal of Experimental Analysis of Behavior,* VI, (April, 1963), 179-88.

The relations among acoustic parameters of a vocal operant were considered and some methods for their measurement described. Four human subjects and one chick were employed in an experiment on the relations among vocal rate, vocal topography, and schedules of reinforcement control human and infra-human vocal responding as they do other operants was replicated and extended to the case of variable-interval reinforcement. An analysis of response amplitude, pitch, and duration showed that the mean and variance of these parameters typically increase from CRF to VI, from VI to EXT and, for a second group of subjects, from CRF to EXT. The topography of the check vocal response appears to stand in the same relation to reinforcement operations as that of the human vocal response. Harlan L. Lane

Lenneberg, Eric H.
"A Probabilistic Approach to Language Learning," *Behavioral Science,* II (January, 1957), 1-12.

Six groups of subjects were taught nonsense languages distributed over stimulus continuum exactly as English words brown, green, blue, pink. If reference relationships in nonsense language were same as subjects' native tongue, learning task was easy. Shift of category location on a stimulus continuum was less disturbing for second-language learning than any change in the aspect of reference. BP

Leopold, Werner F.
Kindersprache," *Phonetica,* IV (1959), 191-214.

Survey of research on child language. Bibliography brought up to date, supplementing *Bibliography of Child Language* (see, above, Part 1). Werner F. Leopold

———.

See Leopold, Part I.

McCarthy, Dorothea
"Language Development in Children," in L. Carmichael (ed.), *Manual of Child Psychology*. New York: John Wiley and Sons, 1954. Pp. 492-630.

A comprehensive and documented study of children's language development, including prelinguistic studies, imitation, gesture language, growth of vocabulary, sentence structure and form, and function of language in child's life. BP

†[Mace, Larry. University of California, Los Angeles, Calif.]
Sequence of Discrimination and Differentiation Training in the Teaching of French in the Early Primary Grades: First Progress Report. July 1, 1963 (ditto).

This project is a Ph. D. dissertation in progress, under a Title VI grant with Paul Pimsleur and Evan Keislar and others as advisers. The report describes three experiments done in connection with an "Exploratory study which viewed the acquisition or differentiation of utterances in French as a problem of verbal chaining." The first two experiments concerned the development of techniques and materials to be used in the third experiment. The third experiment attempted "To compare the efficacy of backward versus forward chaining in shaping vocal echoic responding in French sentences of approximately seven meaningful units (mostly words) in length." The results indicate that "The difference between the means for the backward and forward treatment groups favors the backward chaining procedure but is not statistically significant." DF

†————.

Sequence of Discrimination and Differentiation Training in the Teaching of French in the Early Primary Grades: Second Progress Report. October 1, 1963.

While the experiments described in the first report (see immediately above) dealt with meaningful utterances, the children involved were not aware of the meaning. In the three experiments subsequently carried out, described in this report, meaning was stressed. The three experiments consisted of two initial experiments to develop materials and techniques to be utilized in the third experiment. The third experiment intended "To test the hypothesis that the facility with which third-grade children will learn to associate (A) three spoken French words with their corresponding pictorial representations, and (B) three pictorial representations with their corresponding French grapheme will be a function of the number of related stimulus-response associations previously established." Re-

sults of various tests are presented in the report. Analysis and interpretation of those results are still underway. A summary of the work
of the first six months of the experiment is given. DF

Maclay, Howard S.
Language and Non-Linguistic Behavior: An Experimental Investigation. Unpublished Ph. D. dissertation, University of New Mexico, n.d.
    Experiment, using control groups, based on Sapir-Whorf hypoth-
esis that language has an influence on thought. Results show certain
relationships, but do not consistently confirm the association between
language and nonlinguistic behavior. BP

Mange, Charles V. Syracuse University, Syracuse, N.Y.
An Investigation of the Relationships between Articulatory Develop-
ment of Phonetic Discrimination and Word Synthesis Abilities in
Young Mentally Retarded Children and Normal Children; Project No.
SAE-6420 (United States Office of Education), December, 1956, to
February, 1959.
    The study investigates the "relationships between two auditory
perceptual abilities (phonetic discrimination and word synthesis) and
articulation development." Among the conclusions of the study:
"There is a low but positive relationship between the ability to
articulate accurately and the ability to make accurate phonetic discriminations during the years of articulation development in childhood.
Phonetic discrimination and word synthesis abilities are relatively
independent measures of auditory perceptual ability." JM

Morton, F. Rand, and Harlan L. Lane
Technique of Operant Conditioning Applied to Second Language
Learning," *Proceedings of the XIV International Congress of Applied
Psychology.* (1961), Copenhagen.

Mueller, Theodore
"Perception in Foreign Language Learning," *Modern Language
Journal,* XLII (April, 1958), 167-71.
    The article emphasizes that the student has great difficulty in
accurately hearing the sounds and therefore the acoustic syntactical
signals of the language. This observation has been further amply
demonstrated in my research with programmed learning. See my
First Quarterly Report—Trial Use of the French Program at the
University of Akron, Akron, Ohio. See Mueller, 4.5. Theodore
Mueller

Osgood, Charles E., *et al.*
"Psycholinguistics, a Survey of Theory and Research Problems,"

Supplement to the Journal of Abnormal and Social Psychology, Vol. XLIX (October, 1954).

Reports the 1953 Summer Seminar sponsored by the Committee on Linguistics and Psychology of the Social Science Research Council. Three differing approaches to the language process were explored in order to appraise their utility for handling different problems and to discover in what respects they could be brought into a common conceptual framework: (1) the linguist's conception of language as a structure of systematically interrelated units, (2) the learning theorist's conception of language as a system of habits relating signs to behavior, and (3) the information theorist's conception of language as a means of transmitting information. A number of basic research problems were examined, the theoretical backgrounds of these problems were analyzed, and possible experimental approaches to them were formulated. Also published as *Psycholinguistics: A Survey of Theory and Research Problems.* . . . Bloomington: Indiana University Press, 1965. Includes A. Richard Diebold, Jr., "A Survey of Psycholinguistic Research," pp. 205-91; and George A. Miller, "The Psycholinguists," pp. 293-307.

Pimsleur, Paul

"Incidental Learning in Foreign Language Learning," *Journal of Educational Research,* Vol. LIV (November, 1960).

Purpose of the experiment is to establish whether incidental learning takes place in a language-learning situation, and if so to what extent. Findings show that incidental learning does take place, that its effects are confined to tasks closely resembling the learning situation, that ability to profit from oral incidental learning is more closely related to a student's oral performance than written performance. BP

Pimsleur, Paul, and Robert J. Bonkowski

"Transfer of Verbal Material across Sense Modalities," *Journal of Educational Psychology,* LII (April, 1961), 104-7.

The experiment is designed to discover if aural learning aids visual learning, whether material should be presented first aurally or visually, whether in terms of time it is more economical to teach by aural-visual order than visual-aural order. The findings offer support for the view that aural instruction preceding visual instruction may have an advantage over the traditional system. BP

Proncko, N. H.

"Language and Psycholinguistics, a Review," *Psychological Bulletin,* XLIII (May, 1946), 189-239.

A comprehensive survey of the literature, studies, and theories of language and psycholinguistics of the three decades preceding the study. Primary emphasis: behavioral phases of language events. Bibliography of 201 items. MJS

Rivers, Wilga M.
The Psychologist and the Foreign-Language Teacher. Chicago: University of Chicago Press, 1964.
This book presents an overall study of the many theories of learning and makes a number of suggestions and recommendations for the modification or improvement of audio-lingual techniques which the practical teacher can apply to specific problems of foreign-language teaching. See also bibliography, pp. 194-201. CBC

Rufsvold, Margaret I., and Carolyn Guss
See Rufsvold, Part I.

Saporta, Sol, and Jarris R. Bastian (eds.)
Psycholinguistics: A Book of Readings. New York: Holt, Rinehard and Winston, 1961.
The book attempts to facilitate "interdisciplinary communication [between structural linguistics and behavioral psychology] by providing students of language with materials dealing with a variety of problems where collaboration between psychologists and linguists promises to be fruitful." Contents: (1) The Nature and Function of Language; (2) Approaches to the Study of Language; (3) Speech Perception; (4) The Sequential Organization of Linguistic Events; (5) The Semantic Aspects of Linguistic Events; (6) Language Acquisition, Bilingualism, and Language Change; (7) Pathologies of Linguistic Behavior; (8) Linguistic Processes to Perception and Cognition. DF

Sebeok, Thomas A.
Observations Concerning Analog and Digital Coding in Communication. Stanford, Calif.: Center for Advanced Study in the Behavioral Sciences, Stanford University, n.d. (mimeo).
Likens the elements of the mind's ability to digital counting and analog measuring of control machines. From this observation this paper discusses the hypothesis that human speech is coded both analogously and digitally. JM

Simches, Seymour O., ed. Tufts University, Medford, Mass.
Interdisciplinary Research Seminar of Psycholinguistics. Medford, Mass.: Tufts University, 1964.
Final Report of the seminar.

Skelton, Robert B.

"Factors Governing Retention in College," *Modern Language Journal,* XLIII (March, 1959), 143-46.

This study evaluates two factors related to college success—the sex of the student and previous foreign-language study. The investigator found the attrition rate of women students was approximately 18 per cent; of men, 35.3 per cent. Chances of surviving the first year of college were doubled if the student presented two years of previous foreign-language study. Foreign-language preparation was advantageous to all groups, especially those in the lower intelligence bracket. BP

Smith, Herbert A.

"The Relationship between Intelligence and the Learning Which Results from the Use of Educational Sound Motion Pictures, *Journal of Educational Research,* XLIII (December, 1949), 241-49.

In view of the relationship stated in the title, the experiments show that the gain in learning is related to degree of intelligence as measured by the tests used and is independent of the method of instruction. JM

Spilka, Irène Vachon

" Le rôle des attitudes dans l'acquisition d'une langue étrangère," *Le français dans le monde,* to appear.

Stolurow, Lawrence M.

Prompting vs. Confirmation Sequences and Overlearning in the Automated Teaching of Sight Vocabulary. Paper read at the American Psychological Association Annual Convention, Urbana, Illinois, September, 1961.

In this paper I report the results of a study which supports those of other investigators who used different materials and subjects but related procedures. A Prompting S-R sequence produces more rapid learning of a sight vocabulary than Confirmation S-R sequence. However, the data also extended previous research findings by indicating that retention under these two sequences is relatively different depending upon the amount of *overlearning* that is involved. With smaller amounts of overlearning a Prompt S-R sequence results in both better recall and better recognition for as long as one month, whereas with more overlearning, a Confirmation S-R sequence results in both better recall and recognition over the same period of time following original learning. An important pedagogical implication is that neither method by itself will do both things—produce rapid learning and better retention. The obvious pedagogical danger indicated by the study is the fallacy of assuming that a method which produces better learning also produces better retention. A second fallacy is the assumption that a method which is better for retention under one degree of overlearning also is better under the other degrees of overlearning. Lawrence M. Stolurow, MLabstract #192.

Suppes, Patrick
"Some Current Developments in Models of Learning for a Continuum of Responses," in *American Institute of Electrical Engineers 1962 Joint Automatic Control Conference*. Stanford, California: Stanford Institute for Mathematical Studies in the Social Sciences, Applied Mathematics and Statistics Laboratories, Stanford University, 1960.

The report states assumption and experimental application of the theory that each stimulus is conditioned to exactly one response and that for a continuum of responses the assumption of conditioning to exactly one response is psychologically unrealistic and mathematically awkward. JM

Suppes, Patrick G., Edward Crothers, and Ruth Weir
Application of Mathematical Learning Theory and Linguistic Analysis to Vowel Phoneme Matching in Russian Words. Stanford, Calif.: Institute for Mathematical Studies in the Social Sciences, Stanford University, Technical Report No. 51, Psychology Series, December, 1962.

American seventh-grade students learned an auditory vowel-matching task involving monosyllabic Russian words. The subject heard a word followed by three alternative words. His task was to select the word whose vowel sound was most similar to that in the initial word. The relative difficulty of the vowels was determined and interpreted according to linguistic rationales. The statistical properties of the learning data were analyzed in terms of stochastic models. Patrick G. Suppes

Taylor, Martha L.
"Linguistic Considerations of the Verbal Behavior of the Brain Damaged Adult," *Linguistic Reporter*, VI (June, 1964), 1-2.

Recent research in the field of psycholinguistics has offered the possibility of discovering something about "normal" language by studying aberrations of verbal behavior. This article discusses the two major categories of verbal impairment resulting from brain damage, aphasia and dysarthria. Mrs. Taylor describes the characteristics of these two categories and refers to several notable observations with respect to language "aberration" of considerable interest and possible importance is her statement that "[the] extent to which clusters of language skills are affected by brain damage should cast considerable light on the organization of these skills in normal language function [. . .]." The article is a rewritten abstract of a paper delivered at the 1962 annual conference of the National Association of Foreign Student Advisers (now the National Association for Foreign Student Affairs) in Washington, D. C. DF

Titone, Renzo
La Psicolinguistica Oggi. Rome: Pas-Verlag, 1964.

    I have tried to go beyond the early attempts toward a synthesis of psycholinguistic study and research data. This book runs along the lines drawn by the reports of the 1953 Indiana University Seminar edited by C. A. Osgood and T. Sebeok. The novelty in it consists in an original systematization of the scientific material concerning psycholinguistic problems and data, and especially in a wider and deeper interpretation of such findings from the point of view of an eclectic psychology of language phenomena. Besides the effort aiming at concentrating an imposing mass of data, I have also tried to assemble a vast commented bibliography consisting of 328 items taken from the international literature on the subject. R. Titone, MLabstract # 781

————.

Studies in the Psychology of Second Language Learning. Rome: PAS-Verlag, 1964.

    In this book I call the attention of all concerned with foreign language teaching to the indispensable *psychological premises* which can guarantee successful learning. My efforts have attempted both partial theoretical syntheses and experimental probings with regard to some important factors and aspects of the language learning process. This latest book of mine collects these studies and investigations as an elementary introduction to the psychology of second language learning. The contents of the book are as follows: (1) The psychology of second-language learning, (2) Second-language learning in early childhood, (3) Second-language learning in adolescents, (4) Grammar learning as induction, (5) The aural discrimination of foreign language phonemes: an experimental constrastic study, (6) Problems in phonetic and transcription: an experimental contrastive study. Renzo Titone, MLabstract #724.

Vicory, Arthur C.
The Paired-Associate Task as a Predictor of Foreign Language Fluency. Unpublished Masters Thesis, San Jose State College, August, 1963.

Many linguists have expressed doubt that information from experiments using the paired-associate task has relevancy for the problem of foreign language learning. This study at the Army Language School, Presidio of Monterey, demonstrated almost perfect validity coefficients between an oral paired-associate task of English to Polish items, administered before training, and criterion measures of fluency in Polish (paired-comparison ratings by instructors) collected after the 1st, 2nd, and 6th month of intensive language training. The implications are explored for the paired-associate task as a specific versus a general language predictor. Arthur C. Vicory

von Raffler-Engel, Walburga
"Appunti sul linguaggio infantile," *Scuola e Città,* anno XV, 12 (Dec., 1964) pp. 660-3.
Describes the problems of analyzing the language of children.

———.

Il prelinguaggio infantile, Brescia: Paideia, 1964. Studi grammaticali e linguistici, No. 7.
Summarized in a forthcoming article whose title formulates the main conclusion of the study: "L'intonazione come prima espressione linguistica dell' infante," *Il Lattante, Rivista mensile di fisiologia e clinica della prima infanzia.* [1965].

Weir, Ruth H.
Language in the Crib. The Hague: Mouton, 1962.
Language in the crib can be taken quite literally—the subject matter of this book is an analysis of monologues of a two-and-a-half year old child lying in his crib, talking to himself. The linguistic structure is described on several levels, with regard to the structures which have been learned well, those which are being learned, and those which are still absent in comparison with standard English. On the level of sound, the phonemes are broken down into their component features in order to arrive at a clearer picture of the child's linguistic development. The analysis of sentences as the highest structural unit within the monologues did not provide a complete enough picture of the nature of the material, and hence a paragraph analysis is included. The various functions of language are discussed in their hierarchical arrangements. This book will also be viewed more broadly as a contribution to a better understanding of the linguistic development in children. The material is analyzed by modern descriptive linguistic techniques, and the presence or absence of structural signals in the language of a child between two and three years of age gives us

valuable clues to the identification of linguistic universals. The analysis is based on recorded soliloquies, the child's version of inner speech which has been interiorized psychologically, but not physically. It is suggestive of an insight into adult inner speech. Since the soliloquies are often in the form of dialogues, this could in turn be considered as supportive of the notion that it is the dialogue and not the monologue which is the primary form of language. Ruth H. Weir, MLabstract # 795

Werner, Heinz, and Edith Kaplan
"Development of Word Meaning through Verbal Context: An Experimental Study," *Journal of Psychology,* XXIX (April, 1950), 251-57.

This study concerns the relationship between the semantic and grammatical aspects of language. A test was devised to determine how children reacted to artificial words with assigned meaning. Results indicate a genetic interdependence of meaning and structure. MJS

Wimer, Cynthia, and W. E. Lambert
"The Differential Effects of Word and Object Stimuli on the Learning of Paired Associates," *Journal of Experimental Psychology,* LVII (1959), 31-36.

Subjects learned nonsense syllable responses paired with either words, objects, or a combination of the two as stimuli. Both the word-syllable and the mixed list were significantly more difficult than the object-syllable list. No difference in the "meaningfulness" of the words and objects was found, and the results were attributed to greater intra-list similarity among words than among objects. Implications for the direct vs. the indirect method of language-learning are discussed. Wallace E. Lambert

Wittenborn, J. Richard, *et al.*
"Empirical Evaluation of Study Habits for College Courses in French and Spanish," *Journal of Educational Psychology,* XXXVI (November, 1945), 449-74.

The third in a series of studies conducted among students of freshman and sophomore French and Spanish classes at the University of Illinois, in an effort to determine what if any habits of study are conducive to good results in learning a foreign language. One hundred and seven test items were administered, and later broken down into three broad categories. The French form of the questionnaire was validated against grades earned in courses and against objective examination scores; the Spanish, against course grades. Results: (1)

It was possible to demonstrate important relationships between a large group of study habits and the criteria. (2) Study-habit items retain predictive significance. Other results of interest. Tables included. MJS

Wolfle, Dael
  "Training," in Stanley S. Stevens (ed.), *Handbook of Experimental Psychology*. New York: John Wiley and Sons, 1951. Pp. 1267-86.
    Discusses six general principles of learning that have evolved from laboratory studies: (1) knowledge of results, (2) avoidance of habit interference, (3) variety of practice materials, (4) methods used in training, (5) knowledge of principles involved, and (6) effectiveness of guidance. BP

3.3 Aptitude and Prognosis Tests

Buros, Oscar Krisen (ed.)
  The Fourth Mental Measurements Yearbook. Highland Park, N.J.: Gryphon, 1953.
    The purpose of the volume is to aid test users to locate and evaluate tests available and books on testing. The book covers the fields of education, industry, psychiatry, and psychology. BP

————.
  See Buros, Part I.

Carroll, John B.
  "A Factor Analysis of Two Foreign Language Batteries," *Journal of General Psychology*, LIX (July, 1958), 3-19.
    Identified five factors regarded as relevant to success in learning foreign languages, on the basis of tests administered to Air Force language trainees. John B. Carroll.

————.
  "Language and Education," *The Study of Language*. Cambridge: Harvard University Press, 1953. Pp. 168-95.
    Discusses measurement of aptitude for audiolingual learning. Nine tests. See above, 3.1. Material current to 1952. Daniel F. Delakas

————.
  Modern Language Aptitute Test, Form A. New York: Psychological Corp., 1958.
    This standardized, validated test for predicting success in foreign languages is designed for high school, college, and adult students. It

requires about one hour to administer, or a half-hour for a so-called "short form." John B. Carroll

†————.

A Parametric Study of Language Training in the Peace Corps; Project No. PC-(W)-226 (Peace Corps), June 1, 1963 to June 30, 1965; $53,317.59.

Seeks to establish the parameters of language learning in a well-controlled intensive training situation: given information on the student's level of language aptitude, prior training in the language, motivation, etc., how much achievement can one expect him to attain after a specified number of hours of exposure to foreign language instruction? Data from 12-week training courses in Spanish and Portuguese will be studied, as well as follow-up data on performance of Peace Corps Volunteers in using their language skills in the field. John B. Carroll

————.

"The Prediction of Success in Intensive Foreign Language Training," in Robert Glaser (ed.), *Training Research and Education*. Pittsburgh: University of Pittsburgh Press, 1962. Pp. 87-136.

Reports "research on the measurement of aptitude for foreign language learning," and outlines "the major findings that are applicable to the screening of personnel for military and governmental programs for intensive or semiintensive foreign language training." One of the main propositions demonstrated is that "facility in learning to speak and understand a foreign language is a fairly specialized talent relatively independent of . . . intelligence." JG

Carroll, John B., and Stanley M. Sapon
Cross Validation of Foreign Language Aptitude Tests with a Second Air Force Trial Course Sample. (Harvard Language Aptitude Project, Report No. 2.) Cambridge, Mass.: Harvard University, February, 1955 (ditto).

Describes revised phonetic discrimination tests which expand the use of auditory memory. Describes also four new tests that involve the *learning* of new language material. The results of the new tests show a cross-validation of the first battery of tests set forth in Report No. 1. Statistical evidence is reported. JM Superseded by Psi Lambda Foreign Language Aptitude Battery. Cambridge, Mass.: Harvard University, 1955.

————.

"Prediction of Success in a Work-Sample Course in Mandarin

Chinese," *American Psychologist,* X (1955), 492-93.

Preliminary report of research indicating high validities for certain tests of foreign language aptitude. The results are summarized in my paper called "Prediction of Success in Intensive Foreign Language Training," next entry. John B. Carroll

*Carroll, John B., Stanley M. Sapon, and S. Earle Richards
Construction and Validation of a Test Battery for Predicting Success in Spoken Foreign Language Courses. (Harvard Language Aptitude Project, Report No. 1.) Cambridge, Mass.: Harvard University, June, 1954 (mimeographed).

Cox, F. N.
"The Prediction of Success and Failure in Learning Foreign Languages," *Australian Journal of Psychology,* VII (June, 1955), 56-65.

Description of a study undertaken at the RAAF Language School in Australia. The study dealt with validity of previously used measuring devices and also with the nature of the personality variable associated with success and failure in learning foreign languages. Data and research under the headings Intelligence and Personality are discussed. A discussion of the results of the study points to general verbal proficiency and the measurement thereof as of prime importance rather than any general "aptitude." Stress is placed upon considering personality factors such as motivation and emotional stability. DF

Dunkel, Harold B.
See Dunkel, 3.7.

Elmgren, John
"The Linguistic Maturity Investigation," *School and Psychology: A Report on the Research Work of the 1946 School Commission.* Stockholm: Esselte, 1952. Pp. 225-45.

Chapter 5 refers to the "Linguistic Maturity Investigation." Describes a number of tests directed toward determining the appropriate age level to begin language teaching, what approach is most effective, and stresses differences in ability due to difference in sex. Tests are described. Conclusions show that girls mature linguistically at an earlier age. Testing presupposed knowledge of grammar. JM

*Françoise-Thérèse, Soeur
A quel facteur attribuer la cause principale du peu de succès dans l'enseignement de la langue seconde au cours primaire? Université de Laval, Thèse de licence en pédagogie, 1960.

*Frith, James R.
Selection for Language Training by a Trial Course. Washington, D. C.: Georgetown University Press, 1953. Also published in the Georgetown University *Monograph Series on Language and Linguistics,* 1953.

Harding, Francis D., Jr.
"Tests as Selectors of Language Students," *Modern Language Journal,* XLII (March, 1958), 120-22.

    The conclusion of the study is that a one-hour battery of aptitude tests was as effective as four-week trial course in selecting Russian-language trainees. BP

Harding, Francis D., Jr., and William S. Jenkins
Prediction of Performance in Foreign Language Training Courses. Lackland Air Force Base, Texas: Personnel Laboratory, Wright Air Development Division, Air Research and Development Command, United States Air Force, June 8, 1960 (mimeo).

    This paper reports additional findings concerning a study on the relationships between aptitude measures and success in language training. Using the criterion whether the student finished among the upper half of the graduates in his class or among the lower half, the Psi Lambda Test (see above, John B. Carroll) was found to be valid for predicting performance in Russian as well as in other languages. DF

Hascall, Edward O.
Predicting Success in High School Foreign Language Study. Un-published Ph.D. dissertation, University of Michigan, 1959.

    The purpose of the study was to determine the predictive value of scores in tests on English skills, aptitudes, interests, etc., with a view to improving counseling of high school students in foreign-language study. The findings were that variables showed greater predictive validity for boys than for girls. The best predictors for both sexes were previous marks in English courses, certain Differential Aptitude scores, and the Stanford Achievement Tests. BP See following item.

————.

"Predicting Success in High School Foreign Language Study," *Personnel and Guidance Journal,* XL (December, 1961), 361-67.

    In this article I attempted to determine the relative predictive value of certain variables—skills, aptitudes, interests and personal factors—in relation to success in high school foreign language study. The subjects were eight hundred boys and girls enrolled in first-year foreign language courses. The criteria against which the predictors were validated were teachers' marks and Cooperative Foreign Language Test scores at the end of the first year of language study. The findings indicated that (1) the relative predictve validity of the several variables varies from one sex to the other; (2) variables tend to show relatively greater predictive validity for boys than for girls; (3) the best predictors for both sexes and for both criteria seem to be teachers' marks in previous English courses and certain achievement and aptitude scores; (4) there seems to be no significant relationship between the criteria and inventoried interests, language spoken in the home, parents' educational background, students' educational and vocational plans, and students' expressed reasons for studying a foreign language. Edward O. Hascall, MLabstract #583.

Hocking, Elton, Carroll Weisiger, and W. Merle Hill
See Hocking, 3.1.

Hughes, Vergil H.
A Study of the Relationships among Selected Language Abilities. Unpublished Ph.D. dissertation, University of Missouri, 1950.
      The purpose of the study was to determine the extent of the relationship among certain language abilities and to determine the extent that achievement in one language area is indicative of comparable achievement in another. It was found that high achievement in any one language area was related to higher-than-average achievement in any other area. BP

Leutenegger, Ralph, Theodore Mueller, and Irving Wershow
Auditory Factors in Foreign Language Acquisition. Project No. OE-3-14-024 (U. S. Office of Education), completed August 15, 1963.
      Scores were obtained for 283 French and 177 Spanish students on the following: six subtests of the Seashore Measures of Musical Talents, five scores on the Committee on Diagnostic Reading Survey Test, one score on the ETS English Expression Test, and three scores on the School and College Ability Test (SCAT). French students achieved significantly higher scores than Spanish students on 8 of the 15 variables. On 7 of the variables, females achieved significantly higher scores than males. Course completors had significantly higher scores than drop-outs on Rhythm, Verbal SCAT, Total SCAT, and English. Multiple Regression techniques were applied to the data for each language separately by sex. Language-acquisition prediction equations were evolved for French females and for Spanish males

only. None of the variables emerged as significant for French males and Spanish females. The findings suggest that variables other than those studied need to be considered to achieve more powerful equations. Ralph Leutenegger

Leutenegger, Ralph R., and Theodore H. Mueller
See Leutenegger and Mueller, 2.3 French.

MacNaughton, Jacquelin, and Margarete R. Altenheim
"An Investigation of Prognosis in German," *Modern Language Journal,* XXXIV (November, 1950), 553-60.

An investgation was made at Hunter College to discover a means of predicting success in the study of German. It was found that the prognosis test was a more reliable indicator than the artificial language test. Student background was also taken into consideration. Students of German background achieved greater success than any other group. Hunter College High School students had slightly greater success than students from a Yiddish-speaking background. Students with neither German, Yiddish, nor Hunter College High School background had poorest grades. BP

Manuel, Herschel T.
"Modern Language Aptitude Test," *Personnel and Guidance Journal,* XXXVIII (March, 1960), 582-84.

In this review article, Manuel describes the objectives of the MLAT, which is divided into five parts: (1) number learning, (2) phonetic script, (3) spelling clues, (4) words in sentences, (5) paired associates. The test is a result of five years of research at Harvard. It is designed to predict an individuals' degree of success in learning a foreign language. Manual that accompanies the aptitude tests gives information as to administration and evaluation of tests. JM

Mendeloff, Henry
See Mendeloff, 2.56.

Nardi, Noach
"Test to Measure Aptitude in the Hebrew Language," *Journal of Educational Psychology,* XXXVIII (March, 1947), 167-76.

Description of a test designed to predict the degree of success that a pupil will have in learning Hebrew. Five subtests, whose reliability and validity were determined, were administered to three hundred students, beginners in Hebrew. Correlations were established —after one to four years of Hebrew study—between the aptitude scores and teachers' marks and were found to be quite satisfactory. The Hebrew aptitude scores showed higher prediction in achievement of Hebrew than that obtained by intelligence tests. MJS

Peters, Harold C.
"Prediction of Success and Failure in Elementary Foreign Language Courses," *Journal of Applied Psychology,* XXXVII (June, 1953), 178-81.

A preliminary study of methods of selecting students from enlisted personnel for the Marine Corps Language School, which required a speaking and reading mastery of the Japanese language in six months. Total of eight tests were used, yielding twenty-one separate scores. Two classifications of students tested are described. Tables presented showing ratios of successes and failures give comparative results of the prediction tests. These criteria, however, are not a pure measure of ability. JM

Pike, E. V.
"A Test for Predicting Phonetic Ability," *Language Learning,* IX, Nos. 1 and 2 (1959), 35-41.

This is a report of a pilot test for grouping phonetics students according to potential ability. Tests proved fairly reliable with a high correlation between scores and achievement. BP

Pimsleur, Paul
"Predicting Achievement in Foreign Language Learning," *International Journal of American Linguistics,* XXIX (April, 1963, Part III), 129-36.

In this article I describe a test battery for predicting FL achievement and diagnosing FL learning difficulties. Sample items are given from 4 tests: Linguistic Analysis, Interest, Sound Symbol, and Chinese Pitch. Correlations (multiple R) are reported, ranging from .31 to .86 (average .55) wth various criteria of French and Spanish achievement in high school and college. Highest correlations were obtained when predicting Cooperative Test scores (.55, .65, .86). The main factors in student success were found to be verbal reasoning (IQ) and motivation. It is concluded that (1) in most FL classes, the students' audio-lingual abilities are not fully engaged. (2) Specialized aptitude tests should be used in combination with, or instead of such conventional measures as IQ for choosing, sectioning, and placing FL students. (3) The use of specialized tests for these purposes is particularly necessary in audio-lingual courses, to permit identification of students with high audio-lingual potential but otherwise undistinguished academic records. Paul Pimsleur

———.

"Predicting Success in High School Foreign Language Courses," *Educational and Psychological Measurement,* XXIII (Summer, 1963), 349-57.

This study attempts to predict FL achievement at the secondary level in French and Spanish, using predictive tests found effective in previous studies at the college level. The 8 predictors considered were: Vocabulary, Interest I, Interest II, Linguistic Analysis, Reading Aloud, Rhymes, Chinese Pitch, Sex. The achievement criteria were the Cooperative Test and the Pictorial Auditory Comprehension Test. Linguistic Analysis, which tests the verbal reasoning factor, proved to be the best predictor in both French and Spanish, combined in each case with other tests to accomplish most efficient prediction. For findings of subsequent studies, see Pimsleur, P., Sundland, D., and McIntyre, R., Underachievement in Foreign Language Learning: Final Report, this section. Paul Pimsleur

———.

"A Study of Foreign Language Learning Ability: Part I and II," in Michael Zarechnak (ed.), *Report of the Twelfth Annual Round Table Meeting on Linguistics and Language Studies.* Washington, D.C.: Georgetown University Press, 1961. Also published as No. 14 in the Georgetown University *Monograph Series on Language and Linguistics,* 1961.

In this monograph I report on a 3-year study of FL learning ability. Its goals are: 1) to break down the so-called "talent for language" into specific testable components; 2) to construct a test battery for predicting achievement; 3) to construct a test battery for diagnosing student difficulties. It was found that 2 factors play by far the largest role in student achievement, verbal intelligence and motivation. These and other factors are discussed. Formulas for predicting traditional and audio-lingual achievement are presented. Paul Pimsleur, MLabstract #65.

———.

Under-Achievement in Foreign Language Learning: Report No. 1. Washington, D.C.: Office of Education, U.S. Department of Health, Education, and Welfare, n.d. (mimeo).

The Report consists of the following three articles, which are included in their appropriate places in the present volume: 1) P. Pimsleur, L. Mosberg, A. V. Morrison, "Student Factors in Foreign Language Learning: A Review of the Literature," *Modern Language Journal,* XLVI (April, 1962, 160-69; 2) Paul Pimsleur, Robert P.

Stockwell, Andrew L. Comrey, "Foreign Language Learning Ability," *Journal of Educational Psychology,* LIII (February, 1962), 15-26; 3) A. V. Morrison, "Personality and Underachievement in Foreign Language Learning, A Pilot Study." See also the Final Report (1963), next entry.

Pimsleur, Paul, Ludwig Mosberg, and Andrew L. Morrison
"Student Factors in Foreign Language Learning: A Review of the Literature," *Modern Language Journal,* XLVI (April, 1962), 160-69.
    In this article we review the literature on student characteristics relevant to success in foreign language study. More than 40 studies are cited, under 7 headings: Intelligence, Verbal Ability, Pitch Discrimination, Bilingualism, Study Habits, Motivation and Attitudes, and Personality. It is concluded that verbal intelligence correlates about .45 with FL achievement, and motivation correlates about .40. Together, they account for some 35% of the variance in FL learning, leaving 65% to be explained by further research. The need for good achievement tests is pointed out, as is the paucity of research in all areas of FL learning, especially with pre-college subjects. Paul Pimsleur

Pimsleur, Paul, R. P. Stockwell, A. L. Comrey
"Foreign Language Learning Ability," *Journal of Educational Psychology,* LIII (1962), 15-26.
    In this article, I describe a test battery for predicting FL achievement and diagnosing FL learning difficulties. Sample items are given from four tests: Linguistic Analysis, Interest, Sound-Symbol, and Chinese Pitch. Predictive accuracy is reported, ranging from .31 to .86 (average .55) for various criteria of French and Spanish achievement in high school and college. Highest accuracy was obtained when predicting Cooperative Test scores (.55, .65, .86). The main factors in student success were found to be verbal reasoning (IQ) and motivation. It is concluded that 1) in most FL classes, the students' audiolingual abilities are not fully exploited, and 2) specialized aptitude tests should be used to choose, section, and place FL students, particularly in audio-lingual courses. Paul Pimsleur

Pimsleur, Paul, Donald M. Sundland, and Ruth D. McIntyre
Under-Achievement in Foreign Language Learning (Final Report). Columbus: Ohio State University, April, 1963.
    Final report of a 2-year study (under NDEA) of FL underachievement, a problem affecting 10 to 20 per cent of all FL students. Subjects were students in 12 high schools and junior high schools.

One principal cause of underachievement is shown to be lack of coordination in the schools' FL program. Another is lack of *auditory ability* in some students. Data is presented concerning prediction of FL achievement, and factors which affect achievement, such as intelligence, motivation, attitudes, and personality. The need is stressed for further study of auditory ability. Suggestions are made for improving FL programs to reduce underachievement. Paul Pimsleur

Raybould, A. B.

"Factors Conditioning Achievement in French among a Group of Adolescents; Synopsis of Thesis," *British Journal of Educational Psychology,* XVII (June, 1947), 114-15.

A study of the possible existence and nature of specific abilities involved in learning French; values of prognosis test based on these abilities; aspects of the study of French that should be stressed as indicated by the tests. Nine tests are listed. The results are correlated with tests applied after one and after four years of study. Prognosis tests given at three months of study show a high correlation with tests seven months later. JM

*Reid, Catherine

The Prediction of Grades in Foreign Language at the Freshman Level from a Battery of Tests of Mental Ability and Achievement. Unpublished Ph.D. dissertation, Fordham University, 1951.

Sapon, Stanley M.

"A Work-Sample Test for Foreign Language Prognosis," *Journal of Psychology,* XXXIX (January, 1955), 97-104.

On the assumption that the measurement of learning of an "artificial" language is a valid work sample test for foreign language prognosis, the author describes the design and application of one such device. Phonology, Morphology, Syntax and Lexicon are described. A sample evaluation is presented along with criterion bases. The test's predictive validity has been tentatively confirmed by its successful application to a student sample undergoing a trial course in Mandarin Chinese. DF

Walsh, Donald D.

"College Board Foreign-Language Tests," *Modern Language Journal,* XXXVII (January, 1953), 19-22.

Report on the new form of CEEB tests in Spanish. The new objective-type tests have been checked against the older-type tests, and the new one-hour tests have been found to be as valid for predicting success in college as were the three-hour tests. This was true not only for scholarship candidates but for all applicants for college entrance. MJS

Williams, Stanley B., and Harold J. Leavitt
"Prediction of Success in Learning Japanese," *Journal of Applied Psychology,* XXXI (April, 1947), 164-68.

This study bases its results on scores of the Pennsylvania State College Academic Aptitude Examination. Procedure is described in regard to the students subjected to testing, criteria of success, the nature of the aptitude test, and the method of testing. Results of testing show that the vocabulary test is a valid differentiator between success and failure. There is a statistical evaluation that compares vocabulary testing and paragraph reading, scoring separately the tests in French, Spanish, and German. JM

Wittenborn, J. Richard
See Wittenborn, 2.3 German.

Wittich, Barbara von
"Prediction of Success in Foreign Language Study," *Modern Language Journal,* XLVI (May, 1962), 208-12.

In this research project the technique of multiple regression was used to find an easily accessible predictor of success in foreign language study at the junior high school level. The significance of I.Q., English-, mathematics-, and total grade-point averages as predictors of success was tested. Total grade-point average combined with I.Q. showed the highest correlation with both prediction variables and criterion/teachers marks in foreign languages. The conclusion was reached that success in the study of a foreign language can be assumed to be the result of ability and of motivation as reflected by achievement. Barbara von Wittich

3.5 Bilingualism

Arseniam, Seth
"Bilingualism in the Postwar World," *Psychological Bulletin,* XLII (February, 1945), 65-86.

A review of studies on various problems of bilingualism—its measurement; its relation to mental development, language development, school development, motor functions, and social adjustment; and a list of problems for research. BP

Buxbaum, Edith
See Buxbaum, 3.7.

Cape Educational Department, Union of South Africa

Report on the Experiment Involving the Use of the Second Language as a Medium of Instruction. Cape Town, Union of South Africa: Cape Educational Department, 1952.

    See annotation for experiment under McConkey, 3.5.

Carrow, Sister Mary Arthur

A Comparative Study of the Linguistic Functioning of Bilingual Spanish-American Children and Monolingual Anglo-American Children at the Third Grade Level. Unpublished Ph.D. dissertation, Northwestern University, 1956.

    See annotation under following entry.

————.

"Linguistic Functioning of Bilingual and Monolingual Children," *Journal of Speech and Hearing Disorders,* III (September, 1957), 371-80.

    Comparison of English-language ability and achievement between groups of monolingual and bilingual children, similar in age, grade, socioeconomic status, and intelligence. Results: significant difference in favor of monolingual group in oral-reading accuracy and comprehension, hearing vocabulary, arithmetic reasoning, and speaking vocabulary. No significant difference in silent-reading comprehension and vocabulary, oral-reading rate, spelling, verbal output, length of clause, and degree of subordination. JAD

Chaiyaratana, Chalao

A Comparative Study of English and Thai Syntax. Unpublished Ph.D. dissertation, University of Indiana, 1961.

    This study is a syntactical comparison of English and Thai (incorporating brief generating grammars) to investigate the problems of English and Thai bilingualism, particularly when 1 of the 2 languages is acquired fairly late in school. This contrastive study of the syntactical structures of Thai and English consciously attempts to bring to light possible sources of difficulty to the Language Learner. The differences and similarities between the 2 languages are stated in terms of their syntax. Morphology, lexicon, and phonology are treated only incidently. From the abstract.

*Chiasson, R. J.

Bilingualism in the Schools of Eastern Nova Scotia. Unpublished Ph.D. dissertation, University of London, Institute of Education, n.d.

Cline, Marion, Jr.

    See Cline, 2.53.

Diebold, A. Richard, Jr.
"Incipient Bilingualism," *Language,* XXXVII (January-March, 1962), 97-112.

A theoretical presentation of language contact and bilingualism is followed by a case study of a rural Mexican Indian community's problems with learning a second language (Spanish). The paper includes discussion of measuring the degrees of second language proficiency among a large population, of the impact of Spanish on the Indian language (Huave) in the form of linguistic interference and borrowings, and of the critical sociolinguistic variables in the bilingual community. A. Richard Diebold, Jr.

Fife, Robert Herndon, and Herschel T. Manuel
The Teaching of English in Puerto Rico. San Juan, Puerto Rico: Department of Education Press, 1951.

This book represents an experimental approach to bilingualism. It reports the findings of a study begun in 1941 and ended in 1948. The first phase of the study was devoted to the measurement of bilingual achievement in English and Spanish. A battery of standardized tests for both languages was administered in Puerto Rico. The English tests were also applied in Austin, Texas, and the Spanish tests were applied in Mexico, so that results from the Puerto Rican bilingual area could be compared with those from the monolingual areas. (These tests, revised, were published by the Cooperative Test Division of the Educational Testing Service. They are known as "Inter-American Tests" and are listed in the 1950-51 Catalog, *Cooperative Tests for Educational Purposes.*) Part II of the book discusses "Tests of Achievement" and includes statistical information. The second phase of the study examined the Puerto Rican educational system in reference to (a) the political and social background; (b) the degree of written and oral usage of English within the culture; (c) the competency of the English-teaching staff and their curriculum; and (d) experimentation to further the progress in teaching English. (In January, 1949, the new Puerto Rican government substituted Spanish for English as the medium of instruction. Trends that affected English teaching in this new atmosphere are treated in footnote references.) JM

Fishman, Joshua A.
See Fishman, 3.7.

Haugen, Einar I.
Bilingualism in the Americas: A Bibliography and Research Guide. University, Ala.: University of Alabama Press, 1956. Publications of The American Dialect Society, No. 26.

A survey of studies made in the field of American bilingualism (including both North and South America) and a new theoretical analysis of the linguistic, psychological, and social problems faced by bilinguals. The author finds in the Americas "one of the most interesting laboratories of bilingual experience since the beginning of recorded history." He reports on and analyzes the studies made under the headings "The Scope of the Problem," "Languages of the Americas," "Language Contact," "The Bilingual Individual," "The Bilingual Community," and "Approaches to Research." A 32-page bibliography concludes the volume. Einar I. Haugen.

————.

The Norwegian Language in America: A Study in Bilingual Behavior. 2 vols. Philadelphia: University of Pennsylvania Press, 1953.

"American Norwegian did become the speech of most of the nearly one million people who emigrated from Norway and many of their uncounted descendants. . . . A mode of behavior that is highly typical of American life will be forgotten unless it is preserved in a full and precise description." Vol. I is essentially historical. Vol. II "is more definitely linguistic; being a description of the internal life of the Norwegian dialects in America. . . . It includes a study of the changes in the dialects resulting from their dispersal in the new country, as well as the effect of English on their total structure. Samples of the American Norwegian dialects are presented along with a representative vocabulary of loan words." JG

————.

"The Phoneme in Bilingual Description," *Language Learning,* VII (1956-57), 17-23.

Reports of an experiment to demonstrate the errors in aural perception of a strange system within one's own language. Einar I. Haugen

Jakobovits, Leon A., and Wallace E. Lambert

"Semantic Satiation among Bilinguals," *Journal of Experimental Psychology,* LXII (1961), 576-82.

The phenomenon of semantic satiation was related to the mediation theory of compound and coordinate bilingualism. It was predicted that compound bilinguals, having interdependent language systems, will exhibit a cross-linguistic satiation effect (cross-satiation), while coordinate bilinguals, having functionally independent language systems, would not exhibit the cross-satiation effect. The results supported the prediction that the two types of bilinguals would behave differently and showed that compounds clearly exhibit the cross-satiation effect while coordinates react in the opposite manner. Some additional analyses were discussed which have a further bearing upon the differences in the language structures of compound and coordinate bilinguals. From the Summary at the foot of the article.

Johnson, Granville B., Jr.
"Bilingualism as Measured by a Reaction-Time Technique and the Relationship between a Language and a Non-Language Intelligence Quotient," *Pedagogical Seminary and Journal of Genetic Psychology,* LXXXII (1953), 3-9.

The purpose of this study was to ascertain the relationship between a language and nonlanguage test of intelligence, using a control group of bilingual boys. The bilingual subjects presented problems that possibly invalidated tests used. BP
See Johnson, 5.

Joly, Charles L. Guidance Center, Catholic Charities of Chicago
A Comparison of the Performance of Spanish-Speaking Bilinguals on English and Spanish Forms of the Inter-American Tests of General Ability. (United States Office of Education.) Duration of the Project: 1958-59.

Puerto Rican and Mexican bilingual children were given equivalent forms in English and in Spanish of the Inter-American Tests of General Ability, to determine how much the language affects the results of the examination. HLN

Jones, W. R., and W. A. C. Stewart
"Bilingualism and Verbal Intelligence," *British Journal of Psychology* (Statistical Section), IV (1951), 3-8.

Purpose of investigation was to obtain further information about the comparative performance on verbal intelligence tests of monolingual and bilingual children. Results showed bilingual children to be significantly inferior to monolingual children in scoring. BP

Keston, M. J., and C. Jimenez
"Study of the Performance on English and Spanish Editions of the Stanford-Binet Intelligence Test by Spanish-American Children," *Pedagogical Seminary and Journal of Genetic Psychology,* LXXXV (1954), 263-69.

Because of the incidence of apparent retardation in bilingual children, these investigators gave intelligence tests to a control group of bilingual children in English and in their native Spanish. Because of language difficulties neither test gave an accurate measure, but there

was higher correlation between school grades and I.Q. on English test.
BP

Kinzel, Paul F.
Lexical and Grammatical Interference in the Speech of a Bilingual
Child. Seattle: Linguistics Department, University of Washington,
1964. Studies in Linguistics and Language Learning, Vol. 1.

The data for this study were taken from the active speech of a
six-year-old English-French bilingual child who learned both languages
in infancy and represent on-the-spot borrowings not related by previous usage. Interference is shown as affecting both the child's primary
language, English, and her secondary language, French. Paul F.
Kinzel

Lambert, Wallace E.
"Measurement of the Linguistic Dominance of Bilinguals," *Journal of
Abnormal and Social Psychology,* L (1955), 197-200.

This paper reports a method of measuring linguistic dominance
among bilinguals, relating the measure to cultural and personality characteristics. Results and discussion follow explanation of the method.
Analytic charts included. JM

Lambert, Wallace E., J. Havelka, and R. C. Gardner
"Linguistic Manifestations of Bilingualism," *American Journal of
Psychology,* LXXII (March, 1959), 77-82.

English-French bilinguals were given a series of tests to determine the degree of correlation among various aspects of their linguistic
behavior. It was found that their relative superiority in French or
English is manifested in comparative thresholds for word-recognition,
facility in word completion and word detection, response-sets, and
speed of reading, but not in speed of translation. Intercorrelations
indicate that a single dimension underlies these various measures, suggesting that bilingualism is reflected in many aspects of linguistic behavior. From the Summary to the article.

Lambert, Wallace E., and S. Fillenbaum
"A Pilot Study of Aphasia among Bilinguals," *Canadian Journal of
Psychology,* XIII (1959), 28-34.

A testing of the hypothesis that functional dependence or independence of polyglots' languages, determined by the manner in which
the languages were originally learned, will determine how they are
affected by aphasic insult. SJ

Lambert, Wallace E., J. Havelka, and C. Crosby
"The Influence of Language Acquisition Contexts on Bilingualism,"
Journal of Abnormal Psychology, LVI (1958), 239-44.

Discusses the hypothesis that bilinguals, having learned their two languages in either separated or fused context, effectively use the two languages separately. There is no difference found in the facility to switch from one language to another that can be attributed to contextual influences. The findings were related to the theory of compound and coordinate bilingual language systems. Nine references are listed. JM

Lambert, Wallace E., and Nancy Moore
Word Association Responses: Comparisons of American and French Monolinguals with Canadian Monolinguals and Bilinguals. (Unpublished: McGill University. This research was supported by a subvention from the Carnegie Corporation of New York and by a research grant from the Defense Research Board of Canada, grant No. D77-94-01-10.)

Word association norms were developed for groups of English and French Canadian monolingual students and for Canadian English-French bilinguals responding at one time in English and at another in French. It was found that the French Canadians show the same degree of associational response diversity as do the French French whereas the English Canadians approximate closely the more stereotyped response pattern of the Americans. With regard to studies on response content, the view was developed that associational responses are essential aspects of the meanings of stimulus words and that the fidelity of communication both across and within language communities is limited by associational discordance. In addition, it was found that the French Canadians are similar to the French French only in the relative diversity of responses but are as different from the French French as the Americans are with regard to both the content of their responses and their use of superordinates. From the report summary

Leopold, Werner F.
Speech Development of a Bilingual Child. 4 Vols. Evanston, Ill.: Northwestern University Press, 1939-49.

An exhaustive study of the acquisition by the author's daughter of German and English. Discussion of phonology, morphology, syntax and vocabulary, and accurate phonetic transcription. SS

Lerea, Louis, and Suzanne Kohut
"A Comparative Study of Monolinguals and Bilinguals in a Verbal

Task Performance," *Journal of Clinical Psychology,* XVII (January, 1961), 49-52.

Two experimental groups, 30 bilinguals and 30 monolinguals, matched in chronological age, intelligence, sex, and socio-economic status, participated in this study. During the experimental situation each S was administered the following battery: (a) a bilingualism questionnaire, (b) Columbia Mental Maturity Scale, (c) Micro Utterance-Association (acquisition), (d) Rogers' Test of Personality Adjustment, and (e) Micro Utterance-Association (relearning). The findings indicated: (1) bilinguals learned and relearned the MU-A task more rapidly than monolinguals, (2) a significant correlation was discovered between speech of learning MU-A and intelligence among the monolinguals, and (3) the relationship between social maladjustment and MU-A performances was not significant in either the bilingual or monolingual group. An association factor may have been responsible for bilinguals' superiority in MY-A, i.e., bilinguals may possess a unique potential unacknowledged in past research. Louis Lerea

McConkey, W. G.
"An Experiment in Bilingual Education," *Journal for Social Research,* II (June, 1951), 28-42.

In 1942, the Natal Provincial Council of the Union of South Africa ordained that Afrikaans-speaking students should receive part of their school instruction in English and that English-speaking students should receive part of their instruction in Afrikaans. Statistical studies show a marked second-language improvement for students. Also the second-language achievement seemed closely related to the influence of the community language. BP

Mackey, William Francis
"The Description of Bilingualism," *Canadian Journal of Linguistics,* VII (Spring, 1962), 51-85.

A research framework for the description of individual bilingualism by degree, function, alternation, and interference. The degree of proficiency at the phonological, grammatical, lexical, semantic and stylistic levels of each language in listening, speaking, reading and writing is correlated with their internal and external functions. The latter are determined by measuring the duration, frequency and pressure of all contacts (home, community, mass media, etc.). The rate and proportion of alternation is compared with the proportion of substitution and importation at the cultural, semantic, lexical, grammatical, and phonological levels. William F. Mackey

Mackey, W. F., and J. A. Noonan
"An Experiment in Bilingual Education," *English Language Teaching Monthly*, VI (1952), 125-32.

———.
See Mackey, 2.3, English.

*Ma'ia'i, Fanaafi
Bilingualism in Samoa: Its Problems and Implications for Education. Unpublished Ph.D. dissertation, Institute of Education, University of London, n.d.

Malherbe, E. G.
The Bilingual School: A Study of Bilingualism in South Africa. Johannesburg: Bilingual School Association, 1943.

The author is Director of Census and Statistics for the Union of South Africa, and formerly Director of the National Bureau for Educational and Social Research. In the introduction, T. J. Haarhoff, Professor of Classics at the University of Witwatersrand in Johannesburg, justifies the need for bilingualism based on the need for psychological unity among the peoples through intercommunication. This book concerns a survey of bilingualism in South African schools made in 1938. The purpose of the survey: (1) to determine the degree of bilingualism attained by the students on completion of their secondary training; (2) to study the factors determining linguistic growth, such as individual intelligence, home environment, extrahome influences, and school influences; (3) to study the influence of medium on the pupil's attainment in Afrikaans and English, his progress in other school subjects, and his general mental development. The following chapters are especially relevant: Chapter 3, "The Measurement of Bilingualism in South Africa"; Chapter 7, "Unilingual and Bilingual Schools Compared as Regards Scholastic Achievement"; Chapter 8, "Social Attitudes in Bilingual and Unilingual Schools"; and Chapter 9, "Social Attitudes of Normal College Students." Only some of the main findings of the survey are given in this edition. There is a subsequent, more comprehensive, edition, published in London in 1946 by Longmans, Green and Co. JM

Manuel, Herschel T.
"Bilingualism," *Encyclopedia of Educational Research.* 3rd ed. New York: Macmillan, 1960. Pp. 146-50.

Marie Gabrielle, Sister, F.S.E., and Sister Raymond de Jesus, F.S.E.
See Marie Gabrielle, 6.1.

Orata, Pedro T.

"The Iloilo Experiment in Education through the Vernacular," *The Use of Vernacular Languages in Education*. (Monograph on Fundamental Education No. 8.) Paris: UNESCO, 1953. Pp. 123-31.

A three-year study of bilingual education, using both the vernacular and English. Testing showed that the vernacular was more productive in teaching in grades one through three and that the amount of carry-over from one language to the other was about equal. JM

*Pursley, Alice J.

Effects of Foreign Language Spoken at Home and in the Community on the Achievement of Elementary School Children. Unpublished Master thesis, Kansas State College of Pittsburg [1961?].

Rojas, Pauline M.

"Reading Materials for Bilingual Children," *Elementary School Journal,* XLVII (December, 1946), 204-11.

A study to discover why reading material prepared for native English-speaking children is unsatisfactory for teaching reading in English to foreign-speaking children in our American schools. Analysis was made of vocabulary content of primers as to form and meaning that would affect the learning situation, in this study, for the Spanish-speaking child. These vocabulary items were listed alongside Spanish equivalents in order to determine the learning burden. Frequency of repetition and distribution of words were also included in the analysis. SJ

Smith, Madorah E.

"Measurement of Vocabularies of Young Bilingual Children in Both of the Languages Used," *Journal of Genetic Psychology,* LXXIV (June, 1949), 305-10.

A measurement of thirty bilingual children in Honolulu showed their vocabulary in either English or Chinese was below that of monolinguals, but it was above when both languages were considered together. The author concludes that language instruction during preschool years seems unwise. SJ

————.

"Word Variety as a Measure of Bilingualism in Preschool Children," *Journal of Genetic Psychology,* XC (June, 1957), 143-50.

The word variety of monolingual and bilingual children aged two through five was compared. The monolinguals used a greater variety of words. Among the bilinguals, the more equal the amounts of each language heard, the lower the scores. SJ

Tireman, Lloyd Spencer
See Tireman, 2.3, English.

von Raffler-Engel, Walburga
Investigation of Italo-American Bilinguals. Paper read at the 35th Annual Meeting of the Linguistic Society of America, Philadelphia, December 1956.
Basically the same as the following entry.

————.
"Investigation of Italo-American Bilinguals," *Zeitschrift für Phonetik,* XIV (1961, No. 2), 127-30. Also *Italica,* XXIV (December, 1957), 239-44.
Bilinguals—restricting the term "bilingual" to those who have achieved "phonic equilingualism": that is, who speaks two languages and sound like a "native" in both—use only one semantic system, but operate with two separate systems of phonetics. An individual is equilingual precisely so long as he keeps the two phonic systems apart. Field work has shown that there is no phonic carry-over when the speaker is fully bilingual linguistically and culturally. The only mispronunciations occur at the moment of transition from one language to another. Research indicates that bilinguals may have (semantically) a single set of "signified" which may be expressed in either language. Bilinguals dream in both languages. They may use one language to express a concept in one speech situation, the other language to express it in another, according to which language is normally used in that situation. "Loan-blends"—the adoptions of meaning and morphology from one language, expressed in the phonology of another— illustrate the point that there may be a single "signified." Walburga von Raffler-Engel; English Language Teaching Abstract No. 195.

*Wacker, Charlotte F.
Foreign Language Experience in the Home and Its Relationship to the Learning of English by Fifth Grade Children Attending a School Having a Bilingual Curriculum. Unpublished Masters thesis, City College of New York [1961?].

Weinreich, Uriel
Languages in Contact: Findings and Problems. New York: Linguistic Circle of New York, 1953.
A study of the "linguistic interference" resulting from contact of two distinct language structures. Contents of the book are as follows: (1) The Problem of Approach; (2) Mechanisms and Structural Causes of Interference; (3) The Bilingual Individual; (4) The Socio-Cultural

Setting of Language Contact; (5) Research Methods and Opportunities. In the final chapter, the author poses three basic problems: (1) "In a given case of language contact, which of the languages will be the source of what forms of interference?" (2) "How thoroughly will the effects of interference be incorporated in the recipient language?" (3) "How far in space will they be diffused?" The author urges research coordination between a structural approach and a sociocultural approach in the study of language contact. The bibliography lists 658 items. JM

Williams, Jac L.
See Williams, Part I.

3.7 Sociopsychological Factors of Language Learning

*Adam, R. S.
Social Factors in Second Language Learning—with Special Reference to the Fiji Islands. Unpublished Ph.D. dissertation, Institute of Education, University of London, n.d.

Andersson, Theodore
The Optimum Age for Beginning the Study of Modern Languages. Unpublished, Department of French, Yale University, n.d.
    Attempts to sift available evidence—which is pitifully small—in order to determine *when,* and *how,* instruction in a second language should begin in school. Conclusion: the optimum age seems to fall within the span of ages four to eight; languages should as much as possible be taught by the direct method. JG

Anisfeld, Moshe, Norman Bogo, and Wallace E. Lambert
"Evaluational Reactions to Accented English Speech," *Journal of Abnormal and Social Psychology,* LXV, No. 4 (1962), 223-31.
    Samples of gentile and Jewish college students evaluated the personality characteristics underlying eight voices presented to them on tape. Some voices used standard English while others spoke English with a Jewish accent. The subjects were not made aware that actually the same individuals one time spoke without the accent and at another time with the accent, so that comparisons of evaluational reactions to the two guises could be made for each of the four speakers. The results thus obtained are discussed in terms of ethnic attitudes. Moshe Anisfeld

Anisfeld, Moshe, and Wallace E. Lambert
"Social and Psychological Variables in Learning Hebrew," *Journal of Abnormal and Social Psychology,* LXIII (1961), 524-29.

A study to show that a sympathetic social attitude is important to the success of acquiring a second language. Attitude tests measured the reasons for learning Hebrew as well as attitude toward Jewish culture. Ability tests measured intelligence and aptitude. These tests, correlated with achievement of Hebrew-language learning, support the hypothesis. Sixteen references are listed. JM

Blanton, Wincie Lawton
An Experimental Application of Language Theory, Learning Theory, and Personality Theory to Evaluate the Influence of Music in Language Learning. Unpublished Ed.D. dissertation, University of Texas, 1962.

This theory-research study explores the complexity of the language role, and the close relationship between music, spoken language, and the nature of man. The hypothesis under test is: Language is human behavior learned through imitation and identification, and motivated by psychological and physiological variables operating under social pressure, and music is a medium which may be used to influence both variables motivating goal-directed language behavior. Language theory and its attendant theory of mind are explored, to facilitate an understanding of the different frames of reference that educational thought employs in the conception of the term *language*. Learning theory and personality theory are explored, to facilitate an understanding of the psychological foundations of language behavior characterized by functional articulation defects. Learning theory is explained in terms of social learning and imitativeness, with special emphasis on the principle of "feedback" or interdependence as expressed in cybernetics. Personality theory is explained in terms of identification and the related problems of functional articulation defects. From the abstract.

Buxbaum, Edith
"The Role of a Second Language in the Formation of Ego and Superego," *Psychoanalytic Quarterly,* XVIII (July, 1949), 279-89.

Dr. Buxbaum's report of her analyses of four bilingual patients who had difficulty either with their second language (in the case of two children, as to accent) or with their native language (in the case of two adults, as to repression) is analyzed and commented upon by Dr. Stera, as well as by reference to the literature. ". . . speech development is . . . disturbed when early object relationships conducive to imitations are poor or absent . . . the ability to learn to speak foreign languages may be dependent on unconscious feelings which are under the control of the superego." Bibliography included. MJS

Carroll, John B. Graduate School of Education, Laboratory for Research in Instruction, Harvard University, Cambridge, Mass.
A Study of Possible Influences of Home Background on the Development of Oral Communication Skills in Children. (United States Office of Education.) Duration of the project: 1958-59.

Statistical methods were used to measure the significance of the correlation between home and background influences and sixth-grade children's skill in oral communication. HLN

Carroll, John B., *et al.*
Report and Recommendations of the Interdisciplinary Summer seminar in Psychology and Linguistics. Ithaca, N.Y.: Cornell University, August 10, 1951 (mimeographed).

An exploration of the relationships between psychology and linguistics; includes a section on the possible application of psycholinguistic knowledge in second-language teaching. Special recommendations are made relevant to problems of communication between linguists and psychologists, and to research in the field. JM

Dunkel, Harold B.
"The Effect of Personality on Language Achievement," *Journal of Educational Psychology,* XXXVIII (March, 1947), 177-82.

In 1946-47 Rorschach tests were administered to about 150 students at the 11th grade level. They also all took a placement test in a foreign language. Using the data on those offering two years of Latin in high school (46), the investigators examined it to test the blind hypotheses concerning which students were likely to succeed or fail in the first two years of Latin. "It seemed likely that what may be identified as a mildly 'compulsive' personality would be that with the greatest probability of success in elementary Latin." The original hypotheses were not substantiated during the course of the investigation. Further investigations along these lines, with sub-groups, are described although no positive conclusion, pending further evidence, are advanced. DF

Farber, J. E.
"The Role of Motivation in Verbal Learning and Performance," *Psychological Bulletin,* LII (1955), 311-27.

An analysis of the theories and implications concerning motivation, particularly with reference to the Taylor Anxiety (A-scale) scores. Results indicate "quality of performance in complex learning situations is increasingly related to S's degree of anxiety, as measured by the Taylor scale. . . ." Other considerations and discussion of this scale as related to D (drive): "... experimentally defined variables such as electric shock ... fear and failure may be classed as motivational by virtue of their non-associative (drive) properties. ..." Bibliography of fifty-seven items. MJS

Fishman, Joshua A.
Readings in the Sociology of Language, to appear.
The following sections are projected: The origin and development of language; Language in groups of small and intermediate size; Language in social strata and sectors; Language reflections of sociocultural organization; Language constraints on world view; Multilingualism; Language maintenance and language displacement; The social contexts and consequences of language planning. DF

Gardner, R. C., and Wallace E. Lambert
"Motivational Variables in Second-Language Acquisition," *Canadian Journal of Psychology,* XIII (December, 1959), 266-72.
Montreal high school students studying French were tested on linguistic aptitude, verbal intelligence, and motivational characteristics. Analysis of the data showed that aptitude and motivational factors related equally to achievement in French. The maximum prediction of achievement was obtained from tests of verbal intelligence, intensity of motivation, purpose of study, and one index of linguistic aptitude. BP

Hayman, John L., Jr.
See Hayman, 2.56.

Hosford, Prentiss McIntyre
Characteristics of Science-Talented and Language-Talented Secondary School Students. Unpublished Ed. D. dissertation, University of Georgia, 1961.
The purpose of this study was to identify characteristics or attributes, exclusive of intelligence, socioeconomic background, and education, which may be related to science talent. A null hypothesis was tested: there are no significant differences in personality traits of characteristics of science-talented and language-talented students, as determined by certain measures. [. . .] Certain perceptions, concepts, interests, and characteristics of science-talented girls more nearly approach those of science-talented boys than those of their language talented-peers, supporting the existence of a constellation of characteristics common to scientists, exclusive of sex differences. Conclusive evidence of differences between science-talented and language-talented students indicates a need for studies to investigate

the origin of these differences—whether genetically based as the result of child-rearing or educational practices. From the abstract.

Johnson, James T., Jr.
See Hayman, 2.56.

Lambert, Wallace E.
"Developmental Aspects of Second Language Acquisition," *Journal of Social Psychology,* XLIII (February, 1956), 83-104.

Three groups of subjects—native French speakers, American graduate students in French, and American undergraduate majors—were asked to give associational words to a stimulus word in an attempt to isolate differences in linguistic behavior of subjects at varying stages of language skill. There are a series of barriers to overcome in acquiring language skill—vocabulary is the easiest; cultural barriers, the most difficult. BP

————.
A Study of the Roles of Attitudes and Motivation in Second Language Learning. Montreal, Canada, McGill University, 1961.

Study of high school French students in New York and southwest Louisiana (native speakers of American English), based on Montreal study, which demonstrated relation of aptitude-intelligence factor to certain skills, such as vocabulary and grammar, and of motivational factor of skills leading to bilingualism. Attitudes of native speakers of Canadian and Louisiana French toward standard French are assessed. DG. Available from the author, the U. S. Office of Education, and through Interlibrary Loan of McGill University. This study was prepared with the assistance of Robert C. Gardner Research Associate, and as Research Assistants, Robert Olton, Kenneth Tunstall, and Irene Vachon Spilka.

Lambert, Wallace E., *et al.*
"Attitudinal and Cognitive Aspects of Intensive Study of a Second Language," *Journal of Abnormal and Social Psychology,* LXVI (April, 1963), 358-68.

Students attending a 6-week French Summer School were examined for attitudes toward French people and culture, their orientations toward learning a 2nd language, and their feelings of anomic at the start and end of the course. Attention was also given to modification in the meanings of French and translated equivalent English concepts. Students at 2 levels of skill in French were compared. Results supported the theory that learning a 2nd language efficiently depends on an appropriate pattern of attitudes toward language study. Anomic increased for both groups of students during the course. Students utilized the semantic features of both their languages and permitted the 2 to interact. This linguistic interdependence correlates positively with achievement. From the abstract at head of article.

Lorge, Irving, and Frank Mayans, Jr.
"Vestibule vs. Regular Classes for Puerto Rican Migrant Pupils," *Teachers College Record,* LV (February, 1954), 231-37.

Report of a cooperative experiment undertaken by the Institute of Psychological Research of Teachers College, Columbia University, to get evidence for evaluating differences in outcomes under the two contrasting administrative procedures for teaching English to migrant Puerto Rican, Spanish-speaking children. One procedure is the "vestibule" class, made up entirely of Puerto Rican children who stay together as a group with one teacher until they know enough English to make a good adjustment to the school environment. The other procedure is to induct Puerto Rican children of junior high school age directly into regular classes. "The data show that the children from the regular classes have the advantages of greater mastery of English and the acquisition of more school subject matter than the children in vestibule classes." JG

Mayers, Alan E.
See Hayman, 2.56.

Morrison, Andrew V.
"Personality and Underachievement in Foreign Language Learning, A Pilot Study," in Paul Pimsleur, *Under-Achievement in Foreign Language Learning,* Report No. 1. (q.v. above below, p. 00).

An underachiever was defined as a student whose grade in a foreign language class was one or more letter grades below the average of other academic courses. So defined, a sample of underachieving boys and a sample of underachieving girls were drawn from two junior high schools. A comparison group, matched on age, sex, and intelligence level was also drawn. Three teachers (language teacher, "home room" teacher, gym teacher) rated students chosen using a 15 item semantic differential. Certain differences were found between the underachieving *boys* and the average *boys,* suggesting the average-achieving boys to be more sociable. No differences were found between the girl subjects. Andrew V. Morrison

Pimsleur, Paul, Donald M. Sundland, and Ruth D. McIntyre
See Pimsleur, 3.3.

Pritchard, D. F.

"An Investigation into the Relationship of Personality Traits and Ability in Modern Languages," *British Journal of Educational Psychology,* XXII (1952), 147-48.

A study to find out if there is any specific type of personality related to the successful acquiring of a foreign language. Statistical results and subjective examinations of the group point to connection between sociability and fluency in spoken French. BP

Roca, Pablo

The Construction of an Interest Inventory for Students of Different Linguistic and Cultural Backgrounds. Unpublished Ph.D. dissertation, University of Texas, 1952. A summary appears in the *Journal of Educational Research,* XLVIII (November, 1954), 229-31.

A pool of items in parallel English and Spanish editions thought to be indicative of interests in general types of activities such as fine arts, language, helping people, numbers, science, etc., was administered to high-school students in Texas and Puerto Rico. Through item analyses, items valid for both cultural groups were selected for the inventory, which was shown to give comparable results in both cultures. Pablo Roca

*Weldon, Richard C.

An Investigation of Relationships between Attitudes and Achievement in French. Unpublished Ph.D. dissertation, University of California, 1951.

4. Linguistics

4.1 The Use of Linguistic Concepts in Language Teaching

Asuncion, Nobleza Castro
A Study of English Sounds Difficult for Filipino Students. Unpublished Master's thesis, Michigan State University, 1956.

An attempt to determine which English sounds are difficult for Filipino students to produce. Seven major Philippine languages were considered in the study. Nobleza Castro Asuncion

Balogh, István
Az orosz ige és tanitásának néhány kérdése. Budapest: Tankönyvkiadó, 1955.

A comparative treatment of the verb in Russian and in Hungarian, with methodological advice on the teaching of Russian verbs. From van Willigen, Part I.

Bauer, Eric Wolfgang
"Structural Linguistics, Programmed Learning and Language Laboratory Techniques," in Conference Report, International Colloquy on Audio Visual Aids and the Teaching of Languages, held at International Audio Visual Technical Centre, Antwerp, Belgium, April, 1963.

Report on recent developments in structural linguistics (applied linguistics in language teaching), with reference to teaching techniques developed by such programs as the Multiple Credit Program in French (Valdman Program) at Indiana University and the Intensive German Program (Innsbruck-Program) at the University of Notre Dame. Short reference is made to new findings in the structural analysis of German ("Structural Essentials of German") and the principles of language laboratory techniques correlated with the linguistic approach. (Limited supply of mimeographed copies available from the author.) Eric W. Bauer

Bolinger, Dwight L.
"Around the Edge of Language: Intonation," *Harvard Educational Review*, XXXIV (Spring, 1964), 282-96.

The layering of pitch contrasts in English, with a sketch of contrasts between English and Spanish, in the light of the assumption that the intonational systems are essentially the same. Dwight L. Bolinger

Cárdenas, Daniel N.
Applied Linguistics — Spanish — A Guide for Teachers. Boston, Mass.: D. C. Heath, 1961.

An attempt is made to show what constitutes good *pattern practice,* the vehicle of *applied linguistics.* This is done, not by theorizing, but by presenting concrete problems of language learning and offering a solution. The first part deals with Syntax, the second with Morphology, and last with Phonology. Each problem is developed in seven parts: 1. point in question simply stated, 2. diagrammed and contrasted with English, 3. diagram explained, 4. examples from Glastonbury materials, 5. pattern practice drills, 6. problems for teacher trainee discussion, and 7. references. Daniel N. Cárdenas

Carroll, John B.
"Linguistic Relativity, Contrastive Linguistics, and Language Learning," *International Review of Applied Linguistics,* I (1963), 1-20.

A consideration of the implication of research on linguistic relativity for the teaching and learning of foreign languages. Research carried out in the Southwest Project in Comparative Psycholinguistics is described. [q.v., Carroll, 3.1]. John B. Carroll

Chaiyaratana, Chalao
See Chaiyaratana, 3.5.

Conrad, Joseph Lawrence
See Conrad, 2.3 German.

Delattre, Pierre
Interference of American Diphthongization in Teaching the Pure Vowels of French, German, and Spanish. Paper presented at the Rocky Mountain Modern Language Association Meeting, Denver, 1963.

Articulation of American vowels /i, u, e, o/ is compared to the corresponding vowels of French, German and Spanish by means of motion picture study of tongue (X-ray) and lips. Four precepts for correction of diphthongization are drawn from objective observations of films. Articulatory tenseness vs. laxness appears on facial expression in motion pictures. Pierre Delattre

Delattre, Pierre, Caroll Olsen, and Elmer Poenack
"A Comparative Study of Declarative Intonation in American English and Spanish," *Hispania,* XLV (May, 1962), 233-41.
 In this article we compare through objective spectrographic analysis two extemporaneous lectures by Diego Rivera and Margaret Mead for declarative intonation contours expressing continuation and finality. A sample page of the contours studied statistically illustrates these results: a. Spanish continuation is mainly rising, English mainly falling. b. Spanish has two distinctive contours for major and minor continuation, a contrast not clear in English. c. Spanish is expressed by high unstressed syllable with straight fall on final stressed syllable. English uses low unstressed and rise with winding fall on final stressed. Following unstressed syllables, if any, are more falling in English. Pierre Delattre *et al.,* MLabstract #253.

de Witte, A. J. J., *et al.*
Moedertaalautomatismen en het onderwijs in de levende taalen. s'Hertogenbosch: Publicatie van het Katholiek pedagogisch bureau voor het V.H.M.O., 1960.
 The author gives the result of a study in which an analytical comparison was made between English, French and German on the one hand and Dutch on the other. Identity and difference in "sentence patterns" are examined as part of a first effort to arrange and grade the subject material on a scientific basis. A bibliography for each chapter. From van Willigen, Part I.

Dimock, Edward. University of Chicago, Chicago.
 Research on South Asian Languages (Hindi, Urdu, and Bengali); Project No. 9,500 (National Education Act, Title VI), June 15, 1961, to June 30, 1963; $80,236.
 The Hindi-Bengali contrastive studies of compound verb structure will "constitute the first steps toward a transfer grammar of the two languages. . . . "—From official description, unpublished, July, 1961.

Di Pietro, Robert J., and Frederick B. Agard
The Grammatical Structures of English and Italian [provisional title]. Chicago: University of Chicago Press, to appear.
 Sponsored by the Center for Applied Linguistics of the Modern Language Association, this is part of the Contrastive Study Series. See Kufner, this section. DF

The Phonology of English and Italian [provisional title]. Chicago: University of Chicago Press, to appear.

Sponsored by the Center for Applied Linguistics of the Modern Language Association, this is part of the Contrastive Studies Series. See Moulton, this section. DF

Doros, Alexander

"O niektórych róznicach w klasyfikacji i posowni przuslowków w języku polskim i rosyjskim," *Język rosyjski,* 1956, No. 3, pp. 31-34.

This and the next three entries are a series of articles comparing Polish and Russian spelling, grammar, and sytax. From van Willigen, Part I.

Doros, Aleksander

"O niektórych róznicach w odmianie i pisowni oraz uzyciu składniowym liczebników i zaimkw w języku polskim i rozyjskim," *Jęsyk rosyjski,* 1956, No. 1, pp. 32-38.

Doros, Aleksander

"O niektórych róznicach w odmianie rzeczowników oraz odmianie i budowie i uzyciu syntaktycznym przymiotników w języku polskim i rosyjskim," *Język rosyjski,* 1955, No. 6, pp. 34-39.,

Doros, Aleksander

"O niektórych róznicach w znaczeniu, odmianie oraz pisowni czasowników w języku polskim i rosyjskim," *Język rosyjski,* 1956, No. 2, pp. 33-37.

El-Bettar, Abdul Kadir Said

The Linguistic Concept Underlying the Construction of the Oxford English Course for Iraq. Unpublished Ed. D. dissertation, University of Michigan, 1962.

The purpose of this study is to investigate the linguistic premises and principles underlying the selection and preparation of the language materials included in the Oxford English Course. The structural content of the Course is for this reason examined on the phonological, morphological and syntactic levels with the objective of arriving at the sequential presentation of, and the relative emphasis placed on each grammatical pattern and structure. From the abstract

Engler, Leo Francis

Problems in English/German Contrastive Analysis. Unpublished Ph. D. dissertation, University of Texas, 1962.

[The] purpose of this dissertation is to arrive by contrastive analysis at demonstrations of the nature of the problems faced by speakers of American English learning standard German in order to obtain a basis for the selection of types of drill to overcome these difficulties and, further, to suggest designs and formats for such drills. From the abstract

Fairbanks, Gordon H.
Application of Structural Linguistics to Foreign Language Teaching in the U.S.S.R. Ithaca, New York: Cornell University, 1960. Also in Modern Language Association of America, *Reports of Surveys and Studies* . . . (See Part I.)
Investigation of awareness of, attitude toward, and teaching and research applications of, structural linguistics in the Soviet Union. Includes study of Soviet methods and materials in Oriental languages. DG

Feldman, David M.
See Feldman, 2.3 Spanish.

Ferguson, Charles A. Modern Language Association of America, New York.
Contrastive Studies for the Foreign Language Teaching of French, German, Italian, Russian and Spanish; Project No. 8,354 (National Defense Education Act, Title VI), June 20, 1959, to June 19, 1961; $172,703.
These contrastive studies will bring the results of linguistic science to bear on the teaching of foreign languages. They will include studies of phonemic structure, basic grammatical categories, sentence types, and transformations. BP
See Di Pietro, Gage, Kufner, Moulton, Stockwell, this section.

Ferguson, Charles A., and William A. Stewart
See Ferguson, Part I.

Fishman, Joshua A.
See Fishman, 3.7.

Flores, Francisco Gubaton
A Contrastive Analysis of Selected Clause Types in Cebuano and English. Unpublished Ed. D. dissertation, University of Michigan, 1963.
This study is a contrastive analysis of selected Cebuano and English clause types based on grammatical descriptions of the tagmemic model. It was undertaken with a twofold goal in view. The first purpose is to compare and contrast grammatical categories in

Cebuano and English by examining selected clause types in the two languages. This immediate purpose is related to the larger purpose of improving the instruction of English in Philippine schools. A second aim is to present an analysis of Cebuano based upon a modified version of Pike's original tagmemic model. From the abstract.

*Gage, William N.
The Grammatical Structures of English and Russian. Chicago: University of Chicago Press, 1963.

*Gage, William N.
The Sounds of English and Russian. Chicago: University of Chicago Press, 1963.

Gage, William N.
See Gage, Part I.

Greis, Naguib Amin Fahmy
The Pedagogical Implications of a Contrastive Analysis of Cultivated Cairene Arabic and the English Language. Unpublished Ph. D. dissertation, University of Minnesota, 1963.

  The purpose of this study is to contribute generally to the teaching of foreign languages and specifically to the teaching of Arabic at the beginning stage to English speakers. . . . The method of approach utilizes linguistic principles and techniques supplemented by cultural, psychological, and practical considerations. From the abstract.

Gurren, Louise
The Comparison on a Phonetic Basis of the Two Chief Languages of the Americas—English and Spanish. Unpublished Ph.D. dissertation, New York University, 1955.

  A study of English and Spanish phonetic differences and similarities comparing single sounds, words, group of words, and intonation. JM

Haas, Mary R.
"The Application of Linguistics to Language Teaching," in A. L. Kroeber (ed.), *Anthropology Today.* Chicago: University of Chicago Press, 1953. Pp. 807-18.

  A justification of the linguistic approach to language learning. This approach is described historically by discussing the contributions of Boas and Sapir, as well as those of Bloomfield and his four recommendations for direct application of the approach. These techniques were activated by the Intensive Language Program of the American Council of Learned Societies, and the results were spectacular enough to encourage the ASTP to institute the method. This was the stimulus needed to influence and improve the teaching of languages on the civilian level. Research information of the ASTP is available on major and minor languages. JM

Hill, Leslie A., and R. Derrick S. Fielden
See Hill, 2.3 English.

†Jackson, Kenneth L.
Word Order Patterns Involving the Middle Adverbs of English and Their Lexically Similar Counterparts in Japanese: A Comparative Study for Teaching Middle Adverbs. Unpublished Ed.D. dissertation in progress, Columbia University.

Kallioinen, Vilho
See Kallioinen, 2.3 French.

Kielski, Bolesław
"Struktura języków francuskiego i polskiego w świetle analizy porównawczej," *Zakład im Ossolińskich,* I (1957); II (1960).
The structure of French and of Polish in the light of comparative analysis. This study is of some scientific interest in that it attempts to solve the special problem of types of languages; it is also of educational interest, in that it shows the need for bearing in mind the structure of the mother tongue when studying a foreign language. The author makes a comparative study of linguistic phenomena in both languages in the field of phonetics, phonology, lexicology, morphology and inflexion; in the second volume he deals with problems of syntax. From van Willigen, Part I.

Kim, Soon-Ham Park
"The Meaning of *Yes* and *No* in English and Korean," *Language Learning,* XII (1962), 27-46.
In this article a contrastive analysis of meanings and uses of the response words *yes* and *no* in English and Korean is attempted. English and Korean patterns of responses to five specific types of response-eliciting stimulus sentences are compared through charts. The article describes that in English the response words are used on the basis of the affirmative or negative status of the fact, whereas in Korean they are used on the basis of the relationship between the status of the fact and of the preceding stimulus sentence. Thus the article also points out that due to this different native linguistic background the Korean learner of English has difficulty in producing correct answers to the negative stimulus sentences. Added at the end

are three levels of suggested lesson plans for drills of correct uses of English response words. Soon-Ham Park Kim. MLabstract #239.

*Kimizuka, Sumako
Problems in Teaching English Based upon a Comparative Analysis of Japanese and English. Unpublished Ph.D. dissertation. University of California at Los Angeles, 1962.

Kohmoto, Satesaburo
Phonemic and Sub-Phonemic Replacement of English Sounds by Speakers of Japanese. Unpublished Ed.D. dissertation, University of Michigan, 1960.

The important parts of this study are: (1) the author's efforts to collate previous studies of the Japanese sound system and organize the facts in a succinct form in order to meet a practical and pedagogical need, (2) the comprehensive treatment of both phonemic and allophonic replacement of English sounds made by the Japanese, (3) the prediction of the degrees of difficulty in overcoming various English pronunciation problems, and (4) the testing of these predictions by the use of native informants. The practical value of this study for pedagogical application lies in the fact that the results attained will provide the basis for the selection and arrangement of a number of selected items of English pronunciation for Japanese learners in a properly related sequence with special emphasis upon the chief trouble spots. From the abstract.

*Košelev, A.
"Novi aspekti na priložnoto iazykoznie v S.S.S.R. [New Aspects of of Applied Linguistics in the U.S.S.R.]," *Iazyk i literatura*, XV (1960), 316-23.

Koutsoudas, Andreas, and Olympia Koutsoudas
"A Contrastive Analysis of the Segmental Phonemes of Greek and English," *Language Learning*, XII (1962), 211-30.

This article has a dual purpose: (1) to predict the problems that will arise in teaching English pronunciation to native speakers of Greek and thus to provide a guide for the empirical solution to these and other problems, and (2) to provide an insight as to what will constitute a problem in language learning. The basis for (1) is a contrastive analysis of the segmental phonemes of Modern Athenian Greek and Mid-western American English, while the process of transferring to a second language habits acquired through familiarity with the native language—i.e., the concept of interference—serves as the basis for (2). Andreas Koutsoudas, MLabstract #620.

Kruatrachue, Foongfuang
Thai and English: A Comparative Study of Phonology for Pedagogical Applications. Unpublished Ph.D. dissertation, University of Indiana, 1961.
Pedagogically oriented contrastive phonology of Thai and English designed to aid Thai speakers in learning English. From Simon Belasco, February 1962, Part I.

Kufner, Herbert L.
The Grammatical Structure of English and German. Chicago: University of Chicago Press, 1962.
In this report I describe those areas of the grammatical structure of English and German which cause the greatest difficulties to the learner of German. The study is intended for language teachers and textbook writers, not for the language classroom. The major emphasis is on syntactical problems and divergent grammatical and semantic categories; little space is devoted to morphological questions. Contrastive structual analyses serve as the basis for this study. Herbert L. Kufner, MLabstract #327.

Lado, Robert
"Linguistic Interpretation of Speech Problems of Foreign Students," *Quarterly Journal of Speech,* XLVI (April, 1960), 171-75.
General treatment of problem of interference between two linguistic systems on all levels, including the phonemic. From Simon Belasco, February, 1961, Part I.

Lehn, W., and W. R. Slager
"A Contrastic Study of Egyptian Arabic and American English: The Segmental Phonemes," *Language Learning,* IX, Nos. 1-2 (1959), 25-33.
A contrastive study of the segmental phonemes (consonants and vowels) of Egyptian Arabic and American English. The study points out that the speaker of Arabic has difficulty learning English due to the differences in the number of contrasts with segmental phonemes, in permissible sequences, and in the phonetic expression of "similar" contrasts. JM

McIntosh, Lois
A Description and Comparison of Question Signals in Spoken English, Mandarin Chinese, French and German for Teachers of English as a Second Language. Unpublished Ph.D. dissertation, University of Michigan, 1953.
The purpose of the study is to aid the teacher of English as a

second language to meet the problem of students from many different linguistic backgrounds in the same classroom. BP

†Mackey, William F., and C. E. Rochette, Laval University, Quebec, Canada
Catenation in English and French: A Differential Analysis. Research in progress.

A differential instrumental analysis of the processes of sound linking in English and French, including the different systems of junction (juncture), co-articulation, regressive and progressive assimilation, hiatus, anticipation, the use of special linking and boundary signals, etc. In each case a contextualized corpus is being analyzed with a dozen subjects. Utterances are later taken out of context and matched. They are first analyzed by means of acoustic spectrography, cineradiology, photopalatography and through the tracings on electrokymographs and a five-track photo-oscillograph. A rhythmoscope is used to check compatability of stress. William F. Mackey

Marty, Fernand
See Marty, 2.3 French.

Moulton, William G.
"Linguistics and Language Teaching in the United States, 1940-1960," in *Trends in European and American Linguistics, 1930-1960.* Utrecht: Spectrum, 1961. Pp. 82-109. Reprinted for sale, Washington, D.C.: Superintendent of Documents, U.S. Government Printing Office, 1962. Reprinted in *International Review of Applied Linguistics in Language Teaching,* I (1963), 21-41.

The author describes the role played by linguists in U.S. language instruction during the period 1940-1960, and the linguistic principles underlying their methods. Topics covered, with bibliography, include the wartime language programs, later adaptations of wartime methods, the ACLS Committee on Language Programs, the MLA Foreign Language Program, the first two years of the NDEA, the Center for Applied Linguistics, English as a second language, linguistically oriented textbooks in English for American students, and a look at the future. William G. Moulton

————.

The Sounds of English and German: A Contrastive Analysis. Chicago: University of Chicago Press, 1962.

In this book I contrast the sound systems of English and German in order to reveal the conflicts between them, to explain the errors which our students make (through carrying English pronunciation habits over into German), and to suggest ways of overcoming these errors. Introductory chapters give a brief presentation of phonetics and phonemics, as applied to English and German; later chapters present a contrastive analysis of the two systems and suggest corrective drills. The book is intended for teachers of German and for those preparing to become teachers of German; it is *not* intended for use with students who are learning German. William G. Moulton.

†Mylerberg, Duane W.
Pedagogical Implications of Transformational Analysis. Unpublished Ph.D. dissertation in progress, University of Washington.

This study examines the theoretical foundations of foreign language pedagogy to ascertain which scientific theory of language (word and paradigm, phrase structure, or transformational analysis) is most consistent with the needs of the pedagogical situation. Findings indicate that transformational analysis is the only grammatical model which can form the basis for drill sets which are both explicit and efficient. I attempt to make clear the process of conversion of a scientific transformational grammar to classroom materials. Examples assume Spanish as the target language and English as the native language. Duane W. Mylerberg

Netherlands Didactiekcommissie
"Het Engelse Klanstelsel beschouwd in verband met het Nederlandse onderwijs," *Levende Talen,* No. 201 (October, 1959), 479-90; No. 202 (December, 1959), 623-33.

The pedagogical Commission of the Netherlands association of modern language teachers had produced a study on English phonemes, based on the scientific comparison of the English and Dutch phonetic systems, which provides the English teacher with valuable information on the practical aspect of his work. From van Wililgen, Part I.

Pascasio, Emy Mariano
"A Comparative Study: Predicting Interference and Facilitation for Tagalog Speakers in Learning English Noun-head Modification Patterns," *Language Learning,* XI (1961), 77-84.

This article illustrates the application of a methodology of comparing a part of English syntax with an equivalent Tagalog syntax to predict the points of interference and facilitation that will arise at this syntactical level for Tagalog speakers learning English. These predicted problems are classified under two types, *reception* and *production* after the comparison. Some patterns are assumed to be easier to recognize than to produce. Then these predicted problems are assigned to different levels of ease and difficulty arranged in ascending order from A to D. The findings showed other structural problems of Tagalog speakers beside the predicted problems. Emy M. Pascasio

—————.

A Descriptive-Comparative Study Predicting Interference and Facilitation for Tagalog Speakers in Learning English Noun-head Modification Patterns. Unpublished Ph.D. dissertation, University of Michigan, 1960.

The purpose of this study was threefold: (1) to compare a part of English syntax with an equivalent part of Tagalog syntax; (2) to predict the points of interference and facilitation that will arise at this syntactical level for Tagalog speakers learning English and classify them on different levels of ease and difficulty; (3) to prepare sample testing materials based on the predicted points of interference and facilitation and to administer these tests to a sampling of Tagalog speakers to verify the predictions made. The conclusions and implications made as a result of this study are: (1) there is an effect of previously learned habits upon foreign language learning, the similar elements were found easy and those different ones difficult; (2) a comparison of the students' native language and the language to be learned furnished a basis for better description of the language learning problems involved, preparation of teaching materials, and constructions of tests for diagnostic and evaluation purposes; (3) it is not only possible to predict areas of interference as well as facilitation between the two languages but also to rank them into different levels of ease and difficulty; (4) empirical evidence is helpful in verifying predicted language learning problems and also in unravelling other problems involved; (5) teachers with a knowledge of such problems can be expected to guide their students better. They will understand the cause of an error and be better able to prepare corrective drills; (6) the learning burden can be graded according to difficulty instead of arranging the lesson series in a purely logical sequence. Emy Mariano Pascasio

Pierce, Joe E.
See Pierce, 2.1.

Politzer, Robert L.
Teaching French: An Introduction to Applied Linguistics. New York: Ginn and Co., 1960.
Basic principles and general application of linguistics to teaching

of French at the beginning high school and college levels. Emphasizes the use of linguistics concepts. Points out pattern conflicts in English and French; suggests linguistic solutions to the teaching problems they create. DG

Politzer, Robert L., and Charles N. Staubach
  Teaching Spanish: A Linguistic Orientation. Boston: Ginn, 1961.
    In this book we deal with methods, materials, and especially the linguistic bases for teaching Spanish "in the new key." We treat method in the first part; *applied* linguistics, basic psychological assumptions, linguistic and non-linguistic procedures. Our second part gives a brief introduction to phonetics/phonemics, discusses teaching pronunciation, forms, syntax, vocabulary, and other phases for which linguistics offers specific analyses and suggestions. Pattern drills and other audio-lingual techniques are featured, and the problems arising from native-tongue interferences are studied in some detail; special problems in Spanish for English speakers are carefully treated. Robert L. Politzer and Charles N. Staubach, MLabstract #74. (A revised edition, N.Y., Blaisdell Publishing Co., will be ready by early 1965.)

Pulgram, Ernst (ed.)
  Applied Linguistics in Language Learning. (Georgetown University Monograph Series on Languages and Linguistics, No. 6.) Washington, D.C.: Georgetown University, 1954.
    This is a collection of papers first read at the MLA meeting, December, 1953. The papers present the findings of linguistic science that are useful to the modern-foreign-language teacher. BP

Rivers, Wilga M.
  See Rivers, 3.1.

Saporta, Sol
  See Saporta, 3.1.

Sibayan, Bonifacio Padilla
  English and Iloko Segmental Phonemes. Unpublished Ed.D. dissertation, University of Michigan, 1961.
    The purpose of this study was to find out what English segmental phonemes are difficult to recognize and produce by elementary school pupils whose first language is Iloho. [. . .] Important implications of this study are: (1) that a program of teaching English to Iloho-speaking elementary school children should be based on a contrastive analysis such as this one, and (2) that a study like this is useful to teachers, writers of teaching materials, test constructors, and supervisors in second language teaching. From the abstract.

Simches, Seymour O.
See Simches, 3.1.

Stockwell, Robert P., J. Donald Bowen, and John W. Martin
Contrastive Study of English and Spanish. V. I: Phonology; V. II:
Grammar. Chicago: University of Chicago Press, to appear.

An extensive but (especially for Volume II) still incomplete
comparative study of the linguistic systems of English and Spanish.
Theoretical discussions of patterns and interference are illustrated by
observations from classroom experience. J. Donald Bowen. Sponsored by the Center for Applied Linguistics of the Modern Language
Association, this is part of the Contrastive Studies Series. See Kufner,
and Moulton, this section.

Twaddell, Freeman
"Linguistics and Foreign Language Teaching," *The DFL Bulletin:
Publication of the Department of Foreign Languages of the NEA*, II
(March, 1963).

Dr. Twaddell briefly exposes the common ground upon which
linguistics and foreign language teaching necessarily need to converge
in order to meet the current and future needs of foreign language
learning. He posits specific "conflict points" of pronunciation and
grammar which the foreign language teacher needs to be aware of.
But more than just being aware of these conflict points, the teacher
must be competent enough to help the student overcome them. The
basis of this competency lies in a certain knowledge of linguistics
along with pedagogical skill and an adequate practical command of
the foreign language. CBC

*Velázquez, Mary D. Rivera de
A Contrastive Analysis of the Phonological Systems of English and
Puerto Rican Spanish with Implications for the Teaching of English as
a Second Language. Unpublished Ph.D. dissertation in progress, University of Indiana.

Vinay, J.-P., J. B. Rudnyckyj, W. S. Avis
See Viney, Part I.

Weir, Ruth Hirsch (ed.)
*Report of the Sixth Annual Round Table Meeting on Linguistics and
Language Teaching.* (Georgetown University Monograph Series on
Languages and Linguistics, No. 8.) Washington, D.C.: Georgetown
University, September, 1955.

Contains a number of lectures relating to applied linguistics and the preparation of teaching materials; the terminology of linguistics; problems of translation, which include translation as a research tool and machine translation; and meaning and language structure. JM

*Yolande-de-L'Immaculée, Soeur, F.C.S.C.J.
Une application pédagogique de la linguistique structurale: la méthode "dynamique." Unpublished Master's thesis, University of Montreal, 1960.

Yorkey, Richard Clements
See Yorkey, 2.3 English.

4.3 Theoretical Research with Possible Applications

Anisfeld, Moshe
"A Comment on 'The Role of Grapheme-Phoneme Correspondence in the Perception of Words' by Gibson et al.," *American Journal of Psychology,* to appear.
See Gibson, below. The present note wishes to raise the possibility of an alternative interpretation of Gibson et al.'s data: that high bigram frequencies of four to eight letter pseudo-words yielded more correct tachistoscopic recognition scores than low bigram frequencies. Moshe Anisfeld

Belasco, Simon, Pierre Delattre, Albert Valdman
See Belasco, Part I.

Bolinger, Dwight L.
"A Theory of Pitch Accent in English," *Word,* XIV (August-December, 1958), 109-49.
A series of tests determining that pitch is more important than intensity in English stress. Short section on learning of pitch structures but no experiments directly concerned with this area. (Research supported by a grant from the Carnegie Corporation of New York.) JAD

Borst, John M.
"The Use of Spectrograms for Speech Analysis and Synthesis," *Journal of the Audio Engineering Society,* IV (1956), 14-23.
Engineers at the acoustics laboratory at M.I.T. have built two electrical synthesizers of speech. One synthesizer is a variable transmission line similar to the vocal tract. The other has variable simple-tuned circuits to represent vocal-tract resonances and can be made to generate simple sentences of fair intelligibility, by use of teletype tapes

and relays. (Research supported by the Carnegie Corporation of New York and the U.S. Department of Defense.) BP

†Buiten, R. L., and Harlan L. Lane
On the Correlation Between the Peak Amplitudes of the Speech Wave Form and Those of Its Fundamental Component. (Report expected in 1965).

Carroll, John B., *et al.*
See Carroll, *et al.,* 3.7.

Catania, A. C.
See Lane, 4.3.

Chatman, Seymour
See Chatman, 2.54.

Cooper, Franklin S., Alvin M. Liberman, and John M. Borst
"The Interconversion of Audible and Visible Patterns as a Basis for Research in the Perception of Speech," *Proceedings of the National Academy of Sciences,* XXXVII (May, 1951), 318-25.
    The study of the use of an instrument called a pattern playback, which reconverts spectrograms into sound. The operating principle of the machine is described. The playback produces intelligible speech, which may then be dissected or degraded in various ways. The measurement of intelligibility is 95 per cent. Information perceived visually through the use of the spectrograph can be converted into sound for audial perception so that pattern characteristics may be preserved, giving a new tool for studying the manipulation and synthesis of speech. (Research supported by Carnegie Corporation of New York.) JM

Cooper, Franklin S., *et al.*
Some Input-Output Relations Observed in Experiments on the Perception of Speech. (Paper presented at the 2e Congrès international de cybernétique, Namur, Belgium, September 3-10, 1958.) Namur, Belgium: Association internationale de cybernétique, 1958.
    An explanation of the study of speech in terms of perceptual relationships between the auditory patterns of words and the visual presentation as displayed by spectrographic pictures; and in terms of possible relationships existing between the perception of speech sounds and the articulatory gestures as involved in the production of these sounds. JM

———.

"Some Experiments on the Perception of Synthetic Speech Sounds,"

Journal of the Acoustical Society of America, XXIV (November, 1952), 597-606.

Investigation of acoustic nature of *p, t, k,* using pattern playback. JAD

Cowan, J. M.

Final Technical Report: Development of a Device to Record Graphically Intonations of Speech as They Are Perceived by a Listener. Ithaca, New York: Cornell University, January 15, 1963 (ditto).

From the Final Report: "Intonation is one of the most important components of a language. It is also one of the most elusive because it is overlaid with a sequence of significant phones occurring at an average rate (in most European languages) of about 12-15 per second. These latter place such a load on the attention of the listener that it is very difficult to abstract the underlying intonation from the rest of the sound complex. A device which would analyze out the intonation and represent it graphically (and perhaps reproduce it auditorily as sheer intonation) would give the linguist a new and reliable tool for the analysis and study of this important component. Such a device would have important application in the teaching of foreign languages because it would illustrate vividly to learners the differences between their native intonation patterns and those of the target language." The report includes a general description of the method and instrumentation toward this end, along with an historical and theoretical treatment of the problem. DF

————.

"Graphical Representation of Perceived Pitch in Speech," in *Proceedings of the Fourth International Congress of Phonetic Science* [Helsinki, Finland, September 1961], 's-Gravenhage: Mouton, 1962. Pp. 567-70.

The article is a general introduction to the project, presenting the theoretical and instrumentational background. It is reprinted in the Final Technical Report, q.v., preceding entry.

Cross, D. V., and Harlan L. Lane

"On the Discriminative Control of Concurrent Responses: The Relations among Response Frequency, Latency, and Topography in Auditory Generalization," *Journal of the Experimental Analysis of Behavior,* V (October, 1962), 487-96.

Three experiments using human subjects are described and verified by chart analysis. The results are: "1) The probabilities associated with a specific response were maximal over several stimulus values at the extreme ends of the continuum, then dropped sharply at stimuli intermediate to the initial S^D's as the probability of the alternative response increased; 2) Overall response latency was inversely related to the relative frequency of the two responses at each stimulus value. When the two responses were most nearly equal in probability, latencies were maximal; when one response had close to unit or zero probability, latencies were minimal; 3) Analysis of the latencies of the two responses, taken separately, revealed: (a) an increase in latency as the difference between the test stimulus and the initial S^D increased; (b) a sharp discontinuity in the latency gradient and reversal in trend at intermediate stimulus intensities; and (c) at a given stimulus value, latencies associated with the stochastically dominant response were consistently shorter than those of the non-dominant response. 4) No changes in response topography (fundamental frequency) were correlated with the characteristic changes in probability and latency during stimulus generalizations." JM

Delattre, Pierre

Change as a Correlate of the Consonant/Vowel Distinction. Paper presented at the Linguistic Society of America Meeting, Chicago, 1963.

A number of laboratory experiments are described which indicate that vowels are perceived by frequency steady state of formants and consonants by frequency change of formants. This new acoustic feature correlates better with the distributional distinction of syllable peak vs. syllable margin than any feature proposed in the past. Pierre Delattre

————.

"Comparing the Prosodic Features of English, German, Spanish and French," *International Review of Applied Linguistics in Language Teaching,* to appear.

First results of long range programs of experimental phonetic research by X-ray motion picture, spectrographic analysis and synthesis on eleven non-segmental traits: 1) Declarative intonation, 2) Non-declarative intonation, 3) Place of logical stress in words, 4) Place of logical stress in sense groups, 5) Nature of logical stress, 6) Place of emphatic stress, 7) Nature of emphatic stress, 8) Variations in syllable weight, 9) Syllabication, 10) Syllable types, 11) Tension. Pierre Delattre

————.

A Comparison of the Frequency of Phoneme Occurrence. Paper presented at the Rocky Mountain Modern Language Association Meeting, Utah, 1962.

Frequency of occurrence of English phonemes is found to be more similar to German than to Spanish and French. German and French, however, have much in common. Comparative tables are presented. Pierre Delattre

————.

A Cross-linguistic Comparison of Syllables. Paper presented at the Rocky Mountain Modern Language Association Meeting, Utah, 1962.

English and German are shown to have a greater proportion of closed syllables and of heavy syllables (loaded with consonants) than French or Spanish. Pierre Delattre

————.

Distinctive and Non-distinctive Aspects of German Intonation. Paper presented at the Rocky Mountain Modern Language Association Meeting, Denver, 1963.

German intonation is described as similar to American English intonation regarding pitch levels (pitch phonemes) but very different regarding actual curves. For instance, the prevailing curve of continuation is rising in German, falling in English. Precise and complete frequency curves are analyzed by appropriate instruments. The importance of such curves in teaching is stressed. Pierre Delattre

————.

English Phonetics as Heard by Speakers of German, French, and Spanish. Paper presented at the Meeting of Western Conferences of Foreign Student Advisors, Boulder, 1963.

Largely a presentation of the phonetic differences found among those four languages by statistical study of vowel types, consonant types, syllable types, stress types, intonation curve types, etc. Pierre Delattre

————.

The General Phonetic Characteristics of Language. Boulder, Colo.: University of Colorado, June, 1962.

Includes the description of a four-way technique for the objective phonetic comparison of English to German, Spanish and French: by X-ray motion picture, by spectrographic analysis, by artificial speech synthesis, and by statistical data. Construction of the laboratory is related, and some preliminary results are presented regarding forty phonetic features in each of the four languages. Pierre Delattre

———.

Isolating the Factors of a Foreign Accent by Synthesis. Paper presented at the meeting of the Modern Language Association of America, Chicago, December 28, 1961.

Techniques of phonetic research by spectrographic synthesis of speech are demonstrated in two examples: the isolation of various factors of stress (duration, intensity of vowel and of consonant) and the distinction among seven degrees of open-to-closed syllabication. Paper available from the author. Pierre Delattre

———.

"The Physiological Interpretations of Sound Spectrograms," *PMLA,* LXVI (September, 1951), 864-75.

Relationship shown between formant-one frequency raising and over-all mouth opening; between formant-two frequency lowering and tongue backing; between formant-two frequency lowering and lip rounding; between formant-two frequency lowering and front-cavity lengthening; between formant-three frequency raising and velum lowering, as in nasalizing; between formant-three frequency lowering and tongue-tip raising as in *r*-coloring. (Research supported by University of Pennsylvania Faculty Research Fund and Carnegie Corporation of New York.) JAD

———.

"Research Techniques for Phonetic Comparison of Languages," *International Review of Applied Linguistics,* I, No. 2 (1963), 85-97.

An experimental phonetics laboratory equipped to compare the phonetic features of languages is concretely described. Its purpose is the improvement of foreign language teaching in the United States. The research technique is four-fold: spectrographic analysis, spectrographic synthesis, cineradiography (motion picture x-ray), and statistical study of the sound structure. It is also shown in this article how 35 phonetic features of English—such as stress, intonation, rhythm, vowel duration, syllabic types, sound distribution, sound frequency of occurrence, neutral vowel position, diphthongization, nasality, fronting, aspiration, etc.—can profitably be compared with the corresponding features of French, German or Spanish by the instrumental techniques described above. Pierre Delattre, MLabstract #721.

———.

"Some Factors of Vowel Duration and their Cross-Linguistic Validity," *Journal of the Acoustical Society of America,* XXXIV (August, 1962), 1141-44.

Separates the factors of vowel duration into those that are phonemically learned, such as the *mettre/maître* difference in French, and those that are physiologically conditioned, such as the influence of the following consonant (external) or the degree of vowel opening (internal). Demonstrates that conditioned factors are universal, or cross-linguistically valid. Pierre Delattre

————.

Some Suggestions for Teaching Methods Arising from Research on the Acoustic Analysis and Synthesis of Speech. (Georgetown University Monograph Series on Language and Linguistics, No. 2.) Washington, D.C.: Georgetown University, September, 1952. Pp. 31-45.

Presents and explains the use of spectrograms that immobilize speech sounds, providing a picture to analyze the pronunciation. The use of the spectrogram is practically applied to French nasals and syllables. This type of research is applicable to the use of the direct translator as a teaching device. JM

————.

"Voyelles diphtonguées et voyelles pures," *French Review,* XXXVII (October, 1963), 64-76.

An objective analysis by means of tape recordings, X-rays, and films of the French and English vowels /o, e, u, i/. Conclusions are drawn as to the various comparable and distinguishable characteristics on the basis of the information provided by the various media. DF

Delattre, Pierre C., *et al.*
"An Experimental Study of the Acoustic Determinants of Vowel Color: Observations of One- and Two-Formant Vowels Synthesized from Spectrograph Patterns," *Word,* VIII (December, 1952), 195-210.

A series of 235 two-formant patterns were prepared and changed into sound by an instrument called a "pattern playback." From this series the authors chose those sounds that most approach the sixteen cardinal vowel sounds of the International Phonetic Association. Presented to phonetics students, they were highly identifiable. (Research supported by the Carnegie Corporation of New York and the Department of Defense.) BP

Gibson, Eleanor J., *et al.*
"The Role of Grapheme-Phoneme Correspondence in the Perception of Words," *American Journal of Psychology,* LXXV (1962), 554-70.

The experiment described demonstrates that the spelling-to-sound correlations in English are reflected in the perception (reading)

of written words and pseudo-words, since pseudo-words constructed according to correspondence rules are read significantly more accurately under tachistoscopic exposure that control pseudo-words. Eleanor J. Gibson. See also, Anisfeld, this section.

Harms, L. S.

Self-Instruction in Sound Discrimination of Phonetic Transcription. Interim Report. Baton Rouge, La.: Louisiana State University, February, 1962.

In this research project, I have attempted to develop a single, highly efficient, adaptive program which would permit both foreign and native students to discriminate among the speech sounds of American English and to transcribe these sounds in the IPA system as employed by Kenyon and Knott [John Samuel Kenyon, and Thomas Albert Knott, *A Pronouncing Dictionary of American English* (Springfield, Mass.: G. G. C. Merriam, 1953)]. Both foreign and native students gained substantially in skill as a result of the self-instructional program. The terminal skill of 95% accuracy was sought in the check out test of words selected randomly from the Kenyon and Knott Dictionary. Twenty-three foreign students averaged 79% accuracy; 12 native students averaged 89% accuracy. A revision of this program is now being tested. L. S. Harms, MLabstract #365.

Harris, Katherine S.

"Cues for the Discrimination of American English Fricatives in Spoken Syllables," *Language and Speech,* I (January-March, 1958), 1-7.

It is sometimes assumed that identification of the fricatives of American English in CV syllables depends primarily on the characteristics of the voice (nonvocalic) portion of the sound. Investigation of the possibility that vocalic portions are important showed that differentiation of f and θ is accomplished on basis of cues in vocalic part of the syllable. (Research supported by the Carnegie Corporation of New York and the Department of Defense.) BP

Harris, Katherine S., *et al.*

"Effect of Third-Formant Transitions on the Perception of the Voiced Stop Consonants," *Journal of the Acoustical Society of America,* XXX (February, 1958), 122-26.

Discussion of results of experimentation using synthetic speech to show that third-formant transitions are cues for the perception of the voiced stops b, d, g. Methodology of experiment is explained in relation to apparatus and stimuli and their presentation. Results are presented graphically. (Research supported by Carnegie Corporation of New York and Department of Defense.) JM

Heinberg, Paul
See Heinberg, 2.55.

Hoffman, Howard S.
"Study of Some Cues in the Perception of the Voiced Stop Consonants," *Journal of the Acoustical Society of America,* XXX (November, 1958), 1035-41.

Confirms previous research demonstrating the role of transitions in the perception of voiced stops *b, d,* and *g.* Also demonstrates the relevance of an additional cue, namely the burst frequency, largely independent of other cues. SS

Horowitz, A. E.
The Effects of Variation in Linguistic Structure on the Learning of Miniature Linguistic Systems. Unpublished Ph.D. dissertation, Harvard University, 1955.

Three experiments using artificial language materials (nonsense syllables and nonsense figures) that allow for experimental control of variables while retaining the minimal features of a "full" linguistic system—duality of patterning and productivity. Variables studied were morpheme order, vowel morphemes scaled for phonetic symbolism of size, and variation of semantic rules while holding linguistic structure constant. A. E. Horowitz

Horowitz, A. E., and H. M. Jackson
"Morpheme Order and Syllable Structure in the Learning of Miniature Linguistic Systems," *Journal of Abnormal and Social Psychology,* LIX (November, 1959), 387-92.

Two experiments testing the effect of variation in morpheme order and English vs. non-English syllabification (with English speaking subjects) on the learning of limited, artificial linguistic systems constructed from nonsense syllables and used to symbolize nonsense figures. Essentially a replication of an early study by Esper (*Language Monographs,* No. 1 [1925],) in which these two variables were confounded. Morpheme order had no effect on learning rate, while using non-English nonsense syllables drastically reduced the number of subjects able to reach criterion within 5 days of practice. A. E. Horowitz

House, A. S., *et al.*
"On the Learning of Speechlike Vocabularies," *Journal of Verbal Learning and Verbal Behavior,* I (September, 1962), 133-43.

In this article we describe a series of experiments dealing with the learning of ensembles of speechlike acoustic stimuli. The stimulus ensembles differed with respect to the number of physical dimensions that were manipulated in generating the stimuli, and with respect to the extent to which the stimuli resembled speech. Results show that performance during learning is better when each stimulus is encoded into several physical dimensions than when the stimuli lie along an unidimensional continuum. Furthermore, as the stimuli become more like speech there is a deterioration of performance during learning with the exception that performance is best when the stimuli are actually speech signals. Implications for theories of speech perception are discussed. A. S. House, MLabstract #713.

Lane, Harlan L. The Regents of the University of Michigan, Ann Arbor, Michigan.
Experimental Analysis of the Control of Speech Production and Perception I. Phase I and II; Project No. OE 3-14-013 (National Defense Education Act. Title VI), February 1, 1963, to January 31, 1965; $128,891.

The Contractor will continue and extend the research supported under U.S. Office of Education contract SAE-9265, which has included 28 experiments in such areas as discrimination learning, auditory generalization, programmed instruction, self-shaping of vocal behavior, analysis of foreign accent, and perception of emotion in speech. The purpose of the new work is to increase our understanding of the process of second-language learning and our ability to control that process. The work will proceed along two lines: the control of vocal behavior and the design, construction, and use of an auto-instructional device to teach the prosodic features of language.

The control of language learning is conceived as the shaping, or selective reinforcement of successive approximations to the patterns of the target language. By bringing together the technique of behavioral control (operant conditioning) and of the electro-mechanical measurement of vocal behavior, the investigators hope to develop procedures to enable students to control the segmental and suprasegmental features of language.

The auto-instructional device for teaching the prosodic features of language will present a model pattern to the student; assess his accuracy in imitating this pattern; present reinforcement conditional on his accuracy; then move on to the next step in the program when the student meets a pre-set, adjustable criterion. The device will work with three aspects of language: rhythm, inflection, and stress. In terms of acoustic parameters, the device will measure the spacing of the rhythmic peaks and the changes in pitch and relative amplitude of the model speech stream, and will cross-correlate one or more of these with the student's imitation.

Following are the contents of the first six progress reports on this composite project.

PROGRESS REPORT No. 1, Experimental Analysis of the Control of Speech Production and Perception, Feb. 1 to Sept. 1, 1961. Table of Contents:

Lane, H. L. (1961)	On the discontinuity of auditory discrimination learning in human adults.
Cross, D. V., & Lane, H. L.	On the discriminative control of concurrent responses: the relations among response frequency, latency, and topography in auditory generalization.[1]
Lane, H. L.	The effects of changing vowel parameters on perceived loudness and stress. I: Does autophonic level affect the loudness function? II: Sound pressure, spectral structure, and autophonic level. III: Vocal matching of stress patterns.
Lane, H. L., & Moore, D. J.	Operant reconditioning of a consonant discrimination in an asphasic.
Lane, H. L.	Teaching machines and programmed learning.
Lane, H. L.	Some differences between first and second language learning.
Morton, F. R., & Lane, H. L.	Techniques of operant conditioning applied to second language learning. See 3.2.
Lane, H. L.	Experimentation in the language classroom: guidelines and suggested procedures for the classroom teacher.
Lane, H. L. (1962)	Repertoires in contact: studies of the interaction between first- and second-language learning.

[1] For published report, see same author and title, this section.

Lane, H. L.	Some differences between first and second language learning. *Language Learning,* XII (1962), 1-14.
Lane, H. L.	Experimentation in the language classroom: guidelines and suggested procedures for the classroom teacher. *Language Learning,* XII, No. 2 (1962), 115-123. Reprinted in *U.S.I.A. Eng. Teaching Forum,* I (1963), 3-8.
Lane, H. L.	Psychophysical parameters of vowel perception. *Psychological Monographs,* LXXVI (1962), 1-25.[1]
Lane, H. L., & Moore, D. J. (1962)	Reconditioning a consonant discrimination in an asphasic: an experimental case history. *Journal of Speech and Hearing Disorders,* XXVII, No. 3 (1962), 232-243.
Lane, H. L., & Cross, D. V.	Effects of training on estimates of vowel loudness.[1]
Cross, D. V., & Lane, H. L.	On the discriminative control of concurrent responses: the relations among response frequency, latency, and topography in auditory generalization. *Journal of Experimental and Analytical Behavior,* V (1962), 487-496.
Kramer, E.	Judgment of portrayed emotion from normal English, filtered English, and Japanese speech. Doctoral dissertation, 1962.
Anderson, T., Schneider, B., & Lane, H. L.*	Aural attention, 1962.
Lane, H. L.*	Autophonic falsetto, 1962.
Lane, H. L.*	Autophonic difference linen, 1962.
Lane, H. L., & Cross, D. V.*	Latency in multiple stimulus-response relations, 1962.
Schneider, B.*	Psychophysical scales for visual and auditory speech perception, 1962.

PROGRESS REPORT No. 2, Experimental Analysis of the Control of Speech Production and Perception: II, Sept. 1, 1961, to Feb. 1, 1962. Table of Contents:

Lane, H. L.   Parameters of vowel perception.

Lane, H. L., & Shinkman, P. G.   The relations among response rate, topography, and schedules of reinforcement: methods and findings in an analysis of the vocal operant.

Cross, D. V., & Lane, H. L.   Effects of training on estimates of vowel loudness.

Kramer, E.   Personality stereotypes in voice: a reconsideration of the data.

Lane, H. L.* (1963)   Reaction time in loudness estimation.

Anderson, T., & Lane, H. L.*   Retention of vocal topography.

Kramer, E.   The judgment of personal characteristics and emotions from nonverbal properties of speech. *Psychological Bulletin*, LX (1963), 408-420.

Lane, H. L.   Some relations between verbal and nonverbal behavior in children. Progress Report, Horace H. Rackham School of Graduate Studies, Faculty Research Project 1274, August 1963.

Lane, H. L., & Shinkman, Paul G.   Methods and findings in an analysis of a vocal operant. *Journal of Experimental and Analytical Behavior*, VI (1963), 179-188.

Lane, H. L.   Specifications for auditory discrimination learning in the language laboratory, *International Journal of American Linguistics*, XXIX, No. 2 (1963), 61-69.

Lane, H. L., & Schneider, B. A.   Methods for self-shaping echoic behavior. *Modern Language Journal*, XLVII, No. 4 (1963), 154-160. See annotation below, 3.2.

Lane, H. L.	Foreign accent and speech distortion, *J. acoust. Soc. Amer.* XXXV, No. 4 (1963), 451-453.
Lane, H. L., & Curran, C. R.	Gradients of auditory generalization for blind, retarded children. *Journal of Experimental and Analytical Behavior*, VI (1963), 585-588.[1]
Lane, H. L.	The autophonic scale of voice level for congenitally deaf subjects. *Journal of Experimental Psychology*, LXVI (1963), 328-331.
Schneider, B. A., & Lane, H. L.	Ratio scales, category scales, and variability in the production of loudness and softness. *Journal of the Acoustical Society of America*, XXXV (1963), 1953-1961.
Schneider, B. A., & Lane, H. L.	Some discriminative properties of syntactic structures. *Journal of Verbal Learning and Verbal Behavior*, II (1963), 457-461.

PROGRESS REPORT No. 3, Experimental Analysis of the Control of Speech Production and Perception: III, Feb. 1, 1962 to April 1, 1963. Table of Contents:

Lane, H. L.	Differential reinforcement of vocal duration.
Cross, D. V.	Metric properties of multidimensional stimulus generalization.
Lane, H. L., & Kopp, J. L.	The effects of response-dependent and independent reinforcement in extending stimulus control.
Lane, H. L., & Schneider, B. A.	Some discriminative properties of syntactic structures.[1]
Schneider, B. A.	Ratio scales, category scales, and variability in the production of loudness and softness.
Lane, H. L.	The autophonic scale of voice level for congenitally deaf subjects.
Kopp, J. L., & Lane, H. L.	A new determination of the pure tone equal-loudness contours for earphone listening.

Lane, H. L. Hunting, J. R., Brethower, D. M., & Kopp, J. L.	An effect of native language and musical training on vocal pitch matching.[1]
Kramer, E.	Judgment of portrayed emotion from normal English, filtered English, and Japanese speech.
Benesh, Marijana, Kramer, E., & Lane, H. L.	Recognition of portrayed emotion in a foreign language. See 5.0.
Lane, H. L.	Initial specifications for a speech auto-instructional device.
	PROGRESS REPORT No. 4, Experimental Analysis of the Control of Speech Production and Perception: IV, April 1, 1963 to November 1, 1963. Table of Contents:
Lane, H. L.	Programmed learning of a second language. See 2.55.
Lane, H. L.	The motor theory of speech perception: a critical review.
Cross, D. V., Lane, H. L., & Sheppard, W.	Visual control of phonemic contrasts: a test of the motor theory of speech perception.
Cross, D. V., & Lane, H. L.	Attention to single stimulus properties in the identification of complex tones.
Ross, Strange	A technique for producing known sound pressures at the eardrum.
Lane, H. L. (1964)	Differential reinforcement of vocal duration. *Journal of Experimental and Analytical Behavior*, VII (1964), 107-115. See annotation below, 3.2. *J. exp. Anal. Behav.* VII (1964), 107-115.
Lane, H. L., & Kopp, J. L.	The effects of response-dependent and independent reinforcement in extending stimulus control. *Psychological Records*, XIV, No. 1 (1964), 81-87.

PROGRESS REPORT No. 5, Preliminary Manual for the Speech Auto-Instructional Device, Nov. 1, 1963 to Feb. 1, 1964.

Lane, H. L.   Acquisition and transfer in auditory discrimination. *American Journal of Psychology*, LXXVI (1964), 240-248. See annotation below, 3.2.

Schneider, B. A., & Lane, H. L.   Note on the variability hypothesis in category scaling. *Journal of Acoustical Society of America*, XXXVI, No. 10 (1964), 1958.

Cross, D. V., Lane, H. L., & Sheppard, W.   Identification and discrimination functions for a visual continuum: a test of the motor theory of speech perception. *Journal of Experimental Psychology*, 1964. (in press)

Lane, H. L., & Bem, D.   An effect of changing verbal behavior on non-verbal behavior in retarded children. *Worm Runner's Digest*. VI (1964), 6-14.

Lane, H. L.   Programmed learning of a second language. Chapter 7 in R. Glaser (ed.), *Programmed Learning: Data and Directions:* Washington, D.C.: National Education Association, 1964. (in press)

Buiten, R. L., & Lane, H. L.   Conditioning prosodic accuracy in a second language. *International Review of Applied Linguistics*, 1964 (in press).

Lane, H. L., Hunting, J. R., Brethower, D. M., & Kopp, J. L.   An effect of native language and musical training on vocal pitch matching. *Perceptual and Motor Skills*, 1964 (in press).

Lane, H. L., & Bem, D. J.   *A Laboratory Manual for the Control and Analysis of Behavior.* Belmont, Calif.: Wadsworth Publishing Company, 1964.

Lane, H. L.   *The Control and analysis of speech.* New York: Appleton-Century-Crofts, 1964 (in preparation).

Lane, H. L., & Geis, G. L.   A program for reviews and a review of a program on linguistics. In *Contemporary Psychology*, 1964 (in press).

Cross, D. V.

Metric properties of multidimensional stimulus generalization. In D. Mostofsky (ed.), *Proc. Conf. Stimulus Generalization.* Stanford: Stanford University Press, 1964 (in press).

Kramer, E.

Personality stereotypes in voice: a reconsideration of the data. *Journal of Social Psychology,* LXII (1964), 247-251.

Kramer, E.

The elimination of verbal cues in judgments of emotion from voice. *Journal of Abnormal and Social Psychology,* 1964, 68 (1964), 390-396.

Buiten, R. L., &
Lane, H. L.

A self-instructional device for conditioning accurate prosody. *International Review of Applied Linguistics* (in press, 1964). See also the following speech.

Buiten, R. L., &
Lane, H. L.

A language teaching system with real-time error discrimination. April 24, 1964. See 2.55.

Environmental factors in behavioral research and training in retardation. Committee for Behavioral Research and Training in Retardation, Conference Report, 1964.

PROGRESS REPORT No. 6, Experimental Analysis of the Control of Speech Production and Perception: VI, November, 1964. Table of Contents:

Lane, H. L.

A survey of the acoustic and discriminative properties of speech sounds.

Ross, Strange

Matching functions and equal-sensation contours for loudness.

Cross, D. V., &
Lane, H. L.

An analysis of the relations between identification and discrimination functions for speech and nonspeech continua.

Kopp, J. L., &
Cross, D. V.

Identification and discrimination functions for graphemes and lines.

Kopp, J. L., &
Cross, D. V.

A relation between stimulus generalization and magnitude estimation.

Cross, D. V.	An application of mean value theory to psychophysical measurement.
Buiten, R. L., & Lane, H. L.	A self-instructional device for conditioning accurate prosody.
Lane, H. L., & Geis, G. L.	A program for reviews and a review of a program on linguistics.

* Report not prepared as of 1/1/65

Lane, Harlan L.

"Foreign Accent and Speech Distortion," *Journal of the Acoustical Society of America,* XXXV (April, 1963), 451-53.

Twenty-four Midwest Americans listened to recorded articulation lists rendered by one American and three foreign-born speakers under eight conditions of masking and filtering. Reducing the speech to noise ratio to 20 db or the transmission bandwidth to 500 cps yields approximate 50 per cent reduction in word articulation for both native and foreign accent speech. The latter was approximately 40 per cent less intelligible than native speech under all experimental conditions. Harlan L. Lane

――――.

"Psychological Parameters of Vowel Perception," *Psychological Monographs,* LXXVI, No. 44 (1962), Monograph No. 563.

Psychophysical scales are determined for the amplitude, duration, and fundamental frequency parameters of vowels. Numerical estimates of vowel loudness and of vowel duration grow as a power function of their respective parameter values, while estimates of pitch are a logarithmic function of fundamental frequency. A given change in the amplitude, duration, or fundamental frequency of a vowel appears greater to the speaker than to the listener; in other words, autophonic scales of vowel parameters grow more rapidly as a function of stimulus magnitude than do reception scales. When a subject is instructed to match his vocal response to a vowel stimulus, autophonic and reception scales of vowel perception predict the parameters of echoic responding. The matching function for each stimulus parameter shows some influence of the other parameters; the largest effect is an increase in response pitch associated with an increase in stimulus amplitude. This interaction is predicted quantitatively from a simplified analysis of the mechanics of the glottal source and from an empirical determination of pitch-amplitude relations in free responding. Harlan L. Lane

———.
See Lane, 2.9.

Lane, Harlan L., and D. V. Cross
"Effects of Training on Estimates of Vowel Loudness," *Journal of Experimental Psychology,* to appear.

The effects of prior conditioning on judgments of subjective magnitude were assessed using the method of magnitude estimation to scale vowel loudness under two experimental conditions: (a) following discrimination training utilizing five synthesized vowel sounds (/i/, /I/, /e/, /æ/ and /a/) for which the vocal response "ten" to the middle vowel /e/ was reinforced, and (b) following a neutral task using the same vowel sounds but without reinforcing differential responding. In addition, generalization of the modulus response along the intensity continuum was compared to that resulting when magnitude judgments are not required. The loudness scales obtained under the first two conditions confirmed the power law. Prior conditioning resulted in a function with a significantly steeper slope than that obtained under neutral conditions. Harlan L. Lane

Lane, Harlan L., and Bruce Schneider
"Some Discriminative Properties of Syntactic Structures." *Journal of Verbal Learning and Verbal Behavior,* II (December, 1963), 457-61.

Forty scripts were prepared that contained the same 36 kernel sentences with one of four syntactic structures: declarative, negative, passive, or query. The relative frequency of the structures in each script was varied systematically. Tape recordings of the scripts, read by forty speakers, were presented to listeners who sorted a (different) set of 144 sentences according to their estimate of which speaker was most likely to have said each sentence. The distribution of syntactic structures in the stimulus scripts was compared with the corresponding distribution arrived at by the listener. When a particular syntactic structure predominated in a speaker's corpus, the listeners tended to assign all the sentences of the dominant form exclusively to that speaker. When the relative frequencies of the syntactic structures in a corpus were more nearly equal, the listeners tended to assign structures at random. Most of the confusion in discrimination, that is, assignment of a structure to a speaker much more often than it was uttered, were associated with the declarative and passive sentence structures. These syntactic forms generalized most often with each other and more often with the remaining syntactic forms than either negative or interrogative sentences. Harlan L. Lane. The research reported herein is related to the project under Mr. Lane's name, this section.

Lane, Harlan L., A. C. Catania, and S. S. Stevens
"Voice Level: Autophonic Scale, Perceived Loudness, and Effects of Sidetone," *Journal of the Acoustical Society of America.* XXXIII, No. 2 (1961), 160-67.
The speaker's numerical estimation of his own vocal level, the *autophonic response*, was found to grow as the 1.1 power of the actual sound pressure was produced. When listeners judged the loudness of another speaker's vocalization (the phoneme [a]), the exponent was 0.7. The disparity between these exponents suggests that the speaker does not rely solely upon his perception of loudness in judging his own relative vocal level. The minor role played by loudness in the autophonic judgment is further demonstrated by the fact that the form and exponent of the subjective scale for autophonic responses remain relatively invariant under wide changes in auditory feedback. [. . .] Unless the speaker tries deliberately to hold a constant level, the amount of sidetone gain with which the voice is fed back to the ears alters the voice level. The degree to which the speaker lowers his voice when the sidetone is increased is also predicted by the exponents governing the autophonic scale and the loudness scale. From the abstract at head of article

Lane, Harlan L., *et al.*
"An Effect of Native Language and Musical Training on Vocal Pitch Matching," *Perceptual and Motor Skills,* to appear.
Five Americans with musical training, five without, and five native speakers of a tone language, Thai, were asked to match the pitch of their voice, while producing a vowel, to that of a preceding pure tone. The pitch-matching functions for the three groups, relating mean fundamental frequency of the matching response to the frequency of the stimulus tone, were approximately linear and similar in slope. Americans without musical training had the greatest variance among the slopes of individual functions. The variance for repeated matches by the same individual and for matches by different individuals showed major effects of native language and musical training. Both sources of variance in fundamental frequency were greatest for the Americans without musical training. Harlan L. Lane. The research reported herein is related to the project under Mr. Lane's name, this section.

Liberman, Alvin M., Pierre C. Delattre, and Franklin S. Cooper
"The Role of Selected Stimulus-Variables in the Perception of the

Unvoiced Stop Consonants," *American Journal of Psychology,* LXV (October, 1952), 497-516.

An intensive investigation through simplified spectrograms into the effect of one acoustic variable on the perception of unvoiced stop consonants that introduce a consonant-vowel syllable. Results of experiment show that in the perception of schematic *p* and *k* before schematic vowels, the irreducible acoustic stimulus is the sound pattern corresponding to the consonant-vowel syllable. (Research supported by Carnegie Corporation of New York and University of Pennsylvania Faculty Research Fund.) BP

————.

"Some Cues for the Distinction between Voiced and Voiceless Stops in Initial Position," *Language and Speech,* I (July-September, 1958), 153-67.

Experiments with synthetic speech indicated that voiced stops in initial position could be made to sound like their voiceless counterparts by cutting back the beginning of the first-formant transition. Some suggestions are made as to possible effects of learning on perception. SS

Liberman, Alvin M., *et al.*

"The Discrimination of Relative Onset-Time of the Components of Certain Speech and Nonspeech Patterns," *Journal of Experimental Psychology,* LXI (May, 1961), 379-88.

An experiment "designed (a) to measure the discriminability of certain acoustic differences when they are cues for the perceived distinction between phonemes and when they lie entirely within a single phoneme category, and (b) to compare such discrimination data with those obtained when essentially the same acoustic differences occur in sounds that are not perceived as speech. . . . A set of control stimuli-patterns of sound differing from each other in essentially the same way that speech stimuli differed—was produced by inverting the speech patterns on the frequency scale. . . . To the extent that the inverted stimuli are an appropriate control, it may be concluded that the sharpening of discrimination at the phoneme boundary is an effect of learning." JM

————.

"The Discrimination of Speech Sounds within and across Phonemic Boundaries," *Journal of Experimental Psychology,* LIV (November, 1957), 358-68.

Research in the relation between subjects' phonemic identification of synthetic speech sounds and the extent to which they can detect differences in the sounds—here *b, d, g.* Part of research in effects of learning or discrimination. (Research supported by Carnegie Corporation of New York and Department of Defense.) JAD

————.

"An Effect of Learning on Speech Perception: The Discrimination of Durations of Silence with and without Phonemic Significance," *Language and Speech,* IV (October-December, 1961), 175-95.

Discrimination of an acoustic variable (various durations of silence) was measured when, as part of a synthetic speech pattern, that variable cued a phonemic distinction and when the same variable appeared in a non-speech context. In the speech case the durations of silence separated the two syllables of a synthesized word, causing it to be heard as *rabid* when the intersyllabic silence was of short duration and as *rapid* when it was long. With acoustic differences equal, discrimination proved to be more acute across the /b, p/ phoneme boundary than within either phoneme category. This effect approximated what one would expect on the extreme assumption that the listeners could hear these sounds only as phonemes, and could discriminate no other differences among them; however, the approximation was not so close as for certain other consonant distinctions. In the case of the non-speech sounds the same durations of silence separated two bursts of noise tailored to match the onset, duration, and offset characteristics of the speech signals. There was, with these stimuli, no appreciable increase in discrimination in the region corresponding to the location of the phoneme boundary. If we assume that the functions obtained with the non-speech patterns represent the basic discriminability of the durations of silence, free of the influence of linguistic training, we may conclude that the discrimination peaks in the speech functions reflect an effect of learning on perception. It was found, too, that discrimination of the non-speech patterns was, in general, poorer than that of the speech. From this we conclude that the effect of learning must have been to increase discrimination across the phoneme boundary; there was no evidence of a reduction in discrimination within the phoneme category. From the abstract.

————.

"Minimal Rules for Synthesizing Speech," *Journal of the Acoustical Society of America,* XXXI (November, 1959), 1490-99.

Words and sentences of rather high intelligibility have been synthesized by means of a system of rules, which is framed largely in terms of a small number of distinctive features, rather than in a larger number of phonemes, or considerably larger number of syllables. SS

———.

"The Role of Consonant-Vowel Transitions in the Perception of the Stop and Nasal Consonants," *Psychological Monographs: General and Applied,* LXVIII (1954), 1-13.

Experiment No. 1: The results of this experiment conducted among 132 student volunteers from the University of Connecticut show that the direction and degree of second-formant transitions can serve as cues for the aurally perceived distinctions among the stop consonants. Experiment No. 2: Stimuli the same as for No. 1, except that (a) transitions were placed at the ends of syllables rather than at the beginning, (b) neutral resonances were added after the transitions, and (c) the first formants had no transitions instead of a consonant-minus transition as in 1. Results: The minus transitions heard in 1, as *p* or *b,* are heard as *m;* for *d* or *t,* as *n;* the *n* responses correspond to the *k-g* responses of experiment 1. (Research supported by Carnegie Corporation of New York and the U.S. Department of Defense.) MJS

———.

"Tempo of Frequency Change as a Cue for Distinguishing Classes of Speech Sounds," *Journal of Experimental Psychology,* LII (August, 1956), 127-37.

Research in distinguishing among the sound classes /p, t, k/, /b, d, g/, /m, n, ŋ/, using spectrographic pattern playback. (Research supported by Carnegie Corporation of New York and U.S. Department of Defense.) JAD

Locke, William N.

"Speech Analysis and Synthesis: Development and Prospects," *French Review,* XXVII (May, 1954), 416-23.

Report of research in progress. Hypothesis: "Objective measurements of speech sounds will make possible new communications devices and new teaching aids." JG

Lotz, John, *et al.*

"The Perception of English Stops by Speakers of English, Spanish, Hungarian and Thai: A Tape-Cutting Experiment," *Language and Speech,* III (April-June, 1960), 71-77.

American English stops, including *residual* stops (i.e., stops in *s*-clusters after the removal of the *s*), were presented for identification to native speakers of American English, Puerto Rican Spanish, Hungarian, and Thai-languages differing in the phonetic composition of their phonemes. Speakers of American English identified the residual stops with the voiced (lenis) stop; the others, with the voiceless stop. The results suggest that there is a hierarchic organization among the features of these stops: the lack of aspiration tends to force the evaluation of stops in the direction of *b, d, g* in American English; in the languages where other distinctions exist, the evaluation is different. SS

Mussen, Ethel F.

A Study of the Relationship between Measures of Speech Reception and Measures of Proficiency in Language. Unpublished Ph.D. dissertation, Ohio State University, 1955.

In this study of relationship of speech reception and language proficiency, findings were that hearing acuity at 2,000 cps and language ability are important determiners of speech reception. There are other factors shown to be important as indicated by variability of scores left unexplained. BP

Penfield, Wilder G.

"Consideration of the Neurophysiological Mechanisms of Speech and Some Educational Consequences," *American Academy of Arts and Sciences, Proceedings,* LXXXII, No. 5 (1953), 201-14.

Clinical analysis by a neurologist of the organs of speech with reference to the optimum time of learning languages, both native and foreign. Reference to the theory of the effect of injury to the dominant hemisphere of the brain on ideational speech mechanism. Thesis: Once functional localization of acquired skills has been established, early plasticity tends to disappear. Recommendation for ease of speech: languages should be learned very early. References to the author's published works in this field. MJS

Pierce, Joe E.

"Spectrographic Study of Vocalic Nuclei," *Language Learning,* XII (April, 1963), 241-47.

In human speech the articulators act as filters. Since spectrograms produced by the acoustic spectrograph show which frequencies are present and which are absent in a given stream of speech, the machine should show what articulatory movements occur. On the spectrograms studied for this paper three formants (heavy black bands which represent the frequencies present) appeared, and the following relationships with articulatory movements were found. All three were paralleled with the base line when no articulators were in motion, and the highest one remained parallel with the base line for all movements illustrated. The second formant moved downward when the lips were rounded and up when they were unrounded. Formant two also moved downward as the tongue was moved back, and upward as it moved forward. When the lips were sharply unrounded and the tongue far to the front of the mouth, the second formant rose above the third, but was in second position for all normal speech sounds. Formant number one moved downward as the tongue rose and up as it was lowered. This differs from the two-formant theory of Martin Joos in noting that the same acoustic effect results from both lip rounding and backward motion of the tongue. Joe E. Pierce, MLabstracts #511.

Pollack, Irwin
"Verbal Reaction Times to Briefly Presented Words," *Perceptual and Motor Skills*, XVII (August, 1963), 137-38.
     Author examined the speed of response to words presented briefly in a tachistoscope. The main variable studied was the size of the vocabulary from which the words were chosen. The author found that the speed of response increased in proportion to the logarithm of the size of the vocabulary of 2-1000 words. Irwin Pollack, MLabstract # 769

Pollack, I., H. Rubenstein, and A. E. Horowitz
"Communication of Verbal Modes of Expression," *Language and Speech*, III (July-September, 1960), 121-30.
     Talkers were instructed to read neutral sentences and "sound happy," or "sound bored," etc. Listeners attempted to identify the intended mode of expression drawing their responses from a limited number of alternatives. "Analysis of variance performed on the results of 16 modes showed that: talker, modes, groups, and sentences were statistically significant as were higher order interactions thereof." Results are also presented showing how the identification of modes of expression is affected by: (1) number of response alternatives, (2) noise, (3) whispering, and (4) temporal sampling. Reasonably high levels of performance may be achieved under conditions of reduced acoustic information. A. E. Horowitz

Pulgram, Ernst
Introduction to the Spectrography of Speech. The Hague: Mouton, 1959.
     In this book I introduce the student of language to the spectrograph, a machine which performs a graphic frequency analysis of sounds. The book consists of 21 chapters arranged under four headings: Acoustics; Phonetics, Phonemics; Spectrophonetics; Spectrophonemics. It describes first the acoustic properties of sound and their possible graphic representations, then the articulation and acoustics of

speech sounds in particular, their classification into phoneme classes, and shows finally how their particular construction of the spectrograph and the use of different filters and adjustments are utilized to produce various graphs that provide linguistically significant information, and how these graphs can be interpreted and used for objectivity, quantitative linguistic research. Ernst Pulgram, MLabstract #294.

Rubenstein, H., and I. Pollack
"Word Predictability and Intelligibility," *Journal of Verbal Learning and Verbal Behavior,* II (August, 1963), 147-58.

In this study the intelligibility of monosyllabic English words in noise was investigated under a variety of constraints affecting their probability of occurrence: verbal context, number of prescribed alternative responses, and word frequency. For all these constraint-types, intelligibility is a simple power function of probability of occurrence. This function varies with the signal-to-noise ratio in a simple way which ultimately depends upon the nature of the materials under test— probably upon the number and probability distribution of the alternatives. This complex, however, may be summed up by a single constant, the slope of the log of the intelligibility versus the log of the probability function at 0 db signal-to-noise ratio. An equation relating intelligibility, probability of occurrence, and signal-to-noise ratio is proposed. H. Rubenstein and I. Pollack, MLabstract #734.

Sapon, Stanley M., and Ezra V. Saul
Findings on the Differential Resistance to Noise of French, Spanish and English. (Georgetown University Monograph Series on Language and Linguistics, No. 6.) Washington, D.C.: Georgetown University, July, 1954.

A study to assess not only the differential effects of noise on the intelligibility of these languages but to assess also the influence of verbal context on the intelligibility of the material. Method and materials are described. The results are statistically presented. The summary states that intelligibility is increased in context situations as opposed to isolated words, and in low-noise as opposed to high-noise conditions. Spanish displays the greatest intelligibility in most cases. Bibliography included. JM

Saporta, Sol. University of Washington, Seattle, Washington
Evaluation of Three Grammatical Models in the Teaching of Foreign Languages; Project No. OE-2-4-010 (National Defense Education Act, Title VI), June 15, 1962 to August 15, 1964, $52,946.

Three models representing competing theories of language analysis will be studied to determine their relative effectiveness when applied in the preparation of foreign language teaching materials. A finite-state or Markov process model, a phrase-structure or immediate constituent model, and a transformation model will be used in the project. First, it is expected that three grammars and the corresponding drills and exercises will be constructed using a miniature artificial language. This material will be tested by experimental use with paid students in a psychological laboratory situation. Later, the same techniques will be applied to the teaching of a portion of Spanish structure in an experimental classroom situation, and the results will be analyzed to judge the relative effectiveness of the three approaches. The essential criterion for evaluating the models will be recognition and production by the student of grammatical sentences both from and beyond the original corpus of materials. From the official description.

Saporta, Sol, Arthur L. Blumenthal, and Donald G. Rieff
"Grammatical Models and Language Learning," in Robert J. Pietro (ed.), *Report of the Fourteenth Annual Round Table Meeting on Linguistics and Language Studies*. (Georgetown University Monograph Series on Language and Linguistics, No. 16.) Washington, D.C.: Georgetown University Press, 1963. Pp. 133-42.
See preceding item for a description of this project.

Shannon, Claude L., and Warren Weaver
The Mathematical Theory of Communication. Urbana, Ill.: University of Illinois Press, 1949.
Communication involves reproducing at one point either exactly or approximately a message selected at another point, the selected message being one of a set of possible messages. The transmission of information is a function of the interdeterminacy that results from the number and probabilities of the alternatives. The book describes a theory for quantifying the transmission of information. SS

Sokolov, Alexander N.
"Silent Speech in the Study of Foreign Languages," *Voprosky Psikhologii*, No. 5 (1960), 57-64.
In this article I describe the results of my electrophysiological experiments concerning the participation of "silent speech" (latent articulation) in the process of soundless reading of texts in the native language and in foreign languages. I have been experimenting with students and colleagues who had varied knowledge of the foreign language (English). It was found that the degree of tension of the organs of articulation (tongue and lips) was directly dependent on the grammatical and semantic structure of the texts. The more difficult the text the more latent articulation was expressed. Inversely it was

dependent on the reading skill. The better established the reading skill the less latent articulation was expressed. Analogous results can be observed concerning the audial perception of foreign speech. On the basis of these facts I examine the question of vocalized and latent articulation in the process of teaching foreign languages. Alexander N. Sokolov, MLabstract #236.

Stevens, S. S.
See Lane, 4.3.

Suppes, Patrick G., *et al.*
Some Quantitative Studies of Russian Consonant Phoneme Discrimination. Stanford, Calif.: Institute for Mathematical Studies in the Social Sciences, Stanford University, Technical Report No. 49, Psychology Series, September, 1962.

College students whose native language was American English learned to say "same" to certain Russian consonant-vowel pairs (e.g., "pa-pa") and "different" to other pairs (e.g., "ba-ba"). The pairs were presented auditorily in random order and the subjects were told the correct answer after each response. Analyses of the responses related performance to linguistic structural variables. Statistical learning models were applied to the data. Patrick G. Suppes
See Suppes, 2.1.

Suppes, Patrick G., Edward Crothers, and Ruth Weir
See Suppes, 3.1.

*Swets, John A., *et al.*
"Learning to Identify Nonverbal Sounds: An Application of a Computer as a Teaching Machine," *Journal of the Acoustical Society,* XXXIV (1962), 928-35.

Wiik, Kalevi
"Suomen ja englannin vokaalien eroista," *Vuosikirja/Årsbok,* II (1961), 7-15.

In the light of recent research in Finland, the author describes some of the results achieved by what is known as perceptional phonetics and its implications for classroom teaching. From van Willigen, Part I.

Witkin, Belle Ruth
An Analysis of Some Dimensions of Phonetic Ability. Unpublished Ph.D. dissertation, University of Washington, 1962.

By means of a principal axes factor analysis nine factors were extracted from a pool of twenty-nine variables, which included tests of speech sound discrimination, analysis, synthesis, and imitation, and the abilities to divorce sounds from orthography and to learn new sound systems. At least three separate phonetic factors were identified —a general factor, a segmentation factor, and a possible pitch or intonation factor. The results appear to indicate that phonetic ability is not significantly related to intelligence, verbal facility, academic achievement, age, sex, or speaker intelligibility. There was a high relationship between spelling and phonetic ability. Belle Ruth Witkin

Yates, Aubrey J.
"Delayed Auditory Feedback," *Psychological Bulletin,* LX (May, 1963), 213-32.

In this article I review the literature on delayed auditory feedback, a phenomenon first demonstrated as recently as 1950. When S hears his own voice with a small time delay his speech may be seriously affected. The effects produced by delayed auditory feedback (DAF) include prolongation of vowels, repetition of consonants, increased intensity of utterance, and other articulatory changes. The significance of individual differences in susceptibility to DAF is considered in relation to personality and psychological characteristics. The technique may prove useful in the detection of auditory malingering and has possible implications for the understanding of stammering. The discussion relates the findings to models of speech control. Methodological problems and future research needs are outlined. Aubrey J. Yates, MLabstract #720.

4.5 The Teaching of Pronunciation

Asuncion, Nobleza Castro
The Phonological Problems Involved in Improving the Oral English of Iloko Speakers. Unpublished Ph.D. dissertation, Michigan State University, 1960.

Contains a linguistic analysis of Iloko phonology contrasted with mid-western American English to examine the problems involved in improving the oral English of educated Iloko speakers. Nobleza C. Asuncion

Brière, Eugène J.
See Brière, 2.3 French.

Cárdenas, Daniel N.
Introducción a una comparación fonológica del español y del inglés. Washington, D.C.: Center for Applied Linguistics of the Modern Language Association of America, 1960.

A presentation, in Spanish, of problems of, and solutions to, the pronunciation of Spanish for English-speaking students. The purpose is threefold: (1) to serve as a point of departure for further scientific comparisons between English and Spanish as well as other languages; (2) to serve as a basis for the instruction of Spanish teachers; (3) to serve as a reference for Spanish teachers who are troubled with pronunciation problems. JM

Delattre, Pierre
See Delattre, 4.1.

Di Pietro, Robert J., and Frederick B. Agard
See Di Pietro, 4.1.

Gage, William N.
See Gage, 4.1.

Henning, William Andrew
Phoneme Discrimination Training and Student Self-Evaluation in the Teaching of French Pronunciation. Bloomington, Ind.: Indiana University, August, 1964 (mimeographed).

This report describes a study designed and carried out to seek answers to the following questions: 1) How will students who receive specifically designed discrimination training without pronunciation practice compare, in ability to discriminate between foreign language sounds and between native language and foreign language sounds, with students who have opportunity to practice pronunciation; 2) How will students who receive discrimination training without pronunciation practice compare, in ability to mimic foreign language sounds, with students who have had pronunciation practice; 3) How will students who receive discrimination training compare, in ability to make valid judgments about their pronunciation, with students who receive pronunciation practice? The study arrived at the following answers to these questions: 1) Subjects who received discrimination training during the study were better able to discriminate French sounds from each other and from English sounds, than subjects who received no discrimination training, but received pronunciation practice instead; 2) The subjects who received discrimination training without pronunciation practice were able to pronounce the sounds of French with greater accuracy than those who received pronunciation practice without discrimination training; 3) There were no overall differences between subjects who received discrimination training and those who received pronunciation practice with regard to the ability to make valid judgments about their own pronunciation. Suggestions for further research are made. DF

Hocking, Elton, Carroll Weisiger, and W. Merle Hill
See Hocking, 3.1.

Hoge, Henry W.
See Hoge, 2.52.

Keislar, Evan R. University of California, Los Angeles, Calif.
Effect of Preliminary Training in Pronunciation Discrimination upon Learning of French Pronunciation with Recording Devices; Project No. 8,950 (National Defense Education Act, Title VI), June 15, 1960, to September 1, 1961; $14,971.

A series of experiments to test the hypothesis that preliminary discrimination training renders subsequent language-laboratory practice more effective in producing good French pronunciation. Eleven pilot studies and three final experiments were conducted to develop discrimination training programs, lab practice materials, means of evoking student responses, tests, and judging techniques. The hypothesis was tested as applied to two pronunciation problems: (1) nasal vowel phonemes õ, ã, ɛ̃; and (2) diphthongized versus undiphthongized final o. Discrimination training was effective in the first case, not effective in the second. Problems of training discrimination, testing, evoking responses, and judging pronunciation are discussed, and conclusions are drawn concerning the role of discrimination in foreign-language learning. Evan R. Keislar

Lane, Harlan L.
See Lane, 2.9.

Larew, Leonor
A Study of Spanish Articulation in the Elementary School: A Pilot Study. Unpublished Ph.D. dissertation, University of Missouri, 1960.

This study was undertaken to ascertain the chronological age at which a child is best able to reproduce Spanish phonemes articulated by a teacher. Test results from a group of sixty pupils in each age category seven through eleven and a group of fourteen years, indicated that when articulation is a major factor to be considered in selecting an age group to begin the study of Spanish, best results will be obtained with the seven-year-olds. There appears to be a progressive decline in the ability to articulate Spanish phonemes by the pupils as they progress chronologically from seven to eight, from eight to nine and from nine to ten. The lowest point appears to be reached when the pupils are ten years old. Leonor Larew.

Lundeen, D. J., *et al.*
"The Effects of a Language Training Program on Foreign Sounding-
ness," *Speech Monographs,* XXIV (March, 1957), 74-76.

This is the description of a successful 6-month program at the
University of Minnesota in the improvement of the English pronunciation of a group of non-native students. Instruction was both theoretical and practical, and attempted to be universal in its choice of
areas of difficulty for discussion and practice. The procedure is described and the results are analyzed statistically. DF

Marckwardt, Albert H.
See Marckwardt, 2.3 English.

Moulton, William G.
"Toward a Classification of Pronunciation Errors," *Modern Language
Journal,* XLVI (March, 1962), 101-109.

The author classifies the types of pronunciation errors which
occur in second language learning, and suggests the corresponding
types of corrective drills which might be effective. The classification
is based on a contrastive analysis of the phonemic systems of the
source and target languages. In the examples given, the source language is usually English and the target language is usually German.
Four general classes of errors emerge: phonemic, phonetic, allophonic, and distributional. Most classes consist of several sub-classes.
William G. Moulton.

————.
See Moulton, 4.1.

Mueller, Theodore
Trial Use of the French Program [First Quarterly Report]. Akron,
Ohio: The University of Akron, [1963?].

The report emphasizes the great difficulties the students experience initially in learning to discriminate between correct and incorrect
sounds of the foreign language. It is, however, a skill which eventu-
ally is acquired by all students. The report deals only with trial use of
the first phase of the program (pronunciation). Good results were
achieved by all students. But after one-hundred hours of intensive
work, the new speech habits have not yet been thoroughly established.
They are still in the formative stages. Corrections, however, are meaningful now that they have learned to hear the difference between
sounds. The French program is used with thirty-two students in a
beginning French class chosen at random at the University of Akron,
Akron, Ohio. Each student is expected to spend twelve hours a week

in the language laboratory. Each student progresses at his own pace. Theodore Mueller

————.

Trial Use of the French Program (ALLP) . . . Third Quarterly Report. Akron, Ohio: Modern Language Department, University of Akron, May 15, 1964.

Besides a description of the progress of the students on the program, the addition of a Reading Program is described. Stopgap provisions for introducing writing are mentioned. The display sessions, or conversation classes, which were begun during the first semester are discussed. These sessions intend to make the student talk as much as possible, to demonstrate his own progress to him, and to note his weaknesses. The report goes on to evaluate the success of the project as it finishes its first year. Observations are made on the time element, slow learners, cognates, and laboratory equipment. DF

Pimsleur, Paul
"Discrimination Training in the Teaching of French Pronunciation," *Modern Language Journal,* XLVII (May, 1963), 199-203.

Tests the hypothesis that auditory discrimination training prior to lab sessions will increase the effectiveness of these sessions by making students better judges of their own pronunciation. Controlled experiment done on two French problems, nasal vowels *en, on, in,* and diphthongized versus undipthongized final *o,* as in *beau.* Discrimination training found effective in first case, not effective in second. The findings are discussed as are the general problems of training discrimination, testing, evoking oral responses, and judging pronunciation. Paul Pimsleur

Pimsleur, Paul, Larry Mace, and Evan Keislar
Preliminary Discrimination Training in the Teaching of French Pronunciation. Los Angeles: University of California, 1961.

The report contains the following divisions: Foreword, Introduction and Review of Literature, Pilot Studies, Discussion of Salient Problems (Defining and Testing Discrimination, Training Discrimination, Evoking Student Oral Responses, Judging Pronunciation), Final Experiments, Conclusions and Discussion. References, Appendixes. DF

Roertgen, William F.
"Experiment in Pronunciation," *Educational Screen,* XXXVIII (November, 1959), 588-91.

To see if laboratory training is a marked advantage to the language student, this teacher experimented with two groups, teaching Dutch sounds: one group practiced by imitation in concert; the other group practiced in the laboratory. The laboratory method was 50 per cent more effective. BP

Schneiderman, Norma
"A Study of the Relationship between Articulatory Ability and Language Ability," *Journal of Speech and Hearing Disorders,* XX (December, 1955), 359-64.

Purpose of the study is to investigate the relationship between articulatory ability and certain aspects of language skill among children. Methodology outlined. Three tests were used and proved to be valid measures. Ability in articulation showed an increase with mental-age growth, not with chronological-age increase. Articulatory ability is associated with high scores in language ability when the mental and chronological ages of the subjects are not held constant. Thirteen references are included. JM

Stockwell, Robert P., J. Donald Bowen, and John W. Martin
See Stockwell, 4.1.

Young, Clarence W.
See Young, 2.54.

Young, Clarence W., and Charles A. Choquette
See Young, 2.54.

Zais, Robert S.
"The Linguistic Characteristics of Punctuation Symbols in the Teaching of Pronunciation Skills," *English Journal,* LII (December, 1963), 677-81.

In this research project I have attempted to determine the extent to which linguistic characteristics of punctuation symbols influence the effectiveness of a method of teaching punctuation skills. Fifty high school pupils were taught, by a single method, a variety of punctuation symbols which fall into groups bearing common linguistic features. The data gathered in evaluating pupils' progress in using these punctuation symbols correctly consistently indicate no correspondence between a punctuation symbol's linguistic characteristics and the effectiveness of a method used to teach skill in its use. Differentiated methods based on linguistic classification, therefore, seem unjustified. Robert S. Zais, MLabstract #660.

5. Teaching the Cultural and Intercultural Context

Allwood, Charles
See Allwood, 2.3, English.

American Council on Education, Committee on the Study of Teaching Materials on Inter-American Subjects.
Latin America in School and College Teaching Materials. Washington, D.C.: American Council on Education, 1944.

An analysis of the present treatment of inter-American topics in our teaching materials and a set of recommendations for the future. The history textbooks concern general United States and Latin American history. Other textbook listings are related to biography, foreign policy, modern problems, geography, education, and the Spanish and Portuguese languages. There are also chapters dealing with materials used for literature classes, the study of Latin American arts and crafts, and music. There is an analysis of educational motion pictures. JM

Axelrod, Joseph, and Donald N. Bigelow
Resources for Language and Area Studies: Report on an Inventory of the Language and Area Center Supported by the National Defense Education Act of 1958. Washington, D. C.: American Council on Education, 1962.

A description of the forty-six centers for the study of critically needed but infrequently taught languages. This report brings together information on how the centers were organized, the number of students enrolled in language and area disciplines, the method of teaching languages, including the use of the audio-lingual method, and the relation between language and area studies. Chapter 3 discusses the implications of the language and area centers for the future of both graduate and undergraduate instruction. Publisher's circular.

Beck, Theodore T.
See Beck, 2.3, French.

Benedict, Ruth
"The Study of Cultural Patterns in European Nations," *Transactions of the New York Academy of Sciences*, Series 2, VIII (May 27, 1946), 274-79.

The study of national character is the study of learned cultural behavior. For her work during World War II, author used informants living in the United States. Critics have said that national studies were too difficult because of the size and complexity of the cultures and the amount of material to be handled, but Benedict claims that these will be handicaps only when the problems for investigation are not well formulated.

Anthropologists are not afraid of a lack of homegeneity in area studies. No adequate study of western class structure has been attempted; classes interact in the society as their culture has prepared them to do. Cultural phenomena pervade all classes. The author gives examples of differences in attitude in various countries to authority, property. Roumanian is the only Romance culture considered. HA

———.

"Anthropology and the Humanities," *An Anthropologist at Work; Writings of Ruth Benedict,* ed. Margaret Mead. Boston: Houghton Mifflin Co., 1959.

Author believes anthropology is close to the humanities because both deal with the same problems. Anthropology has shown at times too great a dependence on the sciences. The humanities offer great resources to the anthropologist. She demonstrates Montaigne's interest in cultural differences; suggests that Santayana's theme of individual dependence on the cultural tradition is close to the anthropologist's viewpoint; shows that good literary criticism may often give an insight into the culture of a period. An adequate study of culture can be achieved by drawing upon the humanities as well as the social sciences. HA

*Benesh, Marijana, Ernest Kramer, and Harlan L. Lane
Recognition of Portrayed Emotion in a Foreign Language, in Experimental Analysis and Control of Speech Production and Perception, Progress Report No. 3; February 1, 1962, to April 1, 1963. (See Harlan L. Lane, 4.3).

Berelson, Bernard, and Gary A. Steiner
Human Behavior; An Inventory of Scientific Findings. New York: Harcourt, Brace & World, 1964.

Presents with background information 1045 findings from the

scientific study of human behavior. Chapters: The Individual; The Family; Small Groups; Organizations; Institutions; Strata; Publics; The Society; Culture. Several pages on Language, 189-192, and on Speech development, 58-61. (The latter section repeats the doubtful findings that "children taught two languages from the start are handicapped in both.") HLN

*Bratset, Richard E.
Identification of Cross-Cultural Problems in Reading English as a Second Language. Unpublished Ed.D. dissertation, University of California, 1961.

Brault, Gerard J.
"French Culture: Some Recent Anthropological and Sociological Findings," *French Review*, XXXV (October, 1962), 44-54.

In this article I endeavor to acquaint the reader with certain interesting "cultural" facts about contemporary France which have been established in the past decade by anthropologists and sociologists. Portions of this new data deserve to be incorporated into the curriculum at the appropriate level. I cite observations and conclusions relating chiefly to the special nature of French individualism, *le foyer*, French special class structure, French village life, and religion in France. Two extremes are to be avoided in teaching culture: approaching a highly civilized people, such as the French, solely in a manner befitting a primitive society; dwelling on the more trivial aspects of daily living. Gerard J. Brault, MLabstract #333.

Brown, Roger W., and Albert Gilman
"The Pronouns of Power and Solidarity," in Thomas A. Sebeok (ed.), *Style in Language*. New York: John Wiley and Sons, 1960. Pp. 253-76.

An excellent basic study, financed with help from the Ford Foundation, of the semantic difference between *tu* and *vos:* its history, and its present status in French, Italian, and German. Essential insight for explaining the cultural features expressed by this detail of those languages. HLN

Corrin, Brownlee Sands
Research on Values and Uses of Foreign Languages for Instruction and Study in the Social Sciences (Political Science and International Relations): Final Report. Baltimore: Goucher College, July 31, 1962 (mimeographed).

See original proposal for this project, p. 170, 1962 volume of this Bibliography. The Final Report discusses the ways in which attempts were made to bring together foreign languages and professional competence at the professional level. Recommendations are made for an International Relations Major and for Political Science Courses. Actions at Goucher College under these recommendations are discussed. A list of Immediate Results of these actions is given along with a concluding set of General Recommendations. DF

External Research
See U.S. Department of State, *External Research*, Part I.

Fishman, Joshua A.
See Fishman, 3.7.

Greenberg, Jacob
"Civilization and Cultural Emphasis in Modern Language Teaching at High School and College Levels," *Journal of Educational Sociology*, XXXI (January, 1958), 152-67.

A synopsis of answers received from 135 high schools and colleges in the United States to questionnaire sent by the author asking which phases of language study received major emphasis. The largest number of those polled placed chief emphasis on reading skill, almost as many on speaking, about a third as many grammar and on culture, and another group stressed all four aims equally. Twenty-four other points are analyzed and discussed, as well as results from high schools. Quotes from replies are included, together with summary. Both private and public colleges were included, but the basis for selection was not given. MJS

Hall, Edward T.
The Silent Language. Garden City, New York: Doubleday and Co., 1959.

Examples of friction and frustration caused by transfer of American customs and expectations into foreign milieux. Bibliography, pp. 232-4. HLN

Hall, Edward T., and George L. Trager
The Analysis of Culture. Prepublication edition reproduced for the authors with the assistance of the American Council of Learned Societies; Washington, D.C., 1953.

Authors have drawn heavily from linguistic science in proposing a trilevel system for the study of culture—formal, informal, and technical. Culture comprises many systems, all firmly anchored like linguistic systems in the biological organism: (1) language; (2) social systems; (3 and 4) time and space systems—cyclic and territorial activities of life forms; (5) material systems. Authors found ten types of human activities: (0) interactional (1) organizational; (2) economic; (3) sexual; (4) territorial; (5) temporal; (6) instructional; (7) recreational; (8) protective; (9) exploitational. All these activities interact. These were arranged on a chart showing their interaction and relationships. Communication was the basic factor and became 00. The crossing on the chart of each type of activity with itself became a basic focal system, with each type of activity as a focal point for individuals or groups. The ninety-nine crossings are the culture's foci. 0, 1, 2, and 3 and their interaction are deemed formal; 4 and 5 are informal focal systems. The others are technical. HA

————.

Human Nature at Home and Abroad: A Guide to the Understanding of Human Behavior. Washington, D.C.: Foreign-Service Institute, Department of State, 1953 (mimeographed).

Human behavior falls into three categories—formal, informal, and technical. Formal is deep-seated and emotionally charged; informal is accepted, little discussed, has little emotional import but may arouse feelings if attention is drawn to it; technical is discussed or discussable. The depth of their stability is measured in the same order. HA

Hayes, Alfred S.
See Hayes, 1.

Hoijer, Harry (ed.)
Language in Culture: Proceedings of a Conference on the Interrelations of Language to Other Aspects of Culture. Chicago: University of Chicago Press, 1954.

The conference attempted to define the problems of interrelating language and other aspects of culture, with particular direction toward Benjamin L. Whorf's hypothesis that language predetermines certain modes of observation and interpretation for its speakers. By comparing languages that are remote in historical background and cultural setting we will force ourselves into an awareness of our own linguistic and cultural biases. Discussions of "The Strategy of Research in the Interrelations of Language and Other Aspects of Culture" (pp. 263-79), proposes hypotheses and their experimental design for comparing the cultures of simple societies. JM

Johnson, Granville B., Jr.
"Relationship Existing between Bilingualism and Racial Attitudes," *Journal of Educational Psychology,* XLII (October, 1951), 357-65.

A study of Spanish speakers in the southwest revealed that those who have the least or the most knowledge of the English language show the least bias toward the culture. BP

Kaulfers, Walter V., G. N. Defauver, and H. D. Roberts (eds.)
Foreign Languages and Cultures in American Education. New York: McGraw-Hill Book Co., 1942.

The book consists of a collection of twenty reports by teachers of foreign languages, English, and social studies who participated at the Stanford Language Arts Institute from 1937 through 1940. BP

Kluckhohn, Clyde
"Universal Categories of Culture," *Anthropology Today.* Chicago: University of Chicago Press, 1953. Pp. 507-23.

Author suggests the need for further inquiry into universals, which exist in other fields, notably linguistics. Notes biological, psychological, and environmental limiting factors; and that culture is the adaptation of the group to these. Culture seems to be centered around certain "foci," adequate description of which is needed. HA

Lado, Robert
The Meaning and Role of Culture in Foreign Language Teaching (Conference Report). Washington, D. C.: Institute of Languages and Linguistics, Georgetown University, 1961. Also published in Modern Language Association of America, *Reports of Surveys and Studies* ... (See Part I.)

Final Report of "a study to uncover seeming conflicts between the humanistic definition of culture and the point of view of the cultural anthropologist." From the official description.

Mead, Margaret
"National Character," *Anthropology Today.* Chicago: University of Chicago Press, 1953. Pp. 642-67.

National-character studies utilize the premises and methods of personality-culture research but deal with "nationals" of political states. National-character studies draw upon work that takes in psychological constructs as the conceptual background for the study of complex societies where complete field studies are impossible. The danger of oversimplification can be eliminated if "culture" is recognized and stated as a "mediating variable." National-character studies assume: (1) All races are equal. (2) Individual differences must be taken into account. (3) Cultures have systematic aspects referable to given biological characteristics—age, sex. (4) Cultures have other systematic aspects referable to regularities in nature. (5)

Cultures may be seen as systems of communication between people or between people and their environment. (6) Cultures have holistic tendencies, and changes in parts may be expected to have reverberations in other parts. (7) Unique characteristics have a historical basis. (8) Changes may take place with events from outside the system but should not contradict formulations based on (3), (4), (5), and (6); changes cannot be predicted, but limits to them can be established. (9) Culture is hereditary, and individual change may have repercussions; change in a whole class is expected to result in the change of the whole system. (10) Though cultures differ they may be comparable in some features to others. (11) Wider cultural patterns may be expected to recur in all subgroups but need not include any of the features distinctive of the particular subgroup pattern. (12) Any member of the culture is a valid informant so long as his place in the culture is defined and understood. (13) Statements about a culture must be so made that the addition of knowledge about another class or group will not destroy their value.

National-character studies allow us to analyze the society as a whole because they are based on the anthropological approach to culture study. They provide the basis for interdisciplinary stimulation and teamwork. National-character studies may include data and theory other than anthropological. National-character studies may be divided into the following steps: (1) developing initial hypotheses, using any highly patterned material; (2) systematic scrutiny of hypotheses, using selected materials; (3) determination of sampling techniques of prevalence and incidence of identified behavior; and (4) validation of the findings through prediction and experiment. Step three is impossible for cultures inaccessible to extensive interviewing of other than very special informant types—refugees, etc. Further development of techniques depends on field studies of modern states, which will involve interdisciplinary cooperation, and on further small community studies, which will give further development of theory. HA

Métraux, Rhoda, and Margaret Mead
   Themes in French Culture. (Hoover Institute Studies.) Stanford, Calif.: Stanford University Press, 1954.
      This book is a collection of four studies giving a concentrated analysis of certain patterns in French culture, relevant to the understanding of French national and international behavior. BP

Modern Language Association Interdisciplinary Seminar on Language and Culture [Albert H. Marckwardt, Chairman].
   "Developing Cultural Understanding through Foreign Language

Study: A Report of the MLA Interdisciplinary Seminar on Language and Culture," *PMLA, LXVIII* (December, 1953), 1196-1218.

An exploratory study that appraised typical teaching materials—concentrating upon second-year university courses in modern languages—and recommended ten problems of basic or applied research (pp. 1217-18). The problems have been incorporated into the present list of topics in need of research. HLN

Nostrand, Howard L.

"The Description of Cultures," in Analysis of the Modern Cultural Crisis. Seattle: Department of General Studies, University of Washington, 1960 (mimeographed). Pp. 300-325.

As a principle for organizing the most significant elements of a culture ("significant" either as typical or as excellent), defines a concept of the "highest common themes" of the culture. Refers to previous studies by anthropologists and philosophers. List of tentative theme topics for the United States. HLN

———.

Board of Regents, University of Washington, Seattle, Wash. Experiment in Determining Cultural Content, and Survey of Language Teaching Research; Project No. OE-4-14-008 (National Defense Education Act, Title VI), September 23, 1963, to July 22, 1964; $16,211.

This contract provided for two projects designed to enrich and improve modern foreign language instruction. The first project involved a pilot study to analyze data on attitudes toward contemporary French culture, gathered through questionnaires administered to Americans of diverse occupational background who have lived in France. On the basis of this pilot study, a detailed study may be considered for support. This is expected to help meet the need for improved methods of communicating the essentials of a complex foreign culture to language students.

The contract also provided for the preparation of a second edition of the publication, *Research on Language Teaching: An Annotated International Bibliography for 1945-61*, which was developed under a previous Office of Education contract. From the official description

———.

A Handbook on the Describing and Teaching of Literate Cultures. Prepared under U. S. Office of Education project OE-2-14-031, 1962-63; to be published in 1965.

A digest of principles recommended for the selecting, defining, organizing, and teaching of the essential features of a culture and social structure, assuming the two educational aims of cross-cultural understanding and communication. HLN

————.

"Literature, Area Study, and Hispanic Culture," *Hispania,* XLIV (September, 1961), 465-72.

Proposes that the effort to identify and define the themes or norms present in a literary work can produce insights that admit of integration with data from the social sciences. Enumerates some themes of Hispanic culture that can be studied both in literature and also in institutions and folkways. Appears also in *Tenth Yearbook of General and Comparative Literature* (Bloomington, Ind.: Indiana University Press, 1961). HLN

————.

"Literature in the Describing of a Literate Culture," *French Review,* XXXVII (December, 1963), 145-57.

Literature offers valuable hypotheses concerning a culture and society. It also gives direct evidence both of the excellence achieved by a people and of its usual behavior patterns. On the latter point, however, an author's conscious representation of the patterns—as distinguished from his unconscious exemplification of them—constitutes only one person's view. Literature's relation to society (as reflection, innovator, and instrument of social control) has been more thoroughly studied than its relation to the culture of which it is a part. Studies are needed that will distill literary evidence of values; the "ground of meaning" assumptions of a people; empirical beliefs; language, paralanguage and kinesics; humor; and the expressive forms of literary art related to those of the other imaginative arts. Particularly promising is the kind of study that abstracts main themes, "because it leads to central meanings which confer significance on diverse manifestations of the culture." More studies are needed, finally, which place literary works in two external perspectives: historical and cross-cultural. "Now that Westerners are coming to recognize the necessity of a perspective embracing the non-Western cultures, the pioneering capacity of literary studies is called upon for a further range of service to human understanding—as important, possibly, as is the cherishing enjoyment of literature itself. In my opinion, the two values need not conflict." HLN

Nostrand, Howard Lee, *et al.*

Film-Recital of French Poems; Cultural Commentary. Seattle: Department of Romance Languages and Literature and Audio Visual Services, 1964.

This report presents the content of the film described under Riecks, below, this section. Texts of the recitation material are included, along with selected illustrations of the material. The bulk of this report contains commentaries on the materials written, thus providing the user with an authoritative analysis of the content—both literary and cultural—of the materials to be taught. A final chapter discusses French Versification. DF. See note on same study, above, 2.53.

Opler, Morris E.

"Themes as Dynamic Forces in Culture," *American Journal of Sociology*, LI (1945), 198-206.

Author uses the word "theme" in a technical sense. It denotes a "postulate or position, declared or implied, and usually controlling behavior or stimulating activity, which is tacitly approved or openly promoted in a society." There are a limited number (usually small) of themes in every culture. "Themes" may have many expressions in conduct or belief, which will aid in discovering them. Formalized expression of themes is fixed and there may be no significant variation on the part of those to whom the theme applies. *Unformalized expressions* of themes are not carefully defined by the culture and give the individual greater freedom. Themes may have symbolic expressions, which in themselves are not necessarily related to the themes but have become vehicles for their expression—gestures, figures of speech, etc. A guide to the importance of the theme is the group's concern over the violation of its terms. Themes interact and may limit each other. Other restraints may exist to the unimpeded expression of a theme. HA

————.

"An Application of the Theory of Themes in Culture," *Journal of the Washington Academy of Sciences,* XXXVI (May 15, 1946), 137-65.

Author applies his theory of themes to the Lipan Apache culture. A thorough acquaintance with the material was a prerequisite; he then brought together the beliefs and behavior that seemed to stem from a common affirmation or incentive. He expressed these in a kind of unifying doctrine—a statement or "theme." His method is largely inductive. Emphasis is on values, ideology, and stimuli, rather than on material culture or techniques, but thematic description does not exclude these latter.

This is a study of the culture as it actually functions; although the moral tone of the stated themes would seem to indicate a certain idealism rather than actualities. Author has found twenty themes for the Lipan people. Further study would indicate how themes balance, augment, or limit each other. Studies made by different people would probably yield results with no appreciable or important variation. Author is satisfied with the twenty Lipan themes, which encompass the whole culture. Themes are the broadest directions of a unified nature implict in the culture. Pages 164-65 give a list of other anthropologists who have contributed toward the theory of themes as focal points in cultural content. Reprinted in *Man in Contemporary Society: A Source Book Prepared by the Contemporary Civilization Staff of Columbia College, Columbia University* (New York: Columbia University Press, 1955), I, 145-62. HA

————.

"Component, Assemblage, and Theme in Cultural Integration and Differentiation," *American Anthropologist,* LXI (December, 1959), 955-64.

Author describes an assemblage as a cluster or associated body of ideas, symbols, artifacts, and behavior in a culturally significant event. An assemblage is made up of various components. This paper illustrates the death assemblage and its components in two Apache groups. The author accounts for cultural differentiation as selective emphasis, extension, intensification, or combination of components by diverging groups. Cultural themes link the assemblages to culture. HA

Ray, Punya Sloka
See Ray, 2.3 Bengali.

Raymond, Joseph
"Attitudes and Cultural Patterns in Spanish Proverbs," *Americas,* XI (July, 1954), 57-77.

On the thesis that a people's proverbs reflect cultural patterns, proverbs are studied within four categories of attitudes and patterns. HA

Redfield, Robert
The Little Community: Viewpoints for the Study of a Human Whole. Chicago: University of Chicago Press, 1955.

The little community is an entity and is to be studied as a whole. It is distinctive, at least in the consciousness of the group, as well as homogeneous and self-sufficient. The group may be studied from an ecological point of view. This is a holistic view but will be insufficient for some communities that are only partially dependent on nature. Social structure may provide another kind of holistic insight, but again may prove insufficient. A biographic approach to the study of the community describes the whole of the culture through the life of a typical individual. It, too, has its difficulties and limitations. A community may be characterized by a generalized personality type, but this approach does not distinguish adequately between the group personality and the value system underlying the formation of the personality. Evaluating the system of "world view" is difficult from two standpoints. First, there is the view from inside the group, and the outside observer's view, which are difficult to distinguish at times. Second, it is difficult to determine the role of personality as distinguished from the role of culture in the formation of the world view. Nevertheless, this approach gives insight into the ethics of the community. A historical study allows for comparisons and will be holistic if the writer is an outsider and sees the history as a whole; or if the wholeness of the community is the object of the historical study. A history of the integration process of a community would also be holistic. There are no truly isolated communities: the community's relations with other organizations are to be analyzed, as these relations bear upon the community's self-concept—its distinctiveness. It may prove worthwhile to compare different studies of the same community, since each investigator brings his own values into his study. There may be diverse thought currents active in the community, but to be valuable for comparison these must correspond to real differences in the community and must be susceptible of objective investigation. Studies of parts of the community are valuable for various reasons, but the study of the community as such must be holistic. HA

Riecks, Donald F., Marie-Georgette Steisel, and Howard Lee Nostrand Filmed Recitations of French Literature: Evaluation of the Film and Cultural Commentary. Final Report. Seattle: Department of Romance Languages and Literature and Audio Visual Services, University of Washington, July, 1964.

    The project described in this report involved the preparation of filmed recitations of French poems, monologues and brief short stories by the French actor Pierre Viala. The trial use of the film involved finding answers to the following three questions: 1) Can such a film be used to teach the language, with its characteristic rhythms, intonations and facial expressions; 2) Can it arouse an expectation of enjoying poetry, and contribute to a love of literature; 3) Can such a film be used, finally, to give insight into the cultural and social context of a foreign language and literature, provided the teacher is assisted in formulating the aspects of the people's way of life that are exemplified in the recitations? The procedure employed in seeking answers to these questions is fully described. The Summary of Findings and Recommendations indicate that all three questions were answered affirmatively and that the filmed materials would be successful if rightly used. A list of experimental research questions is included. DF. See Nostrand, Film-Recital . . . , this section.

Roca, Pablo
See Roca, 3.7.

Sebeok, Thomas A., A. S. Hayes, M. C. Bateson
See Sebeok, 2.1.

Silva-Fuenzalida, Ismael
"Ethnolinguistics and the Study of Culture," *American Anthropologist,* LI (July-September, 1949), 446-56.
Language is an integrated system of symbols. New cultures will be learned only when their languages are understood. Morphemic sequences are in harmony with the associated culture. Linguistic analysis aids in understanding functional distinctions in culture. Linguistic changes reflect cultural changes. The author uses examples from the Spanish of Chile to illustrate sociocultural distinctions in language. HA

Steward, Julian H.
Area Research: Theory and Practice. (Social Science Research Council Bulletin 63.) New York: Social Science Research Council, 1950.
The objectives of area research are to provide knowledge of practical value about important world areas; to give students and scholars an awareness of cultural relativity; to provide understanding of social and cultural wholes as they exist in areas; and to further the development of a universal social science. The material presented must come from interdisciplinary research and relate to particular problems. In several interdisciplinary programs described, language and/or literature are usually given important places. The contribution of anthropological studies to area research has been mainly in the form of community studies. This approach has been valuable but often fails to relate the community to the larger area. Some national character studies have failed to recognize important aspects of the sociocultural whole. Research should be centered around particular themes of interest—nationalism, urbanization, international relations, etc. This not only would limit the field of inquiry but help develop interdisciplinary cooperation. Area research must be built upon some

integrating or unifying concept: the author suggests the sociocultural whole. Chapter 4 deals with an area-study project as it was carried out in Puerto Rico. This was primarily the work of anthropologists with help from other disciplines. On the basis of class and economic structure, four villages and one metropolitan subgroup were analyzed; findings related to Puerto Rican institutions as a whole and their development and change under cultural pressures emanating from the United States. Relationships to other areas, crosscultural implications, were established. HA

Sutherland, M. B.
"Study of the Effects of Learning French on Attitudes toward the French; Summary of Thesis," *British Journal of Educational Psychology,* XVI (February, 1946), 4.
    Author found a small increase in favor of the French by those studying French. BP

Taylor, H. Darrel, and John L. Sorenson
"The Culture Capsule," *Modern Language Journal,* XLV (December, 1961), 350-54.
    In this article we present a rationale for the development and use of ten-minute illustrated lectures in a foreign language classroom which will each present one minimal difference or similarity between the United States and Mexico. Each script is written for a given level of student proficiency and is presented live by the teacher. Student participation is induced by carefully framed rhetorical and "open-ended" questions. All paraphenalia for the presentation of a culture capsule is contained in a small box and may be shelved for use by many teachers. Thus, any teacher may present programs on short notice, in an orderly sequence with factual content, dramatic presentation and a high degree of student participation. H. Darrel Taylor and John L. Sorenson, MLabstract #172.

Weber, Jean-Paul
Genèse de l'oeuvre poétique. Paris: Gallimard, 1961.
    This study, originally a principal thesis for the Doctorat ès Lettres, applies the method of thematic analysis to eight French poets: Vigny, Hugo, Baudelaire, Mallarmé, Verlaine, Claudel, Apollinaire, and Valéry. See the notation of Weber's *La psychologie de l'art.* HLN

————.
. .*La psychologie de l'art.* (Initiation Philosophique.) Paris: Presses Universitaires de France, 1961.
    Defines a psychological approach to the interpretation of esthetic

contemplation, artistic creation, and the work of art, which avoids the reduction to either Freudian drives or universal ideas. The proposed middle ground is a thematic approach. It explores "personal" themes recurrent in a given author, presumed to relate his adult life to his childhood and "impersonal" themes characteristic of a given culture or whole civilization. Among Professor Weber's studies preparatory to this monograph are three essays on themes of the "personal" category: "Nerval et les 'mains pleines de feux,' " *La table ronde,* No. 135 (March, 1959), pp. 96-107; "Edgar Poe ou le thème de l'horloge," *Nouvelle revue française,* No. 68 (August, 1958), pp. 301-11, and No. 69 (September, 1958), pp. 498-508; and "Les transpositions du nez dans l'oeuvre de Gogol," *Nouvelle revue française,* No. 79 (July, 1959), pp. 108-20. These and additional studies of Lautréamont, J. Gracq, and Kafka, are expected to be published in one volume by Gallimard in 1962. HLN

Weinreich, Uriel
     See Weinreich, 3.5.

White, Leslie
     The Science of Culture: A Study of Man and Civilization. New York: Farrar, Strauss and Co., 1949.
     Man differs from the other animals in his ability to use symbols. Other primates are capable of using tools, but only man can symbolize his activity. This makes culture possible as it enables man to communicate his activities. "Mind" does not really exist except as "minding"—a function of the body. Scientific study has developed from the physical to the biological and is now on the threshold of the social, of which "culturology" is the most difficult because of man's inability to separate himself from his culture. Psychology interprets the functioning of the organism and has nothing to do with the study of culture, which must be undertaken culturologically. The "mind" is culturally determined. Culture may be studied without reference to humans; it has an existence of its own. Genius is an accident of birth; a good mind in a fortuitous cultural environment will produce a so-called "genius." Cultural achievements are inevitable; when conditions permit an achievement will be made. Author illustrates this thesis with a reappraisal of the activities of Ikhnaton, King of Egypt, in light of the cultural milieu. Mathematics are a produce of culture and there is no mathematical proof outside of culture. Author examines incest regulation culturologically and explains that exogamy leads to greater group security. Culture controls behavior, man adjusts. Culture creates culture. The individual is a catalytic agent making interaction

possible in the cultural process: man is a medium of expression of the cultural process. Invention or novelty is simply a new synthesis of cultural events. Cultural growth is not constant. Energy and its use and development by man determine cultural development and growth. Mankind has passed through agricultural and fuel-energy periods and finds himself on the threshold of a new energy-using period. The cultural growth of the past has been determined by energy exploitation. "Culturology" should be the name of the science of culture. HA

Wylie, Laurence
   See Wylie, Part I.

Young, Eleanor Culver
   An Experimental Study of the Effects of Intensive Reading of Selected Materials in a Foreign Language upon Certain Attitudes. Unpublished Ed.D. dissertation, Rutgers University, 1962.

   The investigation supported the hypothesis that intensive reading of selected materials in a foreign language during a minimal period of three months will effect significant changes in certain attitudes. The study reflects the literature related to moral values and to the objectives of foreign language teaching, which include the nurturing of positive attitudes. Results of a survey of New Jersey foreign language teachers indicated strong agreement supporting the validity of the cultural objective, which embraces the lessening of ethnocentrism. From the abstract.

6. Languages in the Curriculum

6.1 Elementary School

Andrade, Manuel, John L. Hayman, Jr., and James T. Johnson, Jr.
See Andrade, 2.7.

Barcus, Delbert, John L. Hayman, and James T. Johnson
See Barcus, 2.56.

Burns, D. G.
"An Investigation into the Extent of First-Year Vocabulary in French in Boys' Grammar Schools," *British Journal of Educational Psychology,* XXI (February, 1951), 36-44.

Study to determine the actual achievement in vocabulary of selected groups of pupils during one year's study of French, and to determine whether there are significant variations in the rate at which new vocabulary is learned. Mean scores of 7 groups for first-year work were 718 items in recognition and 555 items in recall. Six groups could recall 670 of year's vocabulary and recognize 76 per cent more. Greatest increase of vocabulary took place in first term. Increased by half in second and third terms. Recall at end of year represented four/fifths of estimated recognition vocabularies. BP

Calvert, F. Irene
See Calvert, 2.3 French.

Carroll, John B.
"Foreign Languages for Children," *National Elementary Principal,* XXXIX (May, 1960), 12-15.

Collates research reports in an attempt to determine whether children learn languages faster than adults, at what grade level FLES should begin, the long-term effects of foreign languages on the elementary school—and on other school subjects—and the best teaching techniques for FLES. The reports are, as yet, too few and scattered to be conclusive, except perhaps on one main issue, namely, that there is no correlation between foreign-language aptitude and general intelligence. JG

———.

See Carroll, 1.

Cunning, Carlotta
See Cunning, 2.56.

Dufort, Mary R.
Two Methods of Elementary School Foreign Language Instruction on the Development of Student Audio Ability in the Foreign Language. Unpublished Ed.D. dissertation, University of California at Berkeley, 1962.

This study was designed to determine which of two techniques of foreign language instruction, "Orinda Guided Imitation" or "Folk Tale Unit," is more effective in developing the audio comprehension of elementary school children during their first year of instruction in Spanish. It was hypothesized that the difference in the development of audio comprehension would be significantly greater for subjects taught by the Orinda Guided Imitation method, who were girls, high-achieving subjects, and subjects who received more than the average amount of follow-up instruction by their regular classroom teacher. The subjects were the population of the 35 fourth, fifth, and sixth-grade classrooms in the Orinda School District, Orinda, California, in 1960-61. Students with recognized auding problems were excluded. The special foreign-language teacher gave a weekly 20-minute lesson to each class in the appropriate instructional method and she held bi-monthly in-service training sessions with each of the teacher groups. Subjects were tested by an audio comprehension test constructed, trial administered, analyzed, and revised by the writer. On the basis of the test results the following conclusions were formulated: 1) The difference in development of audio comprehension was significantly greater for subjects taught by the Orinda Guided Imitation method, who were girls, and subjects in high-achieving classes. 2) The difference in relation to the amount of follow-up instruction was not significant. On the basis of the findings it was recommended that districts consider: 1) In-service training and classroom instruction geared to the guided imitation method of instruction. 2) Special audio training for boys. 3) Experimentation with special foreign language materials and techniques for use with children who do not achieve to their capacity. Mary R. Dufort

————.

See Dufort, 2.7.

Dunkel, Harold B., and Roger A. Pillet
"French Program in the University of Chicago Elementary School,"
Elementary School Journal, LVII (October, 1956), 17-27.

Justifies the basis for presenting experimental foreign-language training at elementary level. Method of presentation thoroughly outlined. Tables show estimate of retention of French patterns at midyear, and per cent of correct responses to aural comprehension at the end of one year. Eleven questions are analyzed as an evaluation of the experiment. The conclusion points out that children learn foreign languages readily; and, having learned at the lower levels, they are prepared for college work, which could pursue material more suitable for the mature intellect. JM

————.

"A Second Year of French in Elementary School," *Elementary School Journal,* LVIII (December, 1957), 143-51.

See first article in this series. Comparison continues: no marked difference between groups. See Dunkel and Pillet, 6.1. JG

————.

"A Third Year of French in Elementary School," *Elementary School Journal,* LIX (February, 1959), 264-66.

See first article in this series. Comparison continues: no marked difference between groups. See Dunkel and Pillet, 6.1. JG

Ellison, Fred P., Joseph S. Flores, and Charles E. Johnson
"The University of Illinois Experiment in the Teaching of Foreign Languages in the Elementary Schools," *University of Illinois Modern Foreign Language Newsletter,* XIV (November, 1959), 1-3.

Progress report and summary of University of Illinois Title VI project. See principal entry for this project: Johnson, 6.1.

England. Ministry of Education. Department of Education and Science
See England, 2.3 French.

Estep, Hunter L.
"Carlsbad Spanish Program," *Hispania,* XXXIV (August, 1951), 292-93.

Description of test results of the Carlsbad six-year elementary school Spanish program, administered to selected group of students distributed by achievement-test classifications among high, medium, and low groups. Findings: Average pupil retained 76 per cent of vocabulary regardless of grade, and scores increased consistently by grade levels although grade tests at higher levels were more difficult. The more Spanish a student learned one year, the more Spanish he could successfully assimilate the next year. MJS

Florander, Jesper
See Florander, 2.3 English.

Flores, Joseph S., Charles E. Johnson, and Fred P. Ellison
"The University of Illinois Experiment in FLES: A Progress Report." *Hispania,* XLIV (September, 1961), 511-13.

This report describes the first-year testing of the hypothesis that fourth-grade students can effectively learn a second language taught by nonspecialist teachers using specially prepared audiovisual lessons. Tests between control and experimental groups were conducted to evaluate comparisons in listening comprehension, immediacy of response, appropriateness of response, pronunciation, and response to directions. The statistics presented show that the experimental group achieved a composite score of 92.05 per cent of the score attained by the control group. The conclusion is that the experimental approach is a potential substitute in view of the lack of specialist teachers. It is recognized that there are intangible factors in the personal relationship between a specialist teacher and class that defy testing. For main entry of this project, see Johnson, below. JM

Foster, Dorothy P., and Clarence M. Williams
See Foster and Williams, 2.3, Spanish.

"French in the Elementary Classes."
See Part I.

Galas, Evangeline M.
See Galas, 7.

Garry, Ralph, and Edna Mauriello
See Garry, 2.3 French.

Geigle, Ralph C.
See Geigle, 6.5.

Gordon, Oakley J., Keith M. Engar, and Donald R. Shupe
See Gordon, 2.3 Russian.

Gradnisnik, Anthony J.
See Gradnisnik, 2.3 Spanish.

Griffiths, Ruth E.
See Griffiths, 6.5.

Grinder, R. E., A. Otomo, W. Toyota
    See Grinder, 2.3 Japanese.

Hayman, John L., Jr.
    See Hayman, 2.56.

Hayman, John L., Jr., and James T. Johnson, Jr.
    See Hayman, 2.3 Spanish, 2.56.

Himmler, Mervin L.
    See Himmler, 2.56.

Hunter, Thomas P.
    See Hunter, 2.3 Spanish.

Johnson, Charles E., Joseph S. Flores, and Fred P. Ellison
"The Effect of Foreign Language Instruction on Basic Learning in Elementary Schools," *Modern Language Journal,* XLV (May, 1961), 200-202.
    This study supplies evidence in favor of the hypothesis: "The inclusion of foreign language instruction in elementary school curricula will not reduce the extent of average gain in pupil achievement test scores." The data reveals that generally the experimental group, which received elementary-school foreign-language training, showed gains equal to, or greater than, the control group. Limitations of the experiments are discussed. A three-year study with more stringent control methods will be undertaken by the Foreign Language Instruction Project. See principal entry for this project, Johnson, *The Development . . .* , this section. JM

————.
University of Illinois Foreign Language Instruction Project, Preliminary Report II: A Summary of the Major Findings at the Close of the Second Year of the Study of the Development of Methods and Materials to Facilitate Foreign Language Instruction in Elementary Schools. Urbana, Ill.: University of Illinois, December 15, 1961 (mimeographed).
    Report of research project described on pp. 186-87 of the 1962 volume of this Bibliography. "The main purpose of the study is to develop a procedure, using newer educational media, for teaching foreign languages to elementary school children by an audio-lingual approach which is effective when used by teachers unfamiliar with the foreign language being taught, and to evaluate the devised procedure by comparing its effectiveness with that of a more conventional audio-

lingual approach to foreign language instruction requiring specialist teachers. Originally a total of five classrooms of children . . . was involved in the study. See Preliminary Report, pp. 184-85, 1962 volume of this Bibliography. This second preliminary report provides data and experimental findings obtained from a group of seventy students who continued Spanish instruction through the second year. Summary of findings are given, and the report attempts to discuss five problems which arose from the findings presented. DF

————.

See Johnson, 6.5.

Johnson, Charles E., *et al.*
The Development and Evaluation of Methods and Materials to Facilitate Foreign Language Instruction in Elementary Schools. Urbana: University of Illinois, 1963.
    See also various items in this section above, Ellison, Flores, and Johnson. *"Major Findings.* The differences between the mean Spanish achievement test scores of the control and experimental groups consistently favored the control group in immediacy of response, appropriateness of response, and pronunciation, and gradually became more and more significant over the three-year period. However, the differences between the mean achievement test scores in listening comprehension revealed no significant differences at any time during the three-year period. At the end of the three years, the control group received higher mean scores than the experimental group on all Spanish achivement tests. However, their mean tests ranged from 69 per cent to 94 per cent of those obtained by the control group. The differences in means for the composite scores and for four of the sub-tests (immediacy of response, appropriateness of response, pronunciation, and oral reading) were regarded as significant. The differences in means for the composite scores and for four of the sub-tests (immediacy of response, appropriateness of response, pronunciation, and oral reading) were regarded as significant. The differences in mean scores on the listening and reading comprehension subtests were not regarded as significant." From the summary of the Final Report, issued separately, February 1963.

Johnson, Grace Nichols, and Frances Hardy
See Johnson, 2.56.

Johnston, Marjorie C.
See Johnston, Part I.

Joos, Martin
"Language and the School Child," *Harvard Educational Review.*
XXXIV, No. 2 (1964), 203-10.

This essay is a lesson for the classroom teacher who tries to impose an artificial kind of grammatical structure upon a child who already comes to class equipped with his own norms of speech. Before the child enters the classroom he has already perceived that human differences of grammaticality have many variations and that the artificiality of a narrow "correct" and "incorrect" dimension is unreal. Teachers must alter their approach to what is dogmatically prescriptive in language and to what is commonly acceptable. If not, then there is room for conflict with its accompanying disastrous outcome. CBC

Justman, Joseph, and Martin L. Nass
"High School Achievement of Pupils Who Were and Were Not Introduced to a Foreign Language in Elementary School," *Modern Language Journal,* XL (March, 1956), 120-23.

On the basis of grade achievement in high school for this small group, no apparent advantages resulted from the study of French in elementary school. The pupils who had studied Spanish showed better achievement; however, the advantage did not persist beyond the first term of high school. BP

Keesee, Elizabeth
See Keesee, Part I.

Keislar, Evan R. University of California, Los Angeles, California.
Sequence of Discrimination and Differentiation Training in the Teaching of French in the Early Primary Grades; Project No. OE-3-14-022 (National Defense Education Act, Title VI), April 1, 1963, to October 1, 1964; $33,930.

The purpose of the investigation was to determine the best order of presentation and development of two activities involved in learning a foreign language; learning (1) to say words and phrases of the language and (2) to tell the difference among situations calling for these words and phrases (i.e., knowing the "meaning" of words). The problem under consideration was whether the learner should engage in activity (1) after some practice in activity (2) or vice versa; or whether the two activities should be integrated in some way. The project contributed to the development of improved procedures for teaching young children to understand and speak a foreign language.

The first step in the work was to develop a set of tape-recorded French lessons and accompanying visual aids for children in the early primary grades. Thereafter, the investigator presented this material to several small groups of children, each group being taught in a different way (pronunciation followed by comprehension or vice versa; both activities in every session, or the latter supplemented by review sessions). The pupils were under close observation throughout the trial sessions and their pronunciation and comprehension was carefully evaluated at the end of the experiment. From the official description

Kern, Edith
See Kern, 2.7.

Larew, Leonor A.
See Larew, 4.5.

Larew, Leonor A., and John J. Lottes
See Larew, 2.51.

Leino, Walter B., and Louis A. Haak
See Leino, 6.5.

Lesage, André
See Lesage, 2.53.

Lopato, Esther W.
See Lopato, 6.5.

Loucks, Robert E.
"Teaching Spanish through Games in the Elementary Schools: An Experimental Study," *Hispania,* XLII (May, 1959), 246-47.
    The results of a research project (master's thesis) conducted on parallel groups of third-grade children between ages of eight and nine. Hypothesis: Children can learn a foreign language more effectively through a series of carefully selected games than through the dialogue system. Results bore out the hypothesis that children taught by games had longer retention of material. They made fewer errors in the tests but were more difficult to motivate. MJS

Mace, Larry
See Mace, 3.1.

Marie Gabrielle, Sister, F.S.E., and Sister Raymond de Jesus, F.S.E.
"FLES: A Comparative Study," *Modern Language Journal,* XLVIII (February, 1964), 72-76.
    In this study we proposed to investigate group differences in French listening comprehension and to analyze the predictive value of mental ability and English silent reading with respect to French listening comprehension. The subjects were 621 fourth graders in "mixed-

parishes" in New England parochial schools. The findings seemed to indicate: (1) that the amount of contact with French in the home affected achievement in French listening comprehension, (2) that girls achieved significantly higher than boys, and (3) that scores in mental ability and English silent reading were inefficient predictors of success in French listening comprehension when used alone or as a team. Sister Marie Gabrielle, MLabstract #742.

Matsumoto, Masatatsu
See Matsumoto, 2.52.

Mildenberger, K. W.
Status of Foreign Language Study in American Elementary Schools. Washington, D.C.: United States Office of Education, 1953 (ditto).
    A statistical survey listing foreign-language programs at the elementary level of about 220 communities of the nation. The charts list inception date of the program, number of participating schools, requirements of participation, pupils, grade levels, time devoted to language training, enrollment, and availability of syllabus. JM

Milwaukee Public Schools
See Milwaukee Public Schools, 2.3 Spanish.

†Mueller, Klaus. Beloit College, Beloit, Wisconsin, and Donald W. Johnson, California State Department of Education, Sacramento, California
A Field Test of Four Approaches to the Teaching of Spanish in Elementary Schools. Research Project D-177 (California State Department of Education), June 1, 1964 to November, 1965.
    This research project has been initiated in an attempt to establish the best way in which to meet the California State mandatory requirement in foreign language for sixth, seventh and eighth grades, effective at the beginning of the 1965-66 school year. Four methods of instruction have been selected for field testing: instruction by a linguistically competent teacher using MLA materials; televised instruction using the Pasadena *Una aventura española* materials; the latter, but with supplemental instruction by a linguistically competent teacher two days per week; instruction provided by the TEMAC materials in Spanish. Ten centers for experimentation per method and grade level have been proposed. Evaluation will be on the basis of criterion tests based on the skills being taught. Each method will have its individual criterion test in the areas of vocabulary, structure and pronunciation. Student attitudes before and after will be taken into consideration, as well as teachers and administrators' response. The research proposal describes in detail each method to be used. This project should prove to be

extremely important not only for the relative advantages of each method in terms of the cost of implementation involved, but also in establishing a tentative program in Spanish to meet both the California State requirement and a similar requirement in other states. DF

Naunheim, Elizabeth
"Spanish in Corpus Christi," *Hispania,* XXXVII (March, 1954), 77-78.

Report on the fourteen-year-old experiment in teaching Spanish to elementary-grade students in Corpus Christi, with an appraisal of results as seen in junior and senior high schools. MJS

Newmark, Gerald
FLES—A New Approach. Santa Monica, California: System Development Corporation, 27 September, 1962.

Gives background for the idea that FLES training should be limited to listening comprehension as its initial objective. Research involved would be the development of materials which would provide active experience for the student. JM

————.
"Foreign Languages in Elementary Schools and Implications for Teacher Education," *Journal of Teacher Education,* XIV (December, 1963), 449-55.

In this article I review some recent research related to the teaching of foreign languages in elementary schools without the services of a qualified language teacher (e.g., FLES by TV and by elementary school teachers with little or no foreign language competence). I also summarize research in progress at the System Development Corporation concerning the application of programmed learning to FLES instruction. Gerald Newmark

————.
See Newmark, 2.51.

NHK Radio-Television Cultural Research Institute
See NHK Radio-Television . . . , 2.51.

Pflieger, Elmer F.
See Pflieger, 2.56.

Pursley, Alice J.
See Pursley, 3.5.

Randall, Earle S.
"*Parlons français:* A Large-Scale FLES Program by Television," *French Review,* XXXIV (May, 1961), 571-73.

This article summarizes the first two years of *Parlons français,* a televised and film program for teaching French in the elementary school. The first year's research studied effects on children's learning when (1) moderately fluent and (2) non-fluent teachers conducted follow-up, and also when (3) these teachers planned their own follow-up or (4) they used specially provided audio tapes. In most areas, pupils' achievement was roughly equivalent, whether a non-fluent or a moderately fluent teacher conducted follow-up. Earle S. Randall

Ryan, Henry M.
The Effects of Foreign Language Study in the Elementary School (FLES) on First Year Achievement in a Second Language. Unpublished Ed.D. dissertation, Pennsylvania State University, 1961.
    This study was designed to determine whether any differences in high school second language course could be observed among three groups having had varying amounts of experience with foreign languages in elementary school (FLES) and a group which had none. . . . Significant differences were discovered among the various experience groups on the achievement test results, on the teachers' grades, and on the German oral comprehension test results. This significance, however, when analyzed by separate language experience groups maintained itself consistently only in German where the high school language was the same as that studied in the elementary school. From the abstract.

Sadnavitch, Joseph M., and W. James Popham
See Sadnavitch, 2.7.

Saxton, John B.
"Experiment at McGuffey School, Oxford, Ohio," *Hispania,* XXXIII (August, 1950), 264-67.
    Report and evaluation of techniques used in an experiment in teaching Spanish to fifth-grade students in the training school at Miami University. Emphasis on use of a combination of all techniques used in similar experiments; mention of drawbacks. Article preceded by a listing of articles on this subject as published in *Hispania.* MJS

Schramm, Wilbur, and Kenneth E. Oberholtzer
See Schramm and Oberholtzer, 2.56.

Selvi, Arthur M.
"An Experiment Introducing Modern Language Activities in the Elementary School," *Educational Administration and Supervision,* XXXVII (May, 1951), 312-15.
    An experiment to prove that foreign languages can be taught with

success to fifth- and sixth-grade pupils. Discussion of (1) why teach a foreign language, (2) what elements should be taught at that level, and (3) direct approach as the method of teaching. Description of the test groups of students and tests scores resulting from their studies. Survey of parental evaluation of the experimental course is presented. JM

Selvi, Arthur M., *et al.*
"Report of the Committee on French in the Elementary School," in *Yale-Barnard Conference on the Teaching of French.* New Haven, April, 1952.

A study describing the trends of foreign language teaching in the United States. Description of some state-wide, city-wide, and single school experimental programs. Reasons indicated for some of these programs being limited to gifted pupils, others being open to all pupils. Arthur M. Selvi

————.

"Report of the Committee on French in the Elementary School," in *Barnard-Yale Conference on the Teaching of French.* New York, March, 1953.

An analysis of psychological, pedagogical and sociological reasons underlying language programs limited to the gifted vs. those open to all pupils. Outline of a comprehensive plan of research aiming to determine the effect of the study of a second language upon pupils of elementary school age, and to appraise the value of such study for (a) retarded children, (b) normal children, (c) gifted children with reference to their (1) sociocultural, (2) emotional, and (3) intellectual development. Arthur Selvi.

Shane, Harold G., and June Grant Mulry
"Frère Jacques Is Out of Bed!" in their *Improving Language Arts Instruction Through Research.* Washington, D.C.: Association for Supervision and Curriculum Development, NEA, 1963. Pp. 111-129.

This chapter is an excellent review of FLES in relation to the overall topic of the authors' study. They summarize the FLES controversy by providing abstracts and summaries of the most significant discussions on the subject. Good documentation is provided and several areas of possible research are mentioned. A 94-item bibliography is included. DF

Silagyi, Dezo Vincent
See Silagyi, 2.56.

Stensaasen, Svein
See Stensaasen, 2.3 English.

Stern, J. J.

Foreign Languages in Primary Education, The Teaching of Foreign or Second Language to Younger Children; Report on an International Meeting of Experts 9-14 April, 1962. Hamburg: UNESCO Institute for Education, 1963.

This publication is a general review of the problem of second-language teaching on the elementary level. Opinions, experiments and programs from both European and non-European countries are reported. Particular attention is given to the bilingual teaching situation. Particularly useful is John B. Carroll's chapter on Research Problems, incorporated into the section entitled Recommendations for Practice and Research. A bibliography is appended to the report. DF

Stockton, James C.
See Stockton, 2.52.

Stowell, Ernest
See Stowell, 6.5.

Sturge-Moore, C. J.
See Sturge-Moore, 2.3 English.

Van Willigen, Daam M.
See Van Willigen, Part I.

Vollmer, Joseph H., and Ruth E. Griffiths
See Vollmer, 6.5.

Weiss, Bernard Joseph
See Weiss, 2.3 English.

Xoomsai, M. L. Tooi, and P. Ratamangkala
See Xoomsai, 2.51.

6.2 First Cycle of Secondary Education

Dostal, Naida M.
See Dostal, 2.53.

Gibson, Romain (Mrs. Rodney E.)
See Gibson, 2.54.

International Christian University, Audiovisual Center
See International Christian . . . , 2.56.

Johnson, Grace Nichols, and Frances Hardy
See Johnson, 2.56.

Kilpatrick, Joel Fred
  See Kilpatrick, 3.1.

MacKinnon, A. R.
  See MacKinnon, 2.3 French.

Moore, Patricia
  See Moore, 2.54.

Mueller, Klaus, and Donald W. Johnson
  See Mueller, 6.1.

NHK Radio-Television Cultural Research Institute
  See NHK Radio-Television . . . , 2.51.

Pflieger, Elmer F.
  See Pflieger, 2.56.

Pickrel, Glenn E., *et al.*
  See Pickrel, 2.51.

Pimsleur, Paul, Donald M. Sundland, and Ruth D. McIntyre
  See Pimsleur, 3.3.

Rufsvold, Margaret I., and Carolyn Guss
  See Rufsvold and Guss, Part I.

Suppes, Patrick G., Edward Crothers, and Ruth Weir
  See Suppes, 3.1.

Toronto Board of Education
  See Toronto Board of Education, 2.3 French, 2.56.

Uemura, Hidekichi
  See Uemura, 2.3 Japanese.

Uota, Shoji
  See Uota, 2.3 English.

Van Willigen, Daam M.
  See Van Willigen, Part I.

White, Wayne Hugh
  See White, 2.3 Spanish.

Xoomsai, M. L. Tooi, and P. Ratamangkala
  See Xoomsai, 2.51.

Young, Clarence W., and Charles A. Choquette
  See Young, 2.54.

6.3 Second Cycle of Secondary Education

Bernard, Edward G., and Sarah W. Lorge
See Bernard, 2.54.

Broady, K. O., C. O. Neidt, and G. B. Childe
See Broady, 2.56.

Buch, John N.
See Buch, 2.54.

Carlson, William D.
An Analysis of Achievement Outcomes of the Six-Hour Class Program
at the University of Minnesota High School. Unpublished Ph.D. dissertation, University of Minnesota, 1955.
        Concerns the value of exposing the child to the foreign-language
area in such a manner that he achieves and by achievement his affective
attitude toward schooling is improved. JM

Couch, Sanford Gary
See Couch, 2.3 Russian.

Dostal, Naida Marich
See Dostal, 2.53.

Gideon, Sara B.
See Gideon, 2.51.

Greenberg, Jacob
See Greenberg, 5.

Harmon, John
"Foreign Languages in Independent Secondary Schools," in Modern
Language Association of America, *Reports of Surveys and Studies . . .*
(see Part I.)

Hascall, Edward O.
See Hascall, 3.3.

"Instruction in Classical and Modern Foreign Languages," *National Education Association Research Bulletin,* XXXV (December, 1957), 156-
59.
        Gives statistical information as to foreign-language enrollment in
public high schools from 1890 through 1955 and the per cent of public
high schools offering modern foreign languages in 1954. A greater per
cent of total American youth population is enrolled in language study
today than in 1900, even though the comparison of enrollments indi-

cates that a larger per cent of high school students was registered in foreign-language study in 1900 than in 1955. JM

Johnson, Charles E., and Joseph S. Flores
See Johnson, 6.1.

Johnson, Grace Nichols, and Frances Hardy
See Johnson, 2.56.

Kilpatrick, Joel Fred
See Kilpatrick, 3.1.

LeVois, Camille J.
See LeVois, 2.53.

Lorge, Sarah W.
See Lorge, 2.54.

Matthew, Robert J.
"Language Studies at the Secondary Level," *Education Digest,* XIII (March, 1948), 20-23.
  Report of an experiment by the Commission on Implications of Armed Services Educational Programs in a large New York high school. Two beginners classes each in French, German, and Spanish were used. The direct method of teaching, with modifications, was used. According to tests, the special group in Spanish did perform better than the control group. Results appeared inconclusive, and were based only on teachers' grades and reactions of administrators. MJS

Milholland, John E., and Jason Millman
"The Value of High School Foreign Language for the Study of College Introductory Foreign Language," *Modern Language Journal,* XLVII (October, 1963), 235-38.
  College grades in French, German, and Spanish for 89 University of Michigan Freshmen who had taken no high school foreign language were compared with the grades in the same college languages of 460 Freshmen who had taken two years of high school language work but in a language different from the one they took in college. When controls for tested verbal ability and for grades in other college subjects were applied, there remained a statistically significant advantage in favor of the students who had taken two years language in high school. The authors conclude that it seems to be justifiable to recommend to high school students that if they intend to go to a college where foreign language is required, they begin their language work in high school. John E. Milholland, MLabstract # 633

Pervy, Adolphe
See Pervy, 2.53.

Petrov, Julia A.
See Petrov, 2.3 Russian.

Pflieger, Elmer F.
See Pflieger, 2.56.

Pimsleur, Paul
See Pimsleur, 3.3.

Pimsleur, Paul, Donald M. Sundland, and Ruth D. McIntyre
See Pimsleur, 3.3.

Rathee, R. S., and V. V. Mennes
"Report on High School Foreign Language: Directed Study Experiment 1960-1961," *Journal of Experimental Education,* XXXII (Fall, 1963), 107-14.
    The purpose of the study is to compare the effectiveness of conventional instruction with correspondence study supplemented by monthly visits from the instructor and tape recordings. Subjects are students in Wisconsin high schools who are studying French, German, Latin and Spanish. Scores are obtained from the Henmon-Nelson test and the Kansas Foreign Language Tests. Analysis of variance is applied to the data. It is found that groups of equal ability show no significant differences in achievement whether they are taught by correspondence study method or by regular school teaching methods at .01 level of significance. However, at .05 level of significance the lower ability groups in Latin teaching show significant difference on a comparison of percentile rank scores. Center for Documentation and Communication Research, Western Reserve University.

Ryan, Henry M.
See Ryan, 6.1.

Tezza, Joseph S.
See Tezza, 2.3 Russian.

Tracy, Edward
See Tracy, 2.54.

Van Willigen, Daam M.
See Van Willigen, Part I.

Vollmer, Joseph H., and Ruth E. Griffiths
See Vollmer, 6.5.

Young, Clarence W., and Charles A. Choquette
See Young, 2.54.

Zais, Robert S.
See Zais, 4.5.

6.4 University

Berrett, Donald S., *et al.*
See Berrett, *et al.*, 2.3, German.

Borglum, George P.
See Borglum, 2.53.

Boyd-Bowman, Peter. Kalamazoo College, Kalamazoo, Michigan. Experimentation with Taped Materials and Native Informants to Develop for Small Colleges Some Programs of Independent Study in the Neglected Languages; Project No. OE-4-14-032 (National Defense Education Act, Title VI), October 4, 1963, to September 30, 1964; $9,088.

As a means of developing programs of independent study in the neglected languages at small colleges, Kalamazoo College will test the feasibility of combining basic course materials, language laboratory facilities, and the services of foreign students as native speakers. The college is to offer instruction in three of the neglected languages chosen from among Hindi, Portuguese, Chinese, Japanese, Swahili and Turkish. Students will participate voluntarily, working independently with commercially available texts and drill tapes in one of the languages offered for about 10 hours per week and with a native speaker for an additional 5 hours. Oral proficiency will be measured weekly, utilizing taped recordings which will be evaluated quarterly by language specialists during their visits to the college. From the official description.

Couch, Sanford Gary
See Couch, 2.3 Russian.

Greenberg, Jacob
See Greenberg, 5.

Greenhill, Leslie P., *et al.*
See Greenhill, *et al.*, 2.56.

Hamilton, Daniel L.
See Hamilton, 2.1.

Hanzeli, Victor E.
See Hanzeli, 2.53.

Fendrick, Daniel. U.S. Department of State, Bureau of Intelligence and Research, Washington, D.C.
Revision of "Language and Area Study Programs in American Universities"; Project No. OE-4-14-031 (National Defense Education Act, Title VI), December 1963 to July 1964; $6,532.

This contract provides for a revision of the Department of State publication *Language and Area Study Programs in American Universities, 1962,* prepared with partial support by the U.S. Office of Education under contract OE-2-14-016. The present contract will again cover only half the cost of the project.

The revision will present in tabular form basic information on graduate level language and area study programs in American universities. It will include the following information for each identified university center: (1) title, name, and department of the director; (2) names and area of specialization of faculty members concerned with the program; (3) degrees offered; (4) regional focus; (5) language taught (including number of courses); (6) area study course offerings; (7) library facilities; (8) outside support (foundation. NDEA, etc.); (9) number of national fellowship holders; and (10) special features.

In addition, a brief analytical essay on the present state of undergraduate language and area studies will be prepared, which will include some 20 to 30 profiles on selected undergraduate programs and will give some account of the notable growth of undergraduate language and area programs in recent years. From the official description.

Hocking, Elton, Carroll Weisiger, and W. Merle Hill
See Hocking, 3.1.

Hohfeld, John Maurice
See Hohfeld, 2.3, Spanish.

Lopes, Albert R., and Marshall R. Nason
"Teaching Elementary Foreign Languages," *Hispania,* XXXIX (December, 1956), 462-63.

Experiment in beginning language classes at University of New Mexico, using large lecture sections, small drill sections grouped according to ability, individual work in language laboratory, and bi-weekly tests. In spite of more rigorous standards than for previous program, results show reduction of failure from 38 per cent to 12 per cent, improvement of student attitudes, and increased interest in specialization in the field. DG

Mackey, William F. Université Laval, Quebec, Canada
Foreign Languages in Canadian Universities and Colleges: Preliminary Report, I. Statistics. Research in progress.

While not applicable research, this project deserves mention at this time for the possible information which subsequent reports may yield as to research being conducted in foreign language learning in Canada. DF

McKinney, James Edward, Jr.
See McKinney, 2.7.

Milholland, John E., and Jason Millman
See Milholland, 6.3.

Miller, Roy A. Yale University, New Haven, Conn.
A Survey of Intensive Programs in the Uncommon Languages, Summer 1964; Project No. OE-4-14-047 (National Defense Education Act, Title VI), June 22, 1964, to September 30, 1964; $11,318.

The contractor will organize a team of experts to survey programs of intensive modern foreign language instruction being held during the summer of 1964 at NDEA Language and Area Centers.

NDEA Language and Area Centers at 20 universities conduct summer programs which include intensive study of 27 critically needed languages not commonly taught in the United States. About 1,500 qualified students at all academic levels are enrolled for courses in such languages as Arabic, Chinese, Hindi-Urdu, Japanese, Swahili, and Vietnamese.

The survey involves personal visits by six language experts to most of the NDEA Centers. Points to be evaluated include amount of time spent by students in actual contact with the language, effectiveness of teaching materials and testing devices, problems of coordinating summer work with academic year courses, and the relationship of instruction in a given language to courses pertaining to the area where it is spoken. From the official description.

O'Rourke, Everett
See O'Rourke, 6.5.

Popham, W. James
See Popham, 2.51.

Putter, Irving
"High School-College Articulation in Foreign Languages," *Modern Language Journal,* XXXIX (March, 1955), 123-25.

This study was undertaken to ascertain if a lapse between high school studies of a foreign language and resumption of study in college affected student achievement. The two-year lapse group scored lower than the no-lapse group coming from high school. However, it is significant that both groups scored higher than the group that started language study at the college level. BP

Rufsvold, Margaret I., and Carolyn Guss
See Rufsvold and Guss, Part I.

Saltzman, Irving
See Saltzman, 2.3 Russian.

Scherer, George A. C., and Michael Wertheimer
See Scherer, 2.1.

Schnurer, Herman, Samuel Baskin, and Robert Boyd
See Schnurer, 2.3 French.

Smither, William J., and William S. Woods
An Experimental Restructuring of the Undergraduate Foreign Language Curriculum with Supporting Research in Teaching Techniques: Interim Report No. 2. New Orleans: Tulane University, n.d.
    Experimental revision of four-year foreign-language program to prepare majors to achieve minimal ratings on the MLA teacher proficiency tests. Special comparison of results of monitored and unmonitored language lab practice. Self-pacing for control groups. DG

Uttal, William R.
See Uttal, 2.55.

Valdman, Albert. Indiana University, Bloomington, Ind.
Implementation and Evaluation of a Multiple Credit Intensive Audio-Lingual Approach in Elementary French; Project No. 9,498 (National Defense Education Act, Title VI), June 15, 1961, to June 14, 1963; $97,703.
    An investigation of "the problems, administrative and pedagogical, presented by the establishment of a college-level, beginning foreign language course which provides the high number of contact hours (500-600) required for the acquisition of audio-lingual skills, and which permits each student to proceed at his own learning rate."— From official description, unpublished.

————.

Indiana University Foundation for and on behalf of Indiana University, Bloomington, Indiana.
Continuation and Completion of the Implementation and Evaluation of a Multiple-Credit Intensive Audio-Lingual Approach in Elementary French; Project No. OE-4-14-009 (National Defense Education Act, Title VI), July 1, 1963, to June 30, 1964; $40,422.

This contract provides for the continuation of a project begun under contract SAE-9498, involving the testing and evaluation of an intensive audio-lingual course in elementary French. The students enrolled in the course spent from 10 to 15 hours a week studying French, primarily in the language laboratory. The laboratory work consisted of active drill with minimal step-increment-type materials and was supplemented by 1 hour per week of grammatical analysis in large student groups, and two 30-minute practice sessions in groups of two to four students.

Although the program offers credit equivalent to a three-semester college course, each student is allowed to progress at his own speed and some are able to achieve an acceptable level of proficiency in less than the usual time.

The project findings are expected to point a way to more efficient utilization of student and staff time in language learning. The final report includes the following: (1) recommendations for improvement of the college level foreign language curriculum and procedures; (2) information on the development and use of self-instructional language courses and tests; and (3) comments on factors which influence foreign language learning.

*Valtasaari, Hanna
"Kokeilevaa vieraitten kielten opetusta Raahen seminaarissa" ("Experimentation in Foreign Language Teaching, Raahen Seminar, [i.e., Junior College]"), Kasvatus ja koulu (Child Rearing and Schools), XXXVII (1951), 203-10 and 238-51.

Vamos, Mara, and John Harmon
"Modern Foreign Language Faculties in Colleges and Universities, 1959-1960," in Modern Language Association of America, Reports of Surveys and Studies . . . (see Part I.)

Vamos, Mara, et al.
"Language Learning in American Colleges and Universities: Data on Degrees, Majors, and Teaching Practices," in Modern Language Association of America, Reports of Surveys and Studies . . . (see Part I.)

Wormald, F. L., Association of American Colleges, Washington, D.C.
Survey of Non-Western Studies in Liberal Arts Colleges; Project No. OE-3-14-018 (National Defense Education Act, Title VI), February 4, 1963, to February 3, 1964; $35,000.

The Association of American Colleges undertook a survey of U.S. undergraduate liberal arts college courses or programs dealing with the cultures and languages of the heretofore neglected "non-

Western" areas of the world. These included Africa, the Middle East, South and East Asia, the Soviet Union, and Latin America. The survey sought to provide a national picture of the status of non-Western studies in undergraduate liberal arts colleges. It focused on significant approaches devised by some 20 colleges which are incorporating the study of non-Western cultures, languages, or areas into the liberal arts curriculum. This involved new courses, the infusion of substantial non-Western materials in existing disciplinary courses, or in the general education courses for undergraduates.

Questions of institutional commitment, the mobilization of faculty, library, and other resources, and examples of cooperative endeavors among neighboring colleges were explored. A meeting of representatives of the member colleges discussed the findings of the survey before a report was prepared in April of 1964. From the official description.

Young, Clarence W., and Charles A. Choquette
See Young, 2.54.

6.5 Language Teaching and General Education

Childers, J. Wesley
See Childers, 2.1.

Commission on Secondary School Curriculum.
Language in General Education: A Report on English in General Education. New York: D. Appleton-Century, 1940.

Language is a necessary part of all individual development as well as the vehicle of the culture of any human group. As such, it is an important skill to be well taught in our educational system. The committee advances some theories of language and also criticizes our present teaching methods. The final chapter points out that the practical application of these theories is in the experimental stage; and points also to the need for further experimentation. JM

Corrin, Brownlee Sands
See Corrin, 5.

Doran, Thomas A. Folsom Unified School District, California.
A Program for Coordinating the Teaching and Learning of Biology and Spanish; Project No. OE-4-14-044 (National Defense Education Act, Title VI), February 15, 1964, to November 13, 1964; $6,925.

The contractor will conduct research among pupils in four schools to determine whether a foreign language is learned more efficiently when presented through the content of another school subject.

Specifically, the project involves assigning pupils enrolled in a regular beginning biology class to a concurrent beginning Spanish class where discussion, dialog, narration, and reading are centered on biology. Materials to be used consist in part of films on wildlife and natural resources with Spanish commentary. The study will compare and evaluate the achievement of these students in both Spanish and biology with that of students following conventional courses. The experiment will be conducted in three high schools and one elementary school. From the official description.

Dufort, Mary R.
See Dufort, 6.1.

Geigle, Ralph C.
"Foreign Language and Basic Learning," *Elementary School Journal,* LVII (May, 1957), 418.

A study of achievement of basic learning before and after the inclusion of foreign-language instruction at the elementary level in order to determine the effect of language training on basic learning. Study of test scores showed that the effect of the added training was beneficial rather than detrimental. JM

Gordon, Oakley J., Keith M. Engar, and Donald R. Shupe
See Gordon, 2.3 Russian.

Johnson, Charles E., Joseph S. Flores, and Fred P. Ellison
"The Effect of Foreign Language Instruction on Basic Learning in Elementary Schools," *Modern Language Journal,* XLVII (January, 1963), 8-11.

The pupils in this study who engaged in learning a second language for twenty minutes each school day . . . showed greater achievement in reading vocabulary and reading comprehension[;] . . . in language skills, arithmetic and work-study skills the two groups varied little. . . . From the article.

*Kahan, Anne M.
The Effect of a Second Language (Hebrew) on Reading Achievement at the Elementary School Level. Unpublished Masters thesis, Boston University [1961?].

Kaulfers, Walter V., *et al.*
Foreign Languages and Cultures in American Education. New York: McGraw-Hill Book Co., 1942.

A presentation of twenty reports of practices by teachers of foreign languages, English, and social studies who participated in experimental programs. The objectives are discussed. New-type unified programs are described. JM

Leino, Walter B., and Louis A. Haak
The Teaching of Spanish in the Elementary Schools and the Effects on Achievement in Other Selected Areas. St. Paul, Minn.: St. Paul Public Schools, November, 1963.

"The problems in this study hinge around two points which may be unanswerable but about which a great deal more should be known. The first of these is the amount of time given to study within a certain subject area at a particular grade level. The second evolves around the ability of students at a particular grade level to learn a second language." (pp. 1-2) Major conclusions are: "Perhaps the most unequivocal of all the results of this study is the finding that the deletion of time from arithmetic, language and social studies to devote to the study of Spanish had no detrimental effect upon measured achievement in the subject areas from which time was taken. [. . .] Equally certain is the finding that measured intelligence is positively correlated with measured achievement in the learning of Spanish." (p. 29) Extensive space is devoted to the discussion of selection of sample, measuring instruments, and methods of analysis. Detailed discussions of the data leading to the major conclusions are included. DF

Lopato, Esther W.
An Experiment to Determine the Effect of Learning Conversational French on Academic Achievement of Third Grade Children. Unpublished Ph.D. dissertation, New York University, 1961.

Four third grade classes, an experimental and control class in each of two Metropolitan New York public schools, participated in the research. The experimental and control classes were equated for age, I.Q. and socio-economic status. The experimental groups were given a conversational French course in addition to the prescribed curriculum. Control groups followed only the prescribed curriculum. Achievement tests administered at the beginning and end of the school year revealed: (1) there were positive correlations between academic achievement generally and achievement in French; (2) expert judges considered the French pronunciation and fluency of the children superior to the results generally obtained with beginning high school students after an equivalent period of instruction; (3) there were no adverse effects on achievement for the year in the prescribed curriculum with the introduction of the French program. On the contrary, the groups studying French evidenced greater mean achievement gain in seven out of eight instances. Esther W. Lopato

————.

"FLES and Academic Achievement," *French Review,* XXXVI (April, 1963), 499-507.
This is an abstract of the preceding entry.

MacBride, Mary D.
See MacBride, 2.3 Latin.

O'Rourke, Everett
"An Experiment in Integrating Biology and Spanish," *California Journal of Secondary Education,* XLIV (November, 1960), 427-36.
In this article I am reporting a team teaching project integrating biology and Spanish conducted at three high schools in Tulare County, California. The biology teachers did not know Spanish and the Spanish teachers were not biologists; however, they coordinated basic purposes and learning procedures, defined the objectives for both subjects, developed selected units most suitable for the integrated approach, selected appropriate audio and visual teaching materials and made tapes and devised other materials when none were available. The cooperation of the Tulare County Schools Office helped to assure success of the project. Non-selective students enrolled in the biology and Spanish. All teachers stated that the students learned more Spanish and more biology than students in previous classes. Everett V. O'Rourke, MLabstract #124.

Pursley, Alice J.
See Pursley, 3.5.

Selvi, Arthur, *et al.*
See Selvi, 6.1.

Sherred, Ruth. Exeter High School, Exeter, Calif.
Experimentation to Determine the Extent to Which Close Correlation of Foreign Language Study with Study in Another Subject Area Has a Measureable Effect on Pupil Achievement in Either Area; Project No. 9,066 (National Defense Education Act, Title VI), September 22, 1960, to July 1, 1962; $10,826.
Based on two premises: (a) "the learning of a foreign language is facilitated and increased if the language can be approached as a means to an end rather than as an end in itself. In this experiment Spanish is taught as an essential means of access to another subject area, biology." (b) "Pupils' performance in the correlated area will also be improved by such correlation if they are concurrently enrolled in a regular course in that area . . . use is made of audio-visual aids,

particularly films and film strips." From official description, unpublished.

Skelton, Robert B.
"The Effect of High School Foreign Language Study on Freshman Test Scores at Alabama Polytechnic Institute," *School and Society,* LXXXV (June 8, 1957), 203-5.
     A battery of 6 tests—i.e., basic intelligence, linguistic ability, mathematics, etc.—were given to 1,647 students entering Alabama Polytechnic Institute. They were separated into two groups—those who had had foreign-language background and those who had not. The study showed the marked superiority of the students with foreign-language background in every category. Follow-up study showed better college performance. It was concluded that foreign language does improve the student's command of his own language, thereby improving his control of other subject matter. BP

Sowards, G. W.
"Organization of the Curriculum," *Review of Educational Research,* XXIX (April, 1959), 146-54.
     A bibliographical analysis of general curriculum problems, with attention to foreign-language experimentation in the lower grade levels on p. 150. JM

Starr, Wilmarth H., Mary P. Thompson, and Donald D. Walsh
See Starr, 2.1.

Stowell, Ernest
Final Report . . . Eau Claire, Wisconsin: Wisconsin State College, October, 1963 (mimeographed).
     The purpose of this research project was to investigate the effect on the third grade class of the Campus Elementary School at Eau Claire of a modern language program in which a large percentage of the class day (25 to 50 per cent) was devoted to instruction in Spanish, with an elementary school teacher from Mexico City giving instruction not only in the language but also in arithmetic, science, social studies, art, music and physical education, conducted in Spanish. Observation period—September, 1962, to June, 1963, and continuing 1963 to 1964. [. . .] The over-all results of the research program indicate that a class would normally lose little by the reduction of time in English if such lost time is devoted to supplementary instruction in the foreign language, using that language as a medium of instruction and not simply a goal of instruction. They indicate that a satisfactory advance can be made toward mastery of a second lan-

guage for real use as a medium of instruction. Finally they indicate that with skillful organization and supervision, a program of foreign language instruction could be developed for most elementary schools which would be infinitely more effective than programs now in vogue, and at a lower cost. From the Final Report.

Vollmer, Joseph H., and Ruth E. Griffiths
Evaluation of the Effect of Foreign Language Study in the Elementary School Upon Achievement in the High School. Somerville, New Jersey: Somerville Board of Education, July 1962.

The report discusses research conducted on the basis of the thirteen-year continuous FLES program in the Somerville, New Jersey Public Schools. "The mathematical findings lead one to conclude that in Somerville, at least, systematic study of a foreign language from grade three through grade eight does not undermine the child's foundation in the basic or traditional learnings. He does not compete in high school classes other than foreign language under any discernible handicap. One might further project the hypothesis that in college or life situations he will fare no hardship attributable to deficient elementary school preparation." From the Conclusions and Discussions. DF

6.6 Specific School Programs

Alhinc, J., M. Clay, and Pierre Roger Léon
See Alhinc, 2.54.

Berrett, Donald S., *et al.*
See Berrett, *et al.,* 2.3, German.

Buffington, Albert
See Buffington, 2.3 German.

Carlson, William D.
See Carlson, 6.3.

Carroll, John B.
See Carroll, 3.3.

Carton, Aaron S., and John B. Carroll
See Carton, 2.3 Russian.

Delattre, Pierre C.
See Delattre, 2.54.

Dufort, Mary R.
See Dufort, 6.1.

Dunkel, Harold B., and Roger A. Pillet
    See Dunkel and Pillet, 6.1.

Ellison, Fred, Joseph S. Flores, and Charles E. Johnson
    See Ellison, Flores, and Johnson, 6.1.

Estep, Hunter L.
    See Estep, 6.1.

Forsdale, Louis, and Gerald Dykstra
    See Forsdale, 2.53.

Garry, Ralph, and Edna Mauriello
    See Garry, 2.3 French.

Gibson, Romain
    See Gibson, 2.54.

Hamilton, Daniel Lee, and Ernest F. Haden
    See Hamilton and Haden, 2.3, French.

Hill, Leslie A.
    See Hill, 2.52.

Hocking, Elton
    See Hocking, 2.54.

Johnson, Grace Nichols, and Frances Hardy
    See Johnson, 2.56.

LeVois, Camille J.
    See LeVois, 2.53.

Lopes, Albert R., and Marshall R. Nason
    See Lopes and Nason, 6.4.

Lundeen, D. J.
    See Lundeen, 4.5.

MacBride, Mary D.
    See MacBride, 2.3 Latin.

Mueller, Theodore
    See Mueller, 4.5.

Mueller, Theodore, and George P. Borglum
    See Mueller and Borglum, 2.54.

Naunheim, Elizabeth
    See Naunheim, 6.1.

O'Rourke, Everett
    See O'Rourke, 6.5.

Pickrel, Glenn E., *et al.*
    See Pickrel, *et al.,* 2.51.

Rathee, R. S., and V. V. Mennes
    See Rathee, 6.3.

Reichard, Joseph
    See Reichard, 2.3 German.

Rosselot, LaVelle
    See Rosselot, 2.53.

Saxton, John B.
    See Saxton, 6.1.

Scherer, George A. C., and Michael Wertheimer
    See Scherer, 2.3 German.

Silagyi, Dezo Vincent
    See Silagyi, 2.56.

Stowell, Ernest
    See Stowell, 6.5.

Toronto Board of Education
    See Toronto Board of Education, 2.3 French.

Valdman, Albert
    See Valdman, 2.55.

Vicory, Arthur C.
    See Vicory, 3.1.

Wershow, Irving
    See Wershow, 2.3 French.

7. Teacher Qualifications and Training

Brault, Gerard J.
"The Special NDEA Institute at Bowdoin College for French Teachers of Canadian Descent," *PMLA,* LXXVII (September, 1962), 1-5.

In this article I report on a pioneering effort under NDEA auspices in the summer of 1961 to exploit in the national interest the linguistic resource represented by well over a million persons of French-Canadian descent residing in New England. Special attention was accorded in every aspect of the program to the problems faced by Franco-Americans desirous of acquiring standard French. An experimental set of teaching materials was constructed by the Institute members. Participants who spoke French freely and fluently tended to have strong dialectal traits and resisted efforts at standardization; younger participants were reluctant to identify themselves with an "ethnic" cause. The institute was highly successful in coping with these and other problems, however, and provided much-needed guidance for future efforts. Gerard J. Brault, MLabstract #356.

Cheydleur, F. D.
"Judging Teachers of Basic French Courses by Objective Means at the University of Wisconsin, 1919-1943," *Journal of Educational Research,* XXXIX (November, 1945), 161-92.

Cheydleur establishes some criteria for effective teaching of basic French at the college level, and thereby judges teachers. He finds that the efficiency of the instructor is shown by the end product—the student. He also lists interesting data, e.g., of the two groups of teachers, foreign and American, the latter is more effective. BP
See Brault, 2.3, French

Childers, J. Wesley, *et al.*
"Teacher Education Curricula in the Modern Foreign Languages," in Modern Language Association of America, *Reports of Surveys and Studies* . . . (see Part I.)

Feldman, David M., and Barbara Schindler

"An In-Service Alternative to the Summer Institute Program," *Modern Language Journal*, XLVIII (February, 1964), 88-91.

In this article we describe a unique in-service training program for secondary school teachers of Spanish stressing the application of the findings of linguistic science to teaching all levels of Spanish. Under the sponsorship of the U.S. Office of Education, the following materials were developed for use by experimental groups which utilized self-directing, study-discussion methods: (1) a textbook *(The Modern Teaching of Spanish)* consisting of twelve chapters dealing with the audio-lingual approach and including an extensive, annotated bibliography, discussion questions, and detailed instruction in independent group study techniques, and (2) a comprehensive reference shelf. The results of the MLA Proficiency Tests in applied linguistics and professional preparation revealed that the participants' progress was closely comparable to that of participants in the nationwide summer institutes the previous summer, and are therefore indicative of a program well worth considering when teachers are unable to attend a summer institute. David M. Feldman and Barbara Schindler, MLabstract #739.

Freeman, Stephen A., *et al.*

"The Qualifications of Foreign Language Teachers," *School and Society*, LXXX (November 27, 1954), 165-68.

Report by committee on preparation, certification, placement, and supervision of language teachers. Gives qualifications, problems, and recommendations. BP

Galas, Evangeline M.

Final Report on the Development and Evaluation of an Elementary School Foreign Language Teaching Technique for Use by Teachers with Inadequate Knowledge of the Language Taught. Washington, D.C.: U.S. Office of Education, 1962.

In this Report I give results of research project performed pursuant to a contract with the above Office. During 1960-61, 563 heterogeneously-grouped pupils in 20 elementary classes, 10 Spanish, 10 French, used HRS records guided by teachers with inadequate or no knowledge of the languages. In daily 20 minute classes, observed monthly, teachers never spoke the language, simply employed techniques outlined in the *Manual*. In June teachers and pupils were professionally taped in class as prescribed by consultants. Tapes, evaluated by linguists, showed much language learned but results generally unacceptable due to poor phonetics. Children, teachers, parents were enthusiastic. Evaluators, recommending improved records, weekly remedial work with a specialist, see possibilities in this method with an improved program. Evangeline M. Galas, MLabstract #339.

Keller, Robert J. University of Minnesota, Minneapolis, Minn.
The Effectiveness of Closed-Circuit Television in Teacher Education; Project No. 077 (National Defense Education Act, Title VII), April 1, 1959, to September 30, 1962; $285,890.

Compares closed-circuit television with kinescopes and direct observation, as means of presenting classroom demonstrations in the training of high school teachers of science, mathematics, and modern languages. HLN

As of January 9, 1961, seventy-five kinescopes in all subject areas had been completed. Three of these demonstrate the teaching of beginning German, two in grade four; and one at the high school level. DG

Latimer, John F. George Washington University, Washington, D.C.
Research Study Conference on Problems of State-Level Supervision of Instruction in Modern Foreign Language; Project No. 8,857 (National Defense Education Act, Title VI), June 20, 1960, to August 31, 1960; $11,756.

At a conference, August 1 through 13, 1960, state foreign-language supervisors undertook a study to improve modern foreign-language instruction. BP

MacGowan, Kenneth, *et al.*
See MacGowan, 2.1.

Mildenberger, Kenneth W.
"Three Years of the Language Development Program (NDEA) Title VI," *Modern Language Journal,* XLV (November, 1961), 289-92.

In this article I summarize the objectives and activities of the Language Development Program authorized in the National Defense Education Act of 1958. In the first three years, 133 institutes have been conducted for a total of 6,500 elementary and secondary school teachers. Forty-seven language and area centers were designated for Federal aid to strengthen instruction principally in the languages and related area subjects of Asia, Africa, and the Soviet World. A total of 1412 graduate fellowships were awarded to individuals studying the uncommonly taught languages. And a vast program of studies, research and materials development has been initiated. Kenneth W. Mildenberger, MLabstract #117.

Mueller, Klaus A. Associated Colleges of the Midwest, 60 W. Walton St., Chicago, Ill. 60610.

Experimental, Refining and Strengthening on Undergraduate Foreign Language Curricula with Supporting Research in Teaching Techniques; Final Report. Project No. 8,833 (National Defense Education Act, Title VI), June 15, 1960, to June 14, 1963; $248,798. Extended by supplementary contract to June 14, 1964.

The Associated Colleges of the Midwest—Beloit, Coe, Grinnell, Lawrence, Ripon, Carleton, Cornell, Knox, Monmouth, and St. Olaf—have contracted a three-year project involving experimentation in their language programs aiming to improve instruction in foreign languages and literatures in college at all levels, including the pre-service undergraduate training of prospective foreign-language teachers. Foreign-language majors and teaching majors may be expected to achieve the minimal rating on applicable parts of the Modern Language Association's proficiency tests for teachers of foreign languages. (See Starr, Wilmarth, above, 2.7, for the tests.) The project involves placement tests; electromechanical facilities to increase the amount of audiolingual practice; facilities for self-directed study so that students can advance at their own rates; the use of lay native speakers to assist faculty; optimum methods in class and laboratory; nearly exclusive use of language in upper-level courses; coordination of instruction at cooperative colleges; the use of standardized achievement tests of the listening, speaking, reading, and writing skills; and the use of the Modern Language Association proficiency tests. The project also attempts to determine optimum class size and optimum proportions of laboratory and classroom sessions; to determine the optimum degree of mastery obtainable by the student before introducing new material; to examine the extent of individual self-teaching, and self-pacing; to investigate the relative value of different types of stimuli; to determine the optimum length of the prereading period; and to evaluate the effectiveness of monitoring versus nonmonitoring in a variety of laboratory designs. Klaus A. Mueller. Four appendices available separately on request: I, II, and IV on tests, III on programmed learning.

Newmark, Gerald
See Newmark, 6.1.

Parker, Douglas V.
A Survey of the Literature in the Field of Foreign Language Teacher Education, 1960-1964. Unpublished M.A. thesis, University of Washington, 1965.

This bibliographical essay provides annotated entries for publications related to the field indicated. The author's conclusions suggest possible approaches to such training as well as problems which need to be examined. Douglas V. Parker.

Seminar in Language and Language Learning. Final Report. Seattle: Department of Romance Language and Literature, University of Washington, 1962.

Unpublished work papers of the seminar held at Seattle September 3-14, 1962. The purpose of the seminar was to evaluate the interdisciplinary needs of the doctoral candidate who is preparing himself to organize the teaching of foreign languages in universities, colleges and high schools. Ten work papers were presented by prominent representatives of the fields of Linguistics, Literature, Cultural Anthropology and Psychology. Seminar reports contain discussion based on the work papers and focused on three topics: curricular recommendations, the interrelations of various disciplines, and the particular skills and qualifications that might be expected from the product of such a program. JM

Starr, Wilmarth H.
See Starr, 2.7.

Tan, Jan Cornelis
English Language Teacher Training in Indonesia. Unpublished Ed.D. dissertation, University of Michigan, 1963.

The purpose of this study is to examine ways to contribute toward the improvement of English language instruction in Indonesia in general, and of English language teaching in particular. It seeks to develop a practicable and linguistically sound curriculum for the preparation of Indonesian teachers of English, to be recommended for the English department in Faculties of Teacher Training and Education throughout the country. The study is primarily concerned with the "specialist" aspect of the problem rather than with the "general practitioner" part of teacher training. Information and material pertinent to this study were determined by a careful survey of books, articles, reports, catalogs, and brochures obtained through governmental and other sources. From the abstract.

Thomas, Joseph V.
The Nature and Effectiveness of Special Methods Courses in the Teaching of Modern Foreign Languages. Unpublished Ph.D. dissertation, Ohio State University, 1952.

After a survey of previous studies, questionnaires were sent to 431 instructors of modern-language special-methods courses at 309 institutions in the United States. Information was compiled concerning curricular patterns, content, instructional patterns, background of instructors, and evaluation of effectiveness. As a result of the study, trends, problems and decisive issues in special methods teaching were brought to light, and recommendations drawn from many sources were offered. The best instruction was found to exist where there was cooperation between language and Education departments, and where facilities permitted active practice of theory during the training period, at a point preferably between advanced language learning and student teaching. Joseph V. Thomas.

Walsh, Donald D., Modern Language Association of America, New York.

An Evaluation of the Effectiveness of the 1963 NDEA Language Institutes; Project No. OE-3-14-023 (National Defense Education Act, Title VI), March 11, 1963, to June 11, 1964; $48,980.

The Modern Language Association evaluated the effectiveness of the 79 NDEA Foreign Language Institutes of the summer 1963. Independent, nongovernmental evaluators visited each of the institutes during the summer, and interviewed directors, faculties, and students. After visitation they wrote individual reports of their findings at each institute. The principal investigator incorporated these reports into a summary report that presented the salient features of the 1963 institutes and served as a basis for planning future programs. Before being put into final form, the report was discussed at a fall meeting of Institute directors.

In the fall of 1963, as a second part of the project, the Modern Language Association directed a questionnaire to 1,500 persons who attended the 1961 Summer Institutes to ascertain (1) their evaluation of the Institutes, (2) their judgment of the effectiveness of their preservice preparation to be language teachers, and (3) the influence which the Institutes have had in furthering their careers. From the official description.

————.

An Evaluation of the National Defense Language Institutes, Academic Year 1963-64 and Summer 1964; Project No. OE-4-14-045 (National Defense Education Act, Title IV), March 15, 1964, to December 15, 1964; $45,403.

Under this contract, the Modern Language Association of America will evaluate the 4 National Defense Modern Foreign Language Institutes for the academic year 1963-64 and a sampling of the 81

Institutes scheduled for the summer of 1964. This evaluation will enable the U.S. Office of Education to assess more accurately the extent to which new teaching methods and materials are being utilized successfully in modern foreign language instruction throughout the country, as well as to judge the effectiveness of the institute program and to point the way for further development. Panels of MLA consultant-evaluators will visit the institutes to observe classwork, program of study, and administrative procedures, and to confer with staff members and institute participants. The evaluators will be teachers of modern foreign languages and specialists in teacher training and in school administration. The data obtained will be examined at a fall meeting of institute directors and incorporated into a summary report that will serve as a basis for planning future programs. From the official description.

Agencies, Institutions, and Organizations

American Council of Learned Societies
354 East 46th Street
New York 17, New York

American Council on Education
1785 Massachusetts Avenue, N.W.
Washington 6, D.C.

American Educational Research Association
National Education Association
1201 Sixteenth Avenue N.W.
Washington 6, D.C.

American Library Association
50 East Huron Street
Chicago 11, Illinois

Association for Supervision and Curriculum Development
National Education Association
1201 Sixteenth Street N.W.
Washington 6, D.C.

Audio-Visual Center
Purdue University
Lafayette, Indiana

Audio-Visual Instructional Materials Center
Wayne State University
Detroit 2, Michigan

California Society for the Study of Secondary Education
Subsequently known as:
California Association of Secondary School Administrators
2220 Bancroft Way
Berkeley 4, California

California State Department of Education
Sacramento 14, California

Canadian Education Association
Toronto, Canada

Carnegie Corporation of New York
589 Fifth Avenue
New York 17, New York

Center for Applied Linguistics
1755 Massachusetts Avenue N.W.
Washington 6, D.C.

Center for Documentation and Research
School of Library Science
Western Reserve University
Cleveland, Ohio

Center for Programed Instruction
365 West End Avenue
New York 24, New York

Centre Audio-visuel
École Normale Supérieure de Saint-Cloud
St. Cloud, Seine et Oise, France

Le Comité international permanent de linguistes,
avec une subvention de l'Organisation des nations unies
pour l'éducation, la science, et la culture
Place de Fontenoy
Paris 7, France

Committee on Educational Research
Faculty of Education
University of Alberta
Edmonton, Alberta, Canada

Deutsches Pädagogisches Zentralinstitut
Abteilung Dokumentation und Information
Berlin N 113
Schönfliesser Strasse 7
West Germany

Educational Facilities Laboratories
477 Madison Avenue
New York 22, New York

Ford Foundation
477 Madison Avenue
New York 22, New York

Georgetown University
Institute of Languages and Linguistics
37th and O streets, N.W.
Washington 7, D.C.

Haskins Laboratories
305 East 43rd Street
New York, New York

Joint Council on Educational Television
1785 Massachusetts Avenue N.W.
Washington, D.C.

Laboratory for Research in Instruction
Graduate School of Education
Harvard University
Cambridge, Massachusetts

Language Research Section
Division of College and University Assistance
U.S. Office of Education
Washington 25, D.C.

Language Testing Fund
514 Worcester Street
Wellesley, Massachusetts

Linguistic Society of America
Box 7790 University Street
Austin, Texas

Listening Center
The Ohio State University
Columbus, Ohio

Mental Health Research Institute
University of Michigan
Ann Arbor, Michigan

Modern Language Association
Foreign Language Program Research Center
4 Washington Place
New York 3, New York

Modern Language Audio-Visual Consultation
Wayne State University
Detroit 2, Michigan

National Association of Foreign Student Advisers
500 Riverside Drive
New York 27, New York

National Education Association
Department of Audio-Visual Instruction
1201 Sixteenth Street, N.W.
Washington 6, D.C.

National Education Association
Department of Educational Research
1201 Sixteenth Street, N.W.
Washington 6, D.C.

National Education Association
Department of Foreign Languages
1201 Sixteenth Avenue, N.W.
Washington 6, D.C.

National Educational Television and Radio Center
10 Columbus Circle
New York 10, New York

New York State Education Department
Albany 1, New York

Office of Naval Research
Special Devices Center
Human Engineering Division
Sands Point, Port Washington
Long Island, New York

Pedagogiske Forskninginstitutt [Institute for Educational Research]
University of Oslo
Oslo, Norway

Publications of the Language Laboratory
University of Michigan
Ann Arbor, Michigan

Social Science Research Council
230 Park Avenue
New York 7, New York

Texas Education Agency
Austin 11, Texas

Tokyo Education Research Institute

UNESCO
Division of Special Services for the Advancement of Education
Place de Fontenoy
Paris 7, France

United States Department of Defense
Washington 25, D.C.

United States Office of Education
Cooperative Research Branch
Washington 25, D.C.

United States Office of Education
Division of Higher Education
Washington 25, D.C.

United States Office of Education
Educational Media Program
Washington 25, D.C.

United States Office of Education
Language Development Program
Washington 25, D.C.

University of Michigan
English Language Institute
Ann Arbor, Michigan

Author Index

Adam, R. S., 237
Agard, Frederick B., 7, 41, 246, 247
Ai, Joseph W., 59
Al-Haruny, M. M., 60
Alhinc, J. M. Clay, 128
Al-Karbouli, Hamad D., 190
Allen, Edward David, 129
Allen, William H., xxii, 3, 119, 120
Allport, Gordon Willard, 195
Allwood, Charles S., 61
Altenheim, Margarete R., 86, 221
American Council on Education, 292
Anderson, T., 269, 270
Andersson, Theodore, 237
Andrade, Manuel, 173, 174
Angiolillo, Paul F., 71
Anisfeld, Moshe, 190, 237, 258
Antier, M., 3
Arseniam, Seth, 226
Artemov, V. A., 41
Asher, James J., 144, 145, 190, 191, 192
Assini, Lewis T., 172
Asuncion, Nobleza Castro, 244, 286
Avis, W. S., 17
Axelrod, Joseph, 292
Axelsson, Carl-Axel, 64

Baardman, G. G., 71
Bailey, Judith A., 145
Baker, Hugh Sanford, 3
Balogh, István, 244
Banathy, Bela H., 129, 193
Barcus, Delbert, 158
Barik, Henri C., 193
Barker, M. A. R., 109
Barlow, John A., 145, 149
Barrutia, Richard, 146
Baskin, Samuel, 82, 146
Bastian, Jarvis, 210
Bateson, M. C., 53

Bauer, Eric W., 120, 129, 130, 193, 244
Beck, Theodore T., 72
Beezhold, F. W., 174
Belasco, Simon, 3, 252
Beliaev, Boris Vasilevich, 41, 193
Bellugi, Ursula, 196
Belson, William A., 194
Bem, D., 273
Benedict, Ruth, 293
Benediktov, B. A., 42
Benesh, Marijana, 272, 293
Berelson, Bernard, 293
Bern, Henry A., 120
Bernard, Edward G., 130, 131
Berrett, Donald S., 86
Berry, Catherine M., 57
Bibliographie linguistique . . . , 3
Birkmaier, Emma M., xvi, 4, 42
Blanton, Wincie Lawton, 238
Blayne, Thornton C., 115
Blickenstaff, Channing B., 42
Blumenthal, Arthur L., 284
Bogo, Norman, 237
Bohlen, Adolfo, 43
Bolinger, Dwight L., 245, 258
Bonkowski, Robert J., 209
Book Review Digest, xx
Borglum, George P., 121, 140, 158
Borst, John M., 258, 259
Bottiglia, William F., 53
Bousfield, Weston A., 194
Bovée, Arthur G., 194
Bowen, J. Donald, 257
Boyd, Robert, 82
Boyd-Bowman, Peter, 325
Bratset, Richard E., 294
Brault, Gerard J., 72, 294, 338
Breckwoldt, John P., 174
Brethower, D. M., 272, 273
Brewster, Robert R., 86

351

Brickman, William W., 4
Brière, Eugène J., 73
Broady, K. O., 159
Brooks, Nelson, 43, 100, 174
Broshahan, L. F., 195
Brown, Charles T., 195
Brown, G. I., 159
Brown, Paul A., 4
Brown, Roger W., 195, 196, 294
Brown-Carlsen Listening Comprehension Test, 177
Brushwood, John S., 132
Bryan, Glenn L., 8
Bryan, Quentin R., 146
Buch, John N., 132
Buchanan, M. A., 5
Buchelt, Walter, 133
Buffington, Albert F., 87, 91
Buguslavsky, George W., 172
Buiten, R. L., 147, 259, 273, 274, 275
Buka, Magda, 185
Bundy, Edward Wayne, 159
Burns, D. G., 308
Buros, Oscar Krisen, 5, 216
Burton, H. Cohen, 194
Buxbaum, Edith, 238

Calvert, F. Irene, 73
Candelaria, Martin, 121
Capretz, Pierre J., 43
Cárdenas, Daniel N., 245, 286
Carlos, Lourdes B., 61
Carlson, William D., 322
Carmichael, L., 207
Carpenter, Clarence R., 37, 147
Carpenter, F., 148
Carroll, Brendan J., 175
Carroll, John B., xvii, xviii, xix, 5, 37, 58, 60, 96, 175, 176, 196, 197, 203, 216, 217, 218, 239, 245, 308, 320
Carton, Aaron S., 96, 176, 198
Casagrande, Joseph B., 198
Cassirer, Henry R., 160
Catania, A. C., 277
CEEB French Test, 48
CEEB Placement Test, 178
CEEB Spanish Test, 225
Center for Documentation and Communication Research, Western Reserve University, viii, xviii
Chaiyaratana, Chalao, 227
Chari, Ahalya, 62
Chatman, Seymour, 133
Cheydleur, Frederick D., 182, 338
Chiasson, R. J., 227

Childers, J. Wesley, 43, 338
Childs, G. B., 158
Chou, Kou P'ing, 153
Cline, Marion, Jr., 122
Cloos, Robert I., 176
Coleman, Algernon, 5
Coleman, Arthur P., 96
College Entrance Examination Board, 48. See also CEEB . . .
Commission on Secondary School Curriculum, 330
Comrey, Andrew L., 224
Condie, LeRoy, 62
Conrad, Joseph Lawrence, 87
Conwell, Marilyn, 133
Cooper, Franklin S., 259, 277, 278
Cooper, James G., 62
Cooperative French Test, 130, 132, 139, 141
Corrin, Brownlee Sands, 294
Couch, Sanford Gary, 97
Coulson, John, 156
Council for Cultural Cooperation, 5
Cowan, J. Milton, 260
Cox, F. N., 218
Creore, A. E., 123
Crosby, C., 232
Cross, D. V., 260, 268, 269, 270, 271, 272, 273, 274, 275, 276
Crossman, David M., 134
Crothers, Edward, 115, 212
Curran, C. R., 271
Curran, Charles A., 44

Dale, Edgar, 6
DeBlois, Donald, 44
Defauver, G. N., 297
Delattre, Pierre, 3, 74, 134, 141, 185, 245, 246, 260, 261, 262, 263, 264, 277, 278
DeMandach, André B., 6
Dembowski, Johann, 44
Denver-Stanford Project, 104, 162, 163, 164, 165, 171, 173, 174
Deutsches Pädagogisches Zentralinstitut, Abteilung Dokumentation und Information, xvii, 6, 122
deWitt, A. J. J., 246
DeWitt, Norman J., xvi
Diamond, L. K., 179
Dickens, Milton, 177
Diebold, A. Richard, Jr., 209, 228
Dimock, Edward C., 59, 246
DiPietro, Robert J., 7, 246, 247

"Dissertacii po germanskoj i romanskoj filologii . . .", 7
"Dissertacii po germanskomu i romanskomu jazykoznaniju . . .", 7
Dissertation Abstracts, vii, 7
Doctoral Dissertations Accepted by American Universities, 7
Dodson, C. J., 177
Donahue, Virginia M., 149
Donoghue, Mildred R., 177
Doob, Leonard W., 199
Doran, Thomas A., 330
Doros, Alexander, 247
Dostal, Naida Marich, 7, 122
Dufort, Mary R., 178, 309
Dunkel, Harold B., 41, 44, 239, 310
Dyer, Henry S., 178
Dykstra, Gerald, 123

East European Acquisition List, viii
Edling, Jack V., 134
Edmonston, J. D., 64
Education Index, vii, 7
El-Bettar, Abdul Kadir Said, 247
Ellison, Fred P., 310, 311, 312, 313, 331
Elmgren, John, 218
England. Ministry of Education. Department of Education and Science, 74
Engler, Leo Francis, 247
Estep, Hunter L., 310

Fairbanks, Gordon H., 248
Farber, J. E., 239
Fea, Henry R., 51
Feldman, David Morris, 102, 339
Felt, William N., 110
Fendrick, Daniel, 326
Ferguson, Charles A., 7, 203, 248
Ferster, Charles B., 90, 148, 159
Fielden, R. Derrick S., 65
Fife, Robert Herndon, 228
Fillenbaum, S., 231
Fisher, Ronald A., 37
Fishman, Joshua A., 240
Fleisner, Else M., 18
Florander, Jesper, 63
Flores, Francisco Gubaton, 248
Flores, Joseph S., 310, 311, 312, 313, 331
"Foreign Languages in Elementary Schools . . .", 8
Forsdale, Louis, 123
Foster, Dorothy P., 103
Fox, Bernard, 199

France. Ministère de l'Education Nationale. Direction des Bibliothèques de France, 8, 80
Françoise-Thérèse, Soeur, 218
Frank, Marcella, 8
Freeman, Margaret Z., 185
Freeman, Stephen A., 339
"French in the Elementary Classes . . .," 8
Frey, Harriet, x
Fries, Charles C., 63
Frith, James R., 219
Froelich, G. J., 194
Fry, Edward, 8, 38, 149

Gaarder, Bruce A., 135
Gage, N. L., 38
Gage, William N., 8, 249
Galanter, Eugene H., 149
Galas, Evangeline M., 339
Gardner, R. C., 231, 240, 241
Garry, Ralph, 75
Gavurin, Edward L., 149
Gee, R. D., 8
Geigle, Ralph C., 331
Geis, George L., 150, 273, 275
Gibson, Eleanor J., 264
Gibson, Romain (Mrs. Rodney E.), 135
Gideon, Sara B., 110
Gilman, Albert, 294
Gilpin, John, 150
Giuliano, William, 103
Glaser, Robert, 38, 151, 155, 159, 217
Gonzalez, Simon, 186
Good, Carter V., 38
Gordon, Oakley J., 98
Gorokhoff, Boris I., 45
Gorosch, Max, 64
Gougenheim, Georges, 76, 79, 89
Gradisnik, Anthony J., 104
Greenberg, Jacob, 295
Greene, Olive, 64
Greenhill, Leslie P., 147, 161
Greis, Naguib Amin Fahmy, 249
Griffiths, Ruth E., 335
Grinder, R. E., 94
Grittner, Frank, 136
Grosslight, J. H., 124
Guenot, Jean, 115, 123
Gurren, Louise, 249
Guss, Carolyn, 14
Guxman, M. M., 87

Haak, Louis A., 332
Haas, Mary R., 249

Haas, Stanley, 104
Habostad, Knut, 64
Haden, Ernest F., 76
Hall, Edward T., 295, 296
Hall, Pauline Cook, 9
Halloran, J. H., 76
Hamilton, Daniel L., 45, 76
Hanzeli, Victor E., 123, 150
Harding, Francis D., Jr., 219
Hardy, Frances, 167
Harmon, John, 329
Harms, L. S., 265
Harris, Katherine S., 265
Harvard Language Aptitude Project, 218
Hascall, Edward O., 219
Haugen, Einar I., 228
Havelka, J., 231, 232
Hayes, Alfred S., xxii, xxiii, xxiv, 39, 46, 53, 124, 137, 186
Hayman, John L., Jr., 104, 158, 162, 163, 164, 165, 173, 174
Healey, F. G., 9
Heinberg, Paul, 150, 151
Hempleman, David, 64
Henmon-Nelson Test, 324
Henning, William Andrew, 287
Hill, Leslie A., 65, 116
Hill, W. Merle, 199
Himmler, Merwin L., 166
Hoban, Charles F., Jr., 124
Hocking, Elton, 137, 199
Hodgkinson, H. L., 159
Hoffman, Howard S., 266
Hoge, Henry W., 116
Hohfeld, John M., 105
Hoijer, Harry, 296
Horecky, Paul, 10
Horn, Thomas D., 105
Horowitz, A. E., 266, 282
Hosford, Prentiss McIntyre, 240
Hotyat, Fernand S., 10
House, A. S., 266
Howes, Davis, 199
Hoyt, William George, 200
Hunter, Thomas P., 106
Hunting, J. R., 272, 273
Hutchinson, Joseph C., 135, 137

Index to American Doctoral Dissertations, 10
"Instruction in Classical and Modern Foreign Languages," 322
International Christian University, Audio Visual Center, 65, 166

Jackson, H. M., 266
Jackson, Kenneth M., 250
Jakobovits, Leon A., 200, 201, 229
James, C. V., 193
Japel, Hans, 65
Jarnatovskaja, V. E., 42
Jenkins, William S., 219
Jimenez, C., 230
Johnson, Charles E., 310, 311, 312, 313, 331
Johnson, Donald W., 316
Johnson, Grace Nichols, 167
Johnson, Granville B., Jr., 230, 296
Johnson, James T., Jr., 158, 162, 163, 164, 165, 173, 174
Johnston, Marjorie C., 10, 46
Joly, Charles L., 230
Jones, W. R., 230
Joos, Martin, 282, 314
Josselson, Harry H., 98
Justman, Joseph, 314

Kacnel'son, S. D., 87
Kahan, Anne M., 331
Kale, Shrikrishna V., 98, 124
Kallioinen, Vilho, 76
Kaplan, Edith, 215
Kaulfers, Walter V., 297, 331
Keating, Raymond, 133, 134, 135, 136, 137, 139, 142, 143
Keesee, Elizabeth, 11
Keislar, Evan R., 207, 288, 290, 314
Keller, Robert J., 340
Kenyon, John Samuel, 265
Kern, Edith, 178
Keston, M. J., 230
Khoury, Joseph Farjallah, 58
Kielski, Bolesław, 250
Kilpatrick, Joel Fred, 201
Kim, Soon-Ham Park, 250
Kimizuka, Sumako, 251
Kinney, Jo Ann S., 202
Kinzel, Paul F., 231
Kluckholn, Clyde, 297
Knott, Thomas Albert, 265
Kohmoto, Satesaburo, 251
Kohut, Suzanne, 232
"Kommentierte Bibliographie ausländischer Zeitschriftenaufsätze ...," 11
Koop, James L., 186, 205, 271, 272, 273, 274
Kopstein, Felix, 116
Korchin, S. J., 202
Korwin, Roy, 202
Koselev, A., 251

Koumari, A., 65
Koutsoudas, Andreas, 251
Koutsoudas, Olympia, 251
Kramer, Ernest, 269, 270, 272, 274, 293
Kreidler, Carol J., 12
Kreusler, Abraham, 46
Kroeber, A. L., 249
Kruatrachue, Foongfuang, 252
Kufner, Herbert L., 7, 252
Kumata, Hideya, 11
Kuniyuki, Noriko, 111

Lado, Robert, 11, 179, 252, 297
Lambert, Philip, 203
Lambert, Wallace E., 193, 201, 203, 215, 229, 231, 232, 237, 240, 241
Lampach, Stanley, 7
Lane, Harlan L., 39, 151, 187, 204, 205, 206, 208, 259, 260, 267, 268, 269, 270, 271, 272, 273, 274, 275, 276, 277, 293
Larew, Leonor, 111, 288
Larson, L. C., 11
Larson, Robert P., 93
Latimer, John F., 340
Leavitt, Harold J., 226
Leavitt, Sturgis E., 106
Lehn, W., 252
Leidy, Thomas Ross, 187
Leino, Walter B., 332
Lenneberg, Eric H., 196, 206, 220
Léon, Pierre Roger, 128, 138
Leopold, Werner F., 11, 206, 232
Lerea, Louis, 232
Lesage, André, 124
Leutenegger, Ralph R., 78, 112, 169
Levine, S., 202
LeVois, Camille J., 125
Lewis, Earl N., Jr., 138
Liberman, Alvin, 259, 277, 278, 279, 280
Lilley, Oliver L., xvi, xviii, xxi
Lindeman, Louise, 46, 54
Livesey, Adelis Frances, 66
Locke, W. N., 185, 186, 280
Long, Arthur L., 125
Lopato, Esther W., 332, 333
Lopes, Albert R., 326
Lorge, Irving, 179, 242
Lorge, Sarah W., 130, 131, 138, 143
Lottes, John J., 111
Lotz, John, 280
Loucks, Robert E., 315

Lumsdaine, A. A., 47, 116, 151, 155, 159
Lundeen, D. J., 289

McArdle, Lois, 179
MacBride, Mary D., 95
McCarthy, Dorothea, 207
Mace, Larry, 207, 290
MacGowan, Kenneth, 47
Mackey, William Francis, 47, 66, 201, 233, 234, 253, 326
MacKinnon, A. R., 79
Maclay, Howard S., 208
McClusky, Frederick D., 11
McConkey, W. G., 233
McDonald, Pearl S., 152
McIntosh, Lois, 252
McIntyre, Ruth D., 223, 224
McKinney, James Edward, Jr., 180
MacNaughton, Jacquelin, 221
MacPhee, E. D., 5
McPherson, James J., xxiv
Ma'ia'i, Fannafi, 234
Malcolm, D. J., 48, 180
Malherbe, E. G., 234
Malter, Morton S., 120
Mange, Charles V., 208
Manuel, Herschel T., 180, 221, 228, 234
Marckwardt, Albert H., 67, 298
Marr, N. Ja., 87
Martin, John W., 257
Martinet, André, 7
Marty, Fernand, 79, 150, 152, 158
Mate, Hubert E., 167
Mathieu, Gustave, vii, 139
Matsumoto, Masatatsu, 116
Matthew, Robert J., 323
Mauger, Gaston, 79
Mauriello, Edna A., 75, 167
Mayans, Alan E., 164
Maynes, J. Oscar, Jr., 140
Mead, Margaret, 297, 298
Mechner, M., 67
Mendeloff, Henry, 168
Mennes, V. V., 324
Métraux, Rhoda, 298
Michéa, R., 48, 76
Mildenberger, Kenneth W., 316, 340
Milholland, John E., 323
Miller, George A., 209
Miller, James Dale, 117
Miller, Roy A., 327
Millman, Jason, 323
Milwaukee Public Schools, 107
MLabstracts, vii, 12

MLAS Cooperative Classroom Testing Program, 177, 223, 224
Modern Language Aptitude Test, 60, 177
Modern Language Association of America, 12, 40
Modern Language Association [of America] Foreign Language Proficiency Tests for Teachers and Advanced Students, 175
Modern Language Association of America Foreign Language Program, 54
Modern Language Association [of America] Interdisciplinary Seminar on Language and Culture, 298
Moore, D. J., 268, 269
Moore, Nancy, 232
Moore, Patricia, 140
Moraud, M. I., 150
Morehouse, Ward, 118
Morrison, Andrew V., 223, 224, 242
Morton, F. Rand, 49, 141, 146, 153, 154, 188, 208, 268
Mosberg, Ludwig, 223, 224
Motzko, Gertraud, 126
Moulton, William G., 7, 12, 253, 289
Mueller, Klaus A., 49, 316, 340
Mueller, Theodore, 78, 140, 150, 153, 154, 168, 199, 208, 220, 289, 290
Mulry, June Grant, 319
Mussen, Ethel F., 281
Mylerberg, Duane W., 254

Nardi, Noach, 221
Nason, Marshall R., 326
Nass, Martin L., 314
National Education Association Project on the Academically Talented Student, 54
National Educational Television and Radio Center, 169
Naunheim, Elizabeth, 317
Neale, L. W., 181
Neidt, C. O., 158
Netherlands Didactiekcommissie, 254
New Teaching Aids for the American Classroom, 155
Newmark, Gerald, 126, 155, 316
NHK Radio-Television Cultural Research Institute, 112, 113
Noonan, James A., 66, 234
Northeast Conference on the Teaching of Foreign Languages, 53
Nostrand, Howard Lee, v, x, 126, 299, 300, 301, 303

Nuffield Foundation, 47
Oberholtzer, Kenneth E., 171
O'Brien, Richard J., 95
Oettinger, Katherine B., 12
Ohannessian, Sirarpi, 12
Oinas, Felix J., 141
Olsen, Caroll, 246
Olton, Robert, 241
Opler, Morris E., 301, 302
Orata, Pedro T., 235
O'Rourke, Everett, 333
Osgood, C. E., 203, 208, 213
Oswald, Victor A., Jr., 88
Otomo, A., 94

Palmer, Patricia, 115
Parker, Douglas V., 341
Parker, William Riley, 50, 53
Pascasio, Emy Mariano, 254
Payne Fund Communications Project, 6
Peltier-Durost Test, 161
Penfield, Wilder G., 281
Pervy, Adolphe, 127
Peters, Harold C., 222
Peters, Mary Olga, 141
Petrov, Julia A., 99
Pfeffer, J. Alan, 88, 89, 90
Pflieger, Elmer F., 170
Pick, H., 42
Pickrel, Glenn E., 113
Pictorial Auditory Comprehension Test, 223
Pierce, Joe E., 50, 281
Pike, E. V., 222
Pillet, Roger A., 310
Pimsleur, Paul, 40, 150, 207, 222, 223, 290
PMLA Annual Bibliography, vii
Poenack, Elmer, 246
Politzer, Robert L., 80, 141, 255, 256
Pollack, I., 282, 283
Polmantier, Paul C., 132
Poltoratzky, Marianna A., 50
Popham, W. James, 113, 114, 181
Porter, Donald, 155
Porter, John J., 142
Porter, Sally F., 142
Powers, Francis F., 13
Pritchard, D. F., 243
Proncko, N. H., 209
Psi Lambda Foreign Language Aptitude Battery, 217
Psychological Abstracts, vii, 14
Pulgram, Ernst, 256, 282
Pursley, Alice J., 235

Purvis, H., 81
Putter, Irving, 327

Rabbin, Joseph, 199
Railing, Trudy K., 55
Randall, Earle S., 317
Rathee, R. S., 324
Ray, Punya Sloka, 59
Raybould, A. B., 81, 225
Raymond, Joseph, 302
Razik, Taher, 6
Reader's Guide, vii
Reams, Mary H., 127
Redfield, Robert, 302
Registry of Canadian Theses in Education, 14
Reichard, Joseph, 90
Reid, Catherine, 225
Reid, J. Richard, 170
Reid, L. S., 149
Reiff, Donald G., 150, 284
Research Studies in Education . . . , 14
Rice, Winthrop H., 14
Richards, S. Earle, 5, 218
Richards, Sumner E., 108
Richardson, G., 118
Riecks, Donald F., 126, 303
Rigney, Joseph W., 8
Rivenc, P., 76
Rivers, Wilga M., 210
Roberts, Andrew D., 108
Roberts, H. D., 297
Roca, Pablo, 243
Rocha e Silva, M. I., 90, 156
Rochette, C. E., 253
Roertgen, William F., 290
Rojas, Pauline M., 235
Romeo, Luigi, 14
Roshol, Sol, 116
Ross, Strange, 272, 274
Rosselot, LaVelle, 128
Rothkopf, E. Z., 149
Rovner, Philip, 87, 91
Rubenstein, H., 282, 283
Rudnyckyj, J. B., 17
Rufsvold, Margaret I., 14
Runden, Charity E., 11
Rusowicz, Mieczyslaw, 128
Russell, David H., 51
Russian Acquisition List, viii
Ryan, Henry M., 318
Ryden, Einar R., 51

Sableski, Julia, 12
Sadnavitch, Joseph M., 181

Saltzman, Irving J., 99, 156
Sánchez, José, 14
Sapon, Stanley M., 148, 150, 159, 217, 218, 225, 283
Saporta, Sol, 210, 283, 284
Saul, Ezra V., 283
Sauvageot, A., 76
Sawyer, Jessie O., 50, 52
Sawyer, Robert Graham, 52
Saxton, John B., 318
Schenck, Ethel A., 182
Scherer, George A. C., 52, 53, 91, 92
Schindler, Barbara, 339
Schneider, Bruce, 205, 269, 270, 271, 273, 275
Schneiderman, Norma, 291
Schnurer, Herman, 82
Schramm, Wilbur, 15, 171
Seacroft, W. B., 47
Sebeok, Thomas A., 53, 210, 213
Selvi, Arthur M., 318, 319
Seminar in Language and Language Learning, 342
Seminar on Uses of Television in Education, 170
Shane, Harold G., 319
Shannon, Claude L., 284
Sheppard, W., 272
Sherred, Ruth, 333
Shinkman, P. G., 206, 270
Sibayan, Bonifacio Padilla, 256
Silagyi, Dezo Vincent, 171
Silberman, Harry F., 156
Siliakus, H. J., 142
Silva-Fuenzalida, Ismael, 304
Simches, Seymour O., 210
Sister Françoise-Thérèse. See Françoise-Thérèse, Soeur
Sister Jerome Keeler, 77
Sister John Marguerite. See Moore, Patricia
Sister Marie Gabrielle, 234, 314
Sister Mary Arthur Carrow, 227
Sister Mary Gregoire, 9
Sister Raymond de Jesus, 234, 315
Sister Yolande-de-L'Immaculée. See Yolande-de-L'Immaculée, Soeur
Skelton, Robert B., 211, 334
Skinner, B. F., 203
Slager, W. R., 252
Slichenmyer, H. L., 53
Smith, Herbert A., 211
Smith, Madorah E., 235
Smither, William J., 328
Sociological Abstracts, vii, 15

Sokolov, Alexander N., 284
Sorenson, John L., 305
Sowards, G. W., 334
Spanish Comprehension Test, 181
Spencer, Richard E., 182
Spicer, A., 47
Spilka, Irène Vachon, 211, 241
Stack, Edward M., 142, 143
Stake, Robert E., 172
Stankiewicz, Edward, 7
Starr, Wilmarth H., 54, 182, 183
Staubach, Charles N., 256
Steiner, Gary A., 293
Steisel, Marie-Georgette, 303
Stensaasen, Svein, 68
Stern, H. H., 37
Stern, J. J., 320
Stevens, Stanley S., 216, 277
Stevens, Thomas C., 82
Steward, Julian H., 304
Stewart, William A., 7, 230
Stockton, James C., 119
Stockwell, Robert P., 224, 257
Stodola, Quentin, 183
Stolurow, Lawrence M., 211
Stone, George Wincester, Jr., 54
Stowell, Ernest, 334
Strain, Jeris E., 183
Sturge-Moore, C. J., 68, 69, 115
Sumner, Francis C., 184
Sundland, Donald M., 223, 224
Superior Council on Education of
    Puerto Rico, 108
Suppes, Patrick G., 54, 115, 212, 285
Sutherland, M. B., 305
Sweet, Waldo, xx
Swets, John A., 285
Symposium methodieck en didactiek
    levende talen, 55
Symposium on the State of Research in
    Instructional Television, 155
Szoboszlay, Miklós, 100

Tan, Jan Cornelis, 342
Tardy, M., 115
Tauber, Maurice F., xvi, xviii, xxi
Taylor, E. H., 188
Taylor, H. Darrel, 305
Taylor, Martha L., 212
Taylor, Robert E., 55
TEMAC, 156, 316
Templin, Mildred C., 55
Tewksbury, Malcolm Gardner, 60
Tezza, Joseph S., 100

Tharp, James B., 4, 15
Thomas, Joseph V., 92, 342
Thompson, Mary P., 54
Thorndike-McCall Reading Test, 194
Throop, Joseph F., 172
Tireman, Lloyd S., 69
Titone, Renzo, 213
Toronto Board of Education, 15, 83, 84,
    172
Toyota, W., 94
Tracy, Edward, 143
Trager, George L., 295, 296
Tunstall, Kenneth, 241
Turner, Raymond, 157
Twaddell, Freeman, 257
Twarog, Leon I., 101
Twombly, Neil J., 95

Uemura, Hidekichi, 94
Ulrich, John H., 173
Unbegaum, U. N., 15
UNESCO, 15, 55
United States Department of State, 16
United States Office of Education, 15,
    16
Uota, Shoji, 69
Uttal, William R., 157

Vakar, Nicholas P., 101
Valdman, Albert, 3, 83, 157, 328
Valette, Rebecca M., 184
Valtasaari, Hanna, 329
Valverde Z., Luis J., 56, 70
Vamos, Mara, 329
Van Eenenaam, Evelyn, xvii, 16, 17
Van Riper, Charles, 184
van Willigen, Daam M., viii, 17, 72
Vanormer, Edward B., 124
Varasteh, M., 56
Velázquez, Mary D. Rivera de, 257
Vernon, Philip E., 195
Verslag Conferentie Wondschoten, 55
Vicory, Arthur G., 213
Vinay, J.-P., 17
Vollmer, Joseph H., 335
von Raffler-Engel, Walburga, 214, 236

Wacker, Charlotte F., 236
Walsh, Donald D., 54, 144, 225, 343
Walsh, Donna Rowell, 57
Walter, Felix H., xxi
Warfel, Harry R., 57
Weaver, Warren, 284
Weber, Jean-Paul, 305
Weinreich, Uriel, 236, 306

Weir, Ruth, 54, 115, 212, 214, 257
Weisiger, Carroll, 199
Weiss, Bernard Joseph, 84
Weldon, Richard C., 243
Werner, Heinz, 215
Wershow, Irving, 85, 220
Wertheimer, Michael, 52, 92
White, Leslie, 306
White, Wayne Hugh, 109
Whorf, Benjamin L., 296
Wiersma, William, Jr., 46
Wiik, Kalevi, 285
Wilds, Claudia P., 176
Williams, Clarence M., 103
Williams, Frederick, 177
Williams, Jac L., 17
Williams, Stanley B., 226
Wimer, Cynthia, 215
Witelson, Sandra F., 203
Witkin, Belle Ruth, 285
Wittenborn, J. Richard, 93, 215

Wittich, Barbara von, 226
Wolfle, Dael, 216
Woods, William S., 328
Wormald, F. L., 329
Worth, Dean S., 7
Wykes, Olive, 57
Wylie, Laurence, 18

Xoomsai, M. L. Tooi, 114

Yates, Aubrey J., 286
Yeni-Komshian, Grace, 204
Yolande-de-L'Immaculée, Soeur, 258
Yorkey, Richard Clements, 71
Young, Clarence W., 144, 189
Young, Eleanor Culver, 307

Zais, Robert S., 291
Zarechnak, Michael, 223
Zeydel, Edwin H., 93
Zirmunskij, V. M., 87

Subject Index

Ability grouping. *See* Tests, *aptitude*

Achievement tests. *See* Tests, *achievement*

Acoustics: section 4.3

Adult education in language learning: Alhinc, "Le laboratoire de langues et la classe audio-visuelle dans une expérience d'enseignement de l'anglais parlé . . . ," 128; Guenot, "Etudes sur la lisibilité des vues fixes," 115; Guenot, *Pédagogie audio-visuelle des débuts de l'anglais: une expérience d'enseignement à des adultes,* 123; Livesey, A Study in Developing a Technique of Method Evaluation in the Teaching of English as a Second Language to Adults in Multilingual Classes, 66

Age in language learning: Andersson, The Optimum Age for Beginning the Study of Modern Languages, 237; Elmgren, "The Linguistic Maturity Investigation," 218; Larew, A Study of Spanish Articulation in the Elementary School: A Pilot Study, 288; Penfield, "Consideration of the Neurophysiological Mechanisms of Speech and Some Educational Consequences," 281; Schneiderman, "A Study of the Relationship Between Articulatory Ability and Language Ability," 291. *See also* Tests, *aptitude*

Anxiety in language learning: Korchin, "Anxiety and Verbal Learning," 202; Mueller, "Some Inferences about an Intensified Oral Approach to the Teaching of French Based on a Study of Course Drop-Outs," 169

Applied linguistics. *See* Linguistics in language teaching

Aptitude tests. *See* Tests, *aptitude*

Arabic, study and teaching of: section 2.3, Arabic

Area studies: section 5

Articulation. *See* Pronunciation

Attitudes in language learning: Anisfeld, "Social and Psychological Variables in Learning Hebrew," 237; Belson, "Learning and Attitude Changes Resulting from Viewing a Television Series *Bon Voyage,*" 194; Carlson, An Analysis of Achievement Outcomes of the Six-Hour Class Program at the University of Minnesota High School, 322; Hayman, Causative Factors and Learning Related to Parent Participation, 165; Lambert, "Attitudinal and Cognitive Aspects of Intensive Study of a Second Language," 241; Lambert, A Study of the Roles of Attitudes and Motivation in Second Language Learning, 241; Lopes, "Teaching Elementary Foreign Languages," 326; Silagyi, A Critical Analysis of Attitudes of Selected Elementary Students Toward Television Teaching in the Detroit Television Teaching Project, 171; Spilka, "Le rôle des attitudes dans l'acquisition d'une langue étrangère," 211; Sutherland, "Study of the Effects of Learning French on Attitudes Toward the French: Summary of Thesis," 305; Young, An Experimental Study of the Effects of Intensive Reading of Selected Materials in a Foreign Language Upon Certain Attitudes, 307

Audiovisual aids: section 2.53. *See also* Auditory aids, Motion pictures, Television, Visual aids

Auditory aids: section 2.51. *See also* Radio, Sound recordings

Australia, teaching of foreign languages in: Wykes, "Survey of Language Teaching in Australia," 57

Basque, study and teaching of: section 2.3, Basque

Bilingualism: section 3.5. *See also* Interference

Canada, Teaching of foreign languages in: Mackey, Foreign Languages in Canadian Universities and Colleges: Preliminary Report, I. Statistics, 326

Children, language skills in: Brosnahan, "Some Aspects of the Child's Mastery of the Sounds in a Foster-Language," 195; Brown, "Three Processes in the Child's Acquisition of Syntax," 196; Carroll, "Language Development," 197; Joos, "Language and the School Child," 314; Leopold, *Bibliography of Child Language*, 11; Leopold, "Kindersprache," 206; McCarthy, "Language Development in Children," 207; Templin, *Certain Language Skills in Children: Their Development and Interrelationships*, 55; von Raffler-Engel, "Appunti sul linguaggio infantile," 214; von Raffler-Engel, "Il prelinguaggio infantile," 214; Weir, *Language in the Crib*, 214. *See also* Foreign languages in the elementary school

Chinese, study and teaching of: section 2.3, Chinese

Class size: Hunter, An Analysis of Multivariant Factors in Classroom Structures on Achievement in Spanish in the Third Grade, 106; Mueller, "Experimentation and Research in the Development of Modern Language Materials and Teaching Methods," 49

Cognitive processes: Anisfeld, "A Comment on 'The Role of Grapheme-Phoneme Correspondence in the Perception of Words' by Gibson *et al.*," 258; Asher, "Vision and Audition in Language Learning," 192; Brown, "Linguistic Determinism and the Part of Speech," 195; Brown, "A Study in Language and Cognition," 196; Carroll, *Language and Thought*, 196;

Carroll, "Some Psychological Effects of Language Structure," 197; Carroll, Southwest Project in Comparative Psycholinguistics, 197; Gibson, "The Role of Grapheme-Phoneme Correspondence in the Perception of Words," 264; Jakobovits, Effects of Repeated Stimulation on Cognitive Aspects of Behavior: Some Experiments on the Phenomenon of Semantic Satiation, 200; Kilpatrick, A Differential Analysis of Language and Nonlanguage Abilities of Seventh-Grade Boys and Girls, 201

Communication theory: Carroll, "Communication Theory, Linguistics and Psycholinguistics," 196

Computer data processing technology and language learning: Suppes, Application of Quantitative Analysis and Computer Data Processing Technology. . . ,54

Contrastive studies: Asunción, The Phonological Problems Involved in Improving the Oral English of Iloko Speakers, 286; Asunción, A Study of English Sounds Difficult for Filipino Students, 244; Balogh, *Az orosz ige és tanitásának néhány kérdése*, 244; Cárdenas, *Introducción a una comparación fonológica del español y del inglés*, 286; Chaiyaratana, "A Comparative Study of English and Thai Syntax," 227; Delattre, "Voyelles diphtonguées et voyelles pures," 264; de Witte, *Moedertaalautomatism en het onderwijs in de levende taalen*, 246; Dimock, Research on South Asian Languages, 246; Di Pietro, *The Grammatical Structures of English and Italian*, 246; Di Pietro, *The Phonology of English and Italian*, 247; Doros, "O niektórych róznicach w klaspfikacji i posowni przuslowków w języku polskim i rosyjskim," 247; Doros, "O niektórych róznicach w odmianie i pisowni oraz uzyciu skałniowym liczebników i zaimkw w języku polskim i rozyjskim," 247; Doros "O niektórych róznicach w odmianie rzeczowników oraz odmianie i budowie i uzuciu syntaktycznym przymiotników w języku polskim i rosyjskim," 247; Doros, "O niektórych róznicach w znaczeniu, odmianie oraz pisowni czasowników w języku polskim i rosyjskim," 247; Engler, Problems in English/German Contrastive Analysis, 247; Flores, A Contrastive Analysis of Selected Clause Types in Cebuano and English, 248; Gage, *Contrastive Studies in Linguistics: A Bibliographical Checklist*, 8; Gage, *The Grammatical Structures of English and Russian*, 249; Gage, *The Sounds of English and Russian*, 249; Greis, The Pedagogical Implications of a Contrastive Analysis of Cultivated Cairene Arabic and the English Language, 249; Gurren, The Comparison on a Phonetic Basis of the Two Chief Languages of the Americas—English and Spanish, 249; Jackson, Word Order Patterns Involving the Middle Adverbs of English and Their Lexically Similar Counterparts in Japanese: A Comparative Study for Teaching Middle Adverbs, 250; Kielski, "Struktura języków francuskiego i polskiego w swietle analizy porównawczej," 250; Kim, "The Meaning of *Yes* and *No* in English and Korean," 250; Kimizuka, Problems in Teaching English Based Upon a Comparative Analysis of Japanese and English, 251; Kohmoto, Phonemic and Sub-Phonemic Replacement of English Sounds by Speakers of Japanese, 251; Koutsoudas, "A Contrastive Analysis of the Segmental Phonemes of Greek and English," 251; Kruatrachue, Thai and English: A Comparative Study of Phonology for Pedagogical Applications, 252; Kufner, *The Grammatical Structures of English and German*, 252; Lehn, "A Contrastive Study of Egyptian Arabic and American English," 252; Moulton, *The Sounds of English and German*, 253; Netherlands Didactiekcommissie, "Het Engelse Klanstelsel beschouwd in verband met het Nederlandse onderwijs," 254; Pascasio, "A Comparative Study: Predicting Interference and Facilitation for Tagalog Speakers in Learning English Noun-head Modification Patterns," 254; Pascasio, A Descriptive-Comparative Study Predicting Interference and Facilitation for Tagalog Speakers in Learning English Noun-head Modification Patterns, 255; Sibayan, English and Iloko Segmental Phonemes, 256; Stockwell, *Contrastive Study of English and Spanish*, 257; Velázquez, A Contrastive Analysis of the Phonological Systems of English and Puerto Rican Spanish with Implications for the Teaching of English as a Second Language, 257

Correspondence study: Broady, The Nebraska Experimental Program in the Use of Television and Correspondence Study, 159; Rathee, "Report on High School Foreign Language: Directed Study Experiment 1960-1961," 324

Counseling: Curran, "Counseling Skills Adapted to the Learning of Foreign Languages," 44

Cross-cultural research methods: section 5

Cultural background: section 5

Cultural differences: section 5

Cultural factors in language learning: section 5; Carroll, "An English Language Survey in West Africa," 175

Cybernetics: Artemov, "Kibernetika, teorija kommunikacii i skola," 41; Dembowski, "Über einige Fragen des Sprechens und seiner Entwicklung im Lichte Kybernetischer Anschauungen," 44

Delayed Auditory Feedback: Yates, "Delayed Auditory Feedback," 286

Design of experiments: section 1

Design of surveys: section 1

Dictation exercises: Valette, "The Use of the Dictée in the French Language Classroom," 184. *See also* Writing, teaching of

Discrimination learning: Hocking, Disordered Communication Processes Associated with Foreign Language Learning, 199; Keislar, Effect of Preliminary Training in Pronunciation Discrimination upon Learning of French Pronunciation with Recording Devices, 288; Keislar, Sequence of Discrimination and Differentiation Training in the Teaching of French in the Early Primary Grades, 314; Lane, "Acquisition and Transfer in

Auditory Discrimination," 204; Lane, "The Effects of Response-Dependent and Independent Reinforcement in Extending Stimulus Control," 205; Lane, "Effects of Training on Estimates of Vowel Loudness," 276; Lane, "Methods for Self-Shaping Echoic Behavior," 205; Liberman, "An Effect of Learning on Speech Perception: The Discrimination of Durations of Silence with and without Phonemic Significance," 279; Mace, Sequence of Discrimination and Differentiation Training in the Teaching of French in the Early Primary Grades, 207; Mange, An Investigation of the Relationships between Articulatory Development of Phonetic Discrimination and Work Synthesis Abilities in Young Mentally Retarded Children and Normal Children, 208; Marckwardt, "An Experiment in Aural Perception," 67; Marckwardt, "Phonemic Structure and Aural Perception," 67; Pimsleur, "Discrimination Training in the Teaching of French Pronunciation," 290; Pimsleur, Preliminary Discrimination Training in the Teaching of French Pronunciation, 290; Politzer, "Auditory Discrimination of French Vowels by English Speakers," 80; Suppes, *Application of Mathematical Learning Theory and Linguistic Analysis to Vowel Phoneme Matching in Russian Words,* 212; Suppes, *Some Quantitative Studies of Russian Consonant Phoneme Discrimination,* 285; Swets, "Learning to Identify Nonverbal Sounds: An Application of a Computer as a Teaching Machine," 285

Drills. *See* Grammatical models

Educational television. *See* Television
Elementary school. *See* Foreign languages in the elementary school
English, study and teaching of: section 2.3, English
Enrollments: Childers, *Foreign Language Offerings and Enrollments in Public Secondary Schools, Fall 1959,* 43
Esperanto, study and teaching of: Halloran, "A Four Year Experiment in

Esperanto as an Introduction to French," 76
Exceptional child and language learning: Gordon, "Challenging the Superior Student by Making the Study of Russian Available in the Elementary School Curriculum via Television," 98; Selvi, "Report of the Committee on French in the Elementary School [1953]," 319; Starr, *Modern Foreign Languages and the Academically Talented Student,* 54. *See also* Individual differences, Learning disability, Intelligence and language learning
Extinction in learning. *See* One-trial learning

Factor analysis: Carroll, "Factor Analysis of Two Foreign Language Batteries," 216
Fiji Islands, teaching of foreign languages in: Adam, Social Factors in Second Language Learning—with Special Reference to the Fiji Islands, 237
Filmstrips: Mackey, "Shipboard Language Teaching," 47; Nostrand, An Experiment in Filmed Recitations for Use in Teaching French. . . , 126; Richardson, "An Experiment in the Use of Filmstrip in the Teaching of French," 118; Sturge-Moore, Contrôles d'acquisition de la langue anglaise parlée: une expérience au cours élémentaire 2ème année, 69
Flashcards as visual media: Stockton, "Flashcard Experiment for Teaching Spanish in the Fifth Grade," 119
Foreign languages in the elementary schools: section 6.1
Forgetting. *See* Memory and forgetting
France, teaching of foreign languages in: Antier, "Sur l'enseignement des langues vivantes en France. Bibliographie critique," 3
French, study and teaching of: section 2.3, French
Frequency counts and lists. *See* Vocabulary

German, study and teaching of: section 2.3, German
Germany, teaching of foreign languages in: Bohlen, *Methodik des neusprachlichen Unterrichts,* 43

Grammar: Bundy, An Experimental Study of the Relative Effectiveness of Television Presentational Techniques and Conventional Classroom Procedures in Promoting Initial Comprehension of Basic Verb Form Concepts in Elementary Spanish, 159; Koumari, Certain Uses of the English Passive Voice and Their Teaching to Foreign Students, 65

Grammatical models: Mylerberg, "Pedagogical Implications of Transformational Analysis," 254; Saporta, Evaluation of Three Grammatical Models in the Teaching of Foreign Languages, 283; Saporta, "Grammatical Models and Language Learning," 284; Suppes, Application of Quantitative Analysis and Computer Data Processing Technology. . . , 54

Group relations: Curran, "Counseling Skills Adapted to the Learning of Foreign Languages," 44

Grouping of students. *See* Tests, *aptitude*

Guam, teaching of foreign languages in: Cooper, Teaching Language Arts to Non-English Speaking Children of Guam, 62

Hearing comprehension: sections 2.51, 2.53; Andrade, "Measurement of Listening Comprehension in Elementary-School Spanish Instruction," 173; Brown, "Studies in Listening Comprehension," 195; Donoghue, Measuring Achievement in Listening Skills of First Year Spanish, 177; Dufort, Two Methods of Elementary School Foreign Language Instruction on the Development of Student Audio Ability in the Foreign Language, 309; Marie Gabrielle, "FLES: A Comparative Study," 315; Mueller, "Some Inferences about an Intensified Oral Approach to the Teaching of French Based on a Study of Course Drop-Outs," 169; Newmark, FLES—A New Approach, 317; Tezza, The Effects of Listening Training on Audio-Lingual Learning, 100. *See also,* Cognitive processes

Hebrew, study and teaching of: section 2.3, Hebrew

High school: section 6.3

Honors courses. *See* Intensive courses

Immediate recall. *See* Memory and forgetting

Incidental learning: Pimsleur, "Incidental Learning in Foreign Language Learning," 209

Individual differences: Bauer, An Exploratory Investigation of "Sensory Image Types" in Foreign Language Learning, 193; Carpenter, *Comparative Research on Methods and Media for Presenting Programmed Courses in Mathematics and English,* 147; Carroll, *The Study of Language,* 197; Hosford, Characteristics of Science-Talented and Language-Talented Secondary School Students, 240; Jakobovits, A Psycholinguistic Study of Measurable Factors in Second-Language Learning, 201; Morrison, "Personality and Underachievement in Foreign Language Learning," 242; Pimsleur, "Foreign Language Learning Ability," 224; Pimsleur, "Predicting Achievement in Foreign Language Learning," 222; Pimsleur, "Student Factors in Foreign Language Learning," 224; Pimsleur, "A Study of Foreign Language Learning Ability: Part I and II," 223; Pimsleur, "Underachievement in Foreign Language Learning," 223; Roca, The Construction of an Interest Inventory for Students of Different Linguistic and Cultural Backgrounds, 243

Indonesia, teaching of foreign languages in: Tan, English Language Teacher Training in Indonesia, 342

Instructional films. *See* Motion pictures

Instructional television. *See* Television

Intelligence and language learning: Angiolillo, "French for the Feeble-Minded: An Experiment," 71; Bovée, "Some Observations on the Relationship between Mental Ability and Achievement in French," 194; Gardner, "Motivational Variables in Second Language Acquisition," 240; Gordon, "Challenging the Superior Student by Making the Study of Russian Available in the Elementary

School Curriculum via Television," 98; Jones, "Bilingualism and Verbal Intelligence," 230; Marie Gabrielle, "FLES: A Comparative Study," 315; Reid, The Prediction of Grades in Foreign Language at the Freshman Level from a Battery of Tests of Mental Ability and Achievement," 225; Selvi, "Report of the Committee on French in The Elementary School [1953]," 319; Smith, "The Relationship between Intelligence and the Learning Which Results from the Use of Educational Sound Motion Picture," 211; Starr, *Modern Foreign Languages and the Academically Talented Student,* 54

Intelligence tests. *See* intelligence and language learning

Intensive courses: Carroll, "A Parametric Study of Language Training in the Peace Corps," 217; Carroll, "The Prediction of Success in Intensive Foreign Language Training," 217; Carton, "The 1959 Summer Russian Language Learning Program," 96; Horn, *Comparison between Effect of Intensive Oral-Aural Spanish Language Instruction,* 105; Lambert, "Attitudinal and Cognitive Aspects of Intensive Study of a Second Language," 241; Mackey, "Shipboard Language Teaching," 47; Miller, A Survey of Intensive Programs in the Uncommon Languages, Summer 1964, 327; Oswald, "Progress of Intensive Elementary German at the University of California, Los Angeles," 88; Peters, "Prediction of Success and Failure in Elementary Foreign Language Courses," 222; Valdman, Continuation and Completion of the Implementation and Evaluation of a Multiple-Credit Intensive Audio-Lingual Approach in Elementary French, 328; Vicory, The Paired-Associate Task as a Predictor of Foreign Language Fluency, 213. *See also* Scientific language courses

Interference: Al-Karbouli, Interference as a Function of Certain Factors in Learning Two Foreign Languages Contiguously, 190; Asher, The High Velocity Process in Verbal Training, 191; Delattre, Interference of American Diphthongization in Teaching the Pure Vowels of French, German, and Spanish, 245; Kinzel, *Lexical and Grammatical Interference in the Speech of a Bilingual Child,* 231; Lado, Linguistic Interpretation of Speech Problems of Foreign Students, 252; Marckwardt, "An Experiment in Aural Perception," 67; Marckwardt, "Phonemic Bifurcation as an English Teaching Problem," 67; Pascasio, "A Comparative Study: Predicting Interference and Facilitation for Tagalog Speakers in Learning English Noun-head Modification Patterns," 254; Pascasio, A Descriptive-Comparative Study Predicting Interference and Facilitation for Tagalog Speakers in Learning English Noun-head Modification Patterns, 255. *See also* Contrastive studies

Intonation: section 4.5; Bolinger, "Around the Rim of Language: Intonation," 245; Cowan, Final Technical Report: Development of a Device to Record Graphically Intonations of Speech as They are Perceived by a Listener, 260; Delattre, "A Comparative Study of Declarative Intonation in American English and Spanish," 246; Delattre, "Comparing the Prosodic Features of English, German, Spanish and French," 261; Delattre, "Distinctive and Non-Distinctive Aspects of German Intonation," 262

Italian, study and teaching of: section 2.3, Italian

Japanese, study and teaching of: section 2.3, Japanese

Junior high school: section 6.2

Language laboratories: sections 2.54, 2.9

Languages in the curriculum: section 6.5. *See also* Foreign languages in the elementary schools, Junior high school, High school, University

Latin, study and teaching of: section 2.3, Latin

Learning process: Suppes, *Applica-
tion of Mathematical Learning
Theory and Linguistic Analysis to
Vowel Phoneme Matching in Russian
Words,* 212; Suppes, "Some Current
Developments in Models of Learning
for a Continuum of Responses," 212
Learning rate: Bern, "New Directions
in Audio-Visual Communications:
Toward Educational Engineering,"
120. *See also* Presentation, effect of
order and time of
Lebanon, teaching of foreign languages
in: Yorkey, A Study of the Practical
Application of Structural Linguistics
to the Teaching of English in Leb-
anese Elementary Schools, 71
Lecture method: Hayman, *Reading
and Writing Results in the Second
Year of Research—1961-62: Report
No. 7,* 104; Lopes, "Teaching El-
ementary Foreign Languages," 326;
Popham, Experimental Appraisal of
Effectiveness of Taped Lectures for
College Extension Courses, 113; Pop-
ham, Experimental Appraisal of Tape
Recorded Lectures in the College
Classroom, 114
Linguistic analysis: Carroll, "Linguistic
Relativity, Contrastive Linguistics,
and Language Learning," 245; Hill,
*Prepositions and Adverbial Particles
in English. . . ,* 65. *See also* Contras-
tive studies
Linguistics in language teaching: sec-
tions 4.1–4.5
Listening comprehension. *See* Hearing
comprehension
Literature: Nostrand, Film-Recital of
French Poems; Cultural Commen-
tary, 301; Nostrand, "Literature, Area
Study, and Hispanic Culture," 300;
Riecks, Filmed Recitations of French
Literature. . . , 303; Weber, *Genèse
de l'oeuvre poétique,* 305; Weber,
La psychologie de l'art, 305

Mass media: Greenhill, Research on
the Presentation of Programmed
Instruction to Large Groups over
Closed Circuit Television, 150;
Mackey, "Shipboard Language Teach-
ing," 47; Mueller, TV and Mass-
Instruction Experiments, 169

Memory and forgetting: Asher, "Evidence for 'Genuine' One-Trial Learning," 190; Asher, "Towards a Neo-
field Theory of Behavior," 192; Bousfield, "The Occurrence of Clustering
in the Recall of Randomly Arranged
Words of Different Frequencies of
Usage," 194; Carton, The "Method
of Inference" in Foreign Language
Comprehension, Learning and Retention (Phase I), 198; Doob, "The Effect
of Language on Verbal Expression
and Recall," 199; Fox, "The Retention of Material Presented during
Sleep," 199; Perry, L'audio-vision et
l'enseignement des langues vivantes,
127; Putter, "High School-College
Articulation in Foreign Languages,"
327; Scherer, "The Forgetting Rate
in Learning German," 91; Skelton,
"Factors Governing Retention in College," 211; Stolurow, Prompting vs.
Confirmation Sequence in the Automated Teaching of Sight Vocabulary, 211
Methodology of research. *See* Research
methods
Minimal-step teaching. *See* Programed learning
Miniature linguistic systems: Horowitz,
The Effects of Variation in Linguistic
Structure on the Learning of Minia-
ture Linguistic Systems, 266; Horowitz, "Morpheme Order and Syllable
Structure in the Learning of Minia-
ture Linguistic Systems," 266; Lenneberg, "A Probabilistic Approach to
Language Learning," 206; Sapon, "A
Work-Sample Test for Foreign Lan-
guage Prognosis," 225; Saporta,
Evaluation of Three Grammatical
Models in the Teaching of Foreign
Languages, 283; Saporta, "Gram-
matical Models and Language Learn-
ing," 284
Morphology: Hempleman, The Struc-
turing of Possession and Related
Problems in the Teaching of English
as a Foreign Language, 64; Hill,
*Prepositions and Adverbial Particles
in English,* 65. *See* also Contrastive
studies
Motion pictures: Allen, "Research on
Film Use: Class Preparation," 119;
Allen, "Research on Film Use: Stu-

dent Participation," 119; Borglum, "Modern Language Audio-Visual Project," 120; Carpenter, "A Theoretical Orientation for Instructional Film Research," 37; Capretz, Audio-Lingual Techniques for Teaching Foreign Languages, 43; Forsdale, "An Experimental Method of Teaching Foreign Languages by Means of 8mm Sound Films in Cartridge-Loading Projectors," 123; Hoban, Instructional Film Research, 1918-1950, 124; Kale, *Learning and Retention of English-Russian Vocabulary under Different Conditions of Motion-Picture Presentation,* 99; Long, "Recent Experimental Investigations Dealing with Effectiveness of Audio-Visual Modes of Presentation," 125; Mac-Kinnon, "Experimental Study of Learning of French in the Public Schools Undertaken by the Toronto Board of Education," 79; Motzko, "Die Bedeutung audiovisueller Hilfen für das Gedächtnis," 126; Newmark, A New Design for Teaching Foreign Languages Using Dramatic Motion Pictures and Programmed Learning Materials, 126; Nostrand, An Experiment in Filmed Recitations For Use in Teaching, 299; Nostrand, Film-Recital of French Poems; Cultural Commentary, 301; Riecks, Filmed Recitations of French Literature..., 305; Rosselot, Evaluation of the Otterbein College Film-Text Method of Teaching French, at Five Ohio Institutions, 128; Toronto Board of Education, Experimental Study of Learning French in the Public Schools Undertaken by the Toronto Board of Education, 83; Toronto Board of Education, A Follow-up Study of the Effects of Aural-Oral French Instruction in the Elementary School on Pupil's Achievement in a Secondary School Programme, 84. *See also* Television

Motivation: Borglum, Modern Language and Audio-Visual Research Project, 121; Farber, "The Role of Motivation in Verbal Learning and Performance," 239; Gardner, "Motivational Variables in Second-Language Acquisition," 240; Lambert, A Study of the Roles of Attitudes and Motivation in Second Language Learning, 241

Multiple-choice presentation: Fry, "Teaching Machines: An Investigation of Constructed Versus Multiple-Choice Methods of Response," 149; Korwin, The Learning and Retention of Material Presented by Means of Multiple-Choice Items, 202

Music and language learning: Blanton, "An Experimental Application of Language Theory, Learning Theory, and Personality Theory to Evaluate the Influence of Music in Language Learning," 238; Blickenstaff, "Musical Talents and Foreign Language Learning Ability," 42; Lane, "An Effect of Native Language and Musical Training on Vocal Pitch Matching," 277; Leutenegger, "Auditory Factors and the Acquisition of French Language Mastery," 78

Native speakers, use of in foreign language teaching: Boyd-Bowman, Experimentation with Taped Materials and Native Informants to Develop for Small Colleges Some Programs of Independent Study in the Neglected Languages, 325; Brault, Revision and Expansion of Bowdoin French Materials, 72; Brault, "The Special NDEA Institute at Bowdoin College for French Teachers of Canadian Descent," 338; Cheydleur, "Judging Teachers of Basic French Courses by Objective Means at the University of Wisconsin," 338; Keeler, "Post War Experiment in Teaching First Year French," 77

Netherlands, teaching of foreign languages in: Baardman, Voorlopig rapport betreffende onderzoek didactiek Frans, 71

Norway, teaching of foreign languages in: Stensaasen, "Gjennomførinpen av engelskundervisningen i folkeskolen," 68

One-trial learning: Asher, "Evidence for 'Genuine' One-Trial Learning, 190; Asher, "Towards a Neo-field Theory of Behavior," 192

Orthography: Ai, "Report on Psychological Studies of the Chinese Language in the Past Three Decades," 59; Crothers, *The Role of Transcription in the Learning of the Orthographic Representations of Russian Sounds,* 115; Sawyer, The Utility of Translation and Written Symbols during the First Thirty Hours of Language Study, 52. *See also* Writing, teaching of

Paired-comparison method. *See* Grammatical models

Parent participation in language learning: Hayman, Causative Factors and Learning Related to Parent Participation, 165

Perceptual processes. *See* Cognitive processes

Persia, teaching of foreign languages in: Varaseth, Some Problems of Teaching Modern Languages in Persian Schools with Suggestions for Their Solution, 56

Personality and language learning: Blanton, "An Experimental Application of Language Theory, Learning Theory, and Personality Theory to Evaluate the Influence of Music in Language Learning," 238; Breckwoldt, An Attempt to Measure Academic Achievement Efficiency, 174; Buxbaum, "The Role of a Second Language in the Formation of Ego And Superego," 238; Dunkel, "The Effect of Personality on Language Achievement," 239; Morrison, "Personality and Underachievement in Foreign Language Learning, A Pilot Study," 242; Pritchard, "An Investigation into the Relationship of Personality Traits and Ability in Modern Languages," 243. *See also* Bilingualism

Phonemics: sections 4.3, 4.5

Phonetics: sections 4.3, 4.5; Belasco, "Phonetics," 3

Phonology. *See* Phonemics, Phonetics, Pronunciation

Polish, study and teaching of: section 2.3, Polish

Presentation, effect of order and time of: Bernard, The Relative Effectiveness of Four Types of Language Laboratory Experience, 130; Croth-

ers, *Latency Phenomena in the Prolonged Learning of Visual Representations of Russian Sounds,* 115; Gavurin, "Logical Sequence and Random Sequence," 149; Horn, *Comparison Between Effect of Intensive Oral-Aural Spanish Language Instruction,* 105; Korwin, The Learning and Retention of Material Presented by Means of Multiple-Choice Items, 202; Mace, Sequence of Discrimination and Differentiation Training in the Teaching of French in the Early Primary Grades, 207; Newmark, A New Design for Teaching Foreign Languages Using Dramatic Motion Pictures and Programmed Learning Materials, 126; Pimsleur, "Transfer of Verbal Material across Sense Modalities," 209; Sawyer, The Utility of Translation and Written Symbols during the First Thirty Hours of Language Study, 152; Scherer, Extended Classroom Experimentation with Varied Sequencing of the Four Skills in German Instruction, 91; Stolurow, Prompting vs. Confirmation Sequences and Overlearning in the Automated Teaching of Sight Vocabulary, 211; Suppes, Application of Quantitative Analysis and Computer Data Processing Technology. . . , 54; Weiss, An Investigation of a Synchronous Multilingual Curriculum in a Linguistic Framework, 84

Professional school programs: section 6.6

Prognosis tests. *See* Tests, *prognosis*

Programed learning: section 2.55. *See also* Teaching machines

Pronunciation: section 4.5. *See also* Phonemics; Phonetics; Tests, *pronunciation*

Psycholinguistics: sections 3.1, 3.7

Psychological factors in language learning: section 3.7. *See also* Bilingualism, Interference, Motivation, Personality development and language

Psychology of learning. *See* Psychological factors in language teaching

Puerto Rico, teaching of foreign languages in: Fife, *The Teaching of English in Puerto Rico,* 228

Racial factors in language learning. *See* Cultural factors in language learning

Radio: Felt, "Radio and the Foreign Language Laboratory," 110; NHK Radio-Television Cultural Research Institute, "The Effects of 'Radio Japanese Classroom,'" 112; Uemura, "The Effects of Educational Radio and Related Teaching of Methods on Student's Ability in the Japanese Language," 94; Xoomsai, "A Survey of Results of Using School Broadcast as a Teaching Method," 114

Readiness age in language learning. *See* Tests, *aptitude;* Age in language learning

Reading, teaching of: Blayne, "Building Comprehension in Silent Reading," 115; Bratset, Identification of Cross-Cultural Problems in Reading English as a Second Language, 294; Hayman, *Reading and Writing Results in the Second Year of Research —1961-62; Report No. 7,* 104; Horn, *Comparison Between Effect of Intensive Oral-Aural Spanish Language Instruction,* 105; Mueller, Trial Use of the French Program (ALLP). . . Third Quarterly Report, 289; Neale, "The Development of Reading Ability in French and Its Measurement in the Grammar School Course," 181; Purvis, "A New Approach to the Teaching of French in Secondary Modern Schools," 81; Purvis, "A Reading Course in French," 81; Rojas, "Reading Materials for Bilingual Children," 235; Russell, "Research on Teaching Reading," 51; Scherer, "Reading for Meaning," 53

Repetition of presentation, effects of: Asher, "Evidence for 'Genuine' One-Trial Learning," 190; Hayman, "Exact vs. Varied Repetition in Educational Television," 162; Jakobovits, Effects of Repeated Stimulation on Cognitive Aspects of Behavior: Some Experiments on the Phenomenon of Semantic Satiation, 200; Jakobovits, The Effects of Repetition in Stuttering: A Theoretical Analysis, 200; Jakobovits, Semantic Satiation in an Addition Task, 201; Jakobovits, "Stimulus Characteristics as Determinants of Semantic Changes with Repeated Presentation," 201; Stolurow, Prompting vs. Confirmation Sequences and Overlearning in the Automated Teaching of Sight Vocabulary, 211

Research methods: section 1

Retention. *See* Memory and forgetting

Russian, study and teaching of: section 2.3, Russian

Self-Instructional devices. *See* Programed learning, Teaching machines

Semantics: Jakobovits, "Stimulus Characteristics as Determinants of Semantic Changes with Repeated Presentation," 201

Semiotics: Sebeok, *Approaches to Semiotics.* . . , 53

Skinnerian programing. *See* Programed learning

Sleep, learning during: Fox, "The Retention of Material Presented during Sleep," 199; Hoyt, The Effect of Auditory Material Presented during Sleep, 200

Slides: Borglum, "AV-Active French," 121; Borglum, Modern Language Audio-Visual Project, 121; Matsumoto, "A Study of the Learning Effects of Audiovisual Methods— Learning Through Slides," 116; Morehouse, Survey and Cataloguing of Slide Materials in South Asian Languages and Area Studies (Phase I), 118

Social factors in language learning: section 3.7 *See also* Bilingualism, Cultural factors in language learning

Sound recordings: Boyd-Bowman, Experimentation with Taped Materials and Native Informants to Develop for Small Colleges Some Programs of Independent Study in the Neglected Languages, 325; Dickens, "An Experimental Application of "CLOZE" Procedure and Attitude Measures to Listening Comprehension," 177; Dodson, *Oral Examinations,* 177; Feldman, Elaboration and Experimental Evaluation of Procedures and Specialized Materials for In-Service Training of Secondary School Teachers of Modern Foreign Languages, 102; Kuniyuki, "An Analysis of the Learning Effects of the Use of Magnetic Tape Recordings for English Teaching," 111; Larew, "Tape Recorder Versus the Teacher in the Spanish Class," 111; Motzko, "Die Bedeutung audiovisueller Hilfen für das Gedächnis," 126; Pickrel, "Tape Recordings Are Used to Teach Seventh Grade Students in Westside Junior-Senior High School, Omaha, Nebraska," 113; Popham, Experimental Appraisal of Effectiveness of Taped Lectures for College Extension Courses, 114; Popham, Experimental Appraisal of Tape Recorded Lectures in the College Classroom, 113; Randall, *"Parlons français:* A Large-Scale FLES Program by Television," 317; Rathee, "Report on High School Foreign Language: Directed Study Experiment 1960-61," 324; Sturge-Moore, Contrôles d'acquisition de la langue anglaise parlée: une expérience au cours élémentaire 2éme année, 68; White, A Comparison of Two Methods of Teaching Beginning Spanish in Junior High School, 109

Soviet Union, teaching of foreign languages in: Bauer, "Audiovisual Aids and Language Teaching in the U.S.S.R.," 120; Conrad, Study of the Germanic Languages in the Soviet Union (1934-1960), 87; Fairbanks, Application of Structural Linguistics to Foreign Language Teaching in the U.S.S.R., 248; Gorokhoff, Language Development in the Soviet Union: A Preliminary Survey, 45; Gorokhoff, Review of Language Development in the Soviet Union, 45; Koselev, "Novi aspekti na priloznoto iazykoznie v S.S.S.R.," 251; Kreusler, *The Teaching of Modern Foreign Languages in the Soviet Union,* 46; Poltoratzky, *Methods of Teaching Foreign Languages in the Soviet Union,* 50; Rusowicz, "Sprodki techniczne w nauczaniu jezyko obcych na podstawie doswiadczen w zwiazku Radziockim," 128

Spanish, study and teaching of: section 2.3, Spanish

Spectrographs and spectrograms: Borst, "The Use of Spectrograms for Speech Analysis and Synthesis," 258; Chatman, "Report on Possible Applications of Sound Spectography in the Language Laboratory," 133; Cooper, "The Interconversion of Audible and Visible Patterns as a Basic Research in the Perception of Speech," 219; Cooper, *Some Input-Output Relations Observed in Experiments on the Perception of Speech,* 259; Delattre, "An Experimental Study of the Acoustic Determinants of Vowel Color," 264; Delattre, "The Physiological Interpretations of Sound Spectrograms," 263; Delattre, "Research Techniques for Phonetic Comparison of Languages," 263; Delattre, *Some Suggestions for Teaching Methods Arising from Research on the Acoustic Analysis and Synthesis of Speech,* 264; Hoge, "Visible Pronunciation," 116; Liberman, "The Role of Selected Stimulus-Variables in the Perception of the Unvoiced Stop Consonants," 280; Liberman, "Tempo of Frequency Change as a Cue for Distinguishing Classes of Speech Sounds," 280; Pierce, "Spectographic Study of Vocalic Nuclei," 281; Pulgram, *Introduction to the Spectography of Speech,* 282

Speech processes: sections 4.3, 4.5

Standards in language: Brault, "The Special NDEA Institute at Bowdoin College for French Teachers of Canadian Descent," 338

Study guides: Feldman, Elaboration and Experimental Evaluation of Procedures and Specialized Materials for In-Service Training of Secondary School Teachers of Modern Foreign Languages, 102

Study habits: Wittenborn, "Empirical Evaluation of Study Habits for College Courses in French and Spanish," 215

Syntax: Asher, Sensory Interrelationships in Vocabulary and Syntactic Learning, 145; Brown, "Three Processes in the Child's Acquisition of Syntax," 196; Lane, "Some Discriminative Properties of Syntactic Structues," 276; Mueller, "Programming Morphemic Structure: The Concept of Minute Steps," 154; Pascasio, "A

Comparative Study: Predicting Interference and Facilitation for Tagalog Speakers in Learning English Noun-head Modification Patterns," 254; Pascasio, A Descriptive-Comparative Study Predicting Interference and Facilitation for Tagalog Speakers in Learning English Noun-head Modification Patterns, 255. *See also* Contrastive studies

Tape recordings. *See* Sound recordings
Teachers, *ability:* section 7
Teachers, *training:* section 7
Teaching machines and autoinstructional devices: section 2.55. *See also* Programed learning
Television: section 2.56; Andrade, Measurement of Speaking Skills in Elementary Level Spanish Instruction, 174
Test construction: Andrade, Measurement of Speaking Skills in Elementary Level Spanish Instruction, 174
Tests, *achievement:* section 2.7
Tests, *aptitude:* section 3.3; Anisfeld, "Social and Psychological Variables in Learning Hebrew," 237; Breckwoldt, An Attempt to Measure Academic Achievement Efficiency, 174. *See also* Individual differences
Tests, *aural performance:* sections 2.7, 4.5
Tests, *entrance. See* Tests, *aptitude*
Tests, *intelligence. See* intelligence and language learning
Tests, *prognosis:* sections 2.7, 3.3; Sapon, "A Work-Sample Test for Foreign Language Prognosis," 225; Vicory, The Paired-Associate Task as a Predictor of Foreign Language Fluency, 213
Thai, study and teaching: section 2.3, Thai
Types of learners. *See* individual differences

Union of South Africa, teaching of foreign languages in: McConkey, "An Experiment in Bilingual Education," 233
United States, teaching of foreign language in: Beliaev, "K Khavrakteristike zarubezhnoi (zapadnoevropeiskoi i amerikanskoi) psikhologii

obucheniya inostrannym yazykom," 41; Coleman, *A Report on the States of Russian and Other Slavic and East European Languages* . . . , 96; Harmon, "Foreign Languages in Independent Secondary Schools," 322; "Instruction in Classical and Modern Foreign Languages," 322; Leavitt, "The Teaching of Spanish in the United States," 106; Mildenberger, Status of Foreign Language Study in American Elementary Schools, 316; Mildenberger, "Three Years of Language Development Program (NDEA) Title VI," 340; Moulton, "Linguistics and Language Teaching in the United States, 1940-1960," 253; Reid, "An Exploratory Survey of Foreign Language Teaching by Television in the United States," 170; Ryden, Vocabulary as an Index to Learning in a Second Language, 51; UNESCO, *Modern Languages in the Schools,* 55; Vamos, "Language Learning in American College and Universities: Data on Degrees, Majors, and Teaching Practices," 329; Vamos, "Modern Foreign Language Faculties in Colleges and Universities, 1959-1960," 329; Zeydel, "The Teaching of German in the United States from Colonial Times to the Present," 93
University: section 6.4
Urdu, study and teaching of: section 2.3, Urdu

Visual aids: section 2.52. *See also* Filmstrips, Slides
Vocabulary: Anisfeld, "A Comment on 'The Role of Grapheme-Phoneme Correspondence in the Perception of Words' by Gibson *et al.*," 258; Asher, Factors within the Program of a Teaching Machine Which Influence Foreign Language Learning, 144; Asher, Sensory Interrelationships in Vocabulary and Syntactic Learning, 145; Barker, A Newspaper Wordcount, Newspaper Reader, and Comprehensive Course in Urdu (Phase I), 109; Brewster, Vocabulary Learning Through Reading German Prose . . . , 86; Burns, "An Investigation into the Extent of First-Year Vocabulary in

French in Boys' Grammar Schools," 308; Dale, A Bibliography of Vocabulary Studies, 6; Gibson, "The Role of Grapheme-Phoneme Correspondence in the Perception of Words," 264; Gougenheim, *L'élaboration du français élémentaire,* 76; Josselson, *The Russian Word Count and Frequency Analysis of Grammatical Categories of Standard Literary Russian,* 98; Kale, Exploratory Studies in the Use of Pictures and Sound for Teaching Foreign Language Vocabulary, 124; Kale, *Learning and Retention of English-Russian Vocabulary under Different Conditions of Motion-Picture Presentation,* 98; Kopstein, "Learning Foreign Vocabulary from Pictures vs. Words," 116; Mackey, A Study of Available Vocabulary, 47; Mauger, *Le français élémentaire: Méthode progressive de français parlé,* 79; Michéa, "Limitation et sélection du vocabulaire dans l'enseignement actif des langues vivantes," 48; Ministère Français de l'Education Nationale, *Le français élémentaire,* 80; Pfeffer, Addition of a Semantic Index to the Basic Spoken German Word List, 88; Pfeffer, The Evolution of the Basic Spoken German Word List. Level I, 89; Pfeffer, *Grunddeutsch. Number 1: Basic Spoken German Word List.* Level I, 89; Pfeffer, *Grunddeutsch, Number 2: Basic Spoken German Word List. Level I, with Semantic Index,* 89; Pfeffer, "Grunddeutsch: Werden und Wesen," 90; Pfeffer, A Spoken German Idiom Count, 89; Smith, "Measurement of Vocabularies of Young Bilingual Children in Both Languages Used," 236; Smith, "Word Variety as a Measure of Bilingualism in Preschool Children," 236; Stolurow, Prompting vs. Confirmation Sequences and Overlearning in the Automated Teaching of Sight Vocabulary, 211; Sumner, "Relation of Grades in German Reading Vocabulary to the Method of Testing," 184; Superior Council on Education of Puerto Rico, *Spanish Word Count,* 108; Tireman, "A Study of Fourth-Grade Reading Vocabulary of Native

Spanish Speaking Children," 69; Twarog, Word Count of Spoken Russian, 101

Wire recordings. See Sound recordings
Word counts and lists. See Vocabulary
Word perception: Crothers, *Latency Phenomena in the Prolonged Learning of Visual Representations of Russian Sounds,* 115; House, "On the Learning of Speechlike Vocabularies," 266; Jakobovits, Effects of Repeated Stimulation of Cognitive Aspects of Behavior: Some Experiments on the Phenomenon of Semantic Satiation, 200; Jakobovits, "Stimulus Characteristics as Determinants of Semantic Changes with Repeated Presentation," 201; Lambert, Word Association Responses . . . , 3.5; Pollack, "Verbal Reaction Times to Briefly Presented Words," 282; Reams, "An Experimental Study Comparing the Visual Accompaniments of Word Identification and the Auditory Experience of Word Intelligibility," 127; Rubenstein, "Word Predictability and Intelligibility," 283; Sawyer, The Utility of Translation and Written Symbols during the First Thirty Hours of Language Study, 52; Wimer, "The Differential Effects of Word and Object Stimuli on the Learning of Paired Associates," 215

Writing, teaching of: Ai, "Report on Psychological Studies of the Chinese Language in the Past Three Decades," 59; Carroll, "Research to Determine the Effectiveness of Programed Grafdrils in Teaching the Arabic Writing System, 58; Hayman, *Reading and Writing Results in the Second Year of Research—1961-62; Report No. 7,* 104; Lesage, Le passage de la langue orale à la langue écrite dans un enseignement audio-visuel de l'anglais à des enfants de 8 ans, 125; Mueller, Trial Use of the French Program (ALLP) . . . Third Quarterly Report, 290; Zais, "The Linguistic Characteristics of Punctuation Symbols in the Teaching of Pronunciation Skills," 291. *See also* Orthography